Honor and Personhood in Early Modern Mexico

Honor and Personhood in
Early Modern Mexico

❦

Osvaldo F. Pardo

University of Michigan Press

Ann Arbor

Published in the United States of America by
University of Michigan Press
Manufactured in the United States of America
♾ Printed on acid-free paper

2018   2017   2016   2015   4 3 2 1

A CIP catalog record for this book is available from the British Library.

Library of Congress Cataloging-in-Publication Data

Pardo, Osvaldo F., 1963–.
    Honor and personhood in early modern Mexico / Osvaldo F.
Pardo.
        pages cm
    Includes bibliographical references and index.
    ISBN 978-0-472-11962-2 (hardcover : alk. paper) — ISBN 978-0-
472-12120-5 (ebook)
        1. Church and state—Mexico—History—16th century.
    2. Church and state—Mexico—History—17th century.   3. Indians
    of Mexico—Government relations—History.   4. Honor.
    5. Church and state—Catholic Church—History—16th century.
    6. Church and state—Catholic Church—History—17th century.
    7. Catholic Church—Mexico—History—16th century.   8. Catholic
    Church—Mexico—History—17th century.   I. Title.
    F1219.3.R38P36   2015
    972′02—dc23

                                                           2015011881

To Adelma E. Odriozola

Contents

Acknowledgments

The last time I heard Sabine MacCormack's voice was on the afternoon of Saturday, June 9, 2012. She mentioned a conference paper on the idea of citizenship in the *Siete Partidas* that she had committed to delivering in Rome sometime in September. There was a lot of preliminary work to do: sources and commentaries to go over, Bartolus of Sassoferrato, Baldus. Saturday phone calls had become a summer tradition of sorts; I assumed that she would welcome a break from her garden chores. Exactly a week after our last talk, Sabine suffered a fatal heart attack while tending her flowers. As I sit to rewrite these acknowledgments, I remember many outdoor dinners above a much larger and wilder garden at her house in Ann Arbor summers ago; I remember how that same garden dominated the view from her book-filled studio.

Oblivious to the barren irony that has taken hold in many quarters of the humanities, Sabine dared to talk about "the life of the mind" without quotation marks. Often. Her particular way of thinking and writing about the past hinged on that very notion. I now see that the life of the mind, as she embodied it, contained no distinction between physical and intellectual work: gardening, painting watercolors (Cuzco, Extremadura), knitting, all somehow left their marks on her scholarship. That she managed to turn an accident of time and geography (*that's what all German girls were supposed to learn, you know?*) into tools of inquiry was but one of the many things that made her so special.

Throughout the writing of this book I have counted on the generous advice of many friends and colleagues. Sabine patiently listened to many versions of this project, and offered much needed encouragement once ideas found their way into writing. Once again, Rolena Adorno's painstakingly detailed comments on drafts raised the right questions, saved me from non sequiturs, and made the task of revising and rewriting infinitely easier. I have been lucky to rely on the expertise and friendship of John Charles, who shared his thoughts and editorial suggestions at different stages. In Madrid, Storrs, or by correspondence, James Amelang has been an invaluable source of sound advice and stimulating conversation. Over the years Jacqueline Loss has mastered the art of appearing not to mind answering even the silliest question about style or editing; I thank her for that, and her dear friendship. Special thanks to Norma Bouchard, William Christian Jr., Mary Clayton, Rob Fahrenholz, Gustavo Nanclares, Mark A. Noll, Ryan Pereira, Victoria Pineda, and Martin Rosenstock.

A kind invitation by Betina Kaplan allowed me to present my work in progress before faculty associated with the Latin American and Caribbean Studies Institute of the University of Georgia. Gregory Lee Cuellar provided a similar opportunity at the Cushing Memorial Library and Archives of Texas A&M University. I thank Craig and Hilaire Kallendorff for their insights and kindness on that occasion.

I conducted initial research at the John Carter Brown Library in 2004 as an Andrew W. Mellon Fellow. Norman Fiering, now happily retired, and Susan Danforth made working at the JCB a very special experience. My stay in Providence was greatly enhanced by daily exchanges with a fantastic group of scholars including Carina Johnson, Andrea Lepage, Matthew O'Hara, Rachel O'Toole, and David Tavárez. David's corrections and comments guided much of my last revision of the manuscript, which has benefited from his keen eye for detail and vast command of the sources. A good portion of the original draft was written while a fellow at the Humanities Institute of the University of Connecticut. A Franklin Research Grant from the American Philosophical Society helped fund a research trip to Spain. Further research was conducted at the Newberry Library thanks to a National Endowment for the Humanities / Newberry Fellowship in 2007.

I am indebted to Ross D. MacKinnon, the Dean of the College of Liberal Arts and Sciences at the University of Connecticut, for granting me time away from teaching and administrative obligations.

An earlier version of chapter 4 was previously published in *Comparative Studies in Society and History* 48, no. 1 (January 2006): 79–109.

Introduction

Between March and June 1856 Edward Burnett Tylor joined the archaeologist Henry Christy on a trip through Mexico, affording them both the rare opportunity to learn about the country through conversation with knowledgeable hosts.[1] Tylor was a well-informed traveler, acquainted with the works of sixteenth-century Spanish chroniclers and contemporary authorities on Mexico such as Alexander von Humboldt. (Tylor, however, disagreed with Humboldt's proposals to improve the local economy.) Curious about the reading habits of the Mexicans, Tylor soon learned that half of the titles intended for popular circulation consisted of works on the Virgin of Guadalupe and religious miracles. To his surprise, Ripalda's catechism, a work that dated back to the last quarter of the sixteenth century, still enjoyed a wide readership.[2] His comments on this popular book are worth quoting:

> Zavala speaks of this catechism as containing the maxims of blind obedience to king and pope; but my more modern edition has scarcely anything to say about the Pope, and nothing at all about the government. Of late years, indeed, the Pope has not counted for much politically, in Mexico; and on one occasion his Holiness found, when he tried to inter-

---

1. Edward B. Tylor, *Anahuac: Or Mexico and the Mexicans, Ancient and Modern* (London: Longman, Green, Longman, and Roberts, 1861; New York: Bergman Publishers, 1970), iii.

2. From its initial publication to well into the nineteenth century, the catechism that remained forever attached to the name of its original author, the Jesuit priest Jerónimo de Ripalda, underwent numerous transformations at the hands of various authors from outside and inside Spain, and became one of the most printed books in Spanish. In New Spain, Ripalda's work was adapted into a Zapotec catechism and published in 1687; the Nahuatl version by the Jesuit Ignacio de Paredes was issued in 1758. On the Zapotec version of Ripalda's catechism, see Luis Resines Llorente, *Catecismos de Astete y Ripalda* (Madrid: Biblioteca de Autores Cristianos, 1987), 211; on the Nahuatl version, see *Catecismo Mexicano, que contiene toda la Doctrina Christiana con todas sus declaraciones: en que el Ministro de Almas hallará, lo que a estas debe enseñar* . . . (Mexico City: Imprenta de la Bibliotheca Mexicana, 1758). The Nahuatl version was reprinted in 1878; eight years later a new translation was published in Puebla. Ascensión H. de León Portilla, *Tepuztlahcuilolli: Impresos en Náhuatl*, 2 vols. (Mexico City: Universidad Nacional Autónoma de México, 1988), 1:330–31.

fere about church-benefices, that his authority was rather nominal than real. On the whole, nothing in the Catechism struck me so much as the multiplication-table, which, to my unspeakable astonishment, turned up in the middle of the book; a table of functions followed; and then it began again with the Holy Trinity.[3]

In his recollections, Tylor the traveler—like many of his contemporary countrymen—is ready to be surprised and amused by the idiosyncrasies of Catholic culture. His discovery that the doctrinal works he perused combined religion and mathematics confirmed his suspicions about the negative influence of Catholicism on social and political progress. Had Tylor taken a look at the substantial number of leaflets and popular works bearing the word "catechism" in their titles that circulated in Spain and postindependence Mexico, he might have considered the juxtaposition of religious and nonreligious matters differently. The following sample of titles published between 1811 and 1830 in the two countries attests to the emergence of a new political reality represented by the constitutional experiment undertaken on both sides of the Atlantic: *Catecismo civil de España en preguntas y respuestas* (1808); *Cartilla o catecismo del ciudadano constitucional* (1820); *Catecismo politico mexicano para uso de las escuelas* (1828); and *Catecismo de la independencia en siete declaraciones* (1821).[4] After being closely identified with religious instruction, the original meaning of "catechism" as primer reemerged to be applied to a variety of practical fields, including civil and political life. Two landmark literary projects evidence this shift: while *L'Encyclopedie* only registered the traditional religious meaning, by the time we get to Littré, "catechism" would also stand for learning "quelque science." The Spanish titles above both acknowledged and distanced themselves from the centuries-old religious usage.

---

3. Tylor, *Anahuac*, 124–25. Tylor is referring to Lorenzo de Zavala's *Ensayo crítico de las revoluciones de México*; the first volume was published in 1831 in Paris. Zavala's comment on Ripalda's catechism is found in a description of the state of education under Spanish colonial rule: "La enseñanza primaria era muy rara en las pequeñas poblaciones, y las escuelas que se establecían en las grandes capitales, estaban dirigidas por los frailes y clérigos en sus propios principios e intereses, o por legos ignorantes que enseñaban a mal leer y escribir, y algunos principios de aritmética para llevar la cuenta en los almacenes de comercio. El catecismo del padre Ripalda, en que están consignadas las máximas de una ciega obediencia al papa y al rey, era toda la base de su religión. Los niños aprendían de memoria estos elementos de esclavitud; y los padres, los sacerdotes y los maestros, los inculcaban constantemente." Lorenzo de Zavala, "Ensayo crítico de las revoluciones de México," in *Obras: El Historiador y el Representante Popular*, ed. Manuel González Ramírez (Mexico City: Editorial Porrúa, 1969), 33. On the change in the reading habits of the Mexicans, see 40.

4. See also the many similar titles collected in *Catecismos políticos españoles arreglados a las constituciones del siglo XIX*, ed. Miguel A. Ruíz de Azúa (Madrid: Comunidad de Madrid / Consejería de Cultura, 1989). Tylor might have been further amused by works bearing titles such as *Catecismo de agricultura* and *Catecismo de ambas Trigonometrías*, both published in London in 1828.

For Tylor, who inspected the catechism in the mid-nineteenth century, its apparent strangeness resided in the juxtaposition of the Catholic religion and strictly secular matters. He saw the pervasive presence of the church as a mark of Spain's legacy. This legacy, and the resulting porousness between the religious and the secular, shaped colonial Mexico and the experiences of its European, criollo, and indigenous peoples alike from its beginnings. The Mexican Indians learned that the conquerors recognized two different sources of authority, the ecclesiastical and the civil, which served as the basic organizing principles of society, that is, ways of classifying social activities and obligations. These are the same two sources of authority whose juxtaposition confused and amused Tylor centuries later, when the question of the education of Mexican citizens in the newly formed republic loomed large in both the religious and secular arenas. This study, which focuses on an earlier historical period, considers works that also sought to teach religious doctrine to a new population in a new context, specifically the indigenous inhabitants of early colonial Mexico. This instructional endeavor occurred at a moment when the crown and the church pinned their hopes for the success of the Spanish enterprise on the instruction of the Mexican Indians in worldly as well as otherworldly matters. An examination of the doctrinal literature of that period produced by friars of the mendicant orders can shed light on the uneasy coexistence of spiritual and secular ambitions.

When the newly appointed *juez gobernador*, Juan de los Ángeles, arrived in the town of Tecamachalco in the Valley of Mexico on August 22, 1563, a number of indigenous scribes were on hand to record the event in detail, describing the ceremonial steps that marked the conferral of his title: the celebration of a Mass followed by a visit to the Audiencia for a public reading of the royal decree authorizing his appointment.[5] The scribes who gave shape to the *Codex Aubin* (ca. 1576–96) took note of the communal prayers on behalf of the Spanish king that preceded the festivities in celebration of San Andrés.[6] One of the seven pictorial documents that make up the *Codex Osuna* (1565) shows the second viceroy of Mexico, Luis de Velasco, confirming the election of a group of Indians to municipal offices by handing them their staffs while a Nahua interpreter stands by. The interpreter's task, as the accompanying text indicates, was to translate into Nahuatl a short exhortation in which the viceroy reminded the newly ap-

---

5. *Anales de Tecamachalco, 1398–1590*, ed. Eustaquio Celestino Solís and Luis Reyes García (Mexico City: CIESAS / Gobierno del Estado de Puebla / Fondo de Cultura Económica, 1992), 15 and 47. It is thought that nine different notaries were responsible for this historical document. *Anales de Tecamachalco*, 15.
6. *Historia de la nación mexicana*, ed. Charles E. Dibble (Madrid: J. Porrúa Turanzas, 1963), 72.

Fig. I.1. Viceroy Luis de Velasco and newly elected municipal officers. *Pintura del gobernador, alcaldes y regidores de México* (also known as *Codex Osuna*). (Courtesy of the Biblioteca Nacional de España.)

Fig. I.2. Pedro Moya de Contreras, archbishop of Mexico, appointed viceroy of the New Spain in 1984. *Tira de Tepechpan.* (Courtesy of the Bibliothèque Nationale de France, Paris.)

pointed officers of their duty to inform others of their obligations regarding religion and the king.

A handful of visual symbols often sufficed to indicate the office, rank, and affiliation of royal and ecclesiastical representatives in the records of indigenous towns. In some exceptional cases, as when the third archbishop of Mexico, Pedro Moya de Contreras, was called in 1584 to serve briefly as viceroy, the *tlahcuiloh*, or painter of the last segment of the *Tira de Tepechpan*, conveyed the coexistence of these two offices in one person by drawing both the *silla curul*, the viceroyal seat, and the traditional episcopal staff.[7] Symbols changed over time as notaries, aware of their inherent malleability, found new uses for them. The body of documents known as *títulos primordiales* or primordial titles

---

7. *Tira de Tepechpan*, ed. Xavier Noguez, 2 vols. (Mexico City: Biblioteca Enciclopédica del Estado de México, 1978), 2:164. See also *Historia de la nación mexicana*, 92; Don Domingo de San Antón Muñón Chimalpahin, *Annals of His Time*, ed. and trans. James Lockhart, Susan Schroeder, and Doris Namala (Stanford: Stanford University Press, 2006), 29. Lori Boornazian Diel discerns the work of four different painters in the *tira*. See *The Tira de Tepechpan: Negotiating Place under Aztec and Spanish Rule* (Austin: University of Texas Press, 2008), 15–18.

sheds light on the process by which members of indigenous municipal councils adapted Spanish symbols of power, such as the coat of arms.[8] The authors of the *título* of San Nicolás and San Pedro, for example, invested the coat of arms adopted by these communities with the same authority as royal decrees and privileges.[9]

It did not take long for indigenous notaries to identify with religious or secular authority; some identified themselves as "escribanos de la iglesia" (ecclesiastical notaries), while others identified with the town's council. In many cases the same notary worked for the church and the secular government.[10] Indigenous notaries never stopped learning about the complex nature of justice, and they were careful to distinguish its different sources of authority.[11] These shifting and sometimes multiple identifications point to the realignment of religion and politics in Spanish and colonial civil society that this study addresses.

The indigenous scribes who kept the traditional genre of historical annals alive in colonial Mexico dutifully recorded regular changes in municipal government as well as other events, such as visits by royal officers and ecclesiastical authorities to their towns.[12] These historical annals reveal a cycle of local government and public events that reaffirmed, through repetition, both the separation of and the intimate connection between the secular and the sacred.

A small number of Indians, mainly those who were part of the local government or prominent members of the community, quickly became thoroughly familiar with the legal rituals fundamental to royal administration, such as the public readings of decrees and provisions. Some of these rituals differed little from their ecclesiastical versions, as the Indian noblemen frequently summoned by the bishop for briefing on the most recent papal bulls probably found out.[13] Through service in local government and frequent contact with the Span-

---

8. "Primordial titles are indigenous-language, municipal histories containing extensive descriptions of the communities' territorial boundaries and land-holdings." Stephanie Wood, "The Social vs. Legal Context of Nahuatl Titles," in *Native Traditions in the Postconquest World*, ed. Elizabeth Hill Boone and Tom Cummins (Washington, DC: Dumbarton Oaks Research Library and Collection, 1998), 201.

9. Robert Haskett, "Paper Shields: The Ideology of Coats of Arms in Colonial Mexican Primordial Titles," *Ethnohistory* 43, no. 1 (Winter 1996): 112.

10. Rebecca Horn, *Postconquest Coyoacan: Nahua-Spanish Relations* (Stanford: Stanford University Press, 1997), 65.

11. For instance, when recording the administration of a particular punishment, they took care to indicate whether ecclesiastical or secular judges had sentenced the offender. *Anales de Tecamachalco*, 54.

12. On the most salient features of this genre and its transformation throughout the colonial period, see James Lockhart, *The Nahuas after the Conquest: A Social and Cultural History of the Indians of Central Mexico, Sixteenth through Eighteenth Centuries* (Stanford: Stanford University Press, 1992), 376–92.

13. *Anales de Tecamachalco*, 82, 91–92.

iards, the Nahuas learned what was second nature to the conquerors: that the ecclesiastical body and secular associations, by virtue of being corporate entities, shared many features, including and above all, juridical procedures and protocols.

A significant number of indigenous people also became acquainted with the basic principles of the new colonial order and the administration of justice through contact with the friars of the mendicant orders who were the most visible face of evangelization in Mexico and whose works constitute a large part of the sources for this study. Recipients of papal privileges, the first Franciscans arrived in Mexico in 1523, followed by a second group of Franciscans a year later, the Dominicans in 1526, and the Augustinians in 1533.[14] Among the Nahuas holding positions in local government, some had received advanced education at the Colegio de Santa Cruz de Tlatelolco, founded by the Franciscans in 1536. Such was the case, for example, of Francisco Bautista de Contreras, governor of Xochimilco, or Antonio Valeriano, one of the Colegio's most distinguished graduates, who enjoyed a long career in public life.[15]

As Tylor's chance encounter with Ripalda's catechism shows us, religious didactic works played a prominent role in colonial Mexico; their long association with literacy and basic instruction made them something more than strictly doctrinal tools. Catechisms, *doctrinas*, and sermons taught Mexican Indians to obey the pope, their priests, and the laws of the church, but also the king, his representatives, and his laws. Despite many similarities, these works often differed in their treatment of difficult subjects such as the boundaries between secular and religious obligation, the nature of human justice, and the scope of papal and princely authority. Over time, as Tylor noted, catechisms became records of the changing relations between the church, secular institutions, and the laity. This book deals with an early chapter in the history of these relations.

The religious literature written to facilitate the conversion of the Nahuas and other cultural groups shows that the friars played a significant role in the transmission of legal and social norms, as well as attitudes toward secular law and

14. For a comprehensive account of the goals and activities of the mendicant orders in early colonial Mexico, see Robert Ricard, *The Spiritual Conquest of Mexico*, trans. Lesley Byrd Simpson (Berkeley: University of California Press, 1966).

15. Commenting on the graduates from the college in a letter to the king, the Franciscans revealed their interest in grooming a cadre of Nahuas for positions of authority: "y por la mayor parte a ellos, como a más hábiles y suficientes, se suelen encomendar los oficios de jueces y gobernadores, y otros cargos de república como el que hoy día es gobernador de los indios de México, Antonio Valeriano, que ha sido colegial, y es muy hábil y virtuoso." Joaquín García Icazbalceta, *Códice Mendieta*, 2 vols. (Guadalajara: Edmundo Aviña Levy, 1971), 1:178. Nahua historian Domingo de San Antón Muñón Chimalpahin Quauhtlehuanitzin commented on Antonio Valeriano's unusually long political career in his journal. On Valeriano's death in 1605, see Chimalpahin, *Annals of His Time*, 85.

authorities. This occurrence was not unique to Mexico, as those familiar with the development of ecclesiastical law in the early Middle Ages know.[16] In New Spain, the cultural distance between conqueror and conquered allowed European friars to present indigenous audiences with their own perspectives on both religious and secular institutions. In this sense the early history of colonial law in Mexico—and perhaps later attitudes toward authority among Indians and criollos as well—appears inextricably linked to the missionaries' task of cultural mediation. As we explore the conditions of instruction of the Indians in moral, legal, or religious matters throughout this study, we should remember that for many friars, successful evangelization of Mexico went hand in hand with the consolidation of their own authority, often in direct competition with secular power. The traditional jurisdictional conflicts that continued to be an everyday occurrence in Spain in spite of the Catholic Monarchs' best efforts acquired a new dimension when translated to Mexico, where the friars assumed the duties of diocesan clergy.

While friars and *encomenderos* both opposed the close association between the Mexican Indians and the colonial legal system, they did so on different grounds. The friars of the mendicant orders who laid the groundwork for the evangelization of Mexico had a complicated relationship to ecclesiastical and secular authority. One source of constant tension between friars and royal authorities was the friars' deep reservations toward the crown's decision to transfer and enforce the traditional separation between ecclesiastical and royal jurisdictions in dealing with Indians. As the friars argued, such distinctions could hardly be applied in Mexico if the primary goal of the Spanish presence was to evangelize the Mexican Indians under the guidance and supervision of the religious orders. While the missionaries sought in vain to be recognized by royal authorities as legitimate judges, they wasted little time presenting themselves as such to the Mexican Indians and administering justice and even punishments, a practice they continued well after the issuance of a royal decree in opposition.

As we will see, almost from the very beginning, these and other conflicts between ecclesiastical and secular authorities played out in the open, acquiring a public dimension. This public character appears to have become essential to the articulation of grievances and forging of alliances between different sectors of the population. The law of God and the laws of men vied for the attention of the Indians.[17]

The missionaries in New Spain came to view learning as a process that was

---

16. On the close association between secular laws and medieval penitentials, see Thomas Pollock Oakley, *English Penitential Discipline and Anglo-Saxon Law in Their Joint Influence*, Studies in History, Economics and Public Law 107, no. 2 (New York: Columbia University, 1923), especially 43–54, 138–44, and 164–65.

17. Antonio Manuel Hespanha, "Le Droit et la domination coloniale européenne: Le cas de l'Empire oriental portugais," in *Lois, justice, coutume: Amérique et Europe latines (16e.–19e. siècles)*, ed. Juan Carlos Garavaglia and J.-F. Schaub (Paris: Èditions de l'EHESS, 2005), 203–26.

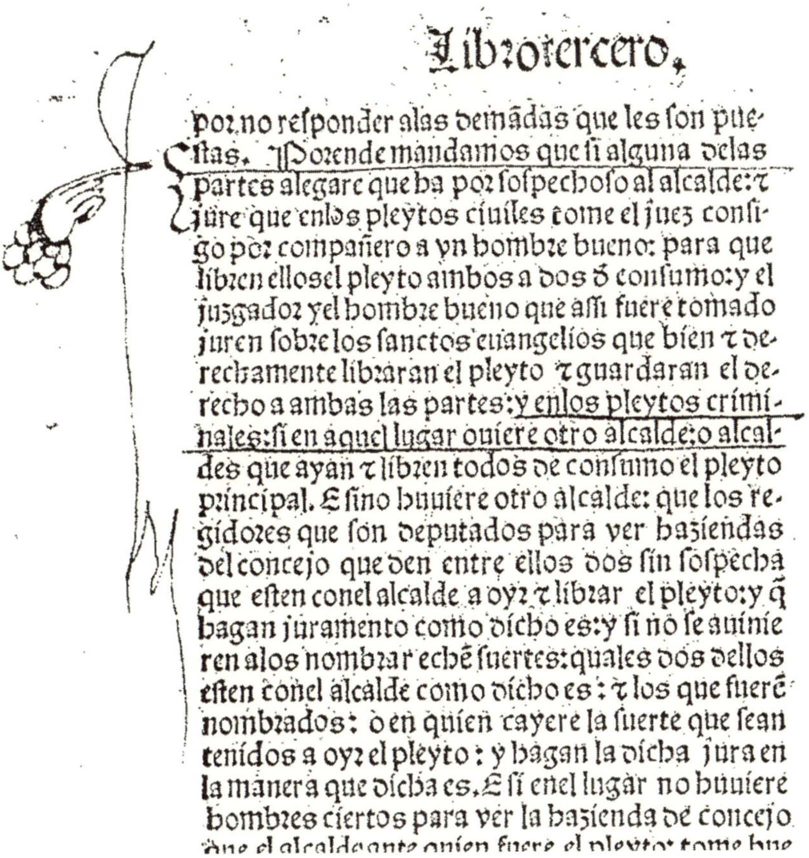

Libro tercero,

poz no refponder alas demādas que les fon pue-
ftas. ¶Pozende mandamos que fi alguna delas
partes alegare que ba poz fofpechofo al alcalde: τ
jure que enlos pleytos ciuiles tome el juez confi-
go poz compañero a yn bombze bueno: para que
libzen ellosel pleyto ambos a dos ō confumo: y el
juzgadoz yel bombze bueno que affi fueré tomado
juren fobze los fanctos euangelios que bien τ de-
rechamente libzaran el pleyto τ guardaran el derecho a ambas las partes: y enlos pleytos criminales: fi en aquel lugar ouiere otro alcalde: o alcaldes que ayan τ libzen todos de confumo el pleyto
principal. E fino buuiere otro alcalde: que los re-
gidozes que fon deputados para ver baziendas
del concejo que den entre ellos dos fin fofpecha
que eften conel alcalde a oyz τ libzar el pleyto: y ḡ
bagan juramento como dicho es: y fi nō fe auinie
ren alos nombzar eché fuertes: quales dos dellos
eften conel alcalde como dicho es: τ los que fueré
nombzados: o en quien cayere la fuerte que fean
tenidos a oyz el pleyto: y bagan la dicha jura en
la manera que dicha es. E fi enel lugar no buuiere
bombzes ciertos para ver la bazienda de concejo
que el alcalde ante quien fuere el pleyto: tome bue

Fig. I.3. Manicule.

not restricted to any particular setting. Teaching became closely associated with showing, with directing Indian eyes to symbols, objects, images, and actions (either devotional or punitive) that affirmed the presence of Christianity in all corners of daily life. An eloquent example is the well-known *nota* sign of a hand with a pointing finger or manicule found in pictographic catechisms, doctrinal books, and documents. First migrating from manuscripts to the printed page, and then enjoying a double life as handwritten sign and movable type, the manicule came to be used in Mexican pictorial catechisms as a conjunction, emphatic particle, and deictic sign that stood for the authoritative hand of the teacher/friar.[18]

If in Spain the boundaries between the secular and the religious were often

---

18. William H. Sherman, *Used Books: Marking Readers in Renaissance England* (Philadelphia: University of Pennsylvania Press, 2008), 25–52.

Fig. I.4. Pictographic catechism attributed to Fr. Bernardino de Sahagún by Lorenzo Boturini. (Courtesy of the Bibliothèque Nationale de France, Paris.)

unclear, in New Spain they became even more porous. In some circumstances, the friars opted to instruct the Mexican Indians about the existence of such boundaries; in others, they chose to keep them in a state of confusion. For instance, they deemed it important to warn the members of indigenous brotherhoods against mistaking their religious duty to tend to the sick for a secular obligation such as "hateful tribute labor" (*tlahiltequitl*).[19] Some high royal administrators who were sympathetic to the friars' cause shared their belief that learning by example was as important as formal instruction in cementing the

---

19. Alonso de Molina, *Nahua Confraternities in Early Colonial Mexico: The 1552 Nahuatl Ordinances of fray Alonso de Molina, OFM*, trans. and ed. Barry D. Sell (Berkeley: Academy of Franciscan History, 2002), 89, 111. On the other hand, secular authorities and even private individuals in some cases tied secular and private obligations to religious holidays, perhaps adding to the confusion that the friars were trying to ameliorate. For example, in 1528, the inspector and captain Juan de Ortega was sent to Michoacán to ensure that the population fulfilled Spanish demands for labor and tribute. Ortega established a tributary cycle that ended on the feast of Saint John and was followed by three months free of obligations. See Rodrigo Martínez Baracs, *Caminos cruzados:* Fray *Maturino Gilberti en Perivan* (Zamora, Michoacan: El Colegio de Michoacán, 2005), 32. Similarly, in 1566, Don Julián de la Rosa, an indigenous nobleman from Tlaxcala, left instructions in his testament for close dependents of his estate (*teixhuihuan*) who received tracts of land to make regular payments in products from that land to his heirs on Christmas, the Feast of the Resurrection, Corpus Christi, and Assumption Day. See Thelma D. Sullivan, ed., *Documentos tlaxcaltecas del siglo XVI* (Mexico City: Universidad Autónoma de México), 1987, 325.

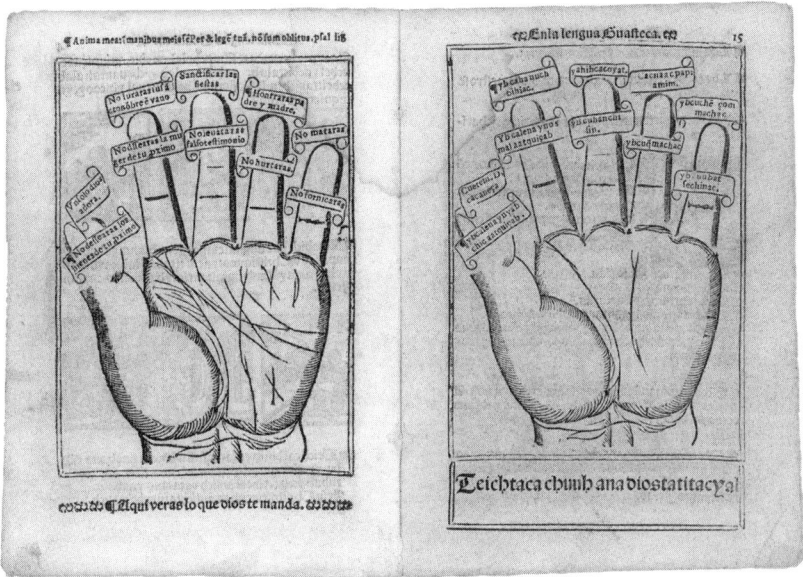

Fig. I.5. The Ten Commandments. Fr. Juan de la Cruz, *Doctrina christiana en la lengua guasteca con la lengua castellana*. Mexico City: Pedro Ocharte, 1571. (Courtesy of the John Carter Brown Library at Brown University.)

faith of the newly converted. Thus, Juan de Ovando asked religious ministers to ensure, first, that all Indians who met certain requirements confess and receive communion, and second, that the gravely ill prepare their testaments and be given extreme unction.[20] Ministers were further urged to surround the sick with other Indians as they received communion so as to foster devotion to the sacrament. This recommendation, when followed, changed the last rites from a domestic, intimate event focused on individual fate into a semipublic affair.

It is no exaggeration to suggest that for some friars instructing the Indians on the breadth of the religious domain meant reducing the scope of the secular, an operation that also left its mark on indigenous languages.[21] For the few but highly influential friars who devoted years to mastering indigenous languages, linguistic knowledge was not only the key to an alien culture but also the source

20. *Gobernación espiritual de Indias, Código Ovandino. Libro 1º*, ed. Angel Martín González (Guatemala City: Instituto Teológico Salesiano, 1978), 166.

21. William F. Hanks, *Converting Words: Maya in the Age of the Cross* (Berkeley: University of California Press, 2010), especially 85–241.

of an unlimited confidence in their power to effect change in local communities. We will encounter a number of these friars in this book; the image of one of them, Bernardino de Sahagún, as he frequently revised the plan for his encyclopedia, evokes both his search for an all-encompassing representation of Nahua society and his unshakable belief as a philologist in his ability to order reality by ordering words. As evidence of the friars' self-assurance, consider the testimony of another of these friars, Bautista de Lagunas, a sixteenth-century Franciscan lexicographer and grammarian based in Michoacán who published a somewhat idiosyncratic dictionary of the Purepecha or Tarascan language in 1574.[22] When discussing the verb *cuera*, glossed as "to untie" and "to absolve," Lagunas pointed out that the derived form *cueratspenstani* had lost all everyday meaning for Purepecha speakers, to become almost exclusively reserved for the sacrament of penance. Lagunas credited Purepecha speakers with having purposely wrought this semantic shift out of reverence for the sacramental act.[23] Notwithstanding a likely dose of wishful thinking behind this explanation, it is worth noting that in portraying the Indians as agents of change, Lagunas made sure that his role as faithful recorder of word usage remained uncompromised. He was almost certainly aware that the successful evangelization of the Tarascans included leaving a mark on their language.

In addition to recording these changes, Lagunas also identified semantic fields that could be expanded to facilitate religious instruction, for example, around the sacrament of penance. One such cluster of words was the verb *cuera* and its conceptual opposite, *kata* ("to tie, to jail, to bind"), which share a rich semantic field associated with the administration of justice. In treating the words jointly, Lagunas noted that they were well suited to convey spiritual states. For instance, he pointed out that *katâgani*, "to be incarcerated," could refer to the imprisonment of the soul as well as the body.[24] Similarly, *katacuhni*, "to wear an anklet," could be turned into "katahuani animaechani," which meant "to make souls prisoners," but also "excommunication," a concept that led missionaries

---

22. The first Tarascan dictionary was published in 1556. Its author, the French-born Franciscan friar Maturino Gilberti, singlehandedly laid the foundation for the study of the Tarascan language through a series of works that included grammars and translations of religious literature.

23. "Aunque ya por reverencia del sacramento quasi no lo usan para otras cosas: sino Cueranstani, para cosas yrracionales como lios, y cargas que por estar assi atadas y liadas se llaman Katacata, y tambien las cargas de leña, o yerva por traerlas atadas, o liadas con aquellas angarillas." Juan Baptista de Lagunas, *Arte y dictionario con otras obras en lengua michoacana*, ed. J. Benedict Warren (Morelia, Michoacán: Fimax Publicistas Editores, 1983), 261. In contrast, Gilberti had years earlier recorded the expression *cueratspenstani thauacurita* for the priest's act of absolving sins. Maturino Gilberti, *Vocabulario en Lengua de Michoacan*, transcription by Agustín Jacinto Zavala (Zamora, Michoacán: El Colegio de Michoacán / Fideicomiso Teixidor, 1997).

24. Lagunas, *Arte y dictionario*, 262–63.

at different points in time to wonder whether the Mexican Indians would ever fully understand it.[25]

At the root of these distinctions lies the friars' preoccupation with making converts aware of the existence of two distinct sources of justice, a topic we will return to more than once in the pages that follow. These few examples show the determination of friars who selectively introduced Spanish terms to create a specialized religious vocabulary from the everyday language of their flock. Lagunas's work, which resembles a technical dictionary of spiritual terms in progress, portrays the Tarascan language as an expanding field of possibilities open for spiritual use. Bringing the spiritual to light by losing oneself in the maze of alien words and usages was itself a religious activity, akin to the exegesis of the Scriptures. What remained implicit in Lagunas becomes more fully articulated by the Dominican Juan de Córdoba in his *Vocabulario castellano-zapoteco* (1574), where he states that God equipped man with a tongue "so that with it he would be able to explain the inner concepts of the soul and make them known to other individuals of his species."[26] Córdoba took this idea to heart; departing from Molina's dictionaries, he introduced lexical distinctions pointing to the inner domain of the soul, a preoccupation of contemporary theologians as well as natural philosophers. Whereas Molina allowed only one entry for "conscience" (*neyoliximachiliztli*), as a good Thomist, Córdoba made room for several entries that covered the rather technical meanings of the word in the scholastic tradition.[27] Taking for granted the universality of the workings of the soul and moral reasoning, he set out to extract philosophical notions identical to those of Christianity from the Zapotec language. In the same spirit, he recorded the introduction of new practices such as the taking of oaths for official appointments and in legal proceedings. When discussing oaths, a subject that we will explore in chapter 3, Córdoba distinguished between the native swearing formulas of old, which he likened to maledictions, and those that indigenous converts had learned from the Spaniards and come to embrace.[28] That

---

25. Lagunas, *Arte y dictionario*, 263. The Augustinian Alonso de la Veracruz suggested that the Mexican Indians barely grasped the meaning of excommunication. Ernest J. Burrus, ed., *The Writings of Alonso de la Vera Cruz*, 5 vols. (Rome: Jesuit Historical Institute; St. Louis: St. Louis University, 1968–75), 5:117–19.

26. Juan de Córdoba, *Vocabulario castellano-zapoteco*, ed. Wigberto Jiménez Moreno (Mexico City: Instituto Nacional de Antropología e Historia, 1942), 5r.

27. Among the entries: "conciencia yd est la potencia o subjeto della"; "conciencia pro vt es acto testificativo de lo que hemos hecho o no hemos hecho"; "conciencia pro ut es acto judicativo de que algo se deve hazer o no." Córdoba, *Vocabulario*, 84–84v.

28. "Iurar echando maldiciones, y este era el modo del jurar los indios tiquèea, cotè, què. . . . Iurar como juran agora los yndios y juramos. Tocònaya pejoanana dios, tozètea, làa, toçacayalàa Pejoànana Dios." Córdoba, *Vocabulario*, 216v.

Córdoba apparently felt the need to distinguish swearing and oath-taking was likely a result of the various meanings of the Spanish verb *jurar*, a multiplicity that did not exist in the Zapotec language. What Córdoba translated as "making an oath" was actually a neologism to describe the action of employing the name of God.[29]

Despite their differences, and with varying degrees of sophistication, the historical characters in this book—friars, royal officers, *encomenderos*, legal scholars—appear to have done their best to understand their world as they strove to transform it. The disconnect between their confidence in their ability to give direction to the constant changes in this fragile colonial society and their struggles with the limits of their own power reminds us that, like the recipients of their endless reports and complaints in Spain, most participants had only a partial understanding of the many forces at work. Yet changes in the behavior of either the indigenous population or fellow Spaniards were duly reported, sometimes with considerable exaggeration or the addition of banal details that may or may not betray the mark of invention.

It has been suggested that distance from the metropolis made it easier for Spanish conquerors who otherwise considered themselves loyal subjects to ignore and even openly defy the king's authority. At the same time, in places like Mexico, the friars reminded *encomenderos* that they should fear the law of God and the sanctions that awaited those who broke it. Religious men viewed loyalty to the king through a somewhat different lens and, as the Mexican case shows, did not hesitate to ignore royal directives or even support conspiracies against the crown. Each group accused the other of disregarding the king's laws. *Encomenderos* and conquerors interpreted the many changes in the laws governing Indian labor during the first decades of the century as unmistakable signs of a shift in the crown's commitment to traditional terms of loyalty. This perception grew stronger as the frequent sight of Mexican Indians seeking redress in local courts came to confirm their status as royal subjects in no uncertain terms. Despite their best efforts, the *encomenderos* failed to convince the crown to grant them noble status and jurisdiction over the indigenous men and women.

The entrance of the indigenous peoples of Mexico into the Christian fold and the legal order of the conquerors revealed the power of baptism. Spanish colonists came to regard baptism as a disruptive force that weakened their status as Christians and royal subjects. As reported by the friars, Spaniards began avoiding any reference to the new converts as Christians, reserving the term

---

29. I am grateful to David Tavárez for pointing this out to me.

for their countrymen.[30] The conquerors' refusal to accept Indians as Christians had as much to do with citizenship as religion, since, as stated in Alphonse X's *Partidas*, conversion was one path to naturalization available to foreigners in Spain.[31] For their part, the Nahuas also attached new meanings to baptism; in the late seventeenth and eighteenth centuries some Nahua members of local ruling families looking back at the time of the Conquest reimagined the baptism of their ancestors as a religious and political ritual that legitimized the authority of their lineage and marked a new beginning for the community and its territory.[32] Back in the sixteenth century, the *encomenderos'* reluctance echoed the controversies surrounding the pure blood statutes, which had restricted access of converted Jews to public and ecclesiastical offices since the fifteenth century.[33] In both the fifteenth and sixteenth centuries, those opposed to the statutes took exception to the use of the term "new Christian" on theological grounds.[34] Some defenses of *conversos* turned into extended commentaries on the theological and legal implications of baptism that revealed how the sacrament had become the very foundation of a social order that rested on the notion of *persona*, or person.[35] At a time when the religious orders wanted

---

30. The accusation is found in a report that the Franciscans sent to the Pope: "Lo sexto, es necesarísimo provea S.S. de remedio en un infernal abuso que los españoles han plantado en toda la región destas Indias occidentales, y es de llamarse ellos cristianos, a diferencia de los naturales de la tierra, puesto que todos son bautizados; y así es plática general de los españoles, hablando con los indios, para decir 'llámame a aquel español,' o 'dile tal cosa a aquel español,' o 've a casa de fulano español,' decir 'llámame a aquel cristiano,' o 'dile esto a aquel cristiano'; cosa absurdísima, y que espanta no haber tenido los Prelados de estas partes de que se ponga remedio en ella, porque es persuasiva a los indios para que nunca se tengan por verdaderos cristianos." García Icazbalceta, *Códice Mendieta*, vol. 1, doc. 57, 258.

31. Tamar Herzog, *Defining Nations: Immigrants and Citizens in Early Modern Spain and Spanish America* (New Haven: Yale University Press, 2003), 122. For the role of religion in the conceptualizations of nativeness in early modern Spain, see 121–28.

32. This is one feature of the body of documents known as "primordial titles" that emerged in the period mentioned above. See, for example, the title from Coatepec de las Bateas, in *Los títulos primordiales del centro de México*, ed. Paula López Caballero (Mexico City: CONACULTA, 2003), 117–18. For an overview of the primordial titles, see Serge Gruzinski, *The Conquest of Mexico: The Incorporation of Indian Societies into the Western World, 16th–18th Centuries*, trans. Eileen Corrigan (Cambridge: Polity Press, 1993), 98–145; and James Lockhart, "Views of Corporate and Self and History in Some Valley of Mexico Towns, Late Seventeenth and Eighteenth Centuries," in *Nahuas and Spaniards: Postconquest Central Mexican History and Philology* (Stanford: Stanford University Press; Los Angeles: UCLA Latin American Center Publications, University of California, Los Angeles, 1991), 39–64.

33. See Albert A. Sicroff, *Les controverses des statuts de "pureté de sang" en Espagne du XVe au XVIIe siècle* (Paris: Didier, 1960).

34. In 1549 Fernán Díaz de Toledo went even further, questioning the application of the term "converso" to Jews. "Instrucción del relator para el obispo de Cuenca a favor de la nación Hebrea," in Alonso de Cartagena, *Defensorium unitatis christianae*, ed. Manuel Alonso (Madrid: Publicaciones de la Escuela de Estudios Hebraicos, 1943), 348.

35. I am referring to the treatise written by Alonso de Cartagena, bishop of Burgos, in response to the statutes of Toledo, which circulated in manuscript form for a very long time. Guillermo

to infuse religious meaning into every aspect of indigenous life, including language, lay Spaniards sought to limit this extension of the sacred sphere and undermined the very idea of an all-inclusive "corpus mysticum."[36] As we will see, however, by identifying closely with their new flock in the name of religion, the friars inadvertently allowed their opponents to cast doubt on their allegiance to their homeland and its king. Having worked hard not to be associated with their countrymen, the religious men found it necessary to remind Philip II that they were also Spaniards.[37]

The education of the Indians in legal matters was also an education in the social and predominantly masculine universe of the Spaniards, and involved learning about rules and procedures as well as the social codes, values, and concepts woven into the law. One of these concepts was honor, which was closely associated with other concepts and institutions such as reputation, social estate, oaths, and punishments. Few social phenomena have received as much attention from historians and anthropologists as honor.[38] Recent decades have generated a rich body of scholarship and a fair amount of debate on the concept.[39]

Verdín-Díaz, ed., *Alonso de Cartagena y el Defensorium Unitatis Christianae* (Oviedo: Universidad de Oviedo, 1992). For the response that the sixteenth-century statutes elicited from a Franciscan theologian, Antonio de Córdoba, see *Quaestionarium theologicum sive Sylva amplissima decisionum, et variarum resolutionum casuum conscientiae* (Venice: Beretii, 1604), book 1, q. 54, 432–47. On the notion of "persona" in medieval canon law, see Jean Gaudemet, "Persona," in *La doctrine canonique médiévale* (London: Variorum), 465–91; and Alain Boureau, "Droit et théologie au XIIIe siècle," *Annales* 47, no. 6 (November–December 1992): especially 1116–21. On the legal implications of baptism as discussed by decretists, see E. F. Vodola, "*Fides et culpa*: The Use of Roman Law in Ecclesiastical Ideology," in *Authority and Power: Studies in Medieval Law and Government Presented to Walter Ullman on His Seventieth Birthday*, ed. Brian Tierney and Peter Linehan (Cambridge: Cambridge University Press, 1980), 83–97. The relationship between baptism and social order has been masterfully examined by Adriano Prosperi in the essay "Battesimo e identitá cristiana nella prima etá moderna," in *Salvezza delle anime, disciplina dei corpi: Un seminario sulla sotria del battesimo*, ed. A. Prosperi (Pisa: Edizioni della Normale, 2006), 1–65.

36. García Icazbalceta, *Códice Mendieta*, vol. 1, doc. 6, 28.

37. "Asimismo suplicamos a V.M. sea servido de considerar que tan bien somos españoles los frailes como los seglares, y que los hábitos no nos hacen de diversa nación, ni que caeteris paribus habiamos de ser contrarios a la propria nuestra por ser favorables a los de la remota y extraña." García Icazbalceta, *Códice Mendieta*, vol. 1, doc. 10, 37.

38. For the concept of honor in Spain, see Julian Pitt-Rivers, "Honour and Social Status," in *Honour and Shame: The Values of Mediterranean Society*, ed. J. G. Peristiany (Chicago: University of Chicago Press, 1966), 19–77, and, in the same volume, Julio Caro-Baroja, "Honour and Shame: A Historical Account of Several Conflicts," 81–137. See also José Antonio Maravall, *Poder, honor y élites en el siglo XVII* (Madrid: Siglo Veintiuno de España, 1979). Among recent works, three stand out. Renato Barahona, *Sex Crimes, Honour and the Law in Early Modern Spain: Vizcaya, 1528–1735* (Buffalo: University of Toronto Press, 2003); Ruth MacKay, "*Lazy, Improvident People*": Myth and Reality in the Writing of Spanish History (Ithaca, NY: Cornell University Press, 2006); and Scott K. Taylor, *Honor and Violence in Golden Age Spain* (New Haven: Yale University Press, 2008).

39. A case in point is the exchange between Julian Pitt-Rivers and Frank H. Stewart triggered by Pitt-Rivers's review of Stewart's *Honor* (University of Chicago Press, 1994). See Julian Pitt-Rivers, "Review of *Honor* by Frank Henderson Stewart," *L'Homme* 143 (July–September 1997): 215–17; and Frank H. Stewart, "De l' honneur," *L'Homme* 147 (July–September 1998): 237–46. I would like

My approach in this book departs from recent scholarship on honor in Latin America on several counts, starting with the period under study, the foundational stage of the colonial order in Mexico. I am conscious that the asymmetry of power during this period meant that each party gained insight into the other's social and moral universe under significantly different conditions. Mexican Indians could always count on direct experience and observation, but many also learned about the conquerors' ways through their codified religious (for example, the Ten Commandments) and legal precepts. Many of these precepts touched directly or indirectly on honor. Refracted through the prism of law and religion, the concept of honor accompanied the transfer of not only other European notions, but also goods and institutions. The following chapters address these processes and explore the discussions that took place around the concept of honor, so deeply ingrained in the Europeans' image of themselves as members of a religious and political body, as Mexican Indians became royal subjects and Christians.[40]

The first Spaniards to arrive in Mexico observed the Nahuas and concluded that the Nahua nobility took honor seriously. During the period of initial contact, a shared sense of honor served Spaniards and Nahua noblemen well and allowed the parties to forge a temporary agreement concerning their respective places and mutual obligations in the new colonial order.[41] The conquerors' initial acceptance of the expectations of the Nahua elite regarding its treatment and privileges was not, however, intended as a long-term or unconditional commitment. The relative autonomy enjoyed by indigenous communities in running their daily affairs under an elective local government composed largely of members of the nobility helped shape the *encomenderos'* perception that the

---

to thank Professor Stewart for sharing this and related material. More recently, Ruth MacKay in her study of Spanish artisans has convincingly called into question Pitt-Rivers's notion that honor is inherently at odds with legality. *Lazy, Improvident People*, 85.

40. By and large, studies on honor in colonial Latin America have emerged in close connection to research on women, marriage, and sexuality. See Ramón A. Gutiérrez, "From Honor to Love: Transformations of the Meaning of Sexuality in Colonial New Mexico," in *Kinship Ideology and Practice in Latin America*, ed. Raymond T. Smith (Chapel Hill: University of North Carolina Press, 1984), 237–63; Lyman L. Johnson and Sonya Lipsett-Rivera, eds., *The Faces of Honor: Sex, Shame and Violence in Colonial Latin America* (Albuquerque: University of New Mexico Press, 1998); Asunción Lavrin, ed., *Sexuality and Marriage in Colonial Latin America* (Lincoln: University of Nebraska Press, 1989); Patricia Seed, *To Love, Honor, and Obey in Colonial Mexico: Conflicts over Marriage Choice, 1574–1821* (Stanford: Stanford University Press, 1988); Ann Twinam, *Public Lives, Private Secrets: Gender, Honor, Sexuality, and Illegitimacy in Colonial Latin America* (Stanford: Stanford University Press, 1999). Among the ethnographic works that touch upon some of the themes explored here is John Beard Haviland, *Gossip, Reputation, and Knowledge in Zinacantan* (Chicago: University of Chicago Press, 1977).

41. See Richard C. Trexler, *Church and Community, 1200–1600: Studies in the History of Florence and New Spain* (Rome: Edizioni di Storia e Letteratura, 1987), 469–92.

social currency that passed for honor among the Mexican Indians was culture-bound.

The sixteenth-century theologian Tomás de Mercado argued that fame and *honra* were goods found across all nations, including those that might appear uncivilized to Europeans.[42] And while all nations had their own ways of determining where fame or reputation lay—Spaniards, he noted, took special pride in matters of lineage[43]—they differed in their conventions for reverence and courtesy. The Mexican friars, in addressing this question of honor across cultural boundaries, tended to adopt a perspective that was, if not entirely determined by the assumptions that guided their own efforts at cultural translation, in large part informed by them. The corpus of traditional expressions and speeches selected and transcribed by the Franciscan Andrés de Olmos and later on by Bernardino de Sahagún in their linguistic research suggests that the friars looked for and found compelling evidence in the Nahuatl language that the Nahuas and Spaniards shared similar notions of honor, reputation, and shame.[44] Over time, as we shall see in the discussions surrounding the administration of oaths, some members of the clergy came to voice a different opinion. For the first generations of missionaries, however, familiarizing themselves with indigenous notions of personhood and morality represented a necessary step in instructing the Nahuas on basic Christian precepts as well as the secular and ecclesiastical laws that were applied to them.

In New Spain, Indian honor was rarely examined during the first decades of the sixteenth century, partly because existing Spanish laws and local provisions, however irrelevant or controversial *encomenderos* may have found them, spelled out the privileges granted to the native elite and offered general guidelines for handling their grievances. From their arrival, the friars pressed the crown to grant the Nahuas and other groups, whom it recognized as free subjects, special protection on account of their precarious economic and spiritual condition. Under this tutelage—in which the religious orders reserved a promi-

---

42. In keeping his promise to avoid scholastic analysis so as to better reach an audience of nonspecialists, Mercado defined *honra* in reference to actions commonly performed to convey reverence, such as standing up upon someone's arrival, kissing hands when greeting, and using honorifics. Tomás de Mercado, *Summa de tratos y contratos* (Seville: Hernando Díaz, 1571), 159v–60.

43. "entre Españoles, que es gente que estima en mucho lo que toca a la sangre, y a los antepassados." Mercado, *Summa de tratos y contratos*, 159.

44. Andrés de Olmos, *Arte para aprender la lengua mexicana*, ed. Rémi Siméon (Paris, 1875; Guadalajara: Edmundo Aviña Levy, 1972), chap. 8, 211–30. Citations are to the Aviña Levy edition. Fr. Bernardino de Sahagún, *Florentine Codex*, ed. Charles E. Dibble and Arthur J. O. Anderson, 12 vols. (Santa Fe: School of American Research / University of Utah, 1969), vol. 6, book 6, chap. 43, 241–60. See also the collection of phrases put together by Fr. Juan de Mijangos and published by Angel Ma. Garibay K., "Frases y modos de hablar, elegantes y metafóricos, de los indios mexicanos," *Estudios de Cultura Náhuatl* 6 (1966): 11–27.

nent role for themselves—the church would have exclusive jurisdiction over the indigenous people. Although the proposal failed to garner support in the court, the efforts that went into making it a de facto reality are one more illustration of the tortuous path of the secular and the spiritual from Europe to America. The missionaries stopped short of openly declaring that the Indians should be protected from royal legislation, but made no effort to hide their negative views on allowing them to become involved in endless and costly lawsuits. Behind the obsession with the litigious Indian lurks the inchoate idea—very much present in the critique launched by religious reformers in Spain—of justice as an imperfect but necessary arrangement that tethers individuals to the material world.

Whereas the crown agreed in general terms that new subjects needed protection, it was reluctant to adopt measures that, like the friars' radical proposal, would dramatically restrict its power. In response to growing concerns over the administration of justice involving Indians, the crown first excluded them from the Inquisitorial jurisdiction of the Holy Office tribunals founded in Mexico and Lima after 1571, and then established the General Indian Court in 1585.[45] By that time, the Indians had been officially granted the protections extended to so-called *personas miserables*, the legal category that traditionally included the poor, women, and orphans. This legal tutelage was complemented by the decision of the Third Mexican Church Council in 1585 to consider all Mexican Indians neophytes, a label that confined them to a conceptually odd state of spiritually arrested development and contradicted the friars' expectations about the new converts. The resulting legal and religious divide among royal subjects only reinforced existing perceptions of a cultural gap between colonizers and colonized, and brought into the open the lingering question of the commensurability of honor across societies.[46]

For sixteenth-century Spanish jurists, canonists, and theologians, honor counted among the many goods enjoyed by men. From a conceptual standpoint, honor posed some problems, since it simultaneously encompassed the abstract and the concrete, the religious and the secular, and the individual and the social. Such conceptual difficulties came to the fore when legal scholars and moral theologians were asked for guidance in dealing with offenses against honor. In confession, for example, penitents were expected to make restitution

---

45. Woodrow Borah, *Justice by Insurance: The General Indian Court of Colonial Mexico and the Legal Aides of the Half-Real* (Berkeley: University of California Press, 1983).

46. An example is the musing of Fernando Zurita: "Utrum omnes Hispani tanquam nobiles sint habiendi, cum honoris impendendi, vel compensandi causa Indis conferuntur. ("Whether all Spaniards when compared to the Indians should be considered noblemen when it comes to the question of how honor should be handled or compensated"). Fernando Zurita, *Theologicarum de Indis quaestionum: Enchiridion primum* (Madrid: Querino Gerardo, 1586), quaestio 4, 12.

for these offenses, as they were when confessing offenses involving other kinds of goods. The questions that this particular brand of restitution posed were not easy to answer, since in order to think of honor as something that could be restored, it had to become commensurable with different worldly goods and, in the case of the Spanish colonies, cultural values.[47]

The recurrent tension between secular and religious authority was of course experienced in different ways by different members of early Mexican colonial society. This study examines the fault lines of this tension as it ran through different arenas of colonial life. I begin the first chapter in the world of goods, where the focus on the distinction between spiritual and earthly possessions revealed the importance of material goods in the spiritual life of colonial subjects. Friars in Mexico wrote extensively about goods and their place in the economic and spiritual life of their indigenous charges, and their repeated involvement in the collection of tribute and tithes among the Indians testifies to the friars' interest in the material culture of the new converts, and the ways it had been transformed under colonial rule. This inquiry furnished a wealth of information on the production and consumption of goods as well as labor, trade, and occupations that soon proved useful. Confessors were often caught between acknowledging the new economic reality and promoting an ideal view of goods as either earthly or spiritual, with honor occupying a somewhat ambiguous place. Indian testaments and ordinances allow a glimpse of the effect that the missionaries' teachings on moral life in relation to goods—their possession, use, and disposal upon death—had on the Indians. This preoccupation with material life, in turn, left its mark on doctrinal works that fashioned the Christian message around ideas of spiritual and earthly goods and brought economy and religion together in unexpected ways.

In the second chapter, I turn from ownership to personhood, particularly to the intervention of the friars in cases involving the restitution of honor. These cases fell within the purview of confessors, and manuals for confessors of Indians show the friars in the process of coming to understand the difficulties of translating, teaching, and enforcing precepts based on notions forged in a different cultural context. These texts help us to understand how the missionaries thought about honor across cultures and how they interpreted secular and ecclesiastical law in the process.

---

47. The restitution of honor occupied a prominent place in the writings of major sixteenth-century Spanish theologians and canonists, including Manuel de Azpilcueta, Juan de Medina, and Manuel Rodríguez. Although these authors revealed a keen perception of the new economic and social realities facing Christians in Spain, they did not address the issues confronting confessors of indigenous penitents.

These cases of restitution of honor also offered the friars an opportunity to convey an alternative view of justice to Indian penitents and their communities, a view that included the friars' own thoughts and designs on the taking of oaths and the administration of punishments, two components integral to the Spanish judicial order. I explore these two issues in the legal order of early colonial Mexico in the third and fourth chapter, respectively. Chapter 3 considers the friars' response to the introduction of oaths—a ubiquitous feature of Spanish social life—into indigenous society in light of their misgivings about secular law and institutions. The fourth and final chapter shows how the friars' critical stance toward the royal administration of justice among Indians led to concrete attempts to turn physical punishments into spiritual forms of discipline. The transplantation of these two European institutions once again compelled Spaniards to look at the concept of honor from a cross-cultural perspective.

Finally, I conclude with a consideration of some very different portraits of the Mexican Indians that were circulating in Spain by the early seventeenth century. Although they diverge in the ways they characterize the Indians, each portrait depicts the Indians simultaneously as religious and political individuals as well as royal subjects. Among the seventeenth-century readers of these portraits and numerous other reports on colonial society and its inhabitants were jurists who sought to make sense of a century of legislation regarding the Spanish colonies, a project that required them once again to consider the notion of honor across cultures. In grappling with these laws, these legal scholars also grappled with the legacy of the project of the colonizers in their guise as instructors on all things religious and civic.

CHAPTER 1

❦

On Things and Possessions

Walk into the house of an Indian, if you please, and the treasures that you will find inside the smoked-filled hut (very much like St. Hilarion's) will consist of a grinding stone, and a few old pots and pitchers, and if he happens to have a worn mat to serve as a bed, he can count himself lucky because many have only the hard soil on which to rest.[1]

Christianity traces its origins to a scene of equivocal domesticity in which a husband and his ready-to-give-birth wife find shelter for a night at a stable. The makeshift room and mundane details of Christ's birth, upon which generations of Christians have been called to meditate, neatly summarized Christianity's critical stance toward earthly possessions.[2]

In the passage cited above, the Franciscan Gerónimo de Mendieta, paraphrasing the chronicler Fr. Toribio de Benavente, invited readers to contemplate the few possessions found in most sixteenth-century Mexican Indian households, as in a spiritual exercise.[3] In doing so, he unwittingly opened the door to a site that future archaeologists and anthropologists would conjure from fragments to address questions that were self-evident to Mendieta's broth-

---

1. Fr. Gerónimo de Mendieta, *Historia eclesiástica indiana* (Mexico City: Antigua Librería, 1870; Mexico City: Editorial Porrúa, 1993), book 4, chap. 21, 440. This and all unattributed translations are mine. See also Fr. Toribio de Benavente (Motolinia), *Historia de los indios de la Nueva España*, ed. Georges Baudot (Madrid: Castalia, 1985), treatise 3, chap. 4, 302.

2. St. Ignatius of Loyola, *The Spiritual Exercises of St. Ignatius*, trans. Anthony Mottola (New York: Image Books / Doubleday, 1989), second week, first day, second contemplation, 70–71.

3. The origin of the devotion to the holy manger, which the Franciscans actively promoted across continents, goes back to an episode in the life of Saint Francis of Assisi. According to his biographer Thomas of Celano, in Greccio Francis enlisted a devoted local nobleman to help with the preparation of a Christmas ceremony; he requested a manger and live animals in order to evoke the Nativity. Francis explained the purpose behind this seemingly odd choice to his aide Giovanni: "poiché quest'anno ho intenzione di ritrarre al vivo la nascita del Bambino di Betlemme, così che tutti possan vedere realmente con gli occhi del corpo i disagi e le privazioni che provò appena nato, come venne adagiato nella mangiatoia e come giaceva sul fieno tra il bue e il asinello." Tommaso Da Celano, *Vita prima*, in *Le due Vite e il Trattato dei Miracoli di San Francesco d' Assisi*, ed. Luigi Macali (Rome: Angelo Signorelli, 1954), no. 84, 110.

ers.[4] From the missionary to the contemporary archaeologist, many would see the Indian household as a repository of information: Mendieta turned its occupants' sparse belongings into objects for reflecting on poverty; contemporary archaeologists, in turn, have transformed shards of pottery into indicators of wealth, and the irretrievable household itself into a unit of production and consumption.[5] This same act of opening the domestic space of the Indian poor to onlookers—together with the questions it raises—survived in modern guise in the visits that Oscar Lewis paid in the 1960s to the living quarters of Mexico City's urban poor to record each and every item owned by their occupants.[6]

The Spanish crown came to see itself as fulfilling various roles in the newly annexed American territories; among them was purveyor of goods through the promotion of transatlantic commerce. As noted by early historians of Spanish trade with the Indies, with the exception of laws governing the traffic of slaves, there were very few restrictions on what could actually be sold across the Atlantic.[7] Embracing the long-held Scholastic view that trade comprised more than the mere exchange of goods for profit, the crown held to the idea that free

---

4. "Sus colchones es la dura tierra, sin ropa ninguna; cuando mucho tienen una estera rota, y por cabecera una piedra o un pedazo de madero, y muchos ninguna cabecera, sino la tierra desnuda. Sus casas son muy pequeñas, algunas cubiertas de un solo terrado muy bajo, algunas de paja, otras como la celda de aquel santo abad Hilarión, que más parecen sepultura que no casa. Las riquezas que en tales casas pueden caber, dan testimonio de sus tesoros." Motolinía, *Historia de los indios de la Nueva España*, treatise 1, chap. 14, 189. The association of the mat with poverty becomes explicit in the rhetoric of self-abasement at work in a Nahua spell aimed at keeping harmful spiritual forces at bay during sleep: "Let it be soon, O my jaguar mat, you who lie opening your mouth wide toward the four directions. You are very thirsty and also hungry. And already the villain who makes fun of people, the one who is a madman, is coming. What is it he will do to me? Am I not a pauper? I am a worthless person. Do I not go around suffering poverty in the world?" Hernando Ruiz de Alarcón, *Treatise on the Heathen Superstitions That Today Live among the Indians Native to This New Spain, 1629*, ed. and trans. J. Richard Andrews and Ross Hassig (Norman: University of Oklahoma Press, 1984), treatise 2, chap. 2, 81.

5. For a compelling examination of the challenges that archaeologists face in the study of social stratification, with special reference to scholarship on Mexico, see Michael E. Smith, "Household Possessions and Wealth in Agrarian States: Implications for Archaeology," *Journal of Anthropological Archaeology* 6 (1987): 297–335; and also Arlen F. Chase and Diane Z. Chase, *Mesoamerican Elites: An Archaeological Assessment* (Norman: University of Oklahoma Press, 1992), 3–17.

6. Oscar Lewis, "Possessions of the Poor," in *Anthropological Essays* (New York: Random House, 1970), 441–60.

7. Rafael Antúnez y Acevedo, *Memorias históricas sobre la legislación, y gobierno del comercio de los españoles con sus colonias en las Indias Occidentales* (Madrid: Imprenta de Sancha, 1797), 130–47. Royal laws such as those issued in 1519 and 1530 banned the export of gold and silver in any form. Diego de Encinas, *Cedulario indiano* (1596), ed. Alfonso García Gallo, 4 vols. (Madrid: Ediciones Cultura Hispánica, 1946), 4:208–9 and 4:135, respectively. With the exception of these metals, very few of those items grouped under the label *cosas vedadas* under medieval law still remained on the books. Joseph F. O'Callaghan, *The Learned King: The Reign of Alfonso X of Castile* (Philadelphia: University of Pennsylvania Press, 1993), 126–29. On royal restrictions and bans on exports in the late medieval period, see Olivia Remi Constable, *Trade and Traders in Muslim Spain: The Commercial Realignment of the Iberian Peninsula, 900–1500* (Cambridge: Cambridge University Press, 1994), 233–39.

commerce between Spaniards and the new subjects would help the latter appreciate and eventually adopt Spanish mores and usages.[8] Much has been made of this commonplace view of the transformative power of commerce among nations. It has been suggested, for instance, that the spread of European products overseas as envisioned by the Spanish monarchs reflected an ingrained attitude toward the customs and material culture of subordinated cultural groups. In an example of this attitude, religious authorities in Granada adopted policies exhorting the Moriscos to abandon, among other things, their traditional garments to dress in Spanish fashion.[9] According to this view, and regardless of whether those policies were actually indicative of a particular mindset, Spain's aspirations to create new markets for European products found a natural ally in religion.

In viceregal America, the consumption of foreign goods by native populations and what has been termed Hispanization refer to two distinct yet overlapping phenomena. With the annexation of new indigenous polities in progress, the Hispanization of the Indians remained, for the most part, a rather inchoate ideal lacking a clear blueprint and any sense of urgency. For instance, in 1550 the crown ordered the Dominicans of New Spain to stop teaching Christian doctrine in native languages in favor of Spanish. Only in passing did the decree, issued to bring to an end to escalating conflict among religious orders over doctrinal uniformity, suggest that learning Spanish might lead the Mexican Indians to adopt the manners and customs of the conquerors ("nuestra policia y costumbres") sometime in the future.[10] Unmoved, the Dominicans and the other religious orders chose to ignore the royal order; eventually Philip II would lend his full support to the friars' decision to use indigenous languages in carrying out their mission.

Throughout the colonial period, however, calls for the Hispanization of the indigenous population never went away, resurfacing every time secular or ecclesiastical authorities made plans for reform, often in the aftermath of rebellions or episodes of social unrest. After the early interactions between Spaniards and Mexican Indians, Hispanization also existed under a slightly different guise, less guiding image for a future society than instrument to secure short-term political or military alliances, as illustrated by the Nahua nobility's easy access to European goods, especially clothing.[11]

8. Antonio de León Pinelo, *Recopilación de las Indias*, ed. Ismael Sánchez Bella, 3 vols. (Mexico City: Miguel Angel Porrúa, 1992), vol. 2, book 7, title 12, law 48, 1871.

9. Arnold J. Bauer, *Goods, Power, History: Latin America's Material Culture* (Cambridge: Cambridge University Press, 2001), 47–49.

10. Encinas, *Cedulario indiano*, 4:340.

11. Robert Haskett, *Indigenous Rulers: An Ethnohistory of Town Government in Colonial Cuer-*

As with the spread of Catholicism, the transfer of European material culture to the indigenous population of the Americas—whether viewed as a concerted effort to change patterns of consumption or as the fluid and less predictable process that it turned into—proved to be a complex affair, complicated by colonists' own misgivings about the transfer and what it might mean for them. Judging by testimonies from friars, royal administrators, and even seasoned entrepreneurs on the lookout for new economic opportunities, Spaniards found it difficult to imagine Mexican Indians fully partaking of the same goods that they themselves coveted, enjoyed, and sometimes bequeathed to their next of kin.

Teaching about Goods

Much like their counterparts on the Iberian Peninsula, the catechisms intended for use in the instruction of the Mexican Indians that circulated in sixteenth-century New Spain in either manuscript or printed form display a wide variety of approaches to the teaching of Christianity.[12] Each approach was informed by different assumptions about the translatability of Christian ideas, in the narrow sense of the linguistic capacity to communicate them but also in the broader, more general sense of comprehending Christian teachings. Underlying this diversity was the authors' shared conviction that the Christian message, by sheer force of its truth, knew no cultural boundaries, as the successful expansion of Christianity across nations and languages over the centuries suggested. This optimistic outward view, inherent to Christianity as a religion of the word, ignores the lessons of the theological controversies that make up the history of Christian dogma, namely that language can be a minefield. In this regard, despite the squabbles over the translation of Christian concepts into indigenous languages that broke out during the sixteenth century in places such as Mexico and Peru—often fueled by long-entrenched animosity between the secular and regular clergy or among religious orders—the missionaries' confidence in the transcendent power of their message remained firm. The opening sections of catechisms or *doctrinas* for the Mexican Indians make clear that the source

---

navaca (Albuquerque: University of New Mexico Press, 1991), 162. See also Haskett's discussion on colonial indigenous elites and material culture, 161–65.

12. The voluminous output of catechetical literature in sixteenth-century Spain has been examined in detail by Luis Resines in *La catequesis en España: Historia y textos* (Madrid: Biblioteca de Autores Cristianos, 1997), 173–92. Among the most comprehensive introductions to the catechetical literature produced during the colonial period are Juan Guillermo Durán, *Monumenta Catechetica Hispanoamericana*, 2 vols. (Buenos Aires: Facultad de Teología de la Pontificia Universidad Católica Argentina Santa María de los Buenos Aires, 1984) and Luis Resines's critical survey, *Catecismos americanos del siglo XVI*, 2 vols. (Castile and Leon: Consejería de Cultura y Turismo, 1992).

of this confidence was not the missionaries' individual linguistic abilities or cultural competence, but rather an awareness of the many possible ways to approach teaching Christianity regardless of the particular medium. The remarkable diversity of the catechisms being published in the Peninsula at the time surely strengthened this belief. That very first encounter between Indians and Christianity implicit in all catechisms loomed large in the missionaries' imaginations; this image preceded all translation and determined what the new religion would stand for, as well as how its tenets, precepts, and rituals would cohere into a whole.

Pedro de Córdoba is forever associated with the early history of the Dominican presence in the Spanish Caribbean. He arrived in La Española in 1510 with a reduced group of brothers that included Antonio de Montesinos, the preacher whose sermon against the mistreatment of the Tainos made a strong impression on the recently ordained Bartolomé de las Casas.[13] Córdoba quickly took a stance in defense of the indigenous population from the abuses of the *encomenderos* and set into motion a program of evangelization of the Indians living in the coastal areas of the continent then known as Tierra Firme. Among Córdoba's personal papers to make it to Mexico after his death in 1521 was the *Doctrina cristiana para instrucción y información de los indios, por manera de historia*, a catechetical treatise that, with additions by Mexican archbishop Juan de Zumárraga and his close associate the Dominican Juan de Betanzos, was eventually printed in 1544.[14] What sets this work apart from the other catechetical treatises published under the archbishop's supervision in the 1540s was its unified presentation of Christian tenets within an all-encompassing narrative (*"por manera de historia"*).[15] Starting with the story of creation as told in Genesis, the text posed history as the stage where the drama of redemption would unfold and eventually reach its resolution. Regardless of whether this particular format was simply dictated by didactic purposes, the organization of Pedro de Córdoba's catechism shows that doctrinal content was not to be separated from either the historical meaning of Christianity or Christianity's conception of history. In this sense, the design of Córdoba's *Doctrina cristiana* could hardly have been more fitting, since the timing of its composition—a few years after

---

13. For an account of the establishment of the Dominican order on the islands and Pedro de Córdoba's role in its expansion, see Daniel Ulloa H., *Los predicadores divididos: Los dominicos en Nueva España, siglo XVI* (Mexico City: El Colegio de México, 1977), 43–82.

14. On the plan for the publication of religious works undertaken by Zumárraga and his fellow bishops, see Luis Resines, *Catecismos americanos del siglo XVI*, 1:35–43.

15. Pedro de Córdoba's *Doctrina* from 1544 served as the basis for the *Doctrina cristiana en lengua española y mexicana por los religiosos de la orden de Santo Domingo*, most commonly known as the "Doctrina de los dominicos," published in Mexico in 1548 and reprinted two years later.

the landing of the first Spaniards in the islands—invited thoughts about beginnings, human and Christian, temporal and geographic.

As unavoidable as references to Genesis in catechetical literature were bound to be, authors had several options at their disposal when deciding which aspects of the biblical book best served the overall architecture of their catechisms. Throughout the ages, the account of creation had been a common starting point for all Christian instruction from the most basic to the most sophisticated, on a host of moral, legal, and theological issues such as human autonomy, the nature of property, and the concept of sin, to name just a few. In the case of Pedro de Córdoba's catechism, creation is above all the event that sets history on a course that includes the encounter of the American Indians with Christianity and thus salvation. Decades after Pedro de Córdoba, the Dominican Pedro de Feria also turned to the story of creation when composing his own catechism, the *Doctrina Christiana en lengua Castellana y çapoteca* (1567), but instead of time he chose another theme as his organizing principle to make the teachings of Christianity intelligible to a Zapotec audience. [16]

Pedro de Feria was born in Extremadura in 1524, and like Pedro de Córdoba and many of his future brothers in religion in Mexico, he studied and was ordained at the Colegio de San Esteban in Salamanca. His formative years (1552–58) as a missionary in New Spain were spent among the Zapotecs in Oaxaca, a region that remained under the exclusive control of the Dominican order until the end of the seventeenth century. According to early biographers, the newly arrived friar mastered the Zapotec language in a remarkably short time and put his considerable linguistic skills to good use by penning a catechism, as well as a Zapotec grammar and a dictionary.[17] Back in Mexico City, he headed the small contingent of Dominican friars that joined a 1559 Spanish

---

16. Pedro de Feria, *Doctrina Christiana en lengua Castellana y çapoteca compuesta por el muy Reverendo padre Pedro de Feria* (Mexico City: Pedro Ocharte, 1567). A transcription of the Spanish text can be found in Luis Resines, ed., *Catecismo del Sacromonte y Doctrina Christiana de Fr. Pedro de Feria: Conversión y evangelización de moriscos e indios* (Madrid: Consejo Superior de Investigaciones Científicas, 2002), 323–90.

17. On Pedro de Feria's linguistic prowess, see Francisco de Burgoa, *Geográfica descripción de la parte septentrional del polo ártico de la América y, nueva iglesia de las Indias occidentales, y sitio astronómico de esta Provincia de Predicadores de Antequera Valle de Oaxaca* (1674), 2 vols. (Mexico City: Editorial Porrúa, 1989), 2:76–77. On his catechism, grammar, and dictionary, see Antonio de Remesal, *Historia general de las Indias Occidentales y particular de la gobernación de Chiapa y Guatemala*, 2 vols. (Mexico City: Editorial Porrúa, 1988), vol. 2, book 11, chap. 1, 511. With the exception of a single page thought to have belonged to Feria's dictionary, neither of these works has survived. Wigberto Jiménez Moreno, introduction to *Vocabulario castellano-zapoteco* by Juan de Córdova, 1942), 18. The Dominican chronicler Dávila Padilla mentions Feria as the author of a "Confessionario Zapoteco," but it is assumed he was referring to the catechism. Agustín Dávila Padilla, *Historia de la fundación y discurso de la Provincia de Santiago de México, de la Orden de Predicadores*, ed. Agustín Millares Carlo (Mexico City: Editorial Academia Literaria, 1955), 653.

expedition to Florida that ended in disaster. After a relatively short hiatus back in San Esteban, Pedro de Feria returned to Mexico for the last time as consecrated bishop of Chiapas, the diocese he oversaw for thirteen years until his death in 1588.

Pedro de Feria's catechism has been described as "systematic" and also naive, on account of its seemingly unsophisticated doctrinal teachings.[18] I suspect the two labels are related and meant to underscore the work's preeminently didactic purpose and tone. By their very nature, sixteenth-century catechisms, whether aimed at children or adults, required some systematization to accommodate what had become the standard repertoire of doctrinal content and religious obligations. In trying to reach an audience from a different cultural universe, some religious authors such as Pedro de Córdoba determined that a step-by-step presentation of Christianity as outlined in the most elementary European catechisms fell short of conveying what was ultimately a new version of the world, founded on a handful of simple yet challenging ideas. As evinced by his Zapotec catechism, Pedro de Feria shared this conviction.

"Formavit Deus homine de limo terrae, et inspirauit in faciem eius spiraculum vite, et factus est homo in animam viventem." Feria skillfully organized the exposition of Christian doctrine (the Articles of Faith, prayers, the Ten Commandments, etc.) around these words from Genesis 2:7. Unlike Pedro de Córdoba, who followed the chronological sequence in Genesis, Feria omitted any reference to the first stages of creation to address man's composite nature directly, its understanding being key to the new religion. Thus, he posited matter and spirit as the foundational principles underlying both the Zapotec reality and the conceptual edifice of Christianity, through which the author would walk his audience.

Medieval theologians, like many of the church fathers whose opinions they followed, tended to cast their arguments on crucial doctrinal issues in a language that reflected contemporary ways of thinking about everyday affairs of the secular world. For example, obligations, debt, satisfaction, and honor played a central role in Anselm's elucidation of the Christian economy of salvation.[19] Similarly, the world of commerce frequently provided similes in medi-

---

18. José Salvador y Conde, "Fray Pedro de Feria y su *Doctrina Zapoteca* (estudio Bio-Bibliográfico)," *Missionalia Hispánica* 4, no. 12 (1947): 417. He also describes it as "metódica y sistemática" on page 459.

19. For the view that the key concepts in Anselm's theory of salvation reflected the legal universe of the feudal society in which he lived, see Adolph Harnack, *History of Dogma*, trans. Neil Buchanan, 7 vols. (New York: Dover Publications, 1961), 6:56–67. Others have argued that Anselm's terminology is already present in the Scriptures and that Harnack's interpretation hinges on an inaccurate translation of the theologian's concepts. See David Brown, "Anselm on Atonement," in *The Cambridge Companion to Anselm*, ed. Brian Davies and Brian Leftow (Cambridge: Cambridge

eval sermons.[20] To the Mexican missionaries who had pursued advanced studies within their orders, the deep connection between theological thought and social experience may or may not have struck them as old news. What seems more certain is that, when faced with explaining Christianity to their new indigenous charges, they found it difficult to do so without referring to the most mundane aspects of human affairs.

Matter and spirit are present in man as body and soul, two incommensurable entities that Christians must balance, mindful of the infinite superiority of the latter over the former and all material things. As Feria explained, when compared to the soul neither precious stones nor the earth or sun have any value, since they are all subject to change, their relative and ultimately modest worth coming from their nature as "corruptible goods and riches" ("bienes y riquezas corruptibles").[21] But what are goods? Man was given *bienes*, *quichàa*, or goods to enable him to tend to his body and soul according to the precepts laid out by the creator. To this end, and reflecting his own composite constitution, man has goods for both the body and the soul at his disposal.[22] Goods for the body include everything needed to ensure man's subsistence on earth and its enjoyment.[23] In discussing of the fifth article of faith, Feria explains that the body, the soul and its powers, and the five senses also belong to these "natural goods."[24] As for the soul, Feria addressed its goods in connection to the sixth and seventh articles, thus distinguishing between goods of *gracia*, or grace (a term that remained untranslated in the Zapotec text), and of glory, respectively. Goods of grace, available to anyone, embrace faith, forgiveness, all virtues, and the powers of the soul, whereas only good Christians enjoy goods of glory.[25]

This classification of goods roughly corresponds to the one found in the Spanish-Zapotec dictionary (1578) composed by the Dominican Juan de Córdoba, with whom Feria worked in Oaxaca and shared an interest in the study of the Zapotec language.[26] In addition to the general term *quichàa*, Córdoba

University Press, 2004), 279–302. Brown explores the meaning of "satisfaction," "debt," and "honor," on pages 290–95. On the impact of Anselm's argument on sixteenth-century legal and theological thought, see Debora Kuller Shuger, *The Renaissance Bible: Scholarship, Sacrifice, and Subjectivity* (Berkeley: University of California Press, 1994), 54–88.

20. Joel Kaye, *Economy and Nature in the Fourteenth Century* (Cambridge: Cambridge University Press, 1998), 150–51.

21. Feria, *Doctrina*, 8r.

22. Feria, *Doctrina*, 9v.

23. Feria, *Doctrina*, 9v–10r.

24. Feria, *Doctrina*, 24v–25r.

25. Feria, *Doctrina*, 25r–27r.

26. Feria was elected provincial in 1565; Juan de Córdoba succeeded him in the position in 1568. On Feria, with whom he also shared a strong commitment to the rules of the order, Córdoba

included entries for *bienes de fortuna* ("quichàa queche làyoo"; "xolopaatào queche làyoo"), or earthy goods; *bienes del alma* ("xiquichàa anima"), or goods of the soul; and *bienes del cuerpo, fuerças, gentileza*, or goods of the body.[27] The two Nahuatl dictionaries published by the Franciscan Alonso de Molina years earlier register only *bienes de fortuna* ("tlaquitl"), also identified as "hacienda" or property.[28]

The exposition of the Articles of Faith shows that Feria was less interested in sketching a taxonomy of goods to be committed to memory than in spelling out the meaning of creation and salvation from the perspective of man. Turned into a sort of building block of the entire catechism, the notion of earthly and spiritual goods lends a more concrete dimension to the explanation of abstract doctrinal points. Moreover, there are enough indications to suggest that Feria may have had in mind the tributary system that was at the heart of Zapotec socioeconomic organization[29] and on which the interactions between individuals and gods were modeled.[30] In striving to render the abstract in familiar terms Feria sometimes stretched the notion of goods, as in his definition of sin as

---

wrote: "Es medianamente doctor, religioso, observante, gran amigo de la pobreza y religion; es buena lengua, de una provincia que se dice la Zapoteca." *Relación de la fundación, capítulos y elecciones que se han tenido en esta Provincia de Santiago de ésta Nueva España, de la Orden de Predicadores de Santo Domingo, 1569* (Mexico City: Vargas Rea, 1944), 54.

27. Juan de Córdoba, *Vocabulario castellano-zapoteco*, 55. On Juan de Córdoba's linguistic works, see Ursula Thiemer-Sachse, "El *Vocabulario castellano-zapoteco* y el *Arte en lengua zapoteca* de Juan de Córdova—intenciones y resultados (Perspectiva antropológica)," in *La descripción de las lenguas amerindias en la época colonial*, ed. Klaus Zimmermann (Frankfurt am Main: Vervuert; Madrid: Iberoamericana, 1997), 147–74. Regarding terminology, Zapotec is not one language but rather a complex or subgroup of languages of the Otomanguean family, spoken mostly in Oaxaca. Jorge A. Suárez, "La clasificación de las lenguas zapotecas," in *Homenaje a Jorge A. Suárez: Lingüística indoamericana e hispánica*, ed. Beatríz Garza Cuarón (Mexico City: El Colegio de México, 1990), 41–68. Córdoba's dictionary reflects his familiarity with the Zapotec spoken in the area around Antequera, where he was based, but also registers regional variants. Juan José Rendón M., "Nuevos datos sobre el origen del *Vocabulario en lengua zapoteca* del padre Córdova," *Anales de Antropología* 6 (1969): 115–29.

28. Alonso de Molina, *Aquí comiença un vocabulario en la lengua castellana y mexicana* (1555), ed. Manuel Galeote (Malaga: Universidad de Málaga, 2001); and Alonso de Molina, *Vocabulario en lengua castellana y mexicana y mexicana y castellana* (1571), ed. Miguel León-Portilla (Mexico City: Editorial Porrúa, 1977).

29. See for instance the address to members of the Zapotec nobility (who happened to have total discretion over the exaction of tribute), and the references to the luxury items that were often requested as tribute. Feria, *Doctrina*, 5–5v and 8r, respectively. For a description of the Zapotec tributary system, see Joseph W. Whitecotton, *The Zapotecs: Princes, Priests, and Peasants* (Norman: University of Oklahoma Press, 1984), 140–41; and Ursula Thiemer-Sachse, "El problema de la definición de regalos, impuestos y tributos en el estado zapoteco en el tiempo precolonial," *Anales de antropología* 33 (1996–99): 285–318.

30. Whitecotton, *The Zapotecs*, 165. On religious offerings, see Thiemer-Sachse, "El problema," 297–300 and José Alcina Franch, *Calendario y religión entre los zapotecos* (Mexico City: Universidad Nacional Autónoma de México, 1993), 123–29. Alcina Franch discusses the place of offerings within communal ceremonies on pages 141–57.

a theft of the highest order. According to this formulation, sinning amounts to stealing God's property ("hacienda de dios"; "xiquichaa Dios").[31] And this property consists of none other than God's laws as spelled out in the commandments.[32] Equating disobedience with theft is a somewhat extreme way to get at the more traditional idea, already present in the Credo, of the sinner's infinite debt to God and the impossibility of cancelation without earned forgiveness.[33] Years later the Franciscan Martín de León, addressing an imaginary audience of Nahuas, would compare the situation of penitents to that of individuals who owe money they do not have.[34]

To talk about goods without acknowledging basic questions about how and to what ends individuals relate to them seems a difficult, if not purposeless, task. Feria found the opportunity to touch briefly on these issues when he expounded on the seventh commandment ("Thou shalt not steal"), which takes the concept of ownership for granted. Having already accounted for the ultimate origins of all goods, he explained that private property arose immediately following creation, when individuals who held everything in common agreed to a general distribution of goods as a means to ensure peaceful coexistence.[35] Feria pointed out that, while private property first emerged as a remedy for social unrest, it quickly became a source of constant worry, as the new arrangement caused individuals to live in fear of losing their possessions to theft or accident.[36]

From the early fourteenth century, when Pope John XXII launched an attack on the very identity of the Franciscan order by questioning its view on evangelical poverty, theologians from different religious corners heatedly debated the origin of ownership and posed questions such as what kind of property regime existed before the Fall.[37] Whereas discussions over the meaning of

---

31. Feria, *Doctrina*, 25v–26r.

32. Feria, *Doctrina*, 26r.

33. Feria, *Doctrina*, 26v.

34. Martín de León, *Camino del Cielo en Lengua Mexicana, en todos los requisitos necessarios para conseguir este fin, con todo lo que un Christiano deve creer, saber, y obrar, desde el punto que tiene uso de razon, hasta que muere* (Mexico City: Diego López Dávalos, 1611), 109.

35. Feria, *Doctrina*, 76v.

36. Feria, *Doctrina*, 27v.

37. For a historical account of the controversy, see John Moorman, *A History of the Franciscan Order From Its Origins to the Year 1517* (Oxford: Clarendon Press, 1968), 307–38. A masterful analysis of the philosophical underpinnings of the dispute and its import on the history of the concept of rights can be found in Brian Tierney, *The Idea of Natural Rights* (Grand Rapids, MI: William B. Eerdmans, 1997), especially 131–69. Also of interest is Roberto Lambertini, "La proprietá di Adamo. Stato d'innocenza ed origine del *dominium* nel *Commento alle Sentenze* e nell' *Improbacio* di Francesco d'Ascoli," *Bulletino dell' Istituto Storico Italiano per il Medio Evo e Archivio Muratoriano* 99, no. 2 (1994): 201–51. On the place of Christ's poverty in Christian thought prior to the Franciscans, see Peter Garnsey, *Thinking about Property from Antiquity to the Age of Revolution*

dominium or *usus* would be out of place in a catechism—especially one aimed at an indigenous audience—it somehow makes sense that in a work so tightly constructed around the concept of goods Feria deemed it appropriate to address that staple of Scholastic debate, the origin of property. And he did so in full awareness that even in the relatively small religious community of New Spain, statements meant for didactic purposes would not be exempted from the close scrutiny generally accorded theological treatises.[38] This may explain why he reminded readers that all goods ultimately belonged to God, framing the relationship between man and God-created goods as one of only nominal ownership.[39]

If fear of theft is the price of ownership of goods that are both necessary and perishable, another kind of earthly good is also subject to loss: fame and honor. Although traditionally conceptualized as goods, the two related and often overlapping notions differ in significant ways from the tangible objects of the seventh commandment. For the sake of simplicity, however, Feria dispensed with definitions and, following his preference for the concrete on pedagogical matters, construed the offenses against honor covered in the eighth commandment ("Thou shalt not bear false witness") as a form of theft, not so much to equate fame and honor with tangible items but rather to highlight the offender's obligation to make restitution.[40] The particular problems that the restitution of honor posed in the context of the evangelization of New Spain will be addressed in the next chapter.

The distinction between spiritual and earthly goods that underlay all Christian teaching coexisted, as it had for quite some time, with Roman law's general classification of things into corporeal and incorporeal, a classification later incorporated into the *ius commune*. It is worth noting that Roman civil law concerned and was organized around persons, things, and actions.[41] As Ber-

---

(Cambridge: Cambridge University Press, 2007), 84–106; on communal ownership in sixteenth-century Spanish thought, see the selection of texts compiled by Carmelo Viñas y Mey, ed., *Doctrinas de los tratadistas españoles de los siglos XVI y XVII sobre el comunismo* (Madrid: Escuela Social de Madrid, 1945).

38. As in Spain, religious literature produced in Mexico was subjected to close scrutiny. For example, in 1559, one of Zumárraga's catechisms was banned for an allegedly scandalous proposition; the same year the French-born Maturino Gilberti faced charges in connection with his *Diálogo de doctrina cristiana* (1559) in the Tarascan language. See Francisco Fernández del Castillo, ed., *Libros y libreros en el siglo XVI* (Mexico City: Fondo de Cultura Económica, 1982), 1–3 and 4–37, respectively.

39. Feria, *Doctrina*, 25r.

40. Feria, *Doctrina*, 78v.

41. "All our law is about persons (ad personas), things (ad res) or actions (ad actiones)." Gaius, *The Institutes of Gaius*, trans. and ed. W. M. Gordon and O. F. Robinson (Ithaca, NY: Cornell University Press, 1987), 1.8, 23; Justinian, *Justinian's Institutes*, trans. and ed. Peter Birks and Grant McLeod (Ithaca, NY: Cornell University Press, 1987), 1.12, 39.

nardino Daza, the Spanish translator of Justinian's *Institutiones*, put it, corporeal things might include "una heredad, el hombre, el vestido, el oro, la plata, y finalmente otras cosas que no tienen cuento" (an estate, man, clothing, gold, silver, and other things too numerous to count), whereas intangible things included legal concepts such as "herencia, el iusufructo, el uso y las obligaciones de qualquier manera que sean" (inheritance, usufruct, use and obligations of any sort).[42] Among the corporeal things, Roman law recognized further distinctions, such as those between movable and unmovable things (*res mobiles* and *res immobiles*), and sacred and religious things (*res sacrae* and *res religiosae*), both of which fell outside the regimes of public and private ownership.[43] Sixteenth-century Spanish authors on contract issues also classified things into three categories: natural, unnatural, and money.[44] The coexistence of religious and legal understandings of goods is seen in Covarrubias's glosses for *bien*, which largely documented usages in scriptural passages, as was common practice in ecclesiastical dictionaries.[45] Preserving the traditional hierarchy of religion over law, Covarrubias devoted the final section to what closely resembles a legal taxonomy.[46]

It seems difficult to overstate the central role that goods—and associated concepts such as ownership—play in Feria's exposition of Christian doctrine. His references to human interactions are so prominent that they have been taken as proof of the work's lack of sophistication—not so much a charge against the work as an implicit acknowledgment of the challenges of introducing Christianity to an Indian audience. Whether or not the Zapotec catechism

---

42. Bernardino Daza, trans., *Las Instituciones Imperiales (o Principios del Derecho Civil) dirigidas al Principe Don Philippe nuestro señor traduzidas por Bernardino Daza, Legista, natural de Valladolid*, by Justinian (Tolosa: Guion Bodauila, 1551), book 2, title 2, 92. The third edition of Daza's translation was published in 1627 with revisions by the classical scholar and grammarian Gonzalo Correas.

43. On the interplay of Roman legal categories and the religious domain, see the brilliant essay by Yan Thomas, "*Res Religiosae*: On the Categories of Religion and Commerce in Roman Law," in *Law, Anthropology, and the Constitution of the Social*, ed. Alain Pottage and Martha Mundy (Cambridge: Cambridge University Press, 2004), 40–72. On medieval developments, see Michel Lauwers, "Le cimetière dans le Moyen Âge latin: Lieu sacré, saint et religieux," in *Annales: Histoire, sciences sociales* 5 (September–October 1999): 1047–72.

44. Francisco García, *Tratado utilísimo y muy general de todos los contratos (1583)* (Pamplona: Ediciones Universidad de Navarra, 2003).

45. Cf. entry for "bonus" in Diego Jiménez Arias, *Lexico ecclesiasticum latino-hispanicum ex sacris bibliis, conciliis, pontificum decretis, ac theologorum placitis, divorum vitiis, variis dictionariis, aliisque probatissimis scriptoribus concinnatum, servata ubique vera etymologiae, orthographiae, et accentus ratione* (Barcelona: Ioannes Piferrer, 1739).

46. "Bienes temporales y espirituales, bienes eclesiásticos y seglares, bienes concejiles y particulares, bienes muebles y rayzes, bienes castrenses y casicastrenses, bienes heredados de otro o adquiridos por sí, bienes dotales y bienes gananciales, bienes partibles y bienes en común, bienes avidos y por aver." Sebastián de Horozco Covarrubias, *Tesoro de la Lengua Castellana o Española*, ed. Martín de Riquer (Barcelona: S. A. Horta, I. E., 1943).

fails to satisfy expectations of expository elegance, its approach reveals an almost paradoxical engagement of the new religion with the material world that is largely absent from similar works produced in New Spain.[47] This engagement is a by-product of Feria's assumptions about how Zapotec Indians thought about matter and spirit, rather than actual knowledge of their particular system of beliefs and practices. From his time in Oaxaca among the Zapotecs until his final years in Chiapas as bishop, Feria remained convinced that the Mexican Indians resisted embracing any religion that did not reflect their attachment to the corporeal.[48] This belief—for which he found evidence in the cases of idolatry that he investigated years later in Chiapas[49]—shaped the from-the-ground-up perspective on Christian doctrine that informed his teaching. This perspective allowed Feria to turn the Zapotec *doctrina* into both a primer on Christianity and a refutation of what he saw as the unabashedly materialistic bent of the Zapotec religion and worldview. The result is a catechism conceived to respond to the dictates of an imagined science of the concrete that the Zapotecs would recognize. And yet Feria felt the need to acknowledge that his transcendent version of the here and now was at odds with the spectacle of his countrymen's reckless pursuit of earthly things.[50] What sets the Zapotec *doctrina* apart from similar works is the pervasive tension between the material and spiritual that its author placed at the core of the relationship between men and goods. The missionaries became aware that this relationship acquired a new and dramatic dimension as

---

47. As far as I know, no European or Mexican catechism has been proposed as a model for Feria's *Doctrina*.

48. "Agora entendereys quan vana y sin fundamento fue vuestra religion antigua, pues solamente pretendiades en ella las cosas corporales y temporales." Feria, *Doctrina*, 5r. In the report to the Third Mexican Council that he sent from Oaxaca, where he was recovering from a fall, Feria wrote: "porque, como ellos eran tan terrestres y sensuales, lo que pretendían y a lo que hordenaban la observançia de su religion, era sólo lo corporal y temporal, conviene a saber: la salud, los hijos, los buenos [sic] temporales, no tener guerras, y, si las tubiessen, alcançar Victoria de sus enemigos, y otros fines semejantes, y ansí hasta el día de hoy les dura esta temeridad, que quando se viene a confesar un indio enfermo, si le pregunta el confessor ¿para qué te quieres confessar? ¿que pretendes en esto? Responde, para sanar de mi enfermedad, y para que Dios me alargue los días de la vida en este mundo." "Memorial del Obispo Fray Pedro de Feria," in Alberto Carrillo Cázares, ed., *Manuscritos del Concilio Tercero Provincial Mexicano (1585)*, 5 vols. (Zamora, Michoacan: El Colegio de Michoacán / Universidad Pontificia de México, 2006), vol. 1, part 1, 296; and also included in José A. Llaguno, *La personalidad jurídica del indio y el III Concilio Provincial Mexicano (1585)* (Mexico City: Editorial Porrúa, 1963), 183–98.

49. The official inquiry took place in 1584 during one of the bishop's *visitas*, or inspections. See Pedro de Feria, "Revelación sobre la reincidencia en sus idolatrías de los indios de Chiapa después de treinta años de cristianos," in *Tratado de las idolatrías, supersticiones, dioses, ritos hechicerías y otras costumbres gentílicas de las razas aborígenes de México*, ed. Francisco del Paso y Troncoso, 2 vols. (Mexico City: Ediciones Fuente Cultural, 1953), 1:381–92.

50. "Los españoles yo confiesso que cometen peccados de hurtos, de homicidios, de fornicios, de odios, y otros pecados, pero creen verdadera y firmemente en un solo dios y no adoran a los ydolos ni confian en ellos." Feria, *Doctrina*, 65v.

the colonial enterprise in which they were essential partners continued to make deeper inroads into the Indian communities under their supervision. Mounting pressures on those communities to meet tributary and labor obligations caused missionaries to take a closer look at the earthly goods on which their and their charges' livelihoods depended. On these less than lofty matters they instructed a different constituency, royal administrators and officers in Mexico and Spain. The instruction of the Indians in the curious intersections between their material lives, Christianity, and colonial institutions, however, would follow less scripted and more circuitous paths.

Things: Moral and Economic

When the economy of thirteenth-century Europe entered a period of commercial expansion that gave rise to an urban merchant class, Catholic theologians began to scrutinize the economic activities of this small but increasingly influential group of individuals that placed themselves under their spiritual care.[51] Medieval manuals of penance conceived of Christian penitents according to different but overlapping criteria; there were husbands, wives, sons, and daughters, each group subject to particular moral precepts derived from the interpretation of the Decalogue. Many Christians drew their social identities from their trade, identities that often rested on their belonging to corporate bodies such as guilds, which had their own religious ties. The church acknowledged this and made penitents accountable for offenses committed when practicing their craft or profession through the penitential forum.[52] Of all the trades and professions, it was merchants who would keep theologians, lawyers, and confessors very busy learning the inner workings of ever more complex commercial

---

51. Lester K. Little, *Religious Poverty and the Profit Economy in Medieval Europe* (Ithaca, NY: Cornell University Press, 1978), 197–219. On the development of Scholastic economic thought among Franciscan theologians, see Odd Langholm, *Economics in the Medieval Schools: Wealth, Exchange, Value, Money and Usury according to the Paris Theological Tradition, 1200–1350* (Leiden: E.J. Brill, 1992), especially 430–53.

52. Jacques Le Goff has explored both the historical consequences of the decision by the Fourth Council of the Lateran (1215) to make annual confession mandatory for all Christians who had reached the age of reason and the change in the perception of manual labor in a Christian society. *Pour un autre Moyen Âge: Temps, travail, et culture en Occident: 18 essais* (Paris: Gallimard, 1977), 162–80, especially 175–78. Just as the new obligation to confess created the need for a body of manuals for confessors, it also gave rise to a literarily significant body of sermons known as *sermons ad status* to instruct parishioners who practiced different trades and occupations. Birgit Van Den Hoven, *Work in Ancient and Medieval Thought: Ancient Philosophers, Medieval Monks and Theologians and Their Concept of Work, Occupations and Technology* (Amsterdam: J. C. Gieben, 1996), 201–43.

transactions and producing opinions on their legality under canon law. In the fifteenth century the Dominican friar Antonine, bishop of Florence, devoted a significant portion of his writings on penance to making confessors aware of the intricate and expanding world of economic arrangements and obligations that their penitents inhabited.[53] Antonine's authority on matters of commerce and Christian morality was quickly acknowledged, especially in Spain, where his opinions remained a point of reference for moral theologians throughout the sixteenth century.[54]

The annexation of the American territories, with their masses of indigenous peoples who found themselves supplying labor to the colonizers under successive systems of economic exploitation, further deepened the concern of theologians about the temptation of an entire generation of Spaniards by new opportunities overseas. As Spanish theologians tried to understand the ensuing transformation of the social and moral landscape, an unprecedented body of treatises arose, revisiting old topics such as usury and monetary exchange and systematizing and dissecting current issues such as slavery, Indian labor, and rights, among many others. In Mexico, the close association between the religious orders and royal administrators during the first decades of Spanish presence had done much to secure both the stability of the region and a steady stream of royal revenue. As a result, the friars had the rare opportunity to become intimately acquainted with the daily economic reality of their Indian charges and to express their often critical opinions, whether called on to do so or not.

The friars' understanding of the material conditions under which the Mexican Indians cared for their families and communities was greatly aided by sharply focused inquiries into pre-Conquest tribute collection, land distribution, and patterns of agricultural production. This deep involvement in all matters related to the economic life of the indigenous communities authorized the friars to make comments and recommendations about tributary policy. Their interest in the Indians' daily material life was of course inseparable from the

53. On Antonine's economic thought, see Raymond de Roover, *San Bernardino of Siena and Sant' Antonino of Florence* (Boston: Baker Library / Harvard Graduate School of Business Administration, 1967). The sixteenth century saw few if any innovations in commercial transactions; their expansion, however, made theologians more aware of the need to instruct priests and confessors on the financial activities of their parishioners. José Antonio Maravall, "La imagen de la sociedad expansiva en la conciencia castellana del siglo XVI," in *Estudios de historia del pensamiento español*, 3 vols. (Madrid: Cultura Hispánica, 1984), 2:275.

54. Alongside the discussion of commercial transactions by theologians concerned with usury, in sixteenth-century Spain a specialized literature on contracts developed that took a wider (and more optimistic) view of commerce as a human activity. Bartolomé Clavero, *Antidora: Antropología católica de la economía moderna* (Milan: Giuffrè Editore, 1991), 109–22.

friars' hopes to forge a distinctive brand of native Christianity; the most fully articulated version of this Christianity proposed drastically reordering the established Spanish boundaries between the secular and the religious.

Early modern European theologians educated themselves about contemporary financial practices and furnished confessors with the necessary tools to oversee, guide, and advise parishioners on matters related to trade and the accumulation of wealth.[55] As shown by their less than kind words about conquerors, *encomenderos*, and assorted entrepreneurs, the Mexican experience reminded missionaries of the challenges that wealth posed to Christians and their confessors as well. What the missionaries learned first-hand about the close-knit group of professional merchants was useful not only in addressing them as representatives of a particular trade in need of specialized instruction, but also in recasting their approach to more general doctrinal and moral teachings for a wider audience. The religious literature directed at indigenous converts showed the native merchants in the same conflictive light as found in contemporary works circulating in Spain. From the beginning of the evangelization in New Spain, converting the native elites was a priority; as a result, the mention of merchants and commerce in the context of indoctrination was inevitable, as shown in a sermon on greed written by the Franciscan linguist and pioneer ethnographer Andrés de Olmos as part of a larger work on the seven deadly sins. When calling on the Nahuas to abandon the pursuit of riches, Olmos turned to the Nahua corpus of ceremonial speeches that codified the behavior and values of the merchant elite—which he had collected and studied for catechetical purposes—to better puncture that group's carefully crafted self-image.[56] In their quest for wealth, he argued, merchants routinely committed a host of sins, such as abandoning their families for long periods and mistreating those who carried their merchandise. For the friars, the much-touted fearlessness that Nahua merchants took as a point of pride amounted to nothing but reckless behavior and disrespect for their own lives.[57] These moral

---

55. Scholastic interest in the moral and religious questions posed by the merchant's role in society dates back to the thirteenth century and gave rise to a significant number of specialized treatises. John W. Baldwin, *The Medieval Theories of the Just Price: Romanists, Canonists, and Theologians in the Twelfth and Thirteenth Centuries. Transactions of the American Philosophical Society*, New Series vol. 49, no. 4 (Philadelphia: American Philosophical Society, 1959), 63–68.

56. At the end of *Arte de la lengua Mexicana*, his 1547 Nahuatl grammar, Andrés de Olmos included a sample of *huehuetlahtolli*, or speeches of the elderly, to further his brothers' knowledge of native language and culture. On Olmos's works, see Georges Baudot, *Utopía e Historia en México: Los primeros cronistas de la civilización mexicana (1520–1569)* (Madrid: Espasa-Calpe, 1983), 167–245.

57. Andrés de Olmos, *Tratado sobre los siete pecados mortales*, ed. Georges Baudot (Mexico City: Universidad Autónoma de México, 1996), 96–99. Fr. Diego Durán derided the lifestyle of contemporary petty merchants from Cholula in similar terms: "que andan unos mercaderejos diez

faults certainly pale in comparison with those of the *pochteca* (merchant) at the center of a seventeenth-century religious play, who engages in usury, repeated perjury, and theft to end up dying untestate strangled by a demon.[58] But just as the Indian poor could further encourage Spaniards with religious inclinations to live in poverty, the life of Nahua merchants, as revealed in the writings of Fr. Bernardino de Sahagún, offered Christians valuable lessons about ownership and the nature of earthly goods.

Sahagún's systematic treatment of all aspects of Nahua culture may give the first impression of a complex, yet static and highly stylized account frozen in time—an impression often reinforced by modern commentators. Other features, such as the transcription of ceremonial speeches or the explanation of ritual life following the agrarian calendar, contribute to this not-unwarranted but certainly partial perception. But the impression does not hold when one turns to Sahagún's examination of trades, which laid out how a widely diverse group of craftsmen, metalworkers, merchants, sellers, and consumers were responsible for reproducing and expanding the technical and geographical boundaries of Nahua material culture.

The Franciscan lavished this same attention on the activities and ritual life of the merchant class. It has been frequently pointed out that the Spanish, soon after their arrival in Mexico, could not help but notice that the social organization of indigenous society closely resembled that of their native Spain in its hierarchy of social groups.[59] In the case of the *pochteca*, the professional merchants who specialized in long-distance trade and worked closely with the state, the similarities went even deeper: they constituted a distinctive class, provided services that were considered indispensable, and yet were still viewed with suspicion by ruling elites and noble families.[60] On both sides of the Atlan-

---

y doce y veinte años ganando y recogiendo doscientos y trecientos pesos y, al cabo de todos sus trabajos y mal comer y trasnochar, sin ningún propósito ni causa, hacen un gran banquete solemnísimo, donde gastan cuanto habían ganado y más." Fr. Diego Durán, *Historia de las Indias de Nueva España e islas de la Tierra Firme*, ed. Angel Ma. Garibay K., 2 vols. (Mexico City: Editorial Porrúa, 1967), 1:68–69.

58. Barry D. Sell and Louise M. Burkhart, *Nahuatl Theater: Death and Life in Colonial Nahua Mexico* (Norman: Oklahoma University Press, 2004), 242–67. The story of the greedy merchant belongs to the medieval repertoire of exempla of usury that found their way into sermons. Jacques Le Goff, *Pour un autre Moyen Age*, 1265–69. Motolinia held that usury, being unknown among the Nahuas in pre-Conquest times, became widespread thanks to the tributary policies introduced by Spaniards. *Memoriales o Libro de las cosas de la Nueva España y los naturales de ella*, ed. Edmundo O'Gorman (Mexico City: Universidad Autónoma de México, 1971), part 2, chap. 18, 360.

59. Lockhart, *The Nahuas after the Conquest*, 94. Las Casas turned the study of these similarities into the basis of his comparative approach of Amerindian and European cultures in the *Apologética historia sumaria*.

60. The threat posed by merchants rising in societal rank through the sheer power of money was clearly articulated in the following passage by the Dominican Fr. Durán: "El tercer modo y me-

tic, the merchant classes were distinguished by an ethos that appeared to be at odds with the values of the governing class and official religion, yet the ruling elites kept their members in check through regulatory mechanisms included public as well as private rituals and obligations.[61] The friars, introducing their ideals of poverty into a culture in a way they saw as the fulfillment of a historical mission that their order was destined to carry out, of course chastised the merchants, but they also praised them for organizing their mundane business affairs around religious observances, however at odds with Christianity they happened to be. Toward the end of the sixteenth century the chronicler Domingo de San Antón Muñón Chimalpahin told of seeing merchants and other tradesmen on a platform, reenacting their daily activities for a crowd during a religious celebration.[62]

Besides the missionaries' obvious interest in learning about Nahua merchants for catechetical purposes, they also found them somewhat alluring. Ceding the public spotlight to the warrior class, the merchants were entrusted to handle precious articles across long stretches of territory, articles that indigenous craftsmen produced and that could make their towns known. As either sellers or bearers of gifts to vassal lords from rulers, the principal merchants dealt with a wide array of luxury commodities, such as ear plugs, gold rings, featherworks, jewelry, and fine textiles, all elite goods that highlighted the subordinate status of their carriers but that the carriers could aspire to enjoy in the form of gifts from their lords for services rendered.[63] According to Sahagún's

nos honroso era el de la mercancía y trato de comprar y vender, hallándose en todos los mercados de la tierra, trocando mantas por joyas, y joyas por plumas, y plumas por piedras, y piedras por escalvos, tratando siempre con cosas gruesas y honrosas y de precio. Estos ensalzaban sus linajes con el dinero, como vemos haber subido muchos hombres del bajo suelo y peor sangre a tanto estado, que han venido a casarse sus hijas con duques y condes y marqueses y hacer grandes y ricos mayorazgos, mezclando su sangre baja con la buena de España." Fr. Diego Durán, *Historia de las Indias de Nueva España*, 1:68. Durán's words point to the ascent and growing influence of a particular group from the merchant ranks in Spanish society, that of the *burgaleses*, or merchants engaged in bulk overseas commerce. Maravall, "La imagen de la sociedad expansiva," 282–83. On the merchants' social organization and hierarchy, see Rudolph van Zantwijk, *The Aztec Arrangement: The Social History of Pre-Spanish Mexico* (Norman: University of Oklahoma Press, 1985), 125–51. On the economic and political roles of the *pochteca* on the eve of the Conquest, see Pedro Carrasco, "La economía del México prehispánico," in *Economía política e ideología en el México prehispánico*, ed. Pedro Carrasco and Johanna Broda (Mexico City: CIS-INAH [Centro de Investigaciones Superiores del Instituto Nacional de Antropología e Historia] / Editorial Nueva Imagen, 1978), 58–64.

61. Inga Clendinnen, *Aztecs: An Interpretation* (Cambridge: Cambridge University Press, 1991), 138. I am indebted to her analysis of the social tensions behind the public persona of the merchant class on pages 132–40.

62. Chimalpahin, *Annals of His Time*, 45.

63. On the production and circulation of elite goods in the late postclassic period and their imperial ideological function, see Johanna Broda, "El tributo en trajes guerreros y la estructura del sistema tributario mexica," in *Economía política e ideología en el México prehispánico*, ed. Pedro Carrasco and Johanna Broda (Mexico City: CIS-INAH [Centro de Investigaciones Superiores

information, merchants seeking to rise through the ranks were expected to participate in ceremonies of thanksgiving upon returning from their travels, thus bringing to a close a cycle of observances that had started with propitiatory rituals before their departure. In their speeches, the returning traders humbled themselves before an audience of senior merchants by declaring that the goods they had successfully transported did not belong to them but to the principal merchants.[64] Even such high-level ownership proved contingent and illusory, since goods ultimately belonged to the deity. They were "his property, his possession" ("in iascatzin in tlatquitzin.")[65] This same phrase would resurface in the recitation of thanksgiving that headed many an Indian testament.[66]

If the religious observances of the merchants served to remind them of the conditions inherent in their recognition as a group with its own social identity, their relationship to religion was not restricted to satisfying the demands of social groups above them. In disavowing any claim to ownership of their precious merchandise, successful Nahua traders both deferred to the powerful and defined their proximity to the religious domain, as fitted their role as carriers of articles with ritual functions and raw materials closely associated with the sacred such as gold, feathers, turquoise, and jadite, among others.

In songs, prayers, and ceremonial speeches Nahua wordsmiths turned these expensive raw materials into ubiquitous metaphors for the sacred and everlasting. The specific ways that Nahua society brought the material and the abstract together to represent the realm of the sacred survived, in liturgical texts composed in indigenous languages. Metaphors, after all, are meant for traveling, and Nahua metaphors certainly did, finding a new home in Christian texts for a Nahua audience as part of a process of translation that revealed the porous

---

del Instituto Nacional de Antropología e Historia] / Editorial Nueva Imagen, 1978), 115–74. On crafts, see Elizabeth M. Brumfiel, "Elite and Utilitarian Crafts in the Aztec State," in *Specialization, Exchange, and Complex Societies*, ed. Elizabeth M. Brumfiel and Timothy K. Earle (Cambridge: Cambridge University Press, 1987), 102–18. Edward E. Calnek has persuasively argued that there are limitations on the understanding of the overall Aztec economy that can be gained by focusing on sumptuary goods and the role of the state. "El sistema de mercado de Tenochtitlan," in *Economía política e ideología en el México prehispánico*, ed. Pedro Carrasco and Johanna Broda (Mexico City: CIS-INAH [Centro de Investigaciones Superiores del Instituto Nacional de Antropología e Historia] / Editorial Nueva Imagen, 1978), 95–114. On *pochtecas*, see Frances B. Berdan, *The Aztecs of Central Mexico: An Imperial Society* (New York: Holt, Rinehart and Winston, 1982), 31–34.

64. "He did not claim the goods, the property as his own. He only told them: They are not my goods which I have carried; they are the goods of our mothers, our fathers, the merchants, the vanguard merchants." Sahagún, *Florentine Codex*, book 9, chap. 6, 31.

65. Sahagún, *Florentine Codex*, book 9, chap. 7, 33.

66. Francisco Sanches from Tecamachalco thanked God in his 1548 testament for having given him a house, land, and cattle ("nochan, notlalpa yguan noyolkaguan"). *Vidas y bienes olvidados. Testamentos indígenas novohispanos*, ed. Teresa Rojas Rabiela, Elsa Leticia Rea López, and Constantino Medina Lima, 5 vols. (Mexico City: CIESAS, 1999), 2:82–83.

boundaries of the sacred.[67] Starting with shipments ordered by Hernán Cortés himself, many elite native crafts, among them shields originally intended for rituals, traveled to Spain for display in churches, friaries, and the private homes of the nobility.[68] While under the friars' supervision, indigenous artisans began to use feathers and other highly regarded materials in devotional images for Christian worship.[69] The function of some works commissioned from indigenous workshops was less clearly defined, as illustrated by a feather miter bearing religious images of European precedence that Philip II donated to El Escorial, where it remains today.[70] The miter was shipped to Spain in an exchange that mirrored the influx of sacred images and relics from Europe to Mexican churches.

However unstable or problematic the status of these objects may appear to us, the laymen and ecclesiastical authorities who commissioned, acquired, gave, and received them showed few religious—or theoretical—concerns. In this regard, the Spanish, already familiar with a gift exchange economy that served political alliances, measured luxury objects of indigenous precedence by their value as tokens of prestige and privilege. These objects rapidly and easily became integrated into the exchange rituals of the Spanish elites, in yet another instance of commonality that the Europeans found with the privileged classes of another culture. Luxury items were supposed to be scarce, possess some degree of uniqueness, and be consumed by the few. Despite evidence that suggested otherwise, Spanish royal and ecclesiastical authorities agreed that

67. See, for example, the set of Christian sacred songs in Nahuatl that Sahagún put together and published in 1583. *Psalmodia Christiana*, trans. Arthur J. O. Anderson (Salt Lake City: University of Utah Press, 1993).

68. The Anonymous Conqueror, drawing a distinction with the weapons employed in war, called attention to the original function of the shields arriving in Spain. Conquistador anonimo, "Relación de algunas cosas de la Nueva España, y de la gran ciudad de Temestitán México," in *Colección de documentos para la historia de México*, ed. Joaquín García Icazbalceta, 2 vols. (Nendeln, Liechtenstein: Kraus Reprint, 1971), 1:373. Cortés's 1526 inventory can be found in Carlos H. Aguilar Piedra, *La orfebrería en el México precortesiano* (Mexico City: Acta Anthropologica II:2, 1946), 102–5. A long inventory of items to be distributed among individuals and religious institutions can be found on pages 105–11.

69. Motolinia described the procession held for the celebration of Corpus Christi in Tlaxcala in 1538 as follows: "Iba en la procession el Santísimo Sacramento y muchas cruces y andas con sus santos; las mangas de las cruces y los aderezos de las andas hechas todas de oro y plumas, y en ellas muchas imágenes de la misma obra de oro y pluma, que las bien labradas se preciarían en España más que de brocado." *Historia de los indios de la Nueva España*, treatise 1, chap. 15, 1592. On feather craftsmen, or *amantecas*, see treatise 1, chap. 12, 180. On the different materials used by local artists to make crosses, see treatise 2, chap. 10, 265–66.

70. According to Francisco de la Maza, the Escorial miter and a second one that became part of the Medicis collection were shipped from Mexico before 1534. "La mitra Mexicana de El Escorial," *Artes de México* 17, no. 137 (1971): 71–72. There are divergent opinions as to the precedence of this artifact. See Teresa Ortíz Salazar, "The Feather Adarga of Philip II and the Escorial Miter," *Coloquios: Nuevo Mundo Mundos Nuevos* (2006), http://nuevomundo.revues.org/1468.

sumptuary laws would help preserve these conditions and the overall integrity of a system that required visble and easily recognizable social hierarchies.[71] That the Nahua ruling class had reached a similar conclusion was further proof that ruling classes thought along similar lines. [72]

Following the traditional view, which was well-represented in the *summae*, manuals for confessors, and other religious treatises, the friars became less concerned with goods as such—whether ordinary or luxury, goods lay outside the realm of morality—and even rightful ownership, and more concerned with the morality of their makers, sellers, or merchants when engaged in their trade.[73] In Sahagún's encyclopedia, the merchants share a book with a select group of craftsmen admired by Nahuas and Spaniards alike for the quality of their work: lapidaries, metalsmiths, and featherworkers. Following the scheme that he applied to all trades, public offices, and family members in general, Sahagún described different craftsmen by way of brief, almost gnomic, portraits that summed up the virtues and vices most commonly associated with their respective trades. These moral portraits served as handy exempla for the friars to use in teaching and preaching. This same approach to the treatment of trades can be found in the pages that his colleague and fellow *nahuatlato* Alonso de Molina dedicated to the confession of penitents according to their profession. In Mexico, this traditional way of organizing the body of penitents for confession found its counterpart in the religious brotherhoods or *cofradías* within guilds, which were fashioned after Spanish brotherhoods and became a fixture in religious and civic festivals.[74] Molina's *Confessionario mayor*, in fact, sheds light on Sahagún's choice by bringing together the ethnographer's cultural insights and the missionary's practical aims. In the case of Sahagún, the frequent subordination of ethnographic inquiry to religious goals should not obscure the significance of the missionary gaze turned toward the material culture of the Mexican

---

71. The importance of sumptuary laws to the debate on indigenous customs is taken up in chapter 4.

72. As defined in the laws proposed by Tlacaelel and enacted by Moctezuma I, only warriors were allowed to wear certain articles of clothing, jewelry, and insignia; given by rulers in recognition for services received, these items were not for sale in the markets. Fr. Diego Durán, *Historia de las Indias de Nueva España*, vol. 2, chap. 29, 236–37. On clothing as a social indicator in Nahua society, see Patricia Hanawalt, "Costume and Control: Aztec Sumptuary Laws," *Archaeology* 33, no. 1 (January–February 1980): 33–43.

73. Probably drawing from the literature on confession, in the fifteenth century Rodrigo Sánchez de Arévalo, bishop of Zamora, discussed each estate and profession of his time by focusing on its contribution or potential harm to the body of society. Especially relevant is his treatment of the mechanical arts. *Spejo de la vida humana* (Zaragoza: Paulo Brus de Constancia, 1491; Valencia: Librerías "Paris-Valencia," 1998), book 1, chap. 23–27, f1–f6v.

74. The statutes of the brotherhoods included the obligation to participate in religious and civic celebrations. Manuel Carrera Stampa, *Los gremios mexicanos: La organización gremial en Nueva España 1521–1861* (Mexico City: EDIAPSA, 1954), 93–94.

peoples, uncovering for his readers the world of man-made objects, the techniques employed in producing them, and their makers.[75] For example, Sahagún gives a step-by-step account of the technique known as lost or wasted wax casting as used by Nahua metalsmiths before and during his time.[76] This particular technique, which of course took for granted the extraction, smelting, and purification of metals, allowed craftsmen to cast a variety of gold, silver, or copper objects such as nose rings, small bells, and animal figurines. The craftsman first made a clay mold, and then applied a layer of beewax and another of charcoal combined with copal. These seemingly dry technical descriptions illustrate human dominion and the Mexicans' mastery over nature in all its diversity. The many Mexican incarnations of *homo faber* that Sahagún's vignettes bring to life conjure up a culturally autonomous universe, an impression reinforced by the Nahuatl text which was left to stand alone without a Spanish glass, on account of its linguistic richness. As in many other instances in which Sahagún justified the inclusion of potentially controversial religious or historical material with its value as a linguistic document, one wonders if in this particular case Sahagún dispensed with a Spanish translation or periphrasis in order to quietly acknowledge and preserve his informants' trade secrets.[77]

Soon after the arrival of the Spanish, native metalsmiths and other craftsmen found themselves making a variety of new objects to meet the demands of the conquering people.[78] Spanish religious writers had come to appreciate

---

75. See Sabine MacCormack, *On the Wings of Time: Rome, the Incas, Spain, and Peru* (Princeton: Princeton University Press, 2007), 137–69.

76. An overview of the development of metallurgy in pre-Colombian Mexico with a special focus on copper and copper alloys can be found in Dorothy Hosler, "Metal Production," in *The Postclassic Mesoamerican World*, ed. Michael E. Smith and Frances E. Berdan (Salt Lake City: University of Utah Press, 2003), 159–71. See also Hosler's in-depth analysis of the production of copper artifacts, ritual functions, and geographical distribution. *The Sounds and Colors of Power: The Sacred Metallurgical Technology of Ancient West Mexico* (Cambridge, MA: MIT Press, 1994), especially chap. 5 and 8. On the relationship between metallurgy and state formation in West Mexico, see Helen Perlstein Pollard, "The Political Economy of Prehispanic Tarascan Metallurgy," *American Antiquity* 52, no. 4 (October 1987): 741–52.

77. On the techniques employed for casting metal figurines of animals that were popular in sixteenth-century Spain, Bernardo Pérez de Vargas commented: "Nótese que es secreto que en nuestra España se sabe entre pocos que lo encubren, estiman y precian, y se hazen bien pagados." *De re metallica: En el qual se tratan muchos y diversos secretos del conocimiento de toda suerte de minerales* (Madrid: Pierre Cosin, 1569), 159v. For a discussion of secrecy and the mechanical arts in light of the transformations wrought by the printing press, see Pamela O. Long, *Openness, Secrecy, Authorship: Technical Arts and the Culture of Knowledge from Antiquity to the Renaissance* (Baltimore: Johns Hopkins University Press, 2001), 175–209.

78. Some indigenous craftsmen entered into long-term contracts with Spaniards; such was the case of Pedro de Quero, a silversmith from Mexico City who provided lead components for ships for more than fourteen years. Silvio Zavala, *Fuentes para la historia del trabajo en Nueva España*, 5 vols. (Mexico City: Fondo de Cultura Económica, 1939), vol. 2, doc. 252, 383–84.

the importance of metalsmiths and other craftsmen to Christian worship.[79] When describing the techniques of indigenous metalsmiths, Sahagún referred in passing to *jarros* (jars) and incense burners.[80] For centuries the burning of copal had been a constant feature in the religious life of diverse Mesoamerican ethnic groups. Traditional copal burners were made of clay and, as surviving pre-Colombian samples show, came in a wide variety of types and sizes for use in either public or private ritual settings. As man-made artifacts designed for the offering of the sacred resin, copal censers took on some of this sacred character, as their widespread presence in burial sites attests. For the celebration of the Catholic liturgy, the Spanish favored elaborate metal incense burners and came to rely on the skills of local metalworkers to furnish ceremonial objects for the new churches. Once created, civil and religious laws dictated the conditions of possession, handling, and disposal of censers and other liturgical objects.[81]

Metal was the material of choice for censers meant for domestic use in affluent Spanish households; on the other hand, some types of traditional ceramic burners remained in use by indigenous families and in communal celebrations.[82] Considered valuable by many in both the monetary and sentimental

---

79. Writing on the mechanical arts of carpentry, masonry, and metalwork, Sánchez de Arévalo said: "Ca por ellas es socorrida la necessidad de los hombres, ca si no fuessen los edificios, no podrian vivir los hombres, y toda la conservacion politica, y el culto divino se perderia." *Spejo de la vida humana*, book 1, chap. 26, fv. More than a century later, Christoval Suárez de Figueroa, translating Tomaso Garzoni's treatise on trades, wrote: "Quien fabrica los calices, cruzes, patenas, candeleros, vinajeras de oro y plata, incensarios y relicarios?" *Plaza universal de todas ciencias y artes* (Madrid: Luis Sanchez, 1615), *discurso* 90, 214. The translator felt free to include a reference to the influx of metals from the Spanish colonies in the Spanish version. 213v.

80. Sahagún, *Florentine Codex*, book 9, chap. 16, 77.

81. On the inalienability of all things given to the church as alms or donations, see Alfonso Díaz de Montalvo, *Los códigos españoles concordados y anotados*, 12 vols. (Madrid: Imprenta de la Publicidad a cargo de M. Rivadeneyra, 1849), vol. 6, book 1, title 2, law 1, 259. On the inalienability of relics, chalices, censers, and other ceremonial objects, including "las imagines que fueron hechas son plata, o sobredoradas, e con piedras preciosas," given to churches by members of the royal family and the nobility, see book 1, title 2, law 10, 261. On prohibition of selling or pawning liturgical objects, articles of clothing, and church ornaments, see book 1, title 2, law 3, 260. See also *Recopilación de las leyes destos reynos, hecha por mandado de la Magestad Catolica del Rey Don Felipe Segundo nuestro señor, que se ha mandado imprimir, con las leyes que despues de la ultima impression se han publicado, por la Magestad Catolica Felipe Quarto el Grande nuestro señor* (Madrid: Catalina de Barrio y Angulo y Diego Diaz de la Carrera, 1640), book 1, title 2, law 7 and book 1, title 2, law 10.

82. An example is the disappearance of long-handled incense burners associated with religious ceremonies in both rural (Otumba) and urban (Tenochtitlán-Texcoco) areas, as well as the sporadic presence of glazed burners without the traditional serpent head in rural areas. Thomas Charlton, Cynthia Otis Charlton, and Patricia Fourier García, "The Basin of Mexico A.D. 1450–1620: Archaeological Dimensions," in *The Postclassic to Spanish-Era Transition in Mesoamerica: Archaeological Perspectives*, ed. Susan Kepecs and Rani T. Alexander (Albuquerque: University of New Mexico Press, 1995), 58, 61.

senses, copal burners were often passed down as heirlooms by the dying. Given metal's long association with social prestige and religion in Mesoamerica, the appearance of this familiar ritual object made of a different material in a church may have further strengthened both the connection and the divide between private and public devotion.

Metalsmiths faced changes that went beyond the mere application of their skills and traditional techniques to the production of new objects, amounting to a substantial transformation of conditions of labor and commerce. For instance, new laws and regulations of trade and commerce included the mandate to adopt Spanish weights and measurements for a wide variety of local products.[83] One such product was cochineal, the expensive dye that, from 1550 on, would rank among Mexico's most important exports.[84] On April 20, 1548 the indigenous *cabildo* of Tlaxcala entrusted the metalsmiths Juan Nezahual and Juan Neza to make the bowls for weighing cochineal.[85] The appointment was to last two years, during which time the two craftsmen from the class of the notables or *principales* were to provide the *cabildo* with measuring bowls made according to official specifications. After passing the required inspection, each bowl would be stamped, as weighing and measuring instruments—and items made of silver—traditionally were.[86] Juan Nezahual and Juan Neza were selected because they were considered "mihmati," careful and conscientious

---

83. See Manual Carrera Stampa, "The Evolution of Weights and Measures in New Spain," in *Hispanic American Historical Review* 29, no. 1 (February 1949): 2–24; Ross Hassig, *Trade, Tribute, and Transportation: The Sixteenth-Century Political Economy of the Valley of Mexico* (Norman: University of Oklahoma Press, 1985), 229–30.

84. It did not take long for the crown to learn about the existence of cochineal in Mexico; as early as 1523 Mexican local authorities were instructed to gather information on its production and quality, and to secure the due payment of tithes from sellers. Encinas, *Cedulario indiano*, 1:195–96. The order to collect tithes from *grana* was repeated in 1539. 1:195. Shipments of cochineal were weighed and parceled in *cargas* of nine *arrobas*. Carrera Stampa, "The Evolution," 14. On the trade of cochineal in Mexico, see Raymond L. Lee, "Cochineal Production and Trade in New Spain to 1600," *The Americas* 4, no. 4 (April 1948): 449. On global trade and production, see A. Donkin, *Spanish Red: An Ethnogeographical Study of Cochineal and the Opuntia Cactus.* Transactions of the American Philosophical Society, New Series, vol. 67, no. 5 (1977). The geographic shift in production during the nineteenth century from America to the Canarias has been traced by Carlos Sánches Silva and Miguel Suárez Bosa. "Evolución de la producción y comercio mundial de la grana cochinilla, siglos xvi–xix," *Revista de Indias* 66, no. 237 (2006): 473–90.

85. *Actas de cabildo de Tlaxcala, 1547–1567*, ed. Eustaquio Celestino Solís, Armando Valencia R., and Constantino Medina Lima (Mexico City: Archivo General de la Nación; Tlaxcala: Instituto Tlaxcalteca de la Cultura, 1984), 248.

86. *Actas de cabildo de Tlaxcala*, 248. Craftsmen were also required to leave an identifying mark on the products of their workshops; see the 1568 ordinance for Mexico City ironsmiths in Francisco del Barrio Lorenzot, *Ordenanzas de gremios de la Nueva España* (Mexico City: Dirección de Talleres Gráficos, 1921), 148. On the official marks required on silverworks, see Manuel Romero de Terreros y Vinent, *Las artes industriales en la Nueva España* (Mexico City: Librería de Pedro Robredo, 1928), 21.

craftsmen who would do a flawless job.[87] This almost formulaic expression of respect calls to mind Sahagún's moral portrait of the good *tepuzpitzqui* and kindred artisans.[88] Sahagún's treatment of Nahua trades reflected a corporate view of society that had been rested on a moral and theological foundation worked out by medieval religious thinkers over time. The city contract appointing the artisans acknowledged their skills and integrity as well as the social value inherent in their craft. Sahagún appeared to agree with this assessment of metalsmithing. Apparently, so did the crown. In 1552, the silversmiths of Palencia, Spain brought an official complaint, based on the broad and seemingly erroneous way that local authorities had interpreted a recent ordinance forbidding tailors, shoemakers, dyers, and weavers, as well as their spouses, from wearing silk.[89] The king immediately issued a provision clarifying that the sumptuary law in question did not apply to silversmiths and similar craftsmen (*artífices*).[90] Taking stock of learned opinion on the hierarchy of disciplines and professions, the king's provision stated that silversmiths should be more highly esteemed than the manual laborers affected by the new law, because their craft required familiarity with some liberal arts such as geometry and mathematics.[91] The silversmiths were thus rewarded with a legal argument that further justified their sense of honor and worth.

Some years later, in 1561, the members of the *cabildo* of Tlaxcala dealt with a similar situation, and again agreed to entrust the same workers to make the *tepozcaxitl* for the official weighing of cochineal.[92] This time, however, the record dispensed with any praise or recognition and instead forcefully spelled out

---

87. "Los harán porque ellos son 'cuidadosos' (*mihmati*). Los hacen muy bien, su *tequitl* (oficio) es sin falta alguna, los cazos de metal serán para la grana que se compre en el mercado." *Actas de cabildo de Tlaxcala*, 248. This passage is not included in James Lockhart, Frances Berdan, and Arthur J. O. Anderson, eds., *The Tlaxcalan Actas: A Compendium of the Records of the Cabildo of Tlaxcala (1545–1627)* (Salt Lake City: University of Utah Press, 1986). On *mati* and the conceptualization of craft and practical knowledge as reflected in Classical Nahuatl, see Marie Noëlle Chamoux, "Dire le savoir-faire en nahuatl classique," in *Dire le savoir-faire: Gestes, techniques et objects*, ed. Salvatore D'Onofrio and Frédéric Joulian (Paris: L'Herne, 2006), 37–54.
88. "The good coppercaster is wise, honest (*mimati*), discreet, imaginative, adroit." *Florentine Codex*, book 10, chap. 7, 26. On the good crafstman (*toltecatl*) and the goldsmith, see page 25.
89. Gaspar Gutiérrez de los Ríos, *Noticia general para la estimacion de las artes y de la manera que se conocen las liberales de las que son mecanicas y serviles* (Madrid: Pedro Madrigal, 1600), book 3, chap. 18, 206. On workers and sumptuary laws in the early modern Spain, see MacKay, *Lazy, Improvident People*, 80–89.
90. Gutiérrez de los Ríos, *Noticia general*, 210.
91. Gutiérrez de los Ríos, *Noticia general*, 206–7. As the document pointed out, although silversmiths were *artífices* from a legal standpoint, popular usage referred to them as *oficiales*, a term generally reserved for manual laborers of a lower order.
92. A full treatment of the semantic change of the word *tepoztli*, from copper to a general term for metal and iron, can be found in Lockhart, *The Nahuas after the Conquest*, 272–74. For linguistic usages in the Mixtecan language, see Terraciano, *The Mixtecs of Colonial Oaxaca*, 85.

the metalworkers' obligations, including the monetary penalty they would in-
cur if their work failed to meet official guidelines.[93] The smelters were reminded
of these guidelines and asked to work under the vigilant eyes of the alcalde
and the *regidores*.[94] Behind this mundane event lay consequential changes. Although we are far removed from Sahagún's highly stylized metalworkers, and
it is hard to know for certain if the deferential treatment of the two craftsmen
upon their first appointment by the *cabildo* was a token of recognition of their
social rank, but whatever clout they may have enjoyed in the past seems to
have faded away, turning the two Juans into mere workers for hire. Starting in
the middle of the sixteenth century, increased European demand for cochineal
brought with it more stringent laws for its production and commercialization.[95]
In this environment, more traditional values soon gave way to the contractual
language describing the obligations of salaried workers whose products were
appraised according to new parameters. That the two Juans made instruments
for weighing destined for overseas markets speaks quite eloquently of the role
that quantification played in transforming old moral notions attached to work,
craftsmanship, and professional integrity. As this example suggests, the same
shift that led indigenous metalworkers to create new and officially commissioned object also significantly altered the ways their work was perceived and
valued. In the case of community-owned objects used for Christian worship, it
did seem to matter who made them. In 1527, the inhabitants of Cuauhtinchan
first heard a bell ringing, which scared them so much that they fled the church
in the middle of mass.[96] One year later, they commissioned a new, larger bell
from Spanish bellmaker Simón de Buenaventura.[97] Years later, Chimalpahin,
a dedicated recorder of Mexico City ceremonial life could not help but report
whether the craftsman of a church bell was Spanish or Indian.[98] Besides the

---

93. *Actas de cabildo de Tlaxcala*, 417–18.

94. *Actas de cabildo de Tlaxcala*, 418.

95. Lee, "Cochineal Production," 468–71.

96. *Libro de los guardianes y gobernadores de Cuauhtinchan (1519–1640)*, ed. Constantino Medina Lima (Mexico City: CIESAS, 1995), 37.

97. *Libro de los guardianes y gobernadores de Cuauhtinchan (1519–1640)*, 55. In 1586 the town
refused the request of a convent in Mexico City to swap bells; it seems there was much at stake in
the ownership of bells, 63. The historical annals of the Cakchiquels register the arrival in 1552 of a
bronze bell sent to the town of Sololá by the king of Spain. *Annals of the Cakchiquels*, in *Annals of
the Cakchiquels* and *Title of the Lords of Totonicapán*, ed. Adrián Recinos and trans. Adrián Recinos,
Delia Goetz, and Dionisio José Chonay (Norman: University of Oklahoma Press, 1953), 137. According to Mendieta, bell-making was among the first crafts brought by Spaniards that the Nahuas
mastered: "Y así fundieron luego muchas campanas, chicas y grandes, muy limpias y de buena voz
y sonido." *Historia eclesiástica indiana*, book 4, chap. 13, 409.

98. Chimalpahin, *Annals of His Time*, 41. Chimalpahin similarly recorded that, by order of the
viceroy, a Nahua master blacksmith departed for New Mexico in July 1609 to train new craftsmen,
159.

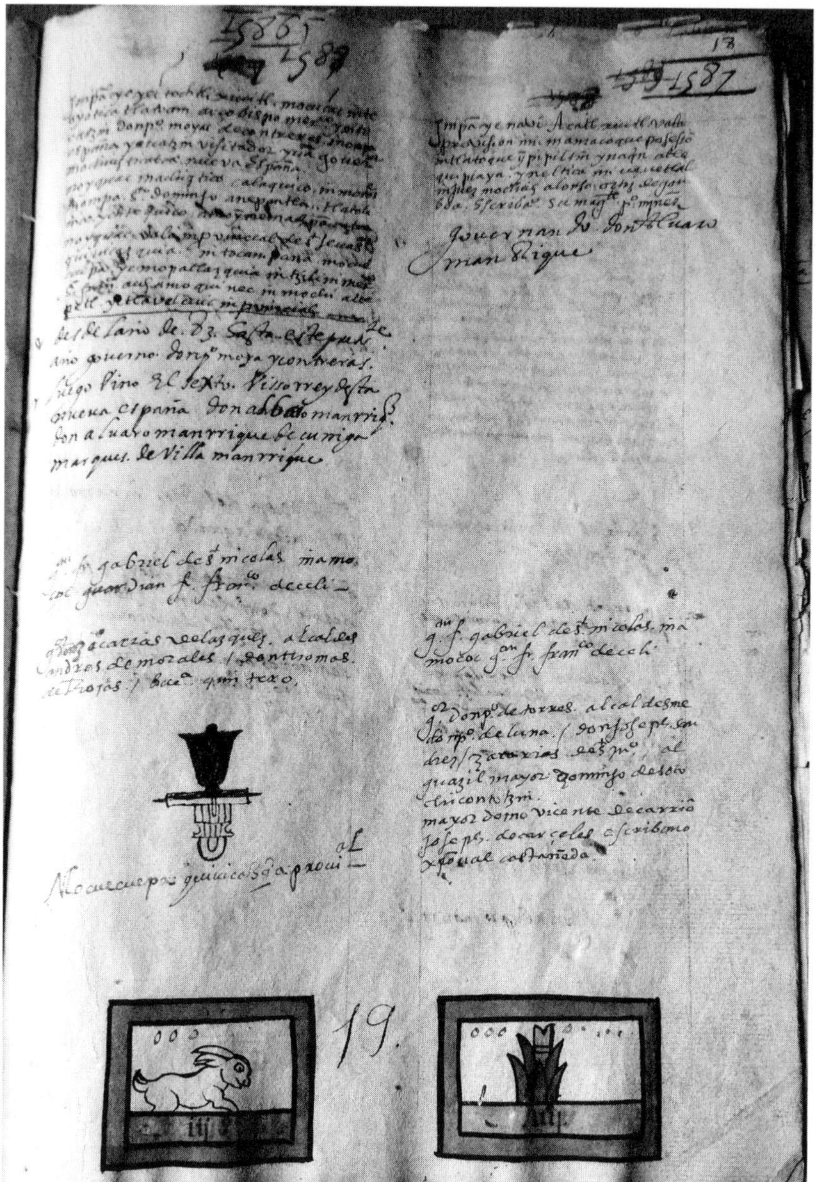

Fig. 1.1. Bell for the church of Cuauhtinchan. *Libro de los guardianes y gobernadores de Cuauhtinchan (1519–1640)*. (Courtesy of the Biblioteca "Jorge Carpizo," Instituto de Investigaciones Jurídicas, Universidad Nacional Autónoma de México.)

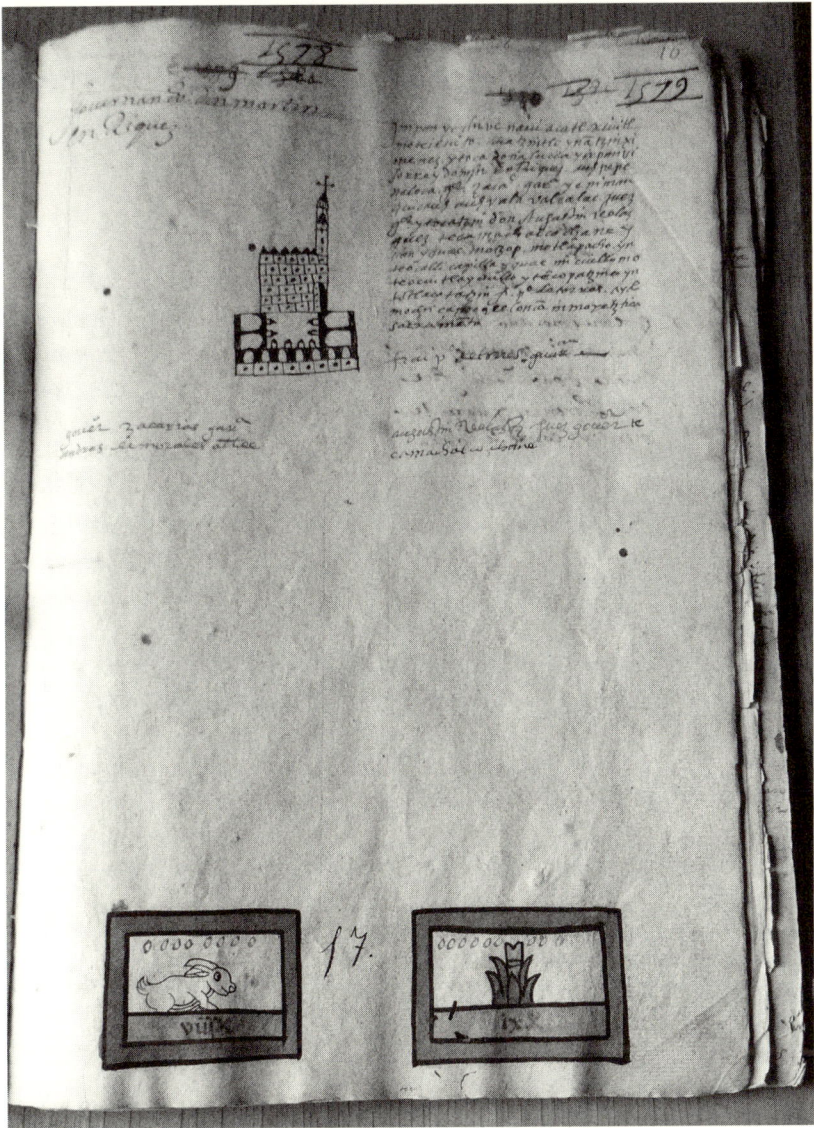

Fig. 1.2. The Church. *Libro de los guardianes y gobernadores de Cuauhtinchan (1519–1640)*. (Courtesy of the Biblioteca "Jorge Carpizo," Instituto de Investigaciones Jurídicas, Universidad Nacional Autónoma de México.)

communal pride that such acquisitions promoted, bells took on more personal connotations, as when the dying paid to be remembered, however briefly, by their tolling.[99]

Possessions of the Poor

In stark contrast to the conquerors' enthusiasm for Moctezuma's palatial quarters and the lavish lifestyle of the Nahua nobility, which they were eager to describe to the Spanish court, Franciscans paid close attention to the living conditions of the *macehuales* or commoners at the same time that they forged close ties to the elites who entrusted them with the education of their children.[100] The friars' engagement with indigenous material culture was an integral part of a calculated effort to bring Christianity to the Mexican Indians; it also prepared them to better respond to those tributary policies they judged unacceptable, in terms that were familiar to the royal administrators that relied on economic and demographic surveys of Indian communities. At the risk of oversimplifying, what the friars learned about the objects surrounding indigenous nobility and commoners, exemplified by jewels and grinding stones, respectively, they put to use in their two main areas of interest, religion and welfare.

Poverty played a fundamental role in the self-definition and teachings of the Franciscans from the order's creation in the thirteenth century. As a way of life

---

99. Rojas Rabiela, Rea López, and Medina Lima, *Vidas y bienes olvidados*, 1:159 and 2:70, 78, 122. For a study of the same phenomenon in a later period, see Caterina Pizzigoni, ed. and trans., *Testaments of Toluca* (Stanford: Stanford University Press; Los Angeles: UCLA Latin American Center Publications, 2007), 60, 65, and 67. It would take a religious person to notice the differences between Mexican and Spanish bells. In 1765, a Spanish Capuchin friar wrote the following impressions of Mexico City in his travel journal: "Las funciones de iglesias las celebran con gran magnificencia. Las campanas son más en número, de mayores tamaños y más sonoras que las de Europa. A las tres de la tarde tocan en todas las iglesias de esta América y dan con pausa tres golpes con la campana mayor en reverencia de las tres horas que Cristo estuvo en la cruz. El modo de tocar las campanas a muerto, a fiesta, a rogativa y a nublado, etc, es uno mismo en toda la América." Francisco Ajofrín, *Diario del viaje que por orden de la Sagrada Congregación de Propaganda Fide hizo a la América septentrional, en el siglo xviii el P. Fray Francisco Ajofrín*, 2 vols. (Madrid: Real Academia de la Historia, 1958), 1:86. As part of his efforts to curb what he saw as the excesses of popular religious devotions, in 1766 Archbishop Francisco Antonio de Lorenzana issued an edict denouncing what he considered to be abuses surrounding the use of bells (like unrestrained tolling and the excessive number of bells in monasteries and churches) and laying out a set of restrictions, such as banning their tolling at night. Francisco Antonio Lorenzana y Buitron, *Cartas pastorales y edictos del Illmo. Señor Don Francisco Antonio Lorenzana y Buitron, Arzobispo de México* (Mexico City: Joseph Antonio de Hogal, 1770), 7–11.

100. On the different meanings of *macehualli*, see Lockhart, *The Nahuas after the Conquest*, 96–102; for a discussion of the Mixtecan terms for "commoners," see Kevin Terraciano, *The Mixtecs of Colonial Oaxaca: Ñudzahui History, Sixteenth through Eighteenth Centuries* (Stanford: Stanford University Press, 2001), 140–44.

rather than just an ideal, however, poverty proved to be a point of contention among members of the order throughout its history.[101] Spain was no exception, and as a wave of reforms swept Spanish monasteries toward the end of the fifteenth century, a community of friars emerged who were committed to living in strict accord with the rules of poverty laid down by the order's founder. The decision by some of these friars to venture into the recently conquered Central Valley of Mexico turned an episode that might have been confined to the order's local historical record into an event in which the friars' ideas and actions took on an unexpected dimension.[102]

In 1524 the Franciscan Toribio de Benavente and eleven brothers arrived in New Spain, tasked with setting the stage for the evangelization of the Nahuas and other indigenous groups. Not long afterward and following the order's tradition of shedding the family name, Benavente proudly adopted the name by which he had become known among the natives: Motolinia, meaning "he/she is poor," a designation that suggested an affinity between the friar and the local population and also marked him as different from his countrymen.[103] The word "motolinia" was already familiar to some Spaniards. Writing from Cuba in 1521, the judge Alonso de Zuazo made reference to an entire class of poor people in Mexico identified as "motolineas."[104]

Naming was very much on the minds of the friars as they worked out guidelines for the mass baptisms of indigenous children and adults.[105] In practice,

---

101. The "Prima regola dei fratri minori" read: "La regola e la vita dei fratri è questa, cioè vivere in obbedienza, in castità e senza proprietà e seguire la dottrina e le vestigia del Signore nostro Gesù Cristo," in San Francesco D'Assisi, *Gli scritti*, ed. Giacomo V. Sabatelli (Assisi: Edizioni Porziuncola, 1971), §1, 39 and 50. The shorter second rule retained this opening paragraph with negligible changes, §1, 72. §2, 73 deals with the disposal of property by sale or donation to the poor. On the emergence of the ideal of religious poverty in the rapidly changing European economy of the thirteenth century, see Little, *Religious Poverty and the Profit Economy in Medieval Europe*, especially 146–69. See also Bronislaw Geremek, *La potence ou la pitié: L'Europe et les pauvres du Moyen Âge à nos jours*, trans. Joanna Arnold-Moricet (Paris: Gallimard, 1987), 23–71.

102. On Franciscan poverty in New Spain, see Antonio Rubial García, *La hermana pobreza: El franciscanismo de la edad media a la evangelización novohispana* (Mexico City: Facultad de Filosofía y Letras, Universidad Nacional Autónoma de México, 1996), 133–46.

103. Mendieta, *Historia eclesiástica indiana*, book 3, chap. 12, 211. On indigenous perceptions of the Franciscans, see Miguel León-Portilla, *Los franciscanos vistos por el hombre náhuatl* (México: Centro de Estudios Bernardino de Sahagún, S. A., 1985).

104. "Hay entre ellos muchos pobres a que llaman *motolineas*. Tienen tal orden que si el tal motolinea es huérfano de padre y madre y mozo, pónenlo luego con señor, de cuyo poder no ha de salir, so pena de muerte, hasta que sea hombre y lo casen." Alonso de Zuazo, *Cartas y memorias (1511–1539)*, ed. Rodrigo Martínez Baracs (Mexico City: CONACULTA, 2000), 190. The close association between poverty and tutelage of fatherless children is worth noting, especially since the Indians would eventually be granted the status of "miserabiles personae." See R. H. Helmholz, *The Spirit of Classical Canon Law* (Athens: University of Georgia Press, 1996), 128–32.

105. The most complete treatment of naming patterns among the Nahuas to date is that of Lockhart, *The Nahuas after the Conquest*, 117–30. For an analysis based on the Cuernavaca censuses, see S. L. Cline, *The Book of Tributes: Early Sixteenth-Century Censuses from Morelos* (Los

the Nahuas adopted a narrow range of Christian baptismal names; out of deference, fear, or indifference, and especially during the early stages of the evangelization, the Nahuas often left the naming decision up to the priests or friars administering the sacrament.[106] The friars also seem to have encouraged Nahuas
to adopt a second name, thus introducing among them a practice common
within religious orders.[107]

The Cuernavaca censuses, which date from approximately 1530 to the
early 1540s, record that a twenty-five-year-old sibling of Atecpanecatl, head of
a household, was named Motolinia;[108] like all his immediate relatives, he was
unbaptized at the time of the census. The name stands in sharp contrast to the
others that tend to appear with some frequency. Later documents attest the usage of Motolinia as a surname.[109] A Tomás Motolinia from Culhuacan owned
several tracts of land at the time of his death and kept all proper documentation
pertaining to these acquisitions in case his will was contested.[110] In an undated
will also from Culhuacan, a Gregorio de San Agustín left a broken boat to two
destitute individuals bearing the same Spanish surname: Domingo Pobre and
Juan Pobre.[111] As I will discuss below, names were one of numerous instances in
which the friars' expectations and assumptions about poverty converged with
indigenous usages.

The first Franciscans anticipated that their message of poverty and salvation
would resonate among the Indians and lead to a faster, smoother conversion
to Christianity. Motolinia did his best to prove his brothers right, recounting
how the Mexicans, following St. Francis, embraced voluntary poverty or gladly
parted with their possessions as death neared. The basic idea of conversion by

---

Angeles: UCLA Latin American Center Publications, 1993), 48–51. On the relationship between
baptism, names, and record keeping in early modern Europe, Adriano Prosperi, "Battesimo e identità cristiana," 18–24.

106. Ordinances were enacted banning the use of indigenous names: "Item: que los dichos
naturales no pongan a sus hijos nombres, divisas nis eñales en los vestidos ni cabezas, por donde se
representen que los ofrecen y encomiendan a los demonios, so pena que sean presos, y luego sean
dados cien azotes, y les sean quitadas las dichas insignias y divisas." Edmundo O'Gorman, "Una
ordenanza para el gobierno de los indios, 1546," *Boletín del Archivo General de la Nación* 11, no. 2
(1940): 189. The full text of the ordinances with the earlier date of 1539 can also be found in *Colección de documentos coloniales de Tepeaca*, ed. Hildeberto Martínez (Mexico City: Instituto Nacional
de Antropología e Historia, 1984), 23–27. Conciliar legislation in colonial Mexico sought to further
weaken indigenous traditions by restricting baptismal names to those found in the New Testament.
Concilium Mexicanum Provinciale III, book 3, title 16, §5, 245.

107. Lockhart, *The Nahuas after the Conquest*, 121.

108. S. L. Cline, *The Book of Tributes*, 265.

109. In 1598 a testator named Verónica Saguanpetla declared as her husband one Tadeo Motolinia. Rojas Rabiela, Rea López, and Medina Lima, *Vidas y bienes olvidados*, 1:290.

110. S. L. Cline and Miguel León-Portilla, eds., *The Testaments of Culhuacan* (Los Angeles:
UCLA Latin American Center Publications / University of California, Los Angeles, 1984), 160–65.

111. Cline and León-Portilla, *The Testaments of Culhuacan*, 258–61.

imitation also led Motolinia to conceive of the Indians themselves as models of poverty to be emulated by prospective friars of the order since, when it came to living in poverty, little separated the strictest Franciscans in Spain from the majority of the Mexicans, whom Motolinia saw as members of a "comunidad" in the religious sense.[112]

Essential to their self-assigned role as spokesmen for and defenders of the natives was the missionaries' characterization of the indigenous masses as "poor," a label that, beyond its obvious but significant resonance within the Franciscan order, was meant to remind royal administrators of the church's long-standing obligation toward those in need. In conflict-ridden Mexico, labels and comparisons carried significant weight and for this reason were sometimes contested.[113] Taught by experience and hoping to benefit from it, missionaries were keenly aware of the power of words to gain currency and shape perception, as their complaint about the *encomenderos'* selective use of the term "Christian" showed.[114] Authorities recognized the obligation of the church toward the poor in various ways, such as allowing religious men who would otherwise be barred from acting as lawyers to represent the poor before secular judges.[115]

The friars' long-lasting identification of the Indians with Christ's poor served as a point of departure for a host of widely-divergent opinions about the economic and moral status of the indigenous population and its potential for transformation under royal policies.[116] As the demographic and social profile of colonial society changed, it became apparent to observers trying to describe the economic conditions of culturally diverse groups living side by side that

---

112. "Y así cuando algún fraile de nuevo viene de Castilla, que allá era tenido por muy penitente y que hacía raya a los otros, venido acá es como río que entra en la mar, porque acá toda la comunidad vive estrechamente y guarda todo lo que puede guardar." Motolinia, *Historia de los indios de la Nueva España*, treatise 3, chap. 4, 302.

113. An eloquent example of the steps that the religious orders took to advance their agenda and discredit alternative views is their insistence that comparisons between the Nahuas and Spanish Moriscos were simply misguided and offered no basis for the creation of new policies.

114. See chapter 3 on the use of the term "Christian."

115. "Otrosi mandamos que ningunos clerigos constituydos en orden sacra no sean abogados ante juezes algunos seglares ni sean recebidos sus escriptos ni peticiones: salvo en causas de sus yglesias o por personas pobres y miserables: y en los otros casos por el derecho permitidos no en otros algunos." *Las pragmaticas del Reyno. Recopilacion de algunas bulas del summo pontifice: concedidas en favor de la jurisdiccion real: con todas las pragmaticas: y algunas leyes del reyno: hechas para la buena governacion y guarda de la justicia: y muchas pragmaticas y leyes añadidas que hasta aqui no fueron impressas* (Valladolid: Juan de Villaguiran, 1540), 47v. The church's claim to spiritual jurisdiction over *miserabiles personae* was met with resistance and successfully challenged by temporal powers across Europe. Helmholz, *The Spirit of Classical Canon Law*, 134–42.

116. A case in point, which is discussed in the conclusion, is the treatise *Virtudes del indio* (1650) by Juan Palafox y Mendoza, bishop of Puebla, whose relations with the religious orders were anything but amicable.

poverty was not a clear-cut category.[117] In this new context, some officials close to the friars reformulated the missionaries' early and positive characterization of the Mexican Indians as a community of the poor, highlighting, among other things, the negative perception of Spanish administrators and *encomenderos* of the local inhabitants' seemingly low productivity and their apparent lack of inclination to work.

Spanish observers paid close attention to the entrance of European-manufactured products into Nahua households.[118] As with all matters concerning the behavior of indigenous subjects, the writings of private individuals, administrators, and friars were affected by debates about viceregal policies and the current state of affairs. The parties, boasting that they knew the Indians' real needs, made claims that were largely conditioned by the widely divergent interests that each represented. Meanwhile, reality took its course and the changes that affected the Indian communities challenged and fulfilled the predictions and wishes of Spaniards in equal measure.

Toward the close of the century, judge and entrepreneur Gonzalo Gómez de Cervantes touched upon the huge gap between the Indian poor and humble Spanish commoners in the Peninsula to argue that the proper administration of economic affairs in Mexico required two separate bodies of laws.[119] He noted that the Mexican Indians went about their lives under conditions of such extreme frugality and deprivation that even the most devout Spanish penitents would find them difficult to endure, whereas the Spanish poor still managed

---

117. Zorita, a sharp observer of the economic realities of Indian communities, tried to convey to royal authorities that the majority of the Indians in Mexico City earned their living by working as carpenters, builders, smiths, and carriers, not as agricultural laborers or peasants. *Colección de libros y documentos referentes a la historia de América*, vol. 9, *Historia de la Nueva España por el Doctor Alonso de Zorita (siglo XVI)* (Madrid: Victoriano Suárez, 1909), 435–36. Michel Mollat has commented on the persistent lack of agreement among European sources on the proper definition of poor. *The Poor in the Middle Ages: An Essay in Social History* (New Haven: Yale University Press, 1986), 232–42. See also Geremek, *La potence ou la pitié*, 139–40.

118. Regarding the opposite phenomenon, archaeologists are analyzing pottery found in Spanish households of different social classes in Mexico City and are raising important questions about Spanish attitudes toward indigenous crafts and their adoption. See, for example, Enrique Rodríguez-Alegría, "Consumption and the Varied Ideologies of Domination in Colonial Mexico," in *The Postclassic to Spanish-Era Transition in Mesoamerica*, ed. Susan Kepecs and Rani T. Alexander (Albuquerque: University of New Mexico Press, 2005), 35–48; and Tomas Charlton and Patricia Fournier's study of the widespread use of Red Ware among the Spanish in the sixteenth-century, "Pots and Plots: the Multiple Roles of Colonial Red Wares in the Basin of Mexico," in *Enduring Conquests: Rethinking the Archaeology of Resistance to Spanish Colonialism in the Americas*, ed. Matthew Liebmann and Melissa M. Murphy (Santa Fe, NM: School for Advanced Research, 2010).

119. "de manera que las cosas de indios no se han de regular con las de los españoles; y no es posible que las cosas del reino se conformen con esta generación." Gonzalo Gómez de Cervantes, *La vida económica y social de Nueva España al finalizar el siglo XVI*, ed. Alberto María Carreño (Mexico City: Antigua Librería Robredo, de José Porrúa e Hijos, 1944), 137.

to avail themselves of adequate food, clothing, and the comfort of a bed, a rare item even among Indian noblemen.[120] Thanks in part to the first Franciscans, who also described their bond with their charges when they described the Indians' material conditions, it became difficult to talk about Indian poverty without reference to religion.

Notwithstanding the comparison to Spanish penitents, Gómez de Cervantes was less interested in the spiritual dimension of the Nahuas' everyday existence than he was in the need for the crown to provide for Spaniards who did not enjoy public offices, lands, mines, or other means to support themselves and contribute to the economic growth of the viceroyalty. To his dismay a considerable number of "neighbors, citizens, and poor people," many of them descendants of conquerors, had been left out of the distribution of Indian labor that lined the pockets of those individuals with close ties to viceregal administrators.[121] As a way of both correcting what he saw as an injustice to faithful subjects and bringing an increasingly visible mass of destitute Spaniards, Indians, and *mestizos* under official control, Gómez de Cervantes proposed a more equitable allocation of native labor (*repartimiento general*) under friars' supervision.[122] The recommendation relies on the idea that the seemingly unbridgeable disparity between the basic needs of the Mexican and Spanish poor translated into a similar gap in the desires of the two groups, an assumption crucial to Gómez de Cervantes's argument about the advantages of applying two separate bodies of law to Spaniards and Indians.

In 1584, having returned to Granada from Mexico, retired and nearing the end of his life, Alonso de Zorita reacted to the crown's decision to start replacing the mendicant friars working in Mexico with secular priests by drafting a lengthy defense of the friars' dedication and spiritual superiority. A reader of French humanist Guillaume Budé, more likely to quote Roman writers and the church fathers than legal sources, Zorita moved to Mexico from Guatemala in 1556 to serve as *oidor* (judge) and inspector of the Audiencia; he would spend

---

120. Gómez de Cervantes, *La vida económica*, 135–36.

121. Gómez de Cervantes, *La vida económica*, 103. Zorita—probably well aware of the ineffectiveness of the royal laws to control vagrants—also called attention to the increasing number of Spaniards, *mulatos*, and mestizos wandering around the city. Alonso de Zorita, *Historia de la Nueva España*, 433. In 1558, a royal order urged Viceroy Luis de Velasco to round up Indians, mestizos, and Spaniards with no known occupation and send them to separate towns, where they were expected to work in the fields or tend to cattle. Vasco de Puga, *Provisiones, cédulas, instrucciones para el gobierno de la Nueva España* (1563) (Madrid: Ediciones Cultura Hispánica, 1945), folio 204v–205. For other ordinances concerning Spanish vagrants in Mexico, see Encinas, *Cedulario indiano*, 4:261 and 340–41.

122. Gómez de Cervantes, *La vida económica*, 105.

ten years there before returning to Spain. Those years of service gave him first-hand knowledge of the local alliances that Spaniards, *mestizos*, and Indians in varying positions of authority had forged in the hope of mutual benefits. He had also acquainted himself with the most minute details of the economic life of Indian households and communities, gathering information about resources, labor, and production to adjudicate cases and make recommendations on tributary policy. Rehashing old accusations against the secular clergy, Zorita questioned the crown's decision to reward priests who differed little from their lay countrymen in their pursuit of earthly gains and indifference to the Indians' well-being. As an example, Zorita pointed to the unequal bartering of goods promoted by priests assigned to Indian towns:

> In exchange for cocoa and the other items already mentioned, to those who have it they give wine, breaches and shoes, and boots and hats and old trinkets and chairs as well as other trifle all at the price they ask for, and they tell the Indians why they should not deserve the same things that the Christians have. And there are Indians who own fifteen and twenty pairs or more of shoes and boots and other things that lay rotting in a corner because they have no need for them, nor they know how to use them, and so that the Indians request wine and pay what they are asked, they are told that in bringing it, they had risked being found out and punished, and everything is transported by *tamemes*, and although the penalty is excommunication, they and their superiors look the other way and no punishment is enough to put an end to these and other transgressions.[123]

The friars on whose behalf Zorita spoke had leveled the same charge many times against parish priests.[124] But the charge was somehow amplified by the implica-

---

123. "En trueque del cacao y de lo demas que se a dicho les dan a los que lo tienen, vino y calças y çapatos, y botas y gorras y paramentos viejos y sillas y otras buxerias al preçio que quieren, y les dizen que ¿por qué no ternan ellos lo que tienen los christianos? Y ay yndios que tienen xv y xx pares y mas de botas y çapatos y de lo demas que se a dicho, a un rincon, todo podrido, porque no la an menester ni saben usar dello y para que tomen el vino y se lo paguen como ellos quieren, les dizen que se an puesto por se lo traer al riesgo de la pena que esta puesta, y todo lo traen en tamemes, y aunque ay puesta pena de excomunion, disimulan con ello ellos y los perlados, y ninguna pena ni ley basta para ympedir estos exçessos y otros que ay en otras cosas." Zorita, *Historia de la Nueva España*, 505. As hinted at by Zorita, parish priests appeared to share the Spanish reluctance to extend the use of the word "Christian" to the Indians.

124. This was also a common accusation against colonial officials such as *corregidores*. See, for example, a royal decree from August 2, 1679, denouncing the widespread practice among *corregidores* of forcing Indians to buy wine and articles of clothing. *Cedulario americano del siglo XVIII*,

tion that in being coerced into buying goods they could not use, the Nahuas were acting against their customs.[125] Underlying this and similar anecdotes was the friars' idealized vision of a culturally autonomous republic of Christianized Indians living side by side with Spaniards. According to this model—which was partially acknowledged in early legislation that sought to protect Indians from economic and other abuses—the Indians' cultural autonomy could only be achieved by keeping exchanges (for example, of laws or goods) between Indians and Europeans to a minimum. To Zorita, since the Indians had no use for European articles, this goal was attainable by enforcing existing laws and, above all, keeping the Mexicans under the supervision of friars.

Despite their divergent perspectives and interests, both Zorita and Gómez de Cervantes portrayed the Mexican Indians as more attached to the familiar objects of their surroundings than to European novelties, a feature that both agreed the crown should preserve. For Zorita, and along the lines of Franciscan thought, the success of the religious enterprise rested on the premise that the material and economic life of the Indians should remain further undisturbed. For Gómez de Cervantes, narrowly focused on the immediate concerns of fellow entrepreneurs, the life of the Mexican Indians was bound to improve as self-interest spurred them to participate in the economic market. As he posed it, however, such an event lay far in the future.[126]

The friars signaled the poverty of Mexican Indians by calling attention to their meager possessions. When compared to the era's debates regarding the poor, the particular interest in what Indians owned is unusual. Spanish treatises about poor relief, largely written in response to controversial new policies, rarely concerned themselves with such a seemingly obvious feature of the state of poverty. Their authors identified the poor by well-established criteria such as an inability to work, taking lack of *hacienda* as a given.[127] Several factors con-

---

ed. Antonio Muro Orejón, 3 vols. (Seville: Escuela de Estudios Hispano-Americanos, 1956–77), 1:33–36.

125. Decades later, the jurist Solórzano Pereira invoked a similar argument when defending the crown's sustained efforts to end the abuse of Indians working in *obrajes* (textile workshops) in Peru and New Spain: "Pues su vestir no necessita de estos texidos, y cada uno antes y despues de introducidos estos obrages le hila, texe, corta y haze conforme al temple, uso, i modo de sus tierras. Con que cessan, o pesan poco las razones que dexe ponderadas por la parte contraria." Juan de Solórzano Pereira, *Política Indiana* (Madrid: Diego Díaz de la Carrera, 1648), book 2, chap. 12, 125.

126. Gómez de Cervantes, *La vida económica*, 85.

127. "Pauperes veri secundum Chrysostomus dicuntur & sunt, qui proprijs manibus sibi victum parare non possunt." Lorenzo de Villavicencio, *De oeconomia sacra circa pauperum curam a Christo instituta, Apostolis tradita* (Paris: Michael Sonnium, 1564), book 2, chap. 9, 107; Domingo de Soto, *Deliberacion en la causa de los pobres* (Salamanca: Juan de Junta, 1545), A7r; A8v. The distinction between able- and non-able-bodied individuals that goes back to John Chrysostom's

verged to make the Indians' possessions (or lack thereof) an unavoidable topic in the conversation among friars, royal administrators, and Spanish entrepreneurs. Among these factors were the mendicants' own religious and moral concerns over earthly goods as well as their early and influential involvement in matters of tributary policy, an outgrowth of the protracted debate within the religious community over whether Indians should pay tithes. Pictorial documents dating to the pre-Conquest era recorded both the kind and amount of goods that different communities paid as tribute. This tradition survived but was transformed during the colonial period, and these *matriculas* served as snapshots of what communities and their households produced at a given point in time, thereby providing a survey of local natural and human resources.

In 1585 the Third Mexican Church Council declared that individuals of no means were to be spared the payment of fees associated with litigation in the ecclesiastical courts, a practice that was followed in civil and criminal cases.[128] The council defined a "persona miserabile" as an adult whose property (movable and ummovable goods) was worth less than fifty pesos.[129] This clear-cut definition helped the church to implement its own legislation and also gave Indians a way to place themselves in colonial society by translating their possessions into the new language of numbers, and the uncertain language of the market. Their familiarity with the market allowed some poor Indians to declare in their testaments not only what their few possessions consisted of, but also their price.[130]

The collection of tribute in the early sixteenth century—with its protocol and attendant complications—thus established particular ways of conceptualizing and perceiving the indigenous masses, according to products and quantities.[131] When European goods erupted onto this perceptual grid, an event that challenged the narrow view of Indians as producers and not consumers, government officials and friars alike surely noticed.

---

writings on Christian obligations toward the poor is also present in Justinian's legislation. Geremek, *La potence ou la pitié*, 25; Mollat, *The Poor in the Middle Ages*, 17–20.

128. Ordinance from 1563. Encinas, *Cedulario indiano*, 2:70.

129. "A Miserabilibus Personis litigantibus, nihil quidquam pecuniae accipiatur ratione litis, eaque miserabilis Persona reputetur, quae in bonis mobilibus, et immobilibus quinquaginta pondo valorem non habuerit." *Concilium Mexicanum Provinciale III* (Mexico City: Joseph Antonio de Hogal, 1770), book 2, title 1, §19, 107. A 1555 royal decree temporarily exempted all Indians from Nueva Galicia who met the definition of poor from paying court fees; the definition included individuals whose possessions did not exceed 6,000 *maravedíes*. Encinas, *Cedulario indiano*, 4:357.

130. See, for example, the brief testament of María Toztecayatl from Tlaxcala in Sullivan, *Documentos tlaxcaltecas del siglo XVI*, 343.

131. Jesús Bustamante, "El conocimiento como necesidad de estado: Las encuestas oficiales sobre Nueva España durante el reinado de Carlos V," *Revista de Indias* 60, no. 218 (2000): 33–55.

A glance at the items listed in Indian wills of the time shows that Zorita's and Gómez de Cervantes's assessment of the Indian response to the flood of European goods did not quite correspond to reality. Spanish missionaries had portrayed the Mexican Indians as fully immersed in a cohesive culture of laudable poverty, a culture that was both more easily recognizable and morally stable than that of the urban poor in Spain, where the dispossessed had become indistinguishable from the growing number of professional fraudsters and entrepreneurial vagrants competing for alms and relief.[132] The friars and allied officers pleaded for lower tributes on behalf of an Indian poor that mainly consisted of laborers who, whether tending fields or practicing the trades on which urban life had come to depend, were overburdened by work and barely able to make ends meet. The friars' insistence on the Indians' disciplined dedication to work—a corrective to the familiar charges of idleness—helped dispel the moral ambiguity traditionally attached to the notion of poverty that humanists, ecclesiastical authorities, and reformers would grapple with for centuries.[133]

Last Things

The teaching of Christian doctrine provided many opportunities for expounding on the nature of spiritual and earthly goods and the superiority of the spiritual over the earthly. This basic truth of the new religion was expressed in clear and succinct fashion in the commandments and the list of deadly sins that Indian converts were asked to learn by rote; its finer points were addressed in sermons and dramatized in plays for large indigenous audiences. Further instruction to prepare new converts to fully participate in the sacraments covered the responsibilities of Christians regarding possessions, such as the repayment of debts, the return of borrowed items to their rightful owners, and the orderly distribution of assets before dying. Very much in line with his optimistic view of the achievements of the Franciscan order during the first decades of

---

132. The kind of impostors referred to in treatises on poverty and brought to life in picaresque novels were certainly not the only ones who deceived or misled about their economic status; individuals had many reasons for claiming poverty when doing so exempted them from obligations or financial burdens. MacKay, *Lazy, Improvident People*, 79–80.

133. On welfare reform and its intellectual underpinnings in sixteenth-century Spain, see Linda Martz, *Poverty and Welfare in Habsburg Spain: The Example of Toledo* (Cambridge: Cambridge University Press, 1983). For a view from Zamora, see Maureen Flynn, *Sacred Charity: Confraternities and Social Welfare in Spain, 1400–1700* (Ithaca, NY: Cornell University Press, 1987), especially 75–114. The Spanish presence in Peru led to a shift in the way that Europeans discussed poverty, as Sabine MacCormack has shown. "Social Conscience and Social Practice: Poverty and Vagrancy in Spain and Early Colonial Peru," in *Home and Homelessness in the Medieval and Renaissance World*, ed. Nicholas Howe (Notre Dame: University of Notre Dame Press, 2004), 91–123.

evangelization, Motolinia praised the disposition of the Nahuas to make restitution, compensate slaves, and selflessly part with their possessions. As the Franciscan chronicler's edifying anecdotes indicate, noblemen, notables, and other individuals of means were a fitting and ideal audience, receptive to the friars' message. Given that the obligations that these new converts assumed had concrete consequences for the economic future of their families, they would have many compelling reasons to listen to the friars. Although the friars' authority on spiritual matters and their prominent role in communal and regional affairs meant that their teachings carried significant weight, they were not the exclusive source for the Nahua elite to learn to handle wealth and property in the new colonial order. By the crown's own design, the administrative, legal, and political education of prominent and not-so-prominent Nahuas took place while they served as elective officers of the *cabildo*, the municipal body of government. As did their Spanish counterparts, indigenous *cabildos* relied on clerical staff and aides to take care of everyday business. From these ranks, an influential group of literate Nahuas-turned-notaries rose to prominence and came to enjoy considerable power both within and across the boundaries of their communities. These officers' influence over other Indians was not lost on the friars, who were themselves instrumental in recruiting literate Indians to serve as notaries of ecclesiastical courts. The close relationship between friars and *tlahcuiloqueh* during the initial period of evangelization is evident in the *Códice de Cuetlaxcohuapan*, the earliest indigenous document to mention these Nahua officers. The codex retells in images and writing how Martín de Valencia, the leader of the first Franciscans in Mexico, pleaded with the lords of Tlaxcala for proper compensation of the services of Nahua notaries, in accord with the dignity of their office.[134] There is something odd in this particular portrait of Fr. Martín de Valencia, whose ascetic practices and apocalyptic visions had set him apart from the rest of his brothers, delivering a speech on a matter as mundane as the need to pay indigenous notaries a fair salary and accord them the same respect as their Peninsular counterparts. Regardless of whether this document was preserved by notaries as an authoritative reminder of an early agreement between them and the town, it also represents an early Franciscan lesson on the transformative power of Spanish law on the lives of the Nahuas and the implicit promise of future support from the friars.[135] Having been educated in schools

---

134. Martín de Valencia must have made his speech between 1531 and 1533. Ascensión H. de León-Portilla, "El Códice de Cuetlaxcohuapan y los primeros escribanos nahuas," in *Códices y Documentos sobre México: Segundo Simposio*, ed. Salvador Rueda Smithers, Constanza Vega Sosa and Rodrigo Martínez Baracs, 2 vols. (Mexico City: Instituto Nacional de Antropología e Historia. Dirección de Estudios Históricos/Consejo Nacional para la Cultura y las Artes, 1997), 2:322.

135. It is now believed that the stylistic features of the drawings place the composition of the

Fig. 1.3. *Códice de Cuetlaxcohuapan*. (Courtesy of the Biblioteca Nacional de Antropología e Historia del INAH, Mexico City.)

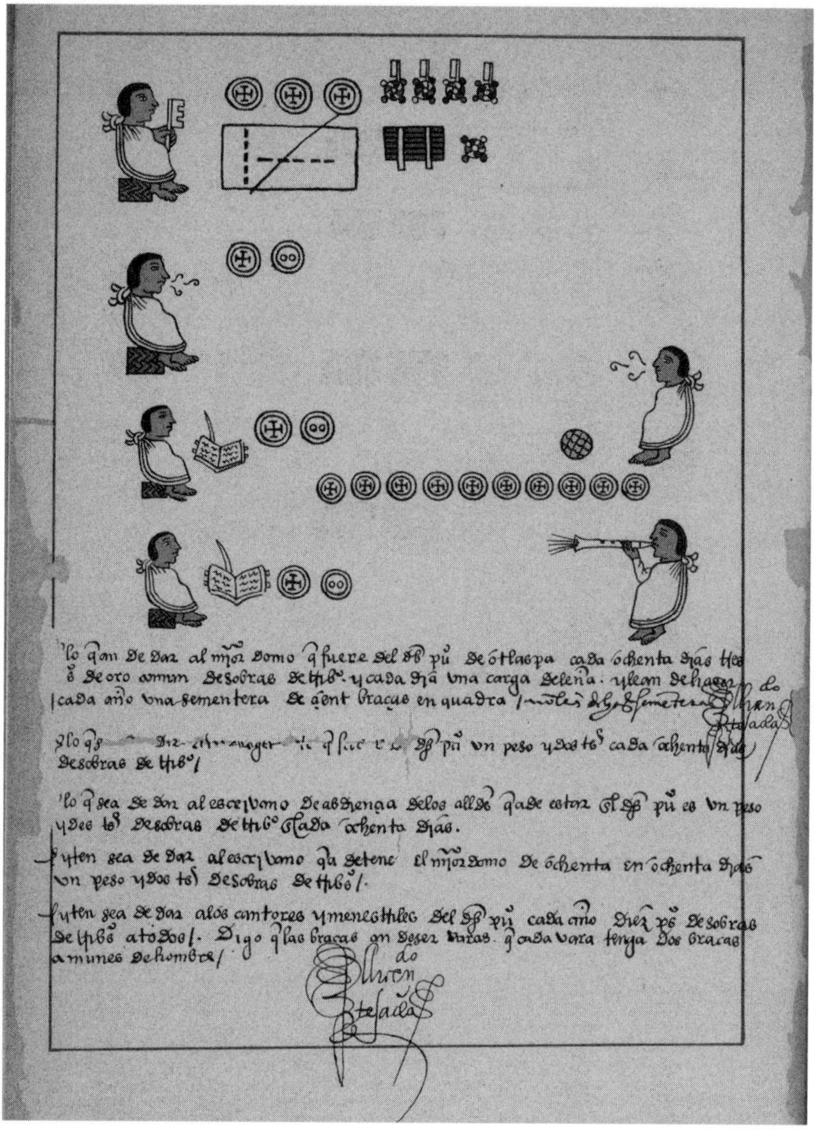

Fig. 1.4. Record of payments received by the town notary (third row of drawing) and the notary of the majordomo, or custodian (fourth row). *Códice de Otlazapan.*

run by missionaries, the would-be notaries were ready for training through what must have been a rather loose apprenticeship at the town hall, where they would acquire and refine the skills necessary to serve in both ecclesiastical and secular courts.[136] As mentioned above, no restrictions prevented these notaries from holding simultaneous appointments.[137]

The most engaged missionaries of the sixteenth century were careful planners who were intent on revising assumptions about the boundaries between royal and ecclesiastical powers and rarely missed an opportunity to put thinking into action. It does not come as a surprise, then, that the Franciscan Alonso de Molina provided notaries with step-by-step instructions in Nahuatl to be followed when recording the last wishes of testators.[138] These instructions called on indigenous notaries to make sure that the testator was in full possession of his or her mental faculties, that no relatives were present during dictation, and that an appropriate number of witnesses of good moral character be present.[139]

---

codex in the second half of the sixteenth century, that is, several years after the events portrayed. See Elena Isabel Estrada de Gerlero, "El Códice Cuetlaxcoapan," in *Estudios acerca del arte novohispano: Homenaje a Elisa Vargas Lugo* (Mexico City: Universidad Nacional Autónoma de México, 1983), 36–41.

136. Regarding the career paths open to Nahuas educated by the missionaries, Lockhart has surmised that "lesser church positions must have sometimes served as a training ground for future high officers of the municipality." Lockhart, *The Nahuas after the Conquest*, 217. For a thorough and well-documented account of the many roles that notaries played in colonial administration, particularly in Guatemala, see Jorge Luján Muñoz, *Los escribanos en las Indias occidentales*, 3rd ed. (Mexico City: Universidad Nacional Autónoma de México / Instituto de Estudios y Documentos Históricos, A.C., 1982). Jesús Bravo Lozano and Patricio Hidalgo Nuchera have focused on the legislation regulating the many types of notaries in the colonial administration, and the careers of several Spaniards who left Madrid to serve as notaries in Mexico at the end of the seventeenth century. *De indianos y notarios* (Madrid: Colegios Notariales de España, 1995).

137. Lockhart, *The Nahuas after the Conquest*, 218. To further or refresh their knowledge, notaries relied on specialized manuals that systematically covered every single aspect of the craft. Gabriel de Monterroso y Alvarado's *Pratica civil, y criminal, y instrucion de escrivanos* was the most successful on both sides of the Atlantic, with editions issued well into the eighteenth century. For a partial catalog of notarial literature printed between 1585 and 1694, see Javier Malagón-Barceló, *La literatura juridica española el siglo de oro en la Nueva España: Notas para su estudio* (Mexico City: Universidad Autónoma de México, 1959), 73–74. Although intended as an update of Malagón-Barceló's titles, Luján Muñoz's additions should be used cautiously, *Los escribanos en las Indias Occidentales*, 78–92. Mexican notaries also had some in-house alternatives, such as *La primera parte de la Política de escrituras* (1605) by Nicolás de Yrolo Calar, a Cádiz-born notary who made the viceregal capital his home as an adult. See Nicolás de Yrolo Calar, *La política de escrituras*, ed. María del Pilar Martínez López-Cano, Ivonne Mijares Ramirez, and Javier Sanchiz Ruíz (Mexico City: Universidad Nacional Autónoma de México, 1996). Only friars or other notaries would have possessed the necessary linguistic skills to produce manuals in indigenous languages; however I am not aware of any such work ever being printed in Mexico.

138. Molina illustrated only one procedure, omitting all reference to other alternatives current in Spain. On the transformation of procedures governing the last will of testators in the Iberian Peninsula from Roman to medieval times, see Alfonso García-Gallo, "Del testamento romano al medieval: Las líneas de su evolución en España," *Anuario de historia del derecho español* 47 (1977): 425–97.

139. Molina does not specify the minimum number of required witnesses. In Spain, open wills

The protocol for the actual dictation of the will leaves little doubt as to Molina's intention to cast the proceedings as a quasi-sacramental ritual in which the notary, assuming a role akin to that of a confessor, was expected to remind the testator of the need to make restitution of ill-gotten goods, settle pending debts, and make provisions for any illegitimate children. Not unlike confessors, notaries were also obliged to keep the content of testaments a secret.[140] To further facilitate the notary's work, Molina included a model testament similar to those in Spanish manuals.[141]

Although the presence of a religious minister was not required during the dictation of the testament, religion cast a long shadow over the proceedings as testators concerned with salvation considered making restitution and liquidating pending debts. If they failed for any reason to honor obligations, this responsibility would survive them and their heirs could be burdened with legal actions. The new converts were reminded, however, that whereas a testator's carelessness could be corrected after death by recourse to civil law, laws had no bearing on matters of conscience and salvation. In a move that may reflect

---

called for five witnesses or three witnesses proven to be *vecinos*; closed wills required seven witnesses. Hernando Díaz de Valdepeñas, *Suma de notas copiosas muy sustanciales y compendiosas* (Toledo: Hernando Díaz y Juan de Medina, 1543), xxv. Indigenous testators needed at least two Indian witnesses: "En los testamentos de los Indios bastan dos testigos varones, o mugeres aunque no sean rogados, y aunque no intervenga escribano publico, como traen Solorzano, y Montenegro." Pedro Murillo Velarde, *Practica de testamentos en que se resuelven los casos mas frequentes, que se ofrecen en la disposicion de las ultimas voluntades* (Manila: Imprenta de la Compañia de Jesús por Nicolás de la Cruz Begay, 1745), 2. In Mexico, Murillo Velarde's work on wills was printed twice in the second half of the eighteenth century; new editions in modified form were printed in the postindependence period.

140. Alonso de Molina, *Confessionario mayor en la lengua mexicana y castellana* (Mexico City: Universidad Nacional Autónoma de México, 1984), 60. A work from a much later date warning Christians not to delay in preparing their testaments described the roles of confessors and notaries in theory and practice as follows: "Para los testamentos es consuelo de los enfermos consultar sus cosas, y negocios con sus Confessores, y estos ordinariamente se hallan con summo desconsuelo en tiempo tan apretado para dar su parecer, reduciendose muchas vezes al de el Escrivano, que aunque ay muchos inteligentes y practicos; ay tambien algunos, o ignorantes, o nuevos en los oficios, que son causa de muchos, y muy graves errores, de que se originan no pocos pleytos." *Dificultad imaginada, Facilidad verdadera: En la practica de testamentos, reducida a ocho Documentos . . .* (Mexico City: Viuda de Miguel de Ribera Calderon, 1714), 2. On the means for testators to safely address sins without making them public during the testamentary proceedings, see pages 9–10. Almost contemporary but of a clear practical nature is the *Formulario de Testamentos* by the Jesuit Gerónimo de Zeballos, a professor of canon law in Córdoba, Argentina. This work circulated in manuscript form but can be found reproduced in Carlos Luque Colombres, "El Formulario de Testamentos del P. Gerónimo de Zeballos S.J.," *Revista de historia del derecho* 7 (1980): 347–433.

141. Molina, *Confessionario*, 61–63v. On Molina's model, see Howard F. Cline, "Fray Alonso de Molina's Model Testament and Antecedents to Indigenous Wills in Spanish America," in *Dead Giveaways: Indigenous Testaments of Colonial Mesoamerica and the Andes*, ed. Susan Kellogg and Matthew Restall (Salt Lake City: University of Utah Press, 1998), 13–33, and Susan Kellogg, *Law and the Transformation of Aztec Culture, 1500–1700* (Norman: University of Oklahoma Press, 1995), 129–37.

the actual teachings of the early missionaries, Motolinia linked the material and spiritual worlds by indicating that once the relatives of the deceased made restitution on his or her behalf, the individual's soul would be ready to leave Purgatory.[142]

The Mexican poor and their counterparts across the Atlantic had more in common than either Zorita or Gómez de Cervantes was willing to acknowledge. That is, when it came to possessions, the Nahua and Spanish poor were remarkably similar. In their testaments, Nahua men and women decided the fate of their few possessions: articles of clothing, *petates* (mats), grinding stones, pots and pans. For example, a Pablo Quechol from Culhuacan ordered that a *metate* (grinding stone) he owned be given to Francisca Tlacoehua, and a second one be sold to pay for future masses on her behalf.[143] Sometimes the inventory included crops ready to be harvested and stored foodstuffs. The Spanish poor left behind equally humble items such as bowls, mortars, and mattresses.[144]

Concerning foreign goods, Nahua testaments from individuals of varied economic means reveal that pieces of furniture such as wooden beds, chairs, and European articles of clothing, far from languishing in forgotten corners, had a place in many of their households.[145] Influential members of indigenous local governments and noble families gladly accepted and sought European goods in exchange for favors. Since the early days of the Conquest, the Spanish had commented, sometimes with amusement, on both the table manners and manners of tables found among the Nahuas, whether they were members of the nobility, merchants, or peasants. Few, however, ventured to predict, as Gómez de Cervantes did, that the Nahuas would be reluctant to give up their customary way of eating, on the floor and without utensils, or to trade their sleeping mats for Spanish mattresses and beds.[146] The habits of the body, molded by the rhythms and everyday objects of household life, died hard, or so Gómez

142. Motolinia, *Historia de los indios de la Nueva España*, treatise 2, chap. 5, 239.

143. Cline and León-Portilla, *The Testaments of Culhuacan*, 88–89; see also 126–27. In 1597, Francisca from Texcoco disposed of two *metates* in similar fashion. Rojas Rabiela, Rea López, and Medina Lima, *Vidas y bienes olvidados*, 1:158; see also 2:142. On goods bequeathed by Nahua testators, see Kellogg, *Law and the Transformation of Aztec Culture*, 137–59.

144. Martz, *Poverty and Welfare in Habsburg Spain*, 201.

145. See, for example, Rojas Rabiela, Rea López, and Medina Lima, *Vidas y bienes olvidados*, 1:131; 2:160; 2:190; 3:134; and Cline and León-Portilla, *The Testaments of Culhuacan*, 41–43. The *relaciones geográficas* also contain information about household items and the trade of European products in indigenous communities.

146. Concerning articles of clothing, the *relaciones geográficas* for Mexico record changes across classes in, for example, the preference for items made of cotton instead of henequen, and the adoption of breeches, shoes, and sandals, as well as hats. See René Acuña, ed., *Relaciones geográficas del siglo XVI: México*, 10 vols. (Mexico City: Universidad Nacional Autónoma de México, 1985–86), 7:157 (Tuzantla); 7:199 (Titlaltepec); and 7:230 (Acolman).

de Cervantes and other Spaniards believed. Zorita showed this same intuition when he suggested Spanish chairs did not belong in the living quarters of the Mexicans.

The belief that converted Mexican Indians were better served spiritually if sheltered from the bearers of foreign goods arriving in droves from overseas was just one view in the debates over which aspects of Spanish society the American Indians should be encouraged to embrace. The crown under Phillip II took the opposite approach, declaring that its mission was to provide the Indies with religion, justice, and a host of goods necessary for sustaining the lives of Spanish colonists and Indians alike.[147]

The drafting of wills was an occasion for testators to declare for the record who they were in society, or at least how they saw themselves in relation to their community.[148] Members of the native elites identified themselves by the offices they had held in local government and often exalted their lineage by remembering kinsmen who had served in the same capacity before them. However extensive, a detailed inventory of landholdings, movable goods, and other possessions could not account for the intangible asset of social prestige. The apparent inadequacy of earthly possessions to convey the individual's sense of self-worth explains at least in part these common declarations.

At the other end of the social spectrum, a significant number of male and female testators, without preambles and a very different act of self-identification, flatly proclaimed their poverty.[149] Some simply opted to declare that they possessed neither goods nor property (*y naxca y notlatqui*).[150] The modest inventories contained in others reveals that some individuals who labeled themselves

---

147. "El Emperador Charlos de gloriosa memoria mi señor y Padre y despues del, nos con zelo de dar Buena quanta delo que la divina Magt. Nos tiene encargado nos hemos occupado con todo estudio y cuidado possible en el descubrimiento y conuersion de las Yndias y habitadores dellas embiando nuestras flotas y armadas cada año a descubrirlas y a las partes descubiertas proveyendolas de predicadores religiosos y ecclesiasticos que predicassen el Santo Euangelio y enseñassen nuestra santta fe Catholica y rigiessen y gouernassen las animas en lo(s) spiritual y de Virreyes y audiencias y Gouernadores y juezes que gouernassen la tierra y la mantuuiessen en justicia proueyendoles y haziendoles proveer assi para los spañoles como para los yndios y naturales de pan, vino azeite, paños, sedas, lienços, cauallos, y ganados armas y herramientas para labrar y cultiuar la tierra, Officios y artifficios y de todas las otras cosas conuenientes para la sustentacion y recreacion humana. " *Gobernacion espiritual de Indias: Código Ovandino, Libro 1°*, ed. Angel Martín González. (Guatemala City: Instituto Teológico Salesiano, 1978), 129.

148. Testament headings sometimes reflected differences in social status; this can be seen in the models for nobility and high-ranking clergymen included by Díaz de Valdepeñas. *Suma de notas copiosas muy sustanciales*, XXIIIv–XXIV.

149. To this declaration, Favian Tamatlaneuh from Ocotelulco, added that he had nothing to hide from the church. Rojas Rabiela, Rea López, and Medina Lima, *Vidas y bienes olvidados*, 1:232–33. A Polonia Tzilotl from the same area declared: "nimotolinia." 1:299 and 2:165.

150. Cline and León-Portilla, *The Testaments of Culhuacan*, 74–75. Miguel Oçoma, also from Culhuacan, described his son and only heir as poor, "y nopiltzin Juan motollinia," 244.

as poor possessed only a few personal items of clothing, while others owned modest patches of land. These variations may or may not be significant in trying to determine what it meant to be poor to Mexican Indians and colonial society at large; they do seem to suggest, however, that for some testators, identifying as poor was neither option nor obligation, but rather an expected and somewhat unavoidable act. In identifying themselves as poor, these Nahuas, consciously or not, approached the spiritual and legal dimensions of the testamentary act from a different perspective than their more fortunate fellows.

Documents like the contracts of the two metalsmiths from Tlaxcala and the testaments of Nahuas from the upper and lower strata of society are just two examples of the new legal and religious order brought about by the Spanish presence in New Spain. These instruments, like many others that Nahuas and other indigenous peoples would encounter during their lifetime, represented new obligations. Many of them also redefined the relationship between individuals and goods—whether tangible or intangible (such as honor or rank), owned or produced by commission—according to Spanish legal norms. Through these and other legal rituals, indigenous people confirmed their status as *personas* in the legal sense, another step in a process that began with baptism. The path to personhood in sixteenth-century Mexico was a gradual one. As noted above, the first contract of the metalsmiths contained traces of gnomic lore, but their second commission was drafted in the cut-and-dry legal language so familiar to Spaniards. On the other hand, testaments, while seeming to offer more transparent access to individuals' wishes, if not their voices, also show the emergence of novel ways for indigenous individuals to talk about themselves in relation to what they did or did not own before notaries and religious figures. A shift in these patterns of self-identification can be traced from the use of "poor" as a proper name to the declaration to the law and church that one is "poor."

Finally, it is worth considering the development over time of ideas of ownership and possession of another category of things: church buildings and the religious artifacts they housed. In Mexico, as in most of the Spanish territories, churches built under the supervision of the religious orders were the product of indigenous labor for which the workers received, for the most part, no remuneration.[151] Over time the new converts would also defray maintenance costs,

---

151. Recounting the construction of the first church in Mexico, Mendieta wrote: "Cubrióse el cuerpo de la iglesia de madera, y la capilla mayor de bóveda, y en ella pusieron las armas de Cortés; no porque él la oviese edificado a su costa (que en aquellos tiempos ni muchos años despues no se les pagaba a los indios lo que trabajaban en edificio de iglesias, sino que cada pueblo hacia la suya, y aun a las obras de México otros muchos pueblos ayudaron a los principios sin paga, y cuando mucho daban de comer en los monesterios a los trabajadores), mas pusiéronse en aquella capilla por el mucho favor que daba a los frailes, no solo en aquella obra, sino en todo lo que se les ofrecia,

as well as the costs of acquisition of liturgical objects, devotional images, and ornaments. For the Franciscan chronicler Gerónimo de Mendieta, the labor and objects furnished by indigenous communities were eloquent examples of almsgiving that Spaniards, still suspicious of the Indians' commitment to the new religion, were well advised to emulate.[152]

As noted above, friars were well aware of how important it was for their indigenous charges to learn the difference between secular and religious obligations, especially when the obligation took the form of labor.[153] It may prove difficult to separate the particular kind of teaching that may have accompanied the early interactions between friars and Indians from the overall conditions that moved indigenous subjects to take part in the construction of religious buildings without expectation of economic reward. What, in the context of evangelization, came to be thought of as teaching cannot easily be disassociated from what could also be construed as an implicit contract between the friars and their new flock. Changing circumstances required the terms of that original and unspoken contract (or lesson on charity) to be more precisely defined, as when the secularization of indigenous parishes was finally set in motion in the second half of the eighteenth century.[154] Recent scholarship has shown that the generally orderly and smooth replacement of friars by secular clergy in Indian parishes was stalled in a few instances by conflicts between parishioners, the mendicant orders, and parish priests over the ownership of buildings and religious objects. In 1753, the parishioners of Santa María la Redonda claimed ownership of the Marian devotional objects housed in the church and opposed

---

así de necesidades temporales como para la conversion y ministerio de los indios." *Historia ecle-siástica indiana,* book 3, chap. 18, 222.

152. "Tratando de lo comun, ¿quién ha edificado tantas iglesias y monesterios como los religiosos tienen en esta Nueva España, sino los indios con sus manos y proprio sudor, y con tanta voluntad y alegría como si edificaran casas para sí y sus hijos, y rogando a los frailes que se las dejasen hacer mayores? ¿Y quién proveyó las iglesias de los ornamentos, vasos de plata, y todo lo demas para su arreo y ornato tienen, sino los mismos indios?" Mendieta, *Historia eclesiástica indiana,* book 4, chap. 17, 422.

153. "También ay neçesidad de que se les enseñe qué cosa son los diezmos y oblaçiones porque por lo común de los indios tienen esto por tributo y por tequío forçoso, y pues se a ofreçido tocar esta materia, me paresçió advertir aquí y suplicar a vuestras señorías sean servidos de proveer que aya enmienda en algunos exçesos que a avido en hazer ofresçer a los indios, señalando a cada uno lo que ha de ofresçer cada vez, al hombre tanto y a la mujer tanto, de que se reçibe escándalo en los indios y aún en los españoles que lo saben." Pedro de Feria, "Memorial del Obispo Fray Pedro de Feria," in Alberto Carrillo Cázares, ed., *Manuscritos del Concilio Tercero Provincial Mexicano (1585),* vol. 1, part 1, 296–97.

154. For a recent discussion of secularization in Mexico in light of the Bourbon project of religious and social reform, see Matthew O'Hara, *A Flock Divided: Race, Religion, and Politics in Mexico, 1749–1857* (Durham: Duke University Press, 2010), chap. 2; also chap. 3, which I draw from in this section.

their transfer to a Franciscan monastery.[155] Almost two decades later, the parishioners of Santiago Tlatelolco challenged the authorities' decision to grant possession of that church to the Franciscan order and require them to make the church of Santa Ana their new house of worship.[156] Indigenous opposition to the transfer rested on the argument (supported by available historical evidence) that the church had been built by their ancestors, and thus belonged to the community. The spokesperson for the Franciscans countered that true charity was incompatible with such claims and notions of ownership.[157] In short, the Franciscans refused to acknowledge any spiritual dimension to the parishioners' claim, reducing it to a primitive act of possession.

Although isolated, these episodes can be framed as the expected or unexpected result of the teachings that accompanied the arrival of Catholicism in Mexico in the sixteenth century, with the position of parishioners reluctant to relinquish churches and religious objects that they considered part of their history construed as the product of an original misunderstanding or a legitimate inference drawn from less than clear instructions on charity. Maybe eighteenth-century indigenous parishioners' claim to communal ownership cannot be fully understood without taking into account the rhetoric of poverty that accompanied the Franciscans' introduction of Christian doctrine and modes of behavior among the Nahuas. There is some irony in the fact that the legal and spiritual dissolution of the long-standing relationship between friars and their parish members resulted from confrontations over spiritual acts, sacred objects, and of all things, ownership. The friars' critique of ownership implicit in their praise of poverty and dispossession may have contributed to making communal giving the basis for a new understanding of ownership of religious things.

---

155. O'Hara, *A Flock Divided*, 103–04.
156. O'Hara, *A Flock Divided*, 106.
157. O'Hara, *A Flock Divided*, 107.

CHAPTER 2

❧

Missionaries, Honor, and the Law

Two *Letrados*

A critique of contemporary law and the institutional hierarchy of magistrates, officers, and the professionals who acted as their warrantors, when not an outright rejection, was both common and essential to the calls for reform that emerged from the Catholic Church and circles of Christian humanists in the fifteenth century and that reached a critical point during the first decades of the Protestant Reformation movement. Such a critical attitude is well represented in sixteenth-century literary utopias, some of which found attentive readers in New Spain.[1] The contempt for what religious reformers, theologians, and moralists across Europe perceived as the ever-growing tyranny of the law was also shared by significant portions of the popular classes that prioritized social change over religious concerns.[2] The Protestant Reformation in Germany successfully tapped into this widespread discontent to highlight the urgency of its message, and was eventually forced to confront the challenge posed by those who took a radical stance against the prevailing social and legal system. The question of the role of human laws in the lives of Evangelical Christians, who now saw themselves in the light of a new economy of salvation, loomed large over Luther and his associates as they took stock of the political and institutional changes that they had set in motion across the German territories by

---

1. See Paul Foriers, "Les Utopies et le Droit," in *Les Utopies à la Renaissance* (Brussels: Presses Universitaires de Bruxelles; Paris: Presses Universitaires de France, 1963), 231–61; a more descriptive approach can be found in Giampaolo Zucchini, "Critica del diritto, difetti della giurisprudenza e problemi di legislazione in utopie del Cinque e Seicento," *Rivista internazionale di filosofia del diritto* (1986): 409–23. On the impact of Thomas More's *Utopia* on Vasco de Quiroga, bishop of Michoacán, see Silvio Zavala, "El humanismo de Vasco de Quiroga," in his *Ideario de Vasco de Quiroga* (Mexico City: El Colegio de México, 1941), 35–66.

2. The negative popular view of law in Germany, for example, has been richly documented by Gerald Strauss. *Law, Resistance, and the State: The Opposition to Roman Law in Reformation Germany* (Princeton: Princeton University Press, 1986), especially 31–55.

severing ties with Rome.[3] The German theologians and jurists who became the intellectual forgers of the Reformation considered the Ten Commandments to be the mandatory starting point for any reflection on the obligations of Christians toward God and civil society as well as the foundation of the new religious and political order.[4] Their teachings on the fourth commandment, for instance, presented the strict obedience that Christians owed to secular authorities in no uncertain terms; questions of how far such obligations should go opened a discussion about civil obedience and the right of Christians to resist tyrannical rulers.[5]

In Spain the response to the Protestants regarding the place of God's law and the scope of royal and ecclesiastical power was mainly the work of the same theologians who were also preoccupied with sorting out the relation between human and divine laws in light of the controversies surrounding the subjugation of entire societies in America.[6] Still, during and after the controversies that sealed the divide between Catholics and Protestants, some Spanish religious writers continued to long for a society that acted according to God's laws, rather than seeking the earthly goods that civil laws appeared to enshrine and promote.[7] In the American territories the friars, whose opinions on human law reflected many of the themes and concerns associated with religious reform, dealt with issues of law and authority on their own terms: geographic distance and effective power over entire communities made even agreed-upon demarcations between church and state porous and movable. As they did so, they enjoyed the support of a delicate alliance of crown and papacy: the friars benefited from

---

3. For a recent account of the making of Reformation legal thought and its theological underpinnings, see Harold J. Berman, *Law and Revolution*, 2 vols. (Cambridge, MA: Belknap Press of Harvard University Press, 2003), 1:71–99; and John Witte Jr., *Law and Protestantism: The Legal Teachings of the Lutheran Reformation* (Cambridge: Cambridge University Press, 2002), 119–64.

4. See Berman, *Law and Revolution*, 2:67 and 74–75. On Melanchton's account of the relation between divine and natural law, see pages 78–87. On the place of the commandments in Oldendorp's conceptualization of laws, see 88–90. On Melanchton's views, see Witte, *Law and Protestantism*, 122–34.

5. On civil obedience and the fourth commandment, see Berman, *Law and Revolution*, 2:43–44 and 65–67. On Luther's and Melanchton's evolving views on obedience and resistance, see Quentin Skinner, *The Foundations of Modern Political Thought*, 2 vols. (Cambridge: Cambridge University Press, 1978), 2:69–74.

6. A compelling account of the theories on political society elaborated by Spanish theologians in response to the Lutherans can be found in Skinner, *The Foundations of Modern Political Thought*, 2:149–73.

7. In his *Epistolario* Juan de Avila, for example, warned rulers as well as ecclesiastical and secular judges against contenting themselves with applying the law and handing down sentences without any concern for the overall spiritual well-being of the Republic, Juan de Avila, *Obras del padre maestro Juan de Avila, predicador en el Andaluzia. Aora de Nuevo añadida a la vida del Autor, y las partes que ha de tener un predicador del Evangelio, por el padre fray Luys de Granada, de la orden de Santo Domingo, y unas reglas de bien bibir del Autor* (Madrid: Pedro Madrigal, 1588), 118v, 119v. On reform, see 122v.

Fig. 2.1. Franciscans administering justice. Diego Valadés, *Rhetorica Christiana* (1579). (Courtesy of the John Carter Brown Library at Brown University.)

both the crown's unprecedented power over ecclesiastical matters and papal privileges bestowed on the mendicant orders overseas.

Just as the exceptional circumstances of the religious orders in New Spain led the friars to reconsider the relationship between law and Christianity, the new and precarious alignment of government and religion brought about by the Spanish presence overseas caused some *letrados* (jurists) in the service of the crown to reflect on the law. For these *letrados*, familiar with the concerns and intellectual endeavors of those Christian humanists with ties to the court, the experiment across the Atlantic provided an opportunity to explore the basic question of justice underlying debates about Spanish rule in the Indies, how to bring together spiritual devotion and service to the king.

The expanding Spanish possessions turned *letrados* into experts on American matters, much as other administrators would become experts on the charged politics of the Low Countries or the papal court. Their expertise on all things American took shape under varied conditions; some, like Juan de Ovando, never set foot on American soil, while others, such as Alonso de Zorita (who corresponded with Ovando), spent years in daily contact with colonizers, religious men, and Indians.[8]

Juan de Ovando had already distinguished himself as a loyal officer known for efficiency and administrative skill when, in 1571, he was appointed president of the Council of the Indies. He knew this governing body well; in 1567, he had been commissioned to conduct an inspection of the council as a *visitador* (inspector).[9] He had studied and taught at Salamanca, and, like most of the administrators of his generation to rise to high administrative offices, he was a man of law but also of books. He collected with zeal, following a trend among wealthy members of the court who had taken to collecting works of art, astronomical instruments, and artifacts from faraway lands. Ovando's collecting, however, also served his professional interests, in that he acquired works useful in his administrative projects at the council. Ovando cultivated the friendship of humanists like the biblical scholar Benito Arias Montano, who arranged the acquisition and shipping of books from Antwerp for his friend. Their correspondence reveals Ovando's fondness for the writings of the church fathers, but also book

---

8. Documents housed at the British Museum include a letter from Zorita in response to an inquiry by Ovando. José María de la Peña y Cámara, "Nuevos datos sobre la visita de Juan de Ovando al Consejo de Indias," *Anuario de historia del derecho español* 12 (1935): 430.

9. On Ovando's inspection of the council, see Stafford Poole, *Juan de Ovando: Governing the Spanish Empire in the Reign of Philip II* (Norman: University of Oklahoma Press, 2004), 117–37. Prior to his duties as inspector of the council, Ovando had been in charge of reforming the university of Alcalá de Henares. See pages 63–77.

catalogs and compendia.[10] An exchange with Arias Montano reveals Ovando's singular preoccupation with ordering and classifying information; on behalf of a friend compiling a bibliographic catalog, Arias Montano asked Ovando for a list of Spanish writers who had written on matters of law. In his reply, Ovando agreed with classifying authors by subject, but not without first pointing out that this criterion had already been used in the *Bibliotheca sancta*.[11]

One of Arias Montano's letters provides a revealing moral portrait of Ovando. Upon hearing of his appointment as president of the Council of the Indies, Arias Montano extended his congratulations and relayed the precise words of praise with which Fernando Álvarez de Toledo, third Duke of Alba, had welcomed the news. The Duke of Alba saw Ovando as the perfect choice for this office that required a devoted Christian who understood the needs of the new church in America and was prepared to meet them, a task for which most men of law were ill suited.[12] Also distinguishing the new appointee from other *letrados* was his proven knowledge of geography, natural history, the military arts, navigation, commerce, and native customs and laws.[13]

Ovando would have heartily agreed with the duke's list of ideal qualifications. When conducting the inspection of the Council of the Indies, he had been struck by the lack of the most basic information on the new territories.[14] This is why, in addition to administrative reforms that he implemented to ensure the proper day-to-day functioning of the council, he developed an ambitious plan to gather detailed information on every aspect of the populated areas under Spanish rule in America, including the number of inhabitants, natural resources, religious practices, and forms of government in pre-Conquest

---

10. Baldomero Macías Rosendo, *La correspondencia de Benito Arias Montano con el Presidente de Indias* (Huelva: Universidad de Huelva, 2008), 169. For a list of titles that Ovando requested, see 177–81. In a letter from 1569, Ovando wrote: "Para lo qual embío crédito de cien ducados, y si en ellos no huviere para [los intrumentos, libros y cosas], se me trayga lo que para que huviere en essos cien ducados por el orden del memorial, excepto que lo primero que quiero son los catálogos de libros y escritores, porque por el oficio que tengo me importan." Macías Rosendo, *La correspondencia*, 185. And the following year: "Y lo que más desseo son los catálogos de los libros, porque para el exercicio de mi oficio importa tenerlos," 200. On Gessner's *Bibliotheca*, see 191.

11. Macías Rosendo, *La correspondencia*, 221.

12. "Porque no bastan leyes solas ni ser uno letrado de leyes, que por la mayor parte los que no han estudiado más que leyes son *rudes in caeteris publicis et privates rebus*." Macías Rosendo, *La correspondencia*, 238.

13. Macías Rosendo, *La correspondencia*, 239.

14. "que en el Consejo no se tiene ni puede tener noticia de las cosas de las Indias sobre que puede y debe caer la gobernación, en lo cual es necesario dar orden para que se tenga." Victor M. Maurtúa, *Antecedentes de la Recopilacion de Yndias* (Madrid: Imprenta de Bernardo Rodríguez, 1906), 3.

times.[15] Once collected and organized, the information was to serve as the basis for policymaking. These reports became known as the *Relaciones geográficas*. The adversarial relation between law and religion that the Duke of Alba saw embodied in the swelling of the ranks of government bureaucracy by the *letrados* had a long history, fueled by equal parts intellectual debate and professional competition. Ovando must have felt reassured by the flattering words of the duke and the scholar who saw in him the qualities that Christian humanists wanted men in government to possess, especially those whose roles bore directly on spiritual matters. It is hard to determine whether Ovando, or anyone for that matter, could have lived up to the expectations of a small circle of scholars and kindred spirits that sought to reconcile religious devotion, politics, and intellectual endeavors in an increasingly fractured European landscape where reason of state soon came to dominate political decisions. But expectations aside, Ovando understood why Catholicism's fate in the American colonies would seem so important to observers in the religiously torn Low Countries.

Ovando's inspection also revealed the council's alarming absence of documentation pertaining to the laws promulgated for the colonies.[16] Using the material gathered by the chronicler and cosmographer Juan López de Velasco in the 1560s, Ovando set out to create what he envisioned as a thorough compilation of all laws and ordinances still in effect in the Indies. Although he planned a work divided into seven books, by the time of his death in 1575, he had completed only the first book and the second title of the second book.[17] Whereas contemporary scholars immersed themselves in the study of Roman law or, as was becoming more common, medieval and more recent Spanish legislation

15. On Ovando's role in the creation of the *Relaciones geográficas*, see Howard F. Cline, "The Relaciones Geográficas of the Spanish Indies, 1577–1648," in *Guide to Ethnohistorical Sources*, part 1, Howard F. Cline, ed., *Handbook of Middle American Indians*, 16 vols. Robert Wauchope, gen. ed. (Austin: University of Texas Press, 1972), 183–93. See also Ismael Sánchez Bella, "El 'Título de las Descripciones' del código de Ovando," in *Dos estudios sobre el Código de Ovando* (Pamplona: Ediciones Universidad de Navarra, 1987), 91–138. For the documentary appendix, see 139–211. Victoria Pineda has discussed the classical roots of Ovando's questionnaires. "La retórica epideíctica de Menandro y los cuestionarios para las *Relaciones geográficas de Indias*," *Rhetorica* 18, no. 2 (May 2000): 147–73. Often overlooked, we find similar royal initiatives under Charles V. Jesús Bustamante, "El conocimiento como necesidad de estado."

16. "Que ni en el Consejo ni en las Indias no se tiene noticia de las Leyes y Ordenanzas por donde se rigen y gobiernan todos aquellos Estados." Maurtúa, *Antecedentes de la Recopilacion de Yndias*, 3.

17. The second title of the second book contained all the ordinances concerning the functioning of the Council of the Indies as an executive, legislative, and judicial body. This set of ordinances, approved in 1571, was published in 1585. Antonio Muro Orejón, "Las ordenanzas de 1571 del Real y Supremo Consejo de las Indias," *Anuario de estudios americanos* 14 (1957): 363–423.

to produce legal and philological commentaries,[18] Ovando faced the task of gathering and systematizing a body of legislation that, although it was still in force, was only half acknowledged, as if due to a glitch in institutional memory. He thus saw the law in a condition rarely revealed to scholars.

The men of learning who had come to know Ovando must have found consolation in the fact that he died having completed the book of the compilation on ecclesiastical matters, or as he put it, "spiritual government."[19] In his legislative proposals, the council president did not seem to view religion, and particularly the religious orders deployed in America, to be a threat to royal authority but rather the very foundation of the ordered society that the crown sought to build. The most radical proposal, never realized, involved creating new officially sanctioned churches run entirely by friars instead of parish priests. Among the many reasons that Ovando cited for this drastic proposition was his belief that "these churches would be well suited to their parishioners, who are exceedingly poor people, and could be maintained at a lesser cost and without the pomp of secular churches."[20] Leaving aside the fact that religious orders were not of one mind on eliminating imposing church buildings, Ovando's words expressed the friars' desire to restore the Primitive Church.[21] In 1570, the Franciscan Gerónimo de Mendieta gave Ovando an illuminated manuscript containing a Nahuatl translation of Thomas à Kempis's *Imitatio Christi*.[22]

In 1583 Philip II, invoking his power under the Real Patronazgo, instructed all bishops in the Indies to begin placing beneficed priests among the Indians.[23] Bishops were told in no uncertain terms that qualified priests would be chosen

---

18. Some examples: Bernardino Daza, the first translator of Alciato's *Emblems* into Spanish, wrote a treatise on the Justinian Code, *Querimonia iurisprudentiae* (Toulouse: Boudeuill, 1551); and Gregorio García's edition of Alfonso X's *Partidas* was published in Salamanca in 1555, the same year that Antonio Gómez's commentaries to the *Leyes de Toro* became publicly available.

19. "Al Visitador le pareçió más conveniente reducirlos a Ordenanças (como lo hizo), las quales dividió en siete libros: el primero, de la Governaçión Spiritual; el Segundo, de la Governaçión temporal; el tercero, de la Justiçia, Tribunales y Ministros della; el quarto, de la República de los Españoles; el quinto, de la República de los Indios; el sexto, de la Real Hacienda; el séptimo, de la Navegaçión y Contrataçión de las Indias." Maurtúa, *Antecedentes*, 8.

20. "Las yglesias serían muy acomodadas al subjeto de los diocesanos, que son gente paupérrima y muy miserable, podríanse sustentar con menos costa y sin el fausto que es menester para yglesias seculars." Maurtúa, *Antecedentes*, 17.

21. "Y finalmente, las yglesias serían de la forma que los Apóstoles al principio las instituyeron, y se seguirían tanto y tan Buenos affectos, que no se pueden referir sin mucha prolixidad." Maurtúa, *Antecedentes*, 17.

22. David Tavárez, "Letras clandestinas, textos tolerados, colaboraciones lícitas: la producción textual de los intelectuales nahuas y zapotecos en el siglo xvii," in *Élites intelectuales y modelos colectivos: Mundo ibérico (siglos xvi–xix)*, ed. Mónica Quijada and Jesús Bustamante (Madrid: Consejo Superior de Investigaciones Científicas, 2000), 67.

23. The 1583 *cédula* is contained in another one dating from 1587. Encinas, *Cedulario indiano*, 1:99–100. *Patronazgo* or *patronato* (patronage) was the authority granted by the papacy to the Spanish crown to control all ecclesiastical affairs in the American territories, including church revenues and ecclesiastical appointments, as well as the power to veto papal bulls.

over, and eventually come to replace, the friars. Juan de Ovando had been dead for almost eight years, but Alonso de Zorita, his contemporary and a retired judge with years of experience in Santo Domingo, Guatemala, and Mexico who shared Ovando's intellectual interests and opinions on the role of the regular clergy in the spiritual government of the Indians, was alive and well enough to draft a rebuttal to the king's new initiative that would have pleased the deceased president.[24] Like Ovando, Zorita had studied law in Salamanca and pursued a career in government that took him to American lands, where as a judge he was directly involved in collecting information about local judicial customs, dispute settlements, and tributary patterns. I will say more about Zorita's activities and thoughts throughout this chapter, but here I would like to draw attention to another facet of his work that he shares with Ovando. Zorita returned to Spain in 1566 and settled in Granada, where, prompted by what appears to be an earlier call by the king for all legislation related to the Indies to be organized in a single work, he took on the task of producing such a compilation.[25] Seemingly unaware of Ovando's simultaneous work under more favorable conditions at the Council of the Indies, Zorita relied on the very limited number of sources that he had at hand, and dedicated the final deficient product to Philip II in the hopes of gaining royal approval that never materialized. This reward would continue to elude loyal *letrados*. The dream of an organized legislative corpus of the Indies finally came true in 1680 with official approval of the *Recopilación de leyes de Indias* under the last Habsburg, Charles II. In the end, the fortunes of Ovando's and Zorita's works fail to give a real measure of how the legislator and the judge, each in his own way, put his efforts into projects with no chance of success but that nonetheless fulfilled the humanist longing to serve king and religion through intellectual labor. Imbued with a friar's sense of ideals and accomplishment, both royal officers believed that their focus was fully warranted by the laws through which the Spanish monarchy had sought to both honor its commitment to religion and avail itself of its extraordinary powers on ecclesiastical matters.

The Mexican Indians and the Law

Within a few years of the fall of Tenochtitlán, secular and religious observers began to report that the Mexican Indians, showing exceptional resolve, were

---

24. Zorita, *Historia de la Nueva España*, 493–527.
25. Alonso de Zorita, *Cedulario de 1574*, ed. Beatríz Bernal (Mexico City: Miguel Ángel Porrúa, 1985), xvii. Departing from previous scholars, Manzano has definitively concluded that the royal order that inspired Zorita dates from 1560. *Historia de la Recopilación de Indias*, 2 vols. (Madrid: Ediciones Cultura Hispánica, 1950), 1:283–86.

pursuing legal disputes at an alarming rate. The Indians attached so much importance to the legal venues opened by the colonizers that some, when disappointed with a judicial decision, waited for a while before returning to the courts in the hope of a better outcome.[26] It appeared that the Mexican Indians were a litigious bunch, and that if nothing were done to curb their claims, the fragile judicial system would soon collapse. While missionaries and secular officers agreed on the basic elements of this characterization, they held widely different opinions about what ultimately drove the Mexican Indians to air their grievances so aggressively and settle their disputes through legal channels.

According to the missionaries, it was contact with Spaniards, rather than their own institutional life or natural inclinations, that had turned the Mexican Indians into compulsive litigants. Whatever the reason, religious ministers agreed that the Nahuas risked losing personal and communal assets in long and drawn-out lawsuits—an undesirable outcome for a population that had been characterized as naturally given to prodigality. For their part, royal officers often blamed the friars for encouraging Indians to get involved in disputes.[27] As time went by, new causes were found to explain what had quickly become yet another "fact" about the Indian population. For instance, Martín Enríquez, the fourth viceroy of Mexico, suspected that Indian noblemen embraced lawsuits as a solution to their problems under the negative influence of mestizos who hoped to benefit economically from them.[28]

Early on, and guided by eminently practical purposes, viceroys, colonists, and missionaries took an interest in learning about the Nahuas' ways of handling interpersonal and communal conflicts in the context of the new viceroyalty. Many observers commented on how the Nahuas made their claims, solved disputes, and related to Spanish ideas of and procedures for administering justice. Notwithstanding the very different interests that motivated these observers, their participation in the colonial enterprise allowed them to make general pronouncements on this area of human behavior, on which little had been written but that was attracting the attention of Spanish administrators and reformers. In Mexico, the unique combination of cultural distance and everyday proximity helped bring into focus a cultural domain that must have seemed both odd and yet strangely familiar to most Spaniards. After all, the Spanish did not attribute their own countrymen's new passion for suing each other to ethnic

---

26. This was the information that Don Antonio de Mendoza, first viceroy of Mexico, passed on to his successor, Don Luis de Velasco. *Instrucciones y memorias de los virreyes novohispanos*, ed. Ernesto de la Torre Villar, 2 vols. (Mexico City: Editorial Porrúa, 1991), 1:101.

27. This is suggested by Viceroy Enríquez. *Instrucciones y memorias*, 1:179.

28. *Instrucciones y memorias*, 1:179.

or regional traits but rather to the growing influence of a professional class of greedy lawyers.[29]

Don Antonio de Mendoza, the first viceroy of New Spain (1535–50), generally refused to take blanket statements about Indian litigiousness at face value, convinced that the knowledge required to govern New Spain could only be attained over time and with skepticism toward many of the Spanish allegations about the behavior of its peoples. As he counseled his successor, Luis de Velasco: "The natives of this land are of such stock that very often they come to complain about things of very little import that they blow out of proportion, while others suffer serious offenses and remain silent. You should be advised that it is necessary to understand what they are referring to even in seemingly inconsequential cases because something important can be learned from little things."[30] "Oir los indios" ("To listen to the Indians") was a lesson that Mendoza learned while in office and passed on to his successor; in practice, it meant that the viceroy should make himself available to all Indians.[31] Ensuring Indian access to royal justice remained a concern for those who occupied the viceregal seat after Mendoza.[32]

The idea of the litigious Indian, a veritable colonial trope created and kept alive by officers, missionaries, and *encomenderos*, coexisted with concerns expressed by high colonial administrators about the lack of access to justice for Indian subjects in many regions under Spanish control. In 1554, for example, Don Luis de Velasco, the second viceroy of Mexico (1550–64), expressed pity for the Indians of the Marquesado—the seignorial territories including the Valley of Oaxaca that the crown had granted to Cortés—who remained cut off from justice altogether, living in ignorance of the law and far from the nearest court.[33] Little had changed for these Indians since the *visitador* Tello de San-

---

29. Richard L. Kagan, *Lawsuits and Litigants in Castile, 1500–1700* (Chapel Hill: University of North Carolina Press, 1981), 17. On the relation between the growth of the legal profession and Spanish law schools, see pages 140–50.

30. *Instrucciones y memorias*, 1:101.

31. *Instrucciones y memorias*, 1:110.

32. The first viceroy's teachings are echoed in the words of Viceroy Luis de Velasco II who laid the groundwork for the establishment of the General Indian Court of New Spain. Writing at the end of his tenure in 1595, he encouraged his successor to heed complaints brought by Indians because they often revealed the existence of real problems. Velasco II also took the opportunity to comment on the alleged penchant of the Mexican Indians to sue over minutiae, a phenomenon that he was inclined to see as an indicator of the developmental stage reached by native societies. *Instrucciones y memorias*, 1:318. For Velasco's view of the role of the viceroy in the administration of justice for Indians, see Mariano Cuevas, *Documentos inéditos del siglo XVI para la historia de México*, 2nd ed. (Mexico City: Editorial Porrúa, 1975), 435–37. The Indians themselves funded the General Indian Court through the imposition of a tribute of one half real. On Velasco's reforms, see Woodrow Borah, *The General Indian Court of Colonial Mexico*, 84–105.

33. Francisco del Paso y Troncoso, *Epistolario de la Nueva España 1505–1818*, 14 vols. (Mexico

doval had reached similar conclusions during a 1545 visit.[34] The gap between these two figures—the Indian ignorant of the law and the Indian too eager to embrace it—points to one of the most persistent and perplexing issues in both the colonial imagination (by which I refer to the imagination of the colonizer) and colonial historiography: the relationship of the colonized to the law or, as often imagined from the perspective of Spanish administrators, the role of the colonizer as lawgiver.[35]

Viceroys relied on the friars to make local and royal public decrees to an Indian audience.[36] In 1558 the same viceroy, Don Luis de Velasco, instructed Lorenzo Librón de Quiñones, a judge of the Audiencia, to visit Oaxaca and ensure that the Indians there got acquainted with the laws of the land through translations into their languages.[37] That same year, Velasco approved a set of ordinances that laid out in great detail the process for payment of tribute in Xochimilco. To ensure their enforcement, the ordinances were to be read and publicly explained four times a year by the governor and the friars, a requirement that betrays the friars' and bishops' active intervention in decisions regarding tribute during Velasco's tenure.[38] Nahua scribes close to the friars left testimony of the Franciscans' instruction of the population on tribute matters; this may explain why Alonso de Molina made sure that the members of the confraternities did not mistake their obligations for a tributary burden.[39] When the king issued the controversial New Laws in 1542, he instructed Viceroy Mendoza to entrust the friars with their translation into indigenous languages as well as their dissemination among the Indians.[40]

City: Antigua Librería Robredo, 1939), 7:188.

34. Paso y Troncoso, *Epistolario de la Nueva España*, 4:210.

35. On this issue in the context of the evangelization of the Mexican Indians, see Osvaldo F. Pardo, *The Origins of Mexican Catholicism: Nahua Rituals and Christian Sacraments in Sixteenth-Century Mexico* (Ann Arbor: University of Michigan Press, 2004), 159–62.

36. Barry D. Sell and Susan Kellogg, "We Want to Give Them Laws: Royal Ordinances in a Mid-Sixteenth Century Nahuatl Text," *Estudios de cultura nahuatl* 27 (1997): 332–34.

37. Paso y Troncoso, *Epistolario de la Nueva España*, 7:223.

38. "Este concierto se lea y dé a entender a todos juntamente con las ordenanzas cuatro veces en el año, y déseles a entender a todos por el gobernador u otro por su mandado, y los religiosos se lo digan también, que ninguna cosa han de dar de cacao ni tomines ni mantas ni leña ni gallinas ni otra cosa alguna, ni más servicio personal, sino solamente las semanas que les cupieren." France V. Scholes and Eleanor B. Adams, *Sobre el modo de tributar los indios de Nueva España a Su Majestad, 1561–1564* (Mexico City: José Porrúa e Hijos, 1958), doc. 24, 109. The word *concierto* appears with no modification in Nahuatl records to refer to the agreements reached by authorities regarding tribute. See, for example, its use in relation to a 1561 agreement that involved Bishop Toral in *Anales de Tecamachalco*, 43.

39. *Anales de Tecamachalco*, 46. For more on Molina, see the introduction.

40. "Y porque todo lo suso dicho sea mas notorio: especialmente a los naturales de las dichas nuestras Indias en cuyo beneficio y p[ro]vecho esto se ordena mandamos que esta nuestra carta sea imprimida en molde y se embie a todas las nuestras Indias a los religiosos q[ue] en ellas entien[n] den en la instruction de los dichos Indios, a los quales encargamos que alla las hagan traduzir en

With this provision the crown gave the *encomenderos* another reason to oppose new legislation that they took as a direct attack on their very existence. This is also how the *encomenderos* interpreted the crown's decision to assume full supervision of Indian laborers after their death, instead of allowing them to remain under the *encomendero*'s family.[41] To the colonists, the friars were both the instigators and unwelcome messengers of these new policies. As the *encomendero* Jerónimo López, a particularly shrewd member of this group, wrote to the king in a 1545 letter:

There are friars who have told the Indians that they owe Spaniards no special veneration, to which the Indians replied that these Spaniards were their lords, and deserving of such treatment because this is how they had done it since early times; but the Indians were warned that they were being deceived because these Spaniards were not lords but *maceguales*, which means commoners; the real lords had stayed in Spain.[42]

López went on to report that after learning about the New Laws, the Mexican Indians had taken to disobeying and attacking Spaniards: in the town of Ayucingo, an Indian bailiff slapped a Spaniard on his beard hard enough to cause profuse bleeding in his mouth.[43]

López's brief and rather casual reference to this episode may have brought home the idea that the Mexican Indians, thanks to the teachings of the friars, had become quite familiar with Spanish codes of behavior and were ready to challenge Spaniards on their own ground, attacking them on their honor. López also told of Indians who, having been appointed bailiffs by their friars, did not hesitate to throw Spaniards to the ground, tie their hands, and shave their beards for no apparent reason.[44] As we shall see below, the ambivalence

---

le[n]gua India, para que major lo entiendan y sepan lo proveydo." *Leyes y ordenanças nuevame[n] te hechas por su Magestad /para/ la governacion de las Indias y buen tratamiento y conservacion de los Indios: que se han de guardar en el Consejo y audiencias reales q[ue] en ellas residen* (Alcalá de Henares: Juan de Brocar, 1543), 9v. On the obligation to provide Indians with translations of laws enacted by the Real Audiencia, see Paso y Troncoso, *Epistolario de la Nueva España*, 8:223.

41. "Ordenamos y ma[n]damos que de aq[ui] adela[n]te ningun[n] Visorrey / governador / audie[n]cia / d[e]scubridor / ni otra persona alguna no pueda encome[n]dar Indios por nueva p[ro]visio[n] / ni por renu[n]ciacio[n] / ni donacio[n] / venta ni otra qualq[ui]er forma modo / nip or vacacio[n] ni here[n]cia: sino q[ue] murie[n]do la p[er]sona q[ue] tuviere los dichos Indios sea[n] puestos en n[uestr]ra real corona." *Leyes y ordenanças*, 7v.

42. Paso y Troncoso, *Epistolario de la Nueva España*, 4:163.

43. Paso y Troncoso, *Epistolario de la Nueva España*, 4:166.

44. "Luego se apellidan e juntan en un credo ciento o mil para uno y lo toman al español y lo derruecan en el suelo e lo atan las manos atrás e le pelan las barbas e hacen diez mil injurias e lo llevan atado al más cercano monesterio que tienen e allí el fraile sin oir al pobre español le da su reprensión por los contentar." Paso y Troncoso, *Epistolario de la Nueva España*, 4:164.

and in some cases outright contempt that the Spanish friars showed toward their countrymen for placing so much importance on an earthly good like honor lent these cases a substantial degree of verisimilitude.

López told the king that the friars were busier in the pulpit glossing civil laws than the Scriptures, thus postulating a sharp distinction between secular and ecclesiastical laws that Spanish laymen in Mexico believed to be increasingly eroding.[45] His concern probably resonated in Spain, where friars were suspected to be unreliable interpreters of papal legislation among other things, as can be gathered from petitions to entrust parish priests to make papal bulls public.[46]

In a world where appearances and legal realities were hard to distinguish, as in the case of *encomenderos* who posed as noblemen, López decried the missionaries' interpretive role in instructing Indians in colonial realities. In López's view, the instruction of Indians, whether in matters of history or law, was inimical to a stable society, because the more the Mexican Indians learned about their rulers, the more vulnerable those rulers became. Through the teaching of history at the Franciscan schools, the Indians learned that outsiders had ruled the Spanish in the past; in the courts of law, the *nahuatlatos* became more aware of their rulers' miseries and weaknesses.[47]

As is true of contemporary historians addressing the interactions between colonizers and colonized, the question of cross-cultural (mis)understanding was very much on Spanish and Indian minds, even as real misunderstandings about each other's beliefs, institutions, and expectations took place as a mat-

---

45. "Es ya la desvergüenza tanta que no lo sé decir, y muy mayor, después que los capítulos que vuestra majestad nos envió por leyes que guardásemos se han publicado y aclarado, y aclarados en los púlpitos en lugar de dotrina y ellos los tienen sacados en su lengua mayormente cuando les dicen que vuestra majestad los hace tan libres que aunque se alcen manda que no se han de ser más encomendados de solo por la vida del encomendatario." Paso y Troncoso, *Epistolario de la Nueva España*, 4:165.

46. "Suplicamos a vuestra Magestad, mande que de aqui adelante no aya predicadores de las bulas, si no que las lean y publiquen los curas y clerigos de las parrochias y lugares, por que es cosa grave la desorden que en estos ay." *Las Cortes de Valladolid del año 1548* (Valladolid: Fernández de Cordova, 1549), petition 177, E7v. Twenty-five years later, during the *cortes* held in Valladolid, it was asked that the papal bulls be read by "personas honestas de buena consciencia y letrados que entiendan lo que predican y no excedan de los casos y cosas contenidos en las bullas." *Quaderno de las cortes que en Valladolid tuvo su magestad del Emperador y rey nuestro señor el año de 1523* (Salamanca: Juan de Junta, 1551). This concern was not new and goes back to legislation passed under Fernando and Isabel. *Recopilación de las leyes destos reynos, hecha por mandado de la Magestad Catolica del Rey Don Felipe Segundo nuestro señor, que se ha mandado imprimir, con las leyes que despues de la ultima impression se han publicado, por la Magestad Catolica del Rey don Felipe Quarto el Grande nuestro señor*, 3 vols. (Madrid: Catalina de Barrio y Angulo y Diego Diaz de la Carrera, 1640; Valladolid: Lex Nova, 1982), book 1, title 10, law 1, 1:45v. The order for the dissemination of papal bulls and other papal documents is spelled out in book 1, title 10, law 12, 1:50.

47. Paso y Troncoso, *Epistolario de la Nueva España*, 4:168–69.

ter of course. Some consequences were negligible, others long-lasting.[48] As the Mexican case shows, communication between the Spanish and Indians did not require an in-depth knowledge of each other's mental makeup. Situations of informal and formal contact in which the actors learned, guessed, made inferences, and reached provisional conclusions about each other gave rise to familiarity with each other's codes, if not understanding. The notion of mutual understanding at the core of contemporary critiques of colonialism, so hard to tell apart from an ethical imperative based on the ideal of mutual cultural transparency, may prove an inadequate point of reference for analyzing the interactions between Spaniards and their new subjects. A history lesson or the rituals and stories of the courtroom revealed something about the Spanish that not everybody, even those convinced of the superiority of Spanish institutions, felt comfortable sharing with the natives. The outcome of disclosing the workings of one's culture may not always be predictable. In one notable example, to López, informing Mexican Indians of the idiosyncratic code that seemed to organize Spanish life meant revealing not only a precious source of masculine power and pride but also the fragile nature of honor itself.

If the first viceroys took pains to make the Indians aware of the laws, it is less clear that similar efforts were made to keep the indigenous population informed of the ultimate fate of some of these laws. The New Laws again present an interesting case; issued in 1542, their implementation and enforcement in Mexico was quickly halted, since violence had erupted in Peru when they were applied there. Some were struck down, including the chapter that ordered the transfer of Indians to the crown upon the *encomendero*'s death, invalidated in 1545.[49] The consequences of the many policy changes were not lost on Viceroy Mendoza; in disarmingly candid words, he told his successor that the number of changes was enough to drive the Mexican Indians crazy.[50]

The Mexican missionaries expressed contradictory opinions about the law's impact on the life of their flock. Depending on the particular issue, they alternately argued that the Indians needed to be sheltered from the law and its likely abuses, or placed under its protection. The crown, for its part, responded to some of the friars' most immediate concerns, as in the provision of the New Laws ordering that lawsuits among Indians be decided summarily and accord-

---

48. The erroneous identification of seemingly similar concepts across Nahua and Spanish cultures was a particular case of misunderstanding with important consequences for the survival of indigenous social structures. For a discussion of this process, see James Lockhart, "Double Mistaken Identity: Some Nahua Concepts in Postconquest Guise," in *Of Things of the Indies: Essays Old and New in Early Latin American History* (Stanford: Stanford University Press, 1999), 98–119.

49. Encinas, *Cedulario indiano*, 2:197.

50. *Instrucciones y memorias*, 1:114.

ing to their customs.[51] The establishment of the legal system in colonial Mexico was the result of an open struggle between the friars and the crown; for quite some time, royal law spoke to Indians with more than one voice and in more than one language.

Noblemen, *Macehuales*, and *Litis*

Prominent members of the Franciscan order espoused the view that the best way to curb lawsuits among Indians was to bring them under the friars' exclusive jurisdiction; acting more like father figures than judges, the friars could swiftly resolve their disputes.[52] With time and their increasingly urgent attempts to stall the crown's plans to replace them with parish priests, Franciscan writers produced detailed legal arguments in support of their claims to full jurisdiction. In the 1550s, the lay brother Pedro de Gante wrote briefly but forcefully on the negative effects of lawsuits and the need for the Indians to live free of worries about earthly matters, a goal that he believed could only be achieved by preventing the new converts from unnecessary contact with Spaniards and assimilated Indians from nonelite families. Gante characterized the widespread lawsuits as a recent development that resulted from individuals meddling in Indian affairs for the sake of economic profit, rather than the unbridled expression of a cultural trait.[53]

The Flemish brother addressed this issue at a time when the crown had asked royal officers to conduct a full review of the apportionment and collection of tribute in Mexico, with the goal of eliminating coerced labor.[54] The assessment of the tributary system would take years; in the meantime, the rift among missionaries, *encomenderos*, and royal officers that had reached new

---

51. "Y que no den lugar a que en los pleytos de entre Indios o con ellos se haga[n] procesos ordinarios ni aya largas como suele acontescer por la malicia de algunos abogados y procuradores, sino que sumariamente sean determinados guardando sus usos y costumbres: no siendo claramente injustos." *Leyes y ordenanças*, 5v–6.

52. This notion was often advanced by friars to argue for their right to punish Indians. Fr. Miguel Navarro described such punishment as follows: "corrigiéndolos y haciéndolos castigar más como padres, según lo requería esta gente nueva y tierna, que como jueces, llevándolos por el rigor y términos del Derecho." García Icazbalceta, *Códice Mendieta*, 1:115.

53. Ernesto de la Torre Villar, *Fray Pedro de Gante, maestro y civilizador de América* (Mexico City: Seminario de Cultura Mexicana, 1973), 93.

54. In response to information received about the tributary system's negative consequences on the welfare of the Indians, the king appointed Diego Ramírez in 1550 to conduct an inspection in the towns between Mexico and Veracruz. Ramírez was to gather information on the collection of tribute and administer justice when needed. Paso y Troncoso, *Epistolario de la Nueva España*, 6:12. For the letters sent by Ramírez to the crown, see doc. 311 in the same volume, and docs. 366, 367, and 382 in volume 8.

heights in the aftermath of the New Laws, only deepened. Already convinced that tributary contributions were a heavy burden for many Indians, Gante suggested that Indian communities stop spending money on lawsuits that only benefited private individuals rather than the crown so that they would be in a better position to satisfy their tributary obligations.

The same themes run through many of the reports and letters written by Pedro de Gante's brethren, among them Gerónimo de Mendieta, who repeatedly voiced the order's opposition to exacting tribute from the formerly exempt Indians of Mexico City. In expanded form, and with the addition of information gathered from his visits to Indian towns, those same themes can be found in the writings of a royal officer closely associated with the Franciscans, the judge Alonso de Zorita.[55] It was during Zorita's time in Mexico that the debate over tribute came to both overshadow and distort other social and political issues, and he took an active role, standing against the *encomenderos* and with the friars and Viceroy Velasco in their opposition to higher tributary contributions. The information that went into some of Zorita's writings, such as his *Breve y sumaria relación*, came out of a 1553 royal order that called for the viceroy to designate an *oidor* (a position that Zorita would come to hold) to inquire about past and present patterns of tribute collection in Indian communities.[56] The crown required information gathered from elderly Indians or indigenous paintings to be corroborated by consultation with the friars, the acknowledged authorities on Mexican antiquities, thus creating the conditions for a convergence of opinion between the judge and the missionaries.[57]

For Zorita, much of the social instability that threatened Indian communities resulted from the erosion of the authority once enjoyed by local lords as *macehuales* became increasingly powerful as they curried favor with Spaniards to secure themselves public offices—some of them newly introduced—related to the administration of justice.[58] Courts were partly to blame for this state of affairs, for they had become the stage on which the *macehuales* challenged

---

55. When serving as a judge of the Audiencia in Guatemala, Zorita was instrumental in the enforcement of the New Laws. On the conflicts that surrounded their enforcement, see Ralph Vigil, *Alonso de Zorita: Royal Judge and Christian Humanist, 1512–1585* (Norman: University of Oklahoma Press, 1987), 121–60.

56. Puga, *Provisiones*, 140v. A *cédula* from the previous year issued in response to complains about excessive tributes paid by Indian commoners to their lords called for a similar inquiry into the old tributary system.

57. Puga, *Provisiones*, 140v. On Zorita's summary of the friars' position, see *Breve y sumaria relación de los señores de la Nueva España* (Mexico City: Universidad Nacional Autónoma de México, 1942), 52. By 1554 the mendicants were conducting their own inquiries into past modes of tribute allocation through interviews with elderly Indians and examination of their paintings. See Paso y Troncoso, *Epistolario de Nueva España*, 7:259–61.

58. Zorita, *Breve y sumaria relación*, 39.

their traditional lords, thus encouraging even more lawsuits.[59] As he accurately noted, the introduction of an elective system of local government, with its host of administrators and enforcers of justice such as alcaldes, *gobernadores*, and *alguaciles*, had weakened the authority of the local lords and contributed to an increase in court cases.[60] In the laconic style of the historical annals kept by local governing bodies, a Nahua notary from Tecamachalco duly recorded that in 1565, the *macehuales* began to serve as alcalde.[61] The confirmation of this phenomenon gives Zorita's definition of the Nahua title *tlahtoani* (from *tlahtoa*, to speak), or "supreme lord," a special weight; he chose to recall the etymology of the word "jurisdiction" to convey the idea of a ruler with absolute power over matters of justice.[62]

Although Zorita did not necessarily share other officers' unfavorable opinion of the Indians and the work of the religious orders, he did also blame mulattoes, mestizos, and Spaniards for instigating quarrels among Indian towns and individuals.[63] Even in cases where Zorita may otherwise have welcomed the intervention of royal justice, as when Indians had legitimate grounds to demand lower and fairer tributes, he concluded that any legal redress gained through traditional procedures would ultimately be prejudicial to the communities due to the expense of legal fees.[64]

---

59. It is thought that members of the indigenous aristocracy started the trend for lawsuits; they were then followed by the *macehuales* by the mid-sixteenth century. Delfina Esmeralda López Sarrelangue, *La nobleza indígena de Pátzcuaro en la época virreinal* (Mexico City: Universidad Autónoma de México / Instituto de Investigaciones Históricas, 1965), 146.

60. The cabildo system was fully in place by the 1560s. Charles Gibson, *The Aztecs under Spanish Rule* (Stanford: Stanford University Press, 1964), 172. On the process of political Hispanization, see pages 166–83. For local perspectives, see S. L. Cline, *Colonial Culhuacan, 1580–1600* (Albuquerque: University of Mexico Press, 1986), 35–47 and 53–58; and Robert Haskett, *Indigenous Rulers*, 60–123; for the legal disputes that followed the establishment of the *cabildo*, see pages 26–59. On the transformation of the indigenous nobility, see Charles Gibson, "The Aztec Aristocracy in Colonial Mexico" in *Comparative Studies in Society and History* 2, no. 2 (January 1960): 169–96; and López Sarrelangue, *La nobleza indígena de Pátzcuaro*, 81–101.

61. *Anales de Tecamachalco*, 50. The same entry registered the absence of *macehuales* from a variety of tasks they had traditionally been asked to fulfill as part of their tributary obligations.

62. "A los señores supremos llamaban y llaman tlatoques, de un verbo que dice tlatoa, que quiere decir hablar, porque éstos, como supremos y meros señores, tenían la jurisdicción civil y criminal, y toda la gobernación y mando de todas sus provincias y pueblo de donde eran señores; y a éstos eran sujetos las otras dos maneras de señores que se dirán adelante." Zorita, *Breve y sumaria relación*, 27. Noblemen often reminded colonial authorities in sworn statements and other legal documents of the scope of the authority that local lords used to enjoy. See, for example, Emma Pérez-Rocha and Rafael Tena, *La nobleza indígena del centro de México después de la conquista* (Mexico City: Instituto Nacional de Antropología e Historia, 2000), 314. For Zorita, a Nahua noble's status was essentially based on either dominion or lineage; on the different noble groups, see *Breve y sumaria relación*, 28–37. On the nomenclature employed in sixteenth-century Mexico to distinguish between noblemen by birth and all others, see López Sarrelangue, *La nobleza indígena de Pátzcuaro*, 96.

63. Zorita, *Breve y sumaria relación*, 42.

64. "Y si algunos hay ladinos que se quejan en nombre de todos, movidos con celo del común, o por la vía que se ha dicho que lo hacen algunos, hay el otro daño que se ha declarado, que gastan

The crown's practical interest in learning about the new subjects' past social and economic conditions in preparation for crafting contemporary policy helped Zorita conjure an image of an Indian past where individuals lived together under only a handful of laws and happily untouched by protracted lawsuits, much like in More's *Utopia*.[65] Given the friars' influence on members of the Indian nobility, it is not surprising that a group of Indian lords ratified this version of the precontact past in a letter to the crown that was certainly penned by missionary hands.[66] As Viceroy Mendoza had already hinted, Zorita also feared that an ever-expanding body of laws, far from securing social order, could instead contribute to its dissolution.

In the same vein as the letter mentioned above, Zorita's indigenous noblemen became a vehicle to express the friars' contempt for secular law. A Nahua noble reportedly reacted strongly to the news of the imminent arrival of yet another royal inspector from Spain: "It is not for our own good. Inspectors and judges come here each day, and we do not know to what effect. Only justice from heaven is true justice."[67] Some friars advanced a more modest version of this heavenly justice. To Mendieta, who opposed the Audiencia's intervention in Indian lawsuits, Zorita was perfect for his proposed appointment as a special judge exclusively charged with resolving disputes within and among indigenous communities.[68] As imagined by the Franciscan, that judge should be "a man closer to God than to the world,"[69] in the same way that the ideal viceroy should be known for his prudence rather than his knowledge of legal compilations.[70] In expressing this opinion, Mendieta joined his predecessors who had reignited on Mexican soil the traditional confrontation between European theologians and *letrados* that would continue into the seventeenth century.[71]

---

la vida y las haciendas en pleitos y corre el tributo por la primera cuenta, y al cabo no alcanzan justicia por lo dicho, o porque no siguen el pleito." Zorita, *Breve y sumaria relación*, 160.

65. Zorita, *Breve y sumaria relación*, 155.

66. "Lo otro, porque en tiempo de nuestra infidelidad usábamos my pocas veces del pleito, y con brevedad se despachaban los negocios de las partes y sin pagárselo, agora que somos ya tornados cristianos tenemos muchos pleitos, ansí con nuestros naturales como con la gente española de V. M." García Icazbalceta, *Códice Mendieta*, 1:132.

67. Zorita, *Breve y sumaria relación*, 53.

68. "Y el remedio es que se señalen dos o tres personas o una sola, en cristiandad y bondad y prudencia y experiencia y afición de los naturales las más señaladas de la tierra, cuales entiendo ser el Dr. Çorita, y el contador Montealegre y el Dr. Sedeño, las cuales personas juntas, o cada una por su parte tengan facultad y autoridad de visitar todos los pueblos, como les cupiere o se les señalaren." Joaquín García Icazbalceta, *Nueva colección de documentos para la historia de México*, 3 vols. (Mexico City: Salvador Chávez Hayhoe, 1941), 1:19. Alcaldes y corregidores were instructed to refer all disputes over boundaries and succession to the Audiencia. Cuevas, *Documentos inéditos del siglo XVI*, 246–47. On the procedures to be followed in other cases according to their seriousness, see 247.

69. García Icazbalceta, *Nueva colección de documentos para la historia de México*, 1:20–21.

70. García Icazbalceta, *Nueva colección de documentos para la historia de México*, 1:36–7.

71. For instance, when discussing the qualifications that bishops in America should meet, the

In Zorita's last few years in New Spain, he had to defend both his authority as a member of the Audiencia and his views on tribute against Jerónimo de Valderrama, an inspector sent by the crown to increase royal revenues through reform of the tributary system, a reform that included taxation of Nahua nobles who had been exempt. An administrator who earned the epithet "scourge of Indians,"[72] Valderrama surely did not endear himself to the Nahua noblemen as he conducted the head count that signaled the imminent loss of their exemption from tribute. He also found little to commend in the way that the friars—especially the Dominicans—and the viceroy fulfilled their obligations to church and crown. His reports elicited strong responses from religious quarters.[73] In one such report, the inspector informed his superiors that the religious orders, with the viceroy's tacit consent, had succeeded in expanding their jurisdiction to the detriment of royal authority.[74] Yet for all his disagreements with the friars, Valderrama concurred with their opinion that litigation overburdened the Nahuas with additional exactions for defraying legal costs and unwittingly contributed to sinking their communities further into poverty. As a remedy, the inspector proposed that the cases be heard and solved at the local or provincial level to avoid the expenses of costly trips of the *principales* and their entourage to the Audiencia. His economic argument differed little from Zorita's;[75] it is in the charges leveled against the *principales* where the two men part company.

The charges of a penchant for pursuing and instigating lawsuits did not pass unchallenged by the nobility. In 1563, for instance, Don Pedro, a cacique from Xochimilco, and a group of noblemen complained to King Philip II that despite the help that their town had provided the Spaniards in the final siege of Tenochtitlán and later campaigns, Cortés and other conquerors had made themselves lords of lands to which they had no right. According to the noblemen, the Spaniards did so in the belief that the Nahuas avoided litigation ("no somos gente de

---

Mexican-born theologian Juan Zapata raised the question of whether theologians or canonists would be better suited for the job. Juan Zapata y Sandoval, *De iustitia distributiva et acceptione personarum ei opposita disceptatio*, ed. C. Baciero, A. M. Barrero, J. M. García Añoveros, and J. M. Soto (Madrid: Consejo Superior de Investigaciones Científicas, 2004). On the tension between theology and law, see Miriam Turrini, "Il giudice della coscienza e la coscienza del giudice," in *Disciplina dell'anima, disciplina del corpo e disciplina della società tra medioevo ed età moderna*, ed. Paolo Prodi (Bologna: Il Mulino, 1994), 279–94.

72. García Icazbalceta, *Códice Mendieta*, 1:182.

73. See García Icazbalceta, *Códice Mendieta*, 1:19, 21–22, and 29–34.

74. "Todo su deseo se resume en dos cosas: jurisdicción y caja de comunidad, y como esto falte, dicen que la cristiandad va por el suelo, y cada día amenazan con que lo quieren dejar todo." France V. Scholes and Eleanor B. Adams, eds., *Cartas del Licenciado Valderrama y otros documentos sobre su visita al gobierno de Nueva España* (Mexico City: José Porrúa e Hijos, 1961), 44. On the alliance between friars and Viceroy Velasco, see pages 141 and 143–44.

75. Scholes and Adams, *Cartas del Licenciado Valderrama*, 47. A similar complaint was also expressed by Archbishop Montúfar. Paso y Troncoso, *Epistolario de Nueva España*, 8:86.

pleitos") and were not adequately prepared to defend themselves. Whereas the complaint proved the Spaniards wrong as to the latter point, the noblemen gave full credence to the idea that they disliked lawsuits by requesting that the lands be returned to their rightful owners through the mere force of truth rather than a protracted legal process.[76]

Just as Nahua noblemen learned of their reputation as legal troublemakers, they also learned—from the friars, most certainly—to express their dislike for lawsuits and their willingness to settle disputes out of court. The town records of Cuauhtinchan in Puebla contain what appear to be well-established linguistic expressions to indicate the resolution of conflicts with or without recourse to the legal system: "mochihua *pleyto*," and "mochihua *amistad*" ("a lawsuit is made," and "friendship is made").[77] The opposition *pleyto-amistad*, which had a long history in Europe and had been commented on by Alphonse X, found its way into Cuauhtinchan, where town officers let the historic record show that they knew how and when to avoid lawsuits.[78] For many indigenous communities the end of legal conflicts with neighboring towns represented an event that merited mention in the historical record. For instance, the annals of Tepeteopan, in the valley of Tepehuan, Puebla, recorded that in 1569 the conflicts over territorial boundaries had been solved: "*nicam otlamqui pleitos*," the lawsuits came to an end.[79]

The arguments and counterarguments about tribute that coalesced around the controversial figure of Inspector Valderrama illustrate the mix of expectations, cold calculations, and ambivalence with which friars and royal officers thought about and dealt with members of the local elites. Valderrama blamed the friars for much of the confusion he encountered when trying to determine

---

76. Pérez-Rocha and Tena, *La nobleza indígena*, 282.

77. *Libro de los guardianes y gobernadores de Cuauhtinchan (1519–1640)*, 82–83; and 136–37. This language could be traced back to the strong Franciscan presence in Cuautinchan. The local indigenous nobility forged a very fruitful alliance with the friars, who played an essential role as mediators in intra and extracommunal conflicts, as Pablo Escalante Gonzalbo has so eloquently shown in "El patrocinio del arte indocristiano en el siglo XVI: La iniciativa de las autoridades indígenas en Tlaxcala y Cuautinchan," in *Patrocinio, colección y circulación de las artes*, ed. Gustavo Curiel (Mexico City: Universidad Nacional Autónoma de México, 1997), 215–35.

78. "Et por ende dixo Aristotiles que si los homes hobiesen entre sí verdadera amistad, non habrien meester justicia nin alcalles que los judgasen, porque la amistad les farie complir et guardar aquello mesmo que quiere et manda la justicia." *Las siete partidas del rey Don Alfonso el Sabio*, 3 vols. (Madrid: Imprenta Real, 1807), part. 4, title 27, law 1, 3:146. On love and friendship, see pages 145–46 and Michael Clanchy, "Law and Love in the Middle Ages," in *Disputes and Settlements: Law and Human Relations in the West*, ed. John Bossy (Cambridge: Cambridge University Press, 1983), 47–67.

79. *Anales de Tepeteopan: De Xochitecuhtli a don Juan de San Juan Olhuatecatl, 1370(?)–1675*, ed. Blanca Lara Tenorio, Eustaquio Celestino Solís, and Elisa Pérez Alemán (Mexico City: CIESAS/ CONACYT/CONACULTA/ INAH, 2009), 61. It is worth noting that the end of the lawsuits appears to have coincided with the return of Franciscan friars to the town.

the status and number of tributary Indians in areas under their direct influence. As he argued, the religious had ensured that those individuals enlisted in the service of the church in any capacity be exempted from tribute, an exemption that only the nobility had enjoyed until then. In 1554, Archbishop of Mexico Alonso de Montúfar, a Dominican supporter of Valderrama who had a bitterly contentious relationship with the Franciscan friars, leveled the same accusations.[80] According to the inspector's reports, those exempted were often granted the rank of *principales* by the viceroy or enjoyed such status de facto by the missionaries' sole decision.[81] The inquiries into tribute that Zorita and Valderrama carried out made them privileged witnesses to the transformation of the indigenous nobility and brought into focus the disparate forces that would ultimately shape its fate. When noblemen and *macehuales* were hard to distinguish, as both officers encountered, the administration of justice became difficult and the laws ineffectual.

The lack of agreement over which social groups were responsible for the rise of lawsuits illustrates the efforts of colonial authorities to come to terms with the unintended consequences of royal laws, local policies, and ad hoc solutions to problems of Indian labor and tribute and the titles of communities and noble families. As viceregal administrators became aware of the changes that their policies had set in motion, the friars addressed the shifting relations between *macehuales* and caciques on their own terms, with an eye toward containment of the social and economic ambitions of the two groups. The desire to strike a balance between these two vying forces becomes apparent in the *Confessionario mayor*, where Molina used the Ten Commandments as a vehicle to address issues of authority, obedience, and obligations that bore directly on the relationships between noblemen and *macehuales*, Indian municipal officers, and the rest of the population. As expected, the fourth and the seventh commandments ("Honor thy father and thy mother;" "Thou shalt not steal") offered a framework that was more than adequate for articulating such concerns. Regarding the seventh commandment, Molina thought that confessors should know not only whether caciques or Indian officers had failed to administer justice to *macehuales*, but also if they had in any way prevented the

---

80. Paso y Troncoso, *Epistolario de la Nueva España*, 7:296–97. The same point was made by Gonzalo Díaz de Vargas, councilman of the *cabildo* of Puebla in 1556. *Epistolario*, 8:105.

81. "Otra introducción había muy prejudicial a la hacienda de Vuestra majestad, y es que en algunos pueblos por ordenanzas de frailes reservan muchas gentes de tributo, cantores, y tañedores y otros que sirven en la iglesia, carpinteros, albañiles, y otros viejos y enfermos, como se verá por las ordenanzas que ahí van; y éstos son muchos, porque el Virrey por cédulas los hace principales, *y a el que un fraile pone don, lo es también, y el que llevare el sombrero de camino cuando no hace sol*" (emphasis added). Scholes and Adams, *Cartas del Licenciado Valderrama*, 69.

macehuales from taking their grievances to the Audiencia.[82] Whereas the gloss on the fourth commandment spelled out the basic requirements of obedience to parents as well as secular and religious authorities, Molina's approach to the seventh highlighted the additional obligations that the new legal and political order imposed on Christian members of the native elite at a time that their loss of power was becoming apparent.

In general terms, Molina's ambivalence toward the native nobility may be an extension of Catholicism's own ambiguous relation with nobility as both an identifiable sociohistorical group and an associated system of values and ideas (about moral virtues, authority, etc.). If we look more closely, the missionaries' mixed feelings appear to have emerged as a response to the gap between their own designs and the rather fluid dynamic that actually dominated social relations on the ground. The friars had counted on the nobility to ensure their success in the creation of a Christian community that, as they envisioned it, would enjoy considerable cultural autonomy. For their part, the nobility was drawn to the world of Spanish conquerors and administrators, where they learned about government and the symbols of Spanish social status that they soon adopted.

In their capacity as town officers involved in everyday matters of government and justice, members of the native elite found themselves subject to the scrutiny of the Spanish colonial administration; like their Spanish counterparts, they faced the prospect of a *residencia*, or an investigation into their tenure upon leaving office. Such legal oversight was designed to evaluate officer conduct and correct possible wrongdoings by determining, for example, if restitution of goods or lands should be made to adversely affected parties. In addition to these practices, with their potential to weaken the authority and social standing of local figures,[83] members of the native elite were also likely to

---

82. "Estorvaste {por ventura} a los macehuales, que querian yr a algunos pueblos, a morar y hazer su habitación, vedandoles que no vendiessen sus casas y heredades propias, o otras haziendas suyas: o los estorvaste e impediste, que no apelassen, ni fuessen a quexarse delante el audiencia real quando les heziste algun agravio e injusticia, e los sentenciaste injustamente o recebiste algun cohecho: y quando recebiste lo que te dieron, fuiste contra la justicia." Molina, *Confessionario mayor*, 43r.

83. "Conviene saber, que los oficiales del Rey, que han poderio de juzgar a muerte o perdimiento de miembro, no pueden ser demandados durantes sus officios, y por esto al Rey pertenece embiar juezes de residencia a las ciudades, villas e lugares de sus Reynos, para que tomen residencia a los otros juezes, que en ellas antes estavan, para saber las cosas que mal han hecho en la republica a donde han sido juezes, assi por aver castigado demasiadamente a los vezinos y moradores de sus juzgados è jurisdiciones, donde tuvieron cargos y administracion de su justicia, como por los no aver castigado el y sus oficiales, como por aver llevado individamente lo que no podian llevar, y por otras cosas y casos que por el Rey les era mandado que hiziessen y cumpliessen, para que sean castigados como conviene a su servicio, y a la administracion de su Real justicia, o sean por ello gratificados como buenos juezes, que hizieron lo que devian: a los cuales toman las dichas residencias por tiempo de treinta dias: tambien de lo que hizieron por via de comission, como por via de

face an examination from their confessors about their performance in office; according to Molina, this examination amounted to a test of their allegiance to the colonial legal system.

Molina, like many of his brethren, thought that secular laws had little to offer converted Indians. Like many friars across religious orders, he was also concerned about the Indians' perception of the daily interactions between native, religious, and viceregal authorities and their assumptions about their respective places in the colonial hierarchy. The metajudicial dimension of the Ten Commandments that comes through in the teachings of friars like Molina addresses both concerns, reminding Indians in a position of authority that their decisions were subject to review by a higher judicial body through an appellate process with which they were not to interfere.

Europeans across the confessional divide as well as Indians were reminded that the fourth commandment went beyond the obligation to honor one's parents to include religious and secular authorities regardless of rank.[84] Some catechisms further explained that it entailed the obligation of all Christians to respect and follow the law.[85] In the name of preserving a semblance of social order through the routine affirmation of class hierarchies, the crown unwittingly did its part to highlight this Christian duty when it required under penalty that high administrators, ecclesiastical authorities, and titled members of the

---

juezes ordinarios." Gabriel de Monterroso y Alvarado, *Pratica civil, y criminal, y instrucion de escrivanos* (Madrid: Pedro Madrigal, 1603), treatise 9, 225. In Mexico the *residencia* "was introduced into the new Indian governments as soon as they were created." Gibson, *The Aztecs under Spanish Rule*, 180. Residents of indigenous towns were to be informed that a *residencia* for local officers who had finished their tenure would take place. *Anales de Tecamachalco*, 74. In 1556, however, the crown notified the Audiencia of New Spain that this was not always the case. Encinas, *Cedulario indiano*, 4:359.

84. "Y esto avemos de entender: no solo de los padres carnales que nos engendraron/ mas aun de los perlados ecclesiasticos: y de los que tienen cura de nuestras almas. Estos que nos han tornado a engendrar en christo Jesu; y generalmente de todos los otros perlados: a nosotros superiores. Assi como maestros: benefactores/principes, justicias: o governadores que tienen cargo de nosotros aca en la tierra." *Tripartito del Christianissimo y Consolatorio Doctor Juan Gerson de Doctrina Christiana a cualquiera muy provechosa*, ed. Alberto Ma. Carreño (Mexico City: Juan Cromberger, 1544; Mexico City: Ediciones "Libros de México," 1949), Br. With characteristic verbal economy Francisco de Vitoria expressed the expectations regarding this commandment as follows: "Si a los principes, y a las personas que estan puestas en dignidad no les cató la honrra y reverencia, y subjeción devida de palabra y obra." *Confessionario muy util y provechoso. Agora nuevamente corregido y enmendado* (Valladolid: Francisco Fernández de Córdoba, 1568), 26v. The interpretations of the fourth commandment found in the catechetical literature of the Reformation have been carefully examined by Robert James Bast in *Honor Your Fathers: Catechisms and the Emergence of a Patriarchal Ideology in Germany, 1400–1600* (Leiden: Brill, 1997). On the (largely ignored) convergence of Catholic and Lutheran perspectives on the fourth commandment, see 196–204.

85. "Tambien se peca si los subditos no obedecen a sus mayores, o a las leyes y mandamientos por ellos puestos en cosas graves, si los despreció en su coraçon, y si murmuró, y se quexó dellos." Bartholome de Medina, *Breve instruction de como se a de administrar el Sacramento de la penitencia, dividida en dos libros* (Zaragoza: Juan Alterache, 1580), 120.

nobility receive the treatment they were due when addressed either in person or in writing.[86] Although the crown's commitment to reinforcing existing social hierarchies by regulating and codifying forms of address—attempts that paralleled the frequent promulgation of sumptuary laws—undermined religious men's increasing opposition to titles as vain, the state interest in securing social order took precedence.[87]

The fourth commandment's call for Christians to obey domestic, civil, and religious authorities can be taken as a straightforward obligation as long as the sites of authority are easily recognizable. As the traditional nobility came to realize, forces within and outside their communities were transforming the old system of allegiances and obedience. If the friars played their part in trying to protect the traditional jurisdiction of caciques against the Spanish encroachment, for example, their efforts alone could not prevent the challenges that an elective local government, new tributary policies, and an emboldened mass of *macehuales* posed to their traditional authority.

Confessors, Honor, and Restitution

Honor had a prominent place in the letters that Jerónimo López wrote in defense of his fellow *encomenderos* against the charge that they mistreated Indians. In them, as noted above, he reported that the Indians, coached by the friars, had taken to affronting Spaniards in public. In López's view, by encouraging the Mexican Indians to subvert long-held principles of social order, the religious orders were undermining royal power and endangering the well-being of the colonies.

---

86. *Pragmática en que se da la orden y forma que se ha de tener y guardar, en los tratamientos y cortesias de palabra y por escripto, y en traer coroneles, y ponellos en qualesquier partes y lugares* (Alcalá: Juan Iñiguez de Lequerica, 1586); and *Quaderno de las leyes añadidas a la Nueva Recopilacion que se imprimio el año de 1598 en que van las leyes y prematicas que desde el dicho año, hasta principio deste de 1610 se han publicado* (Madrid: Juan de la Cuesta, 1610), book 4, title 1, law 18, 53v. Later decrees dealing with the same issue are found in *Prematica de tratamientos, y cortesias, y se acrecientan las penas contra los transgresores de lo en ella contenido* (Madrid: Juan de la Cuesta, 1611); *Prematica en que su Magestad manda que se guarden las que ultimamente se promulgaron en cinco de Enero, y doze de Àbril de seiscientos y onze, y los Capitulos de reformacion de onze de Hebrero de seiscientos y veinte y tres, en razon de las cortesias con las declaraciones y penas que en ella se declara* (Madrid: Maria de Quiñones, 1636).

87. "Pues la verdadera honra no consiste en vanidades de títulos dados por escripto y por palabra, sino en otras causas mayores, a que estos no añaden ni quitan. Y aviendose diversas vezes tratado y platicado por nuestro mandado por los de nuestro Consejo, y consultado con nos, avemos acordado, proveydo y ordenado en lo susodicho." *Pragmática en que se da la orden y forma*, 2v. Displeased with the lack of compliance with this ordinance in Mexico, Viceroy Gaspar de Zúñiga y Azevedo reissued it in 1600; its printer was Henrico Martínez.

The notion of honor grounded the Spanish legislation that aimed to protect the special status and privileges of the upper social classes, or *estamentos*. Some Spanish theologians did not hide their critical view, pointing out that honor contained the seed for beliefs and behavior inherently at odds with Christian teaching. Yet these religious writers were bound to acknowledge on practical grounds that honor was, for better or worse, an inescapable feature in the social life of their fellow countrymen.[88]

Writing about the sins of envy, pride, and sloth, the thirteenth-century theologian Thomas de Chobham noted how confessors struggled to determine an appropriate penitential act for those who had harmed their neighbor's reputation.[89] More troubling, most penitents paid no attention to these so-called spiritual crimes and only a few cared to confess them.[90] Chobham's words describe a state of affairs that Spanish confessors would deplore for centuries.

Sixteenth-century Spanish manuals on confession, whether written for priests or laypeople, reflect a growing concern over the lack of understanding of spiritual sins, and verbal offenses in particular, among the faithful and their confessors. These manuals and the significant number of treatises on the sins of the tongue printed at the time also point to the determination of royal and ecclesiastical authorities to hold Spaniards accountable for verbal offenses and other actions, which, contrary to church teachings, they considered inconsequential to their salvation. Whereas Thomas de Chobham had wrestled with the question of a fitting penitential act, sixteenth-century Spanish theologians tried to discern appropriate ways for penitents to make restitution to wronged parties in a society that was both far more complex and increasingly obsessed with lineage, honor, and social status. The new urgency to educate confessors on verbal offenses can be seen in the 1537 edition of *Arte para bien confessar*, which contained an additional chapter on "restitution of honor" meant to "to

---

88. This acknowledgment is commonly found in the context of religious discussions of the notion of nobility and the role of temporal goods in Christian life. See, for example, Martín Carrillo, *Memorial de Confessores* (Zaragoza: Miguel Ximeno Sánchez, 1596), 17. As Maravall has pointed out, the Spanish church, which eventually became entirely subordinated to the absolutist monarchy, resisted viewing the nobility as a body comparable to the ecclesiastical estate. However, the church in general agreed that lineage was a vehicle of virtue, a notion that sixteenth- and seventeenth-century moralists questioned. Maravall, *Poder, honor y elites en el siglo XVII*, 43–50.

89. "De his tamen supradiximus quod est difficile est talibus peccatis assignare condignam penitentiam per contrarium, et iniugenda est pro talibus peccatis quia sepe per invidiam vel superbiam nocet homo in multis proximo suo detrahendo ei, diminuendo famam eius, auferendo ei bona sua, et in multis aliis modis." Thomas de Chobham, *Thomae de Chobham Summa confessorum* (Louvain: Éditions Nauwelaerts / Paris: Bêatrice-Nauwelaerts, 1968), 534.

90. "Paucis enim vident talia criminalia spiritualia in se, et pauciores de eis confitentur." Chobham, *Summa confessorum*, 534.

muzzle the loose tongues of slanderers who eat away the life of their brothers."[91]

Some penitents were confused by the distinction between restitution and satisfaction; many of them mistook satisfaction—traditionally considered, along with contrition and confession, an integral part of the sacrament of penance—for restitution.[92] In the unadorned words of Domingo de Valtanás, to make restitution "is to pay your neighbor what is owed to him, because through this act he will be put back in possession of what belongs to him, which someone unlawfully took away; and restitution should be made before the penitent comes to confession."[93] "Satisfaction," on the other hand, was those acts that confessors required of the penitent, in the form of prayers, fasting, or alms.[94]

The Spanish-born friar Tomás de Mercado, who entered the Dominican order in Mexico and continued his studies in Salamanca, considered restitution important enough to warrant a small treatise of its own in his widely read *Summa de tratos y contratos*, a collection of opuscula to instruct merchants and bankers to practice their trade without violating Christian precepts.[95] In closing his *Summa* with a general exposition on restitution, Mercado seemed eager to

91. "poner freno a las bocas desenfrenadas de los maledizientes/murmuradores roedores de las vidas de sus hermanos." *Arte para bien confessar fecha por un devoto hieronymo. Agora de nuevo corregida* (Seville: Juan Cronberger, 1537), 5r. This title appears among other books confiscated from friars and booksellers in Yucatán. Fernández del Castillo, ed., *Libros y libreros en el siglo XVI* (Mexico City: Fondo de Cultura Económica, 1982), 320–22. The *Index* prepared by the Spanish Inquisition from 1551 and 1559 targeted books with no indication of author, printer, time, or place of edition. See J. M. de Bujanda, *Index de L'Inquisition Espagnole 1551, 1554, 1559* (Sherbrooke, Quebec: Centre d'Études de la Renaissance; Geneva: Librarie Droz, 1984), no. 73, 257 and no. 306, 407.

92. The sixteenth-century moral Spanish moral theologian Juan de Medina noted that restitution was traditionally understood in both a broad and a restricted sense. In its broad sense restitution was interchangeable with satisfaction. "Accipitur autem restitutio dupliciter, large, et stricte. Primo modo, extendit se ad omnem recompensam alicui, loco damni illati, agendam. Quanquam haec potius satisfactio dicenda sit, quam restitutio; iuxta capit." *De Poenitentiae, Restitutione, & Contractibus*, 2 vols. (Ingolstadt: David Sartori, 1581; Farnborough, UK: Gregg Press, 1967), 2:1.

93. Domingo de Valtanás, *Confessionario muy cumplido con un tractado de materia de excomuniones y de usura, de matrimonio, y de votos . . . Agora nuevamente corregido y añadido en esta tercera impression* (Seville: Sebastián Trugillo, 1555), 6v.

94. Valtanás, *Confessionario muy cumplido*, 8r. There were other significant differences as well, namely, that restitution involved exterior things and occurred between individuals, whereas satisfaction concerned sinful acts or passions and took place between penitent and God. Manuel Rodriguez (Lusitano), *Summa de casos de consciencia con advertencias muy provechosas para confessores*, 2 vols. (Salamanca: Juan Fernández, 1595), 2:142. Earlier theologians had written about making restitution to both men and God: "Unde debet et iniungi ut faciat restitutionem omnibus deo et hominibus." Thomas of Chobham, *Summa confessorum*, 534.

95. Earlier treatises aimed at merchants and the growing number of individuals from all social stations engaged in commerce include Doctor Saravia de la Calle, *Instrucion de mercaderes muy provechosa* (Medina del Campo: Pedro de Castro, 1547). On the groundwork by theologians and canonists to rationalize and codify the practice of restitution in response to the ascent of the merchant classes in medieval Europe, see Giacomo Todeschini, *I mercanti e il tempio: La società cristiana e il circolo virtuoso della ricchezza fra Medioevo ed Età Moderna* (Bologna: Società Editrice Il Mulino, 2002), 133–85.

remind his specialized readers that, although the world of natural and man-made things appeared vast, certain intangible goods demanded even more care because their loss compromised salvation.[96] The most precious of these, such as grace and the theological as well as moral virtues, were bestowed by God and could not be stolen. They could, however, be lost. While each individual was ultimately responsible for their loss, confessors conceded that human will is known to falter when exposed to malicious advice, lies, flattery, or bad examples from persons meaning harm.[97] Mercado counted among these "spiritual thieves" those individuals who dissuade others from pursuing a religious vocation, or succeed in persuading nuns or ministers to abandon their profession, two transgressions that required restitution on the part of the instigator.[98]

Christians and non-Christians alike acquired a wide range of natural goods of variable durability and value throughout their lives; Mercado instructed his readers that the more lasting among them were invisible or spiritual, such as wit or the knowledge of sciences, letters, or mechanical arts.[99] Next came external and far less durable corporeal goods that included life, fame, *honra* (which he identified with reverence and courtesy), and movable goods, all of which could be stolen either literally or figuratively.[100]

As proof that men were innately conditioned for spiritual pursuits, Mercado noted how far they were willing to go in search of intangible goods such as fame.[101] Located at the outer edge of the vast domain of worldly goods, fame comes closest to resembling a spiritual entity; the difficult paths leading to it even recall the treacherous roads that await the virtuous. If, as Mercado remarked, men freely abandoned readily available corporeal pleasures and goods

---

96. Mercado quite aptly opened the considerably revised second edition with an added opusculum on natural law and justice.

97. Mercado, *Summa de tratos y contratos*, 132v.

98. Mercado, *Summa de tratos y contratos*, 133v. In the case of a friar who left his order due to malicious advice (a classic example in manuals for confession), authorities such as Raymond de Penafort recommended that the guilty party enter a religious order, a suggestion that points to the difficulties to determine not only the appropriate form of restitution but also to whom it should be made. Anthonino de Florencia, *La summa de confession llamada defecerunt*, 75v.

99. Mercado, *Summa de tratos y contratos*, 134. Azpilcueta spoke of "bienes del alma." *Tractado de alabança y murmuracion en el qual se declara quando son merito, quando peccado venial, y quando mortal* (Valladolid: Adrian Ghemart, 1572), 111. A more detailed and far more inclusive classification of spiritual things can be found in Manuel Rodríguez's discussion of simony. *Summa de casos de consciencia*, vol. 2, chap. 55, 205.

100. Mercado, *Summa de tratos y contratos*, 136v.

101. "Uno de los eficaces argumentos, con que suelo mostrar el gran desseo que ay en todos, aunque no lo sentimos, de los bienes espirituales, e invisibles, es ver con quanto conato apetescen los hombres la fama, que es bien invisible y esta en el entendimiento." Mercado, *Summa de tratos y contratos*, 159.

when emboldened by the promise of fame, then this quest resembles a prepara-
tory step or exercise for attaining even higher goods.

Restitution was an eminently practical affair. As such, any final judgment
had to be based on realistic expectations in order for it to be enforceable. By
accepting in principle that it was impossible to determine the value of life,
honor, and reputation, moral theologians could preserve the integrity of their
teachings on different orders of goods and better define the scope and aims of
restitution.[102] In cases of homicide or assault resulting in the loss of a limb, the
compensation to victim or family members was to be an estimation of the economic damages that the household was likely to suffer. Calculating the damage
was only the first step to a final decision; other steps included assessing the social and economic status of perpetrators, victims, and relatives and working out
how the restitution would take place—for example, out of the public eye. Beyond the specific guidelines for confessors, restitution also required a different
kind of knowledge, one that came from an intimate familiarity with the community's social dynamics and even the idiosyncrasies of its members. When in
need of such information, confessors were instructed to rely on the judgment
and interpersonal skills of a well-respected community member (*buen varón*,
or *prohom* in Catalan), a figure whose role in the settlement of disputes had
been established in medieval law.[103]

Although it was widely acknowledged that restitution was limited by the
many variables at work in each case—for example, the obligation imposed on
the party at fault should be reasonable so that it could be fulfilled—theologians
had trouble translating immaterial objects into money. This reticence might
have had less to do with residual prejudices against money than the awareness
among educated religious men of the "materialization" of incorporeal things

---

102. "Y la razon y causa deste discrimen es, que estos bienes primeros, como el saber, vivir y
valer exceden tanto en reputacion y estima al dinero que si se recompensan con el aviendose inju-
riosamente quitado, no es por llegar el dinero a su valor, sino porque no ay cosa mejor con que se
pague despues de perdidos." Mercado, *Summa de tratos y contratos*, 136v.

103. Cajetan, *Summa Caietana, trasladada en lingoajem Portugues com annotaoes de muytas
duvidas, & casos de consciencia. Por ho Doctor Paulo de Palacio* (Coimbra: Ioão de Barreyra, 1566),
387v; and Antonio de Córdova, *Tratado de casos de conciencia*, q. 18, 160. On the role of *prohoms*
in the Catalonian Christian and Jewish communities during the Middle Ages, see Elka Klein, *Jews,
Christian Society, and Royal Power in Medieval Barcelona* (Ann Arbor: University of Michigan
Press, 2006), 64–69. The concept was used in reference to the administration of justice in the Valley
of Mexico before the Conquest. Commenting on the body of individuals appointed by the ruler of
Texcoco to administer justice and determine punishments, the mestizo historian Juan Bautista Pomar wrote: "Todos los demás delitos y excesos castigaban a albedrío de buen varón, arrimándose a
lo q[ue] les parecía más justo, y más conforme a razón." "Relación de Tezcoco," in *Relaciones geográficas del siglo XVI: México*, ed. René Acuña, 3 vols. (Mexico City: Universidad Nacional Autónoma
de México, 1986), 3:78.

such as duties or services that resulted from the European economic expansion that began in the thirteenth century.[104] As money continued making inroads in areas traditionally considered beyond quantification, casuists further examined existing distinctions in an effort to better discern (if not preserve) the receding boundaries of the unquantifiable. At the end of the sixteenth century, the Portuguese Franciscan theologian Manuel Rodríguez engaged in this kind of exercise when he elaborated on the difference between the fame earned from a virtuous life and from a high social estate.[105] With the increasingly widespread use of money for restitution, some confessors feared that monetary compensation might soon turn into a universal solution, one ill suited to restoring the honor and reputation of affected individuals.[106] For this reason, confessors insisted that penitents satisfy the offense according to established custom—most commonly, public retraction—unless attendant circumstances prevented it, in addition to any economic reparation.[107] An offender who retracted in public as many times as deemed necessary was considered to have restored the honor or reputation that his words had damaged. And, as Mercado made a point of highlighting, this reparatory act also entailed the shaming of the slanderer necessary to balance the loss of highly valued social currency.[108]

---

104. Janet Coleman, "Medieval Discussions of Property: *Ratio* and *Dominium* according to John of Paris and Marsilius of Padua," *History of Political Thought* 4, no. 2 (1983): 209–28; and Joel Kaye, *Economy and Nature in the Fourteenth Century* (Cambridge: Cambridge University Press, 1998). Kaye's book is an in-depth examination of the theological underpinnings of medieval discussions on money and economic exchange.

105. "Es de notar, que ay gran differencia entre la perdida de la fama, y del estado: porque la fama es una cosa que se sigue a la virtud, la cual es cosa inestimable: mas el estado, y la fama del, no es propriamente fama de bondad, mas es una fama alcançada de obras grandiosas: conviene a saber, la fama del ingenio de las fuerças, ligereza, riquezas, y otras cosas temporales, las quales tienen precio. Por lo qual, aunque la fama del estado parezca mas alta que las riquezas, pues la fama del estado se sirve dellas, poco o casi nada excede el valor dellas." Manuel Rodríguez, *Summa de casos de consciencia*, 2:167.

106. Mercado, in contrast, embraced the use of currency in cases of restitution: "Digo, que quando commodamente se puede bolver la fama en propria specie, se ha de hazer, mas no aviendo opportunidad, o possibilidad, puede y deve restituyr en dinero, especialmente si esta la parte en necessidad. Porque el dinero es precio y valor de todas las cosas temporales, y tanto puede dar, que el leso quede satisfecho y contento." Mercado, *Summa de tratos y contratos*, 171v. But he also noted that monetary compensation was not always welcome by the victims themselves, who were under no obligation to accept it: "Y aun quando fuere evidente y notorio que no han de querer, no ay necessidad de hazer les offertas, en especial, si teme lo tomarán por affrenta. Que ay personas que tienen por injuria rescebir dinero, aviendo rescebido semejante agravio, y a quien se les haría mas grave, applacarse con oro, que suffrir la muerte del hijo, o del padre." Mercado, *Summa de tratos y contratos*, 154v. Taylor has explored the way that disputes over debts in seventeenth-century Castile revealed the relation between economy and honor. Taylor, *Honor and Violence in Golden Age Spain*, 119–29.

107. Mercado, *Summa de tratos y contratos*, 163–63v.

108. "Ansi la regla mas acertada, y cierta, para cumplir con su obligacion, que es bolverle su fama cumplida, es desdezirse, cuantas vezes fuere menester, y padescer tanta verguença, por una, que tan en daño del proximo se desvergonço." Mercado, *Summa de tratos y contratos*, 163v.

Viewed from a theological perspective, earthly possessions eloquently expressed human control over the material world. Worldly possessions were also a source of potential distress, not because of any particular feature of the things themselves—since they are morally neutral—but the unavoidable consequences of living in society and being exposed to its members' moral weaknesses. The more men devoted themselves to honor and fame, the more vulnerable they became. Laws spelled out how far individuals could go to defend their honor, but moralists and religious reformers did not fail to notice that laws could not protect people from hasty decisions that could ultimately jeopardize their salvation. For instance, individuals might find themselves unnecessarily risking their own or someone else's life when doing so could and should have been avoided. In holding that Christians were under no obligation to defend their property, theologians tried to clearly chart the safest moral path without losing sight of the fact that this path might run counter to existing social expectations and norms in some circumstances.[109] Regardless of whether these norms represented a burden, a confirmation of privilege, or both, confessors were instructed to be mindful of their importance in the lives of penitents. Theologians who had come to accept that homicide was justified under certain circumstances, as when committed to prevent theft, were inclined to conclude that it was even more justified when a victim of physical assault found it impossible to leave the scene with his honor intact, since honor exceeded material possessions in value.[110]

Honor's special status vis-à-vis the material and the immaterial informed the competing opinions in religious circles regarding its relative worth in comparison to other goods subject to restitution, such as life and material possessions. Theologians suspected that, in failing to discern which goods were more important than others, a growing number of Spaniards risked their salvation by carelessly choosing to settle matters of honor through duels.[111] Acknowl-

---

109. Francisco de Vitoria, *On Homicide, and Commentary on Summa Theologiae II-IIae Q. 64*, ed. and trans. John P. Doyle (Milwaukee: Marquette University Press, 1997), 97.

110. "Y lo mesmo nos parece, quando no se defendiendo con armas, quedaría injuriado en su honra, o persona, pues segun lo susodicho, por defender la hazienda, puede matar, y la honrra vale mas que la hazienda, y la injuria personal excede a qualquiera de la hazienda." Martín de Azpilcueta, *Manual de confessores, y penitentes, que clara y brevemente contiene la universal, y particular decission de quasi todas la dubdas, que en las confessiones suelen occurrir de los peccados, absoluciones, restituciones, censuras, irregularidades* (Toledo: Juan Ferrer, 1554), 103; for Vitoria's discussion of the possible solutions to this scenario, see *On Homicide, and Commentary on Summa Theologiae II-IIae Q. 64*, a. 7, 201. The most immediate point of reference for homicide and defense of property was Cajetan, who found justification in Ambrose: "E a quem lhe quer levar o que lhe e necessario, nao somente pra viver, mas ainda tambem pera viver virtuosamente, qual e a fazenda, sua, ou dos suos." *Summa Caietana*, 210v.

111. The most comprehensive study of duel in early modern Spain to date is Claude Chauchadis,

edging that theologians had different opinions on the matter, Mercado sided with those who, like Martín de Azpilcueta, thought that Christians should put life before honor, but honor before property when facing imminent danger from an assailant.[112] This scale was somewhat relative, however, owing both to the lack of expert consensus and the tendency for the analysis to shift depending whose actions were under scrutiny. Thus when turning his attention to *murmuratio* (slander) and related sins of the tongue, Azpilcueta concluded that, when committed by slanderers, the offense amounted to homicide, recasting the traditional and abstract formula that the tongue kills in concrete legal terms.[113] The bluntness of this assertion could just be a rhetorical flourish

---

La loi du duel: Le code du point d'honneur dans l'Espagne des XVIe–XVIIe siècles (Toulouse: Presses Universitaires du Mirail, 1997). On the positions adopted by theologians and the church, see 173–204. The Italian *tratattistica* on matters of honor had considerable influence in Spain; still worth consulting are Frederick Robertson Bryson, *The Point of Honor in Sixteenth-Century Italy: An Aspect of the Life of the Gentleman* (New York: Columbia University / Publications of the Institute of French Studies, 1935); F. Erspamer, *La biblioteca di don Ferrante: Duello ed onore nella cultura del Cinquecento* (Rome: Bulzoni, 1982); and Carlo Dionisotti, "La letteratura italiana nell'età del concilio di Trento," in *Geografia e storia della letteratura italiana* (Turin: Einaudi, 1999), 227–54.

112. "Tratemos de la satisfacion, que se ha de hazer, de la fama y honra, cosas que en valor tiene en segundo lugar. Y aun son de suyo tan amables, y de muchos en tanto tenidos que les paresce aun mejores, que el mesmo ser y vivir natural. Pero de los varones que florescieron en sabiduria, cuyo entendimiento fue illustrado, y el animo ageno de presumpcion, o passion, de tal modo ensalçan la honra y fama, que la ponen sobre todas las riquezas, siguiendo en esto la escriptura divina, mas debaxo, y a los pies de la vida. A quien del todo dan el primado. A estos segui, como era razon en la particion passada, y seguire en lo restante de la obra." Mercado, *Summa de tratos y contratos*, book 6, chap. 8, 158; Martín de Azpilcueta, *Tractado de alabança y murmuracion*, 120–21. A different view can be found in Huarte de San Juan's ruminations on the dispositions necessary for the military arts: "De manera que, según esto, no es repugnancia juntarse la prudencia con el ánimo y valentía; porque el prudente y sabio tiene entendido que por el ánima ha de poner la honra, y por la honra, la vida, y por la vida, la hacienda; y así lo secuta." *Examen de ingenios*, ed. Guillermo Serés (Madrid: Cátedra, 1989), chap. 13, 534.

113. "Todo murmurador es homicida y matador." Martín de Azpilcueta, *Tractado de alabança y murmuracion*, 218. The term *susurratio* was used interchangeably with *murmuratio*. Andrés de Escobar, *Modus confitendi* (Paris: Antoine Caillaut, ca. 1483), A4r. Originally identified and discussed in the context of monastic life, in the Middle Ages the sins of the tongue began to be scrutinized and dutifully labeled in light of their effects on society at large. Medieval theologians distinguished between face-to face offenses (*contumelia*) from those committed in the victim's absence (*detractio*). By the sixteenth century, competing classifications and terminologies appear to have done more to obfuscate than clarify what distinguished each sin. This was the prevailing sentiment among Thomists at the time. By way of illustration, Azpilcueta reported that a gentleman once asked Cardinal Cajetan, a highly esteemed authority on Aquinas, why Aquinas and Cajetan himself neglected to mention *murmuración* as a sin. The cardinal responded by pointing out that Aquinas taught that *murmuración* was neither a genus nor a species, since it was present in every sin of the tongue. Azpilcueta, *Tratado de alabança y murmuracion*, 224. Aquinas's alleged oversight was also explained away via Cajetan by Bartolomé de Medina, *Breve instruccion de como se a de administrar el sacramento de la penitencia*, 210v. By favoring this inclusive meaning, Azpilcueta sought to restore a distinction between *murmuración* and the sin of *detracción* (or *detractio*) that had been lost. For a comprehensive study on the subject, see Carla Casagrande and Silvana Vecchio, *I peccati della lingua: Disciplina ed etica della parola nella cultura medievale* (Rome: Istituto Enciclopedia Italiana, 1987). On blasphemy in Spain, see Maureen Flynn, "Blasphemy and the Play of Anger in Sixteenth-Century Spain," *Past & Present* 149 (1995): 29–56.

intended to convey the gravity of a sin that, as writers before him had complained, remained stubbornly ignored. But it should also be remembered that rumor and anonymous accusations could land an individual in the jails of the Inquisition, as eventually happened to Azpilcueta's old friend, the theologian and archbishop of Toledo, Bartolomé de Carranza. Thus, Azpilcueta had good reason to consider the gravity of the sins of the tongue in light of new social and political realities. In any event, Azpilcueta's unqualified word choice signals an unmistakable reassessment of the labels attached to verbal offenses in medieval classificatory systems of sins, labels that would be abandoned over the course of the sixteenth century. Medieval theologians, considering sins such as *detractio* (slander) from the perspective of the sinner's intention, construed them as spiritual homicide (*homicidium spirituale*).[114] Later writers, perhaps prompted by perceived inconsistent or unclear Scholastic classifications, referred to *detractio* as a "quasi quoddam homicidium spirituale occultum."[115] It seems that the progressive disappearance of the label "spiritual" is the result of moral theologians' movement away from medieval models of analyzing sins. For our purposes, it is important to highlight that when Azpilcueta equated *detractio* to homicide he was redefining the sin according to what was then understood to be a crime with far more serious consequences that his forebears had thought.

While sixteenth-century theologians brought new insight into the dynamics of Spanish society through their analysis of the sins of the tongue, theirs would not be the last word on the topic. Even if, as was commonly observed, Spaniards were obsessed with honor, "slander" may not have meant the same thing across social hierarchies. By 1600, slander had become a topic of conversation in the political and intellectual circles associated with the court, where Neostoicism had established itself as the doctrine du jour. Politicians did not just need reminding that slanderers were sinners; they also needed advice for dealing with being the object of gossip and calumny. Drawing on classical authors such as Lucian, Justus Lipsius penned an *oratio* offering such advice.[116] In

---

114. "Item est homicidium corporale et est homicidium spirituale; corporale quo homo occiditur corporaliter; spirituale quo spiritualiter et quadam fictione iuris quasi occidi videtur, quod fit plurivus modis, odiendo, detrahendo, opprimendo, male consulendo, nocendo, victum subtrahendo." Bernardus Papiensis, *Summa Decretalium*, ed. Theodor Laspeyres (Ratisbon: Joseph Manz, 1860), 220. See also Raymond of Penyafort, *Summa de poenitentia, et matrimonio cum glossis Ioannis de Friburgo* (Rome: Johannes Tallini, 1603; Farnborough, UK: Gregg Press, 1967), book 2, t. 1, 147. For an overview on "spiritual homicide" in medieval sources, see Judith Shaw, "Corporal and Spiritual Homicide, the Sin of Wrath, and the 'Parson's Tale,'" *Traditio* 38 (1982): 281–300.

115. Matthew of Krakow, *De modo confitendi et de puritate conscientiae* (Paris: [Guy Marchant?] for Denis Roce, ca. 1501), chap. 21, 18v. Most likely because it was attributed to Aquinas and printed under his name, this small treatise enjoyed wide circulation. A brief description can be found in Pierre Michaud-Quantin, *Sommes de casuistique et manuels de confession au moyen âge (xii–xvi siècles)* (Louvain: Edit. Nauwelaerts/Lille: Librairie Giard, 1962), 79–80.

116. Toon Van Houdt and Jan Papy, "*Modestia, Constantia, Fama*: Towards a Literary and Phil-

1626 Sancho Bravo de Lagunas dedicated his translation of Lucian's treatise to the Count Duke of Olivares.[117] Three years earlier, *Espejo de murmuradores* by Carlos de Tapia, Marquis of Belmonte, was translated into Spanish from Italian by Tapia's son, the nobleman and occasional playwright Francisco de Tapia y Leyva.[118]

Law and Christian Precepts: Honor Translated

The contested perspectives on honor found in Spain acquired an entirely new dimension when Spanish legal institutions, values, and practices were transferred to the American colonies, where friars and administrators tried to reconcile European and indigenous social notions, concepts, and norms. The friars' role in the transmission of law went beyond fulfilling the occasional royal request. It was through the friars that the Mexican Indians readied themselves for confession, becoming familiar with laws, legal notions, and social values. These teachings were often shaped by the friars' conflicting views about both the society they had left behind and the one taking shape before their eyes. Almost inevitably, these and other tensions become apparent in the missionaries' approach to notions of honor, reputation, and related concepts as they sought to make Christianity intelligible to the Nahuas.

In 1569, the Franciscan Fr. Alonso de Molina's two bilingual (Nahuatl-Spanish) manuals for confessors were published. Molina built each work around an exposition of sins, structured in the form of questions asked by a priest and organized into two consecutive sections that followed the Ten Commandments and the Seven Deadly Sins, respectively. The *Manipulus curatorum*, a fourteenth-century manual for priests by the Spaniard Guido de Monte Roquerio that the First Church Council of Mexico recommended for the preparation of confessors, also used this format of two sections that cover similar material but are organized under different principles—along with the use of questions, although only in the section dealing with deadly sins.[119]

---

osophical Interpretation of Lipsius's *De Calumia Oratio*," in *Iustus Lipsius Europae Lumen et Columen: Proceedings of the International Colloquium, Leuven 17–19 September 1997*, ed. G. Tournoy, J. de Landtsheer, and J. Papy (Leuven: Leuven University Press, 1999), 186–220.

117. *Discurso de Luciano que no deve sarse credito facilmente a la murmuracion* (Lisbon: Pedro Craesbeeck, 1626).

118. Carlos de Tapia, Marqués de Belmonte, *Espejo de murmuradores: Traduzido de la lengua italiana por Francisco de Tapia y Leyva* (Madrid: Viuda de Alonso Martín, 1623).

119. Recommended for confessors were "una Suma Silvestrina, o Angelica, Manipulus Curatorum, y un Confesionario, como *Defecerunt*, u otro semejante, y la Suma Caetana." *Concilios provinciales primero, y segundo, celebrados en la muy noble, y muy leal ciudad de Mexico* (Mexico

Both of Molina's manuals follow the same expository sequence, dealing first with the commandments followed by the deadly sins. If this arrangement meant to reflect a hierarchy of sorts (as may very well be the case), it was in agreement with the importance that the First Church Council in 1555 had assigned to the commandments in the teaching of Christian doctrine.[120]

Within the Ten Commandments, the injunction against homicide had come to include other transgressions such as wounding, maiming, and even wishing someone's death. Among the questions that confessors were to ask Nahua penitents regarding the fifth commandment ("Thou shalt not kill"), Molina's *Confessionario mayor* includes the following: "Have you hurt anyone with a stick? Have you broken anyone's arm or leg? Have you made a dent in anyone's head or hurt anyone's eye? Have you grabbed [*mesaste*] or kicked anyone?"[121] If the penitent admitted to any of these offenses, the confessor was to inform him or her of the obligation to make proper restitution to the victim or the victim's relatives. The actions condemned under this commandment differed in both seriousness and kind, as an examination of them in light of secular law will show.

The confessor's questions refer to common punishable crimes that had been

---

City: Antonio de Hogal, 1769), 110. The *Manipulus curatorum* enjoyed a long life in manuscript form; it was first published in Paris in 1473 and many times after that across Europe. In Spain, its publication in Zaragoza in 1475 gives this work a special place in the history of the book in the Iberian Peninsula. On the printing of the work and its intended use in the instruction of the clergy, see Manuel José Pedraza Gracia, "La introducción de la imprenta en Zaragoza: La producción y distribución del *Manipulus Curatorum* de Guido de Monterroterio, Zaragoza, Matheus Flanders, 15 de octubre de 1475," *Gutenberg-Jahrbuch* 71 (1996): 65–71. New and much-needed documentary evidence of the life of the author of the *Manipulus* can be found in Conrado Guardiola, "Los primeros datos documentales sobre Guido de Monte Roquerio, autor del 'Manipulus Curatorum,'" *Hispania: Revista española de historia* 48, no. 170 (1988): 797–826. The book was included in the *Index*, and copies were confiscated from Mexican clergy. Fernández del Castillo, *Libros y libreros en el siglo XVI*, 472, 475, 477.

120. "Otrosi, que los instruyan en los Mandamientos, y santos Sacramentos de la Iglesia, y en los diez Mandamientos de nuestra ley Christiana, amonestandoles se guarden de los traspasar, y venir contra ellos. Assimismo les digan, quales son los siete Pecados mortales, para que major puena guardarse de caer en ellos." *Concilios provinciales primero, y segundo*, 38. The recommendations of the Second Council included more recent works such as the *Summa* by Martín de Azpilcueta: "algunas Sumas de casos de conciencia en latin, o en romance, assi como la Suma de Navarro, o *Defecerunt* de S. Antonino, o Silvestrina, o Angelica, 199. An arrangement similar to Molina's (including the use of questions) can be found in Martín de León's *Camino del cielo*. For sake of both accuracy and expediency, the author made clear that he had decided to focus on deadly sins exclusively. *Camino del cielo*, 109v.

121. "Heriste a alguno, distele de palos; quebrastele el brazo, o la pierna; o hendistele la cabesa: o quebrastele el ojo; mesaste a alguno, o distele de coces . . . ?" Molina, *Confessionario mayor*, 30v. Molina's short manual for confessors does not depart from this sequence: "Maltrataste a alguno, distele de palos quebrastele el braço, quebrastele la cabeça, mesastele, o distele con algo en la cabeça, o distele de coxcorrones, o de cabeçadas, hendistele la cabeça?" *Confessionario breve, en lengua Mexicana y Castellana* (Mexico City: Antonio de Espinosa, 1565), 9v.

codified since early medieval times; the law traditionally assigned the aggressor different penalties, according to the circumstances and social rank of the individuals involved. Molina's definitions by the injured body part and the instrument that caused the injury give the passage an archaic flavor that recalls the old *fueros* (municipal codes) in which physical violence could extend to an attack on the victim's honor if the injury were serious enough.[122] The offenses at hand, considered in light of these old *fueros*, may fall into what was for a long time a nebulous category of crimes against honor (or what in Spanish legal terminology is known as *injuria fáctica*).[123] Among them *messar* (*momotzoa* in Nahuatl), the act of grabbing or plucking a part of the body such as hair or a beard, became the best example of a crime in which the affront caused by the act was acknowledged to be more important than the act itself.[124]

The absence of clear boundaries between symbolic and physical injury, characteristic of the Spanish *fueros*, eventually gave way to the conceptual demarcation of a separate legal category of crimes against a person's honor.[125] This shift, however, had little impact on the actions that Molina described, the meaning of which remained culture-bound.

Around the turn of the century, the Franciscan Fr. Juan Bautista Viseo, who wrote extensively on the difficulties that confessors of Indians faced and was thoroughly familiar with Molina's works, gave the fifth commandment a more systematic treatment, guiding the penitent through a variety of offenses from homicide to insults. Significantly, he distinguished between acts of aggression specifically aimed at the victim's head from others such as slapping, attacking with a stick, or breaking someone's arm.[126] As for the seriousness of those acts

---

122. As can be expected, penitentials reflected many of the features found in the *fueros*. For example the *Paenitentiale Silense* registered the following offenses and penalties under homicide: "Qui percussierit et sanguine fuderit, xl dies peniteat. . . . Si per poculum, x annos peniteat." Ludger Körntgen and Francis Bezler, eds., *Paenitentialia Hispaniae* (Turnholt: Brepols, 1998), 23.

123. "Si algun omne tira por el pie a otro omne libre sin derecho, o por los cabellos, si non paresce nenguna sennal de laga, por cada uno destos tuertos de suso dichos el que lo fizo peche L. sueldos al qui lo recibió el tuerto." *Fuero juzgo* in *Los códigos españoles concordados y anotados*, vol. 1, book 12, title 8, law 8, 193–94. A detailed list of offenses arranged according to the affected body part can be found in the *Fuero viejo de Castilla*, in the same volume at book 2, title 1, law 6, 274. See also *The Code of Cuenca: Municipal Law on the Twelfth-Century Castilian Frontier*, trans. and ed. James F. Powers (Philadelphia: University of Pennsylvania Press, 2000), chap. 12, laws 4–18, 86–89.

124. Regarding the plucking of a beard, the old *fueros* distinguished different degrees of seriousness by measuring how much beard had been pulled. See *Los códigos españoles concordados y anotados*, vol. 1, book 2, title 1, law 2, 273.

125. Rafael Serra Ruiz has painstakingly traced the evolution of the concept of *injuria* in medieval Spanish law. *Honor, honra e injuria en el derecho medieval español* (Murcia: Sucesores de Nogués, 1969), especially 240–77. On the judicial process around *injuria*, see Marta Madero, *Manos violentas, palabras vedadas: La injuria en Castilla y León (siglos XIII–XV)* (Madrid: Taurus, 1992).

126. "Quebraste la cabeça a alguno o mesastele o diste con algo en la cabeza, o distele de coscorrones, o de cabezadas, o hendistele la cabeça?" and "Por ventura diste de bofetadas a alguno

aimed at the victim's head, it will suffice to recall López's reports of Indians slapping and shaving Spaniards.

Although Molina followed the traditional pattern and reserved discussion of verbal offenses for the section on the eighth commandment ("Thou shalt not bear false witness"), his discussion of the fifth commandment included the question whether the penitent had ever called someone a "sodomite." In the *fueros* "sodomite" was one of five words that were considered to damage someone's honor when used as insults.[127] *Cuiloni*, the Nahuatl word for sodomite that Molina and other authors employed, appears in sources as an insult that the Nahuas directed at Tezcatlipoca, an elusive and powerful deity that they called *cuilonpol*, or "big sodomite," in a form of ritual imprecation.[128]

By Molina's time, Spanish law drew a clear distinction between injuries to body and to honor; in everyday life, however, this distinction proved somewhat illusory. In the case of the colonies, the crown did not consider verbal offenses (*palabras injuriosas*) between Indians serious enough to merit legal process so long as it was not aggravated by the use of weapons.[129] This law—which did not preclude the resolution of the conflict by recourse to third parties or lo-

---

o de palos o le quebraste el braço?" Juan Bautista, *Confessionario en lengua mexicana y castellana* (Tlatelolco: Melchior Ocharte, 1599), 47v and 48, respectively.

127. The others were *gafo* (leper), *cornudo* (cuckold), *traidor* (traitor), and *hereje* (heretic)—and for a woman, *puta* (whore). *Novísima Recopilación*, book 12, title 25, law 1, 86. See also the *Ordenanzas reales de Castilla* in *Los códigos españoles*, book 8, title 9, law 2, 6:510. The *Fuero juzgo* includes a different set of insults; see *Los códigos españoles*, book 12, title 3, laws 1, 2, 3, 4, 5, and 6, 191–93. Some religious writers found some words to be more hurtful than others. When discussing the fifth commandment the Franciscan Francisco Ortíz Lucio singled out words like *ladrón, ciego*, and also "poor." *Compendio de todas las summas que comunmente andan, y recopilacion de todos los casos de conciencia mas importantes y comunes, assi para el penitente examinar su conciencia, como para el confessor exercitar bien su oficio* (Mallorca: Gabriel Guasp, 1599), 87. As mentioned above, the social status of victim and offender ultimately determined the seriousness of all verbal offenses. The Augustinian Juan Henríquez, for example, following Pedro de Navarra, concluded that while it was a mortal sin to call a nobleman "insane," the same word applied to "un hombre común" was not. Ioan Henríquez, *Compendio de casos morales ordinarios* (Seville: Francisco de Lyra, 1634), 58.

128. Sahagún, *Florentine Codex*, book 4, chap. 9, 35. See also Bernardino de Sahagún, *Coloquios y doctrina cristiana con que los frailes de San Francisco, enviados por el papa Adriano IV y por el emperador Carlos V, convirtieron a los indios de la Nueva España, en lengua mexicana y española de Bernardino de Sahagún* (1524), ed. Miguel León-Portilla (Mexico City: Universidad Nacional Autónoma de México, 1986), chap. 4, 125. The use of *cuiloni* as an insult appears associated with the domain of the devil in the "general confession" found in Martín de León, *Camino del cielo*, 110v. For a discussion of the term *cuiloni* and its meanings in precolonial and colonial times, see Pete Sigal, "The Cuiloni, the Patlache, and the Abominable Sin: Homosexualities in Early Colonial Nahua Society," *Hispanic American Historical Review* 85, no. 4 (2005): 555–93.

129. León Pinelo, *Recopilación de las Indias*, book 6, title 1, 13, 2:1568–69. This law appears to draw from a similar one dating from 1518 that focused exclusively on the use of "palabras livianas." See *Novísima recopilación de las leyes de España* in *Los códigos españoles*, book 12, title 25, law 2, 10:87. In the case of verbal offenses involving clergymen, conciliar legislation took a similar approach, leaving it to the offended party to bring charges. *Concilium Mexicanum Provinciale III*, book 1, title 9, §4, 64–65.

cal procedures—differed from Molina's teachings on the fifth commandment in that it placed offenses against honor on a par with physical injuries. Going beyond secular laws, the missionaries reserved for themselves the duties of interpreting and arbitrating matters of honor for the Indians, much as they had with other cultural matters.

There were established precedents in manuals for confessors and commentaries on the commandments for the inclusion of offenses against honor, particularly insults, with homicide and physical attacks. Hernando de Talavera's *Confessional* (1496), for example, made clear that in addition to death, the fifth commandment prohibited any type of injury to someone's body or reputation.[130] Insults and hurtful remarks about a person, whether present or not, belonged to the category of injuries to reputation.[131] In the sense that such actions could lead to an individual's "social death" or because of a threat to a nonphysical quality intimately identified with the physical person, some authors on the fifth commandment, including Guido de Monte Roquerio in the fourteenth-century *Manipulus curatorum* mentioned above, used the expression "spiritual homicide" to better highlight the seriousness that the church placed on the "sins of the tongue."[132] Odd but instructive is the way that Molina, a careful examiner of cultural differences, chose to present these seemingly alien distinctions to the Nahuas. Molina's treatment stands out for both its rather oblique way of making reference to honor and for the inclusion of highly culturally codified gestures such as *messar*. The treatment of the fifth commandment found in the 1565 *Doctrina Christiana breve* by the Dominican Domingo de la Anunciación is remarkably close to Molina's in form, yet it differs from the Franciscan's in that it spells out that physical aggression may damage the body as well as honor.[133]

Authors of manuals for confessors made decisions about what to include

130. "El quinto mandamiento es no mataras. En el qual vieda nuestro señor no solamente la muerte corporal y qualquier lesion y injuria que al cuerpo del proxymo ynjustamente se pueda hazer o a su fama." Hernando de Talavera, *Confessional*, in *Breve y muy provechosa doctrina de lo que deve saber todo christiano* . . . (Granada: Meinardo Ungut and Juan Pegnitzer, ca. 1496), F7v.

131. Talavera, *Confessional*, F8.

132. *Detractio* fits into this category when born out of hatred. *Manipulus curatorum officia sacerdotum* (Cologne: Heinrich Quentell, 1498), T4r.

133. "Y assi mismo nos manda que tampoco le offendamos ni lisiemos la mano, el pie, el ojo ni dar bofetada ni de açotes ni con palo ni con otras cosa alguna ni que le hagamos injuria." Domingo de la Anunciación, *Doctrina christiana breve y compendiosa por via de dialogo entre un maestro y un discipulo, sacada en lengua castellana y mexicana* (Mexico City: Pedro Ocharte, 1565), 46v. Anunciación's use of the word *injuria* (which he renders in Nahuatl as *pinahualiztli*, a deverbative noun from *pinahua*, "to feel shame") brings honor into focus. The *Doctrina de los dominicos* includes shaming someone but makes no reference to the means employed. *Doctrina cristiana en lengua española y mexicana por los religiosos de la orden de Santo Domingo* (1548) (Madrid: Ediciones Cultura Hispánica, 1944), L4r.

under the fifth commandment and what to leave out or deal with elsewhere. In making these decisions, they wrestled with the problems posed by offenses against honor. For instance, the Franciscan Fr. Francisco de Alcocer, the Spanish author of a *Confessionario breve* (1568) that enjoyed wide circulation, noted that the fifth commandment was mainly concerned with homicide and physical aggression. But he also recognized that physical assaults may sometimes bring dishonor to the victim; when this was the case, the aggressor was required to make restitution for both the physical injury and the affront.[134] For all his efforts to narrowly define the commandment, Alcocer also chose to include verbal offenses under it, a decision he felt the need to clarify since such offenses may be considered under the eighth commandment. He explained that "dishonor can proceed from a slap, [and from] sticks as well as from words," and that tradition had associated all these acts as sins.[135] Although he was aware that there was room to refine the treatment of sins within the scheme of the commandments, Alcocer saw no reason to resist tradition. Unlike the penitents that Molina's questions were designed to address, Alcocer's penitents hardly needed to be reminded of the many ways in which they could be affronted.[136]

Molina's interpretation, as well as the systematic approach employed by Juan Bautista, raises questions about the means and goals of cross-cultural translation. Considering these bilingual manuals from the perspective of the confessor or the Indian penitent may give rise to different explanations of the criteria that guided the choices of these two missionaries. For instance, Molina's preference for a list of specific actions over the more general formulations favored in contemporary laws may have been an attempt on his part to make the fifth commandment more easily accessible to Nahua penitents. Or Juan Bautista's more methodical approach may have been an expeditious way for the confessor to gather information from penitents without burdening them with

---

134. "o si de los palos, o bofetón resultó deshonra como se suele seguir, que ay obligación de restituyr el daño, y satisfazer la injuria, y deshonra." Francisco de Alcocer, *Confessionario breve y muy provechoso para los penitentes* (Salamanca: Juan de Cánova, 1568), 68v.

135. "Las injurias de palabras y maldiciones puse aquí, aunque tambien se pudieran poner en el octavo mandamiento, porque la deshonra también sucede de bofetón, y palos como de palabras. Lo segundo lo tracté quí por ser ordinario yr encadenados estos pecados, conviene saber, dezir palabras injuriosas, intentar, o hazer alguna injuria corporal, y echarse maldiciones." Alcocer, *Confessionario breve*, 70v.

136. Many seventeenth-century authors reserved the fifth commandment for the commission of physical harm either by deed or thought. In Mexico, Bartholome de Alva and Gabino Carta were two such authors. Bartholome de Alva, *Confessionario mayor y menor en lengua mexicana* (Mexico City: Francisco Salbago, 1634), 21v. "Prohíbese en este mandamiento principalmente el homicidio, y qualquier daño que se haze contra la vida, y salud corporal del próximo." Gabino Carta, *Guía de confessores* (Mexico City: Biuda de Bernardo Calderón, 1653), 60v. See also Juan Machado de Cháves, *Perfeto confessor, y cura de almas* (Madrid: Viuda de Francisco Martínez, 1655), book 2, part 3, treatise 16, 297 and ss.

technical distinctions. Whatever the reasons, the passages in question reveal honor's important place in the minds of the colonizers and show how difficult it was at times for missionaries to separate unwelcome secular notions from religious precepts.

Teaching Christian precepts to Mexican Indians raised the question of how to talk about honor across cultures. The inherent difficulty was not so much a conceptual one of the translatability of alien concepts—a type of challenge that Spanish friars had learned to relish—but rather a moral one, given the deep reservations that friars and reformers shared toward a notion of honor that many Spaniards had embraced with an almost religious fervor. As expected, these reservations found their way into the friars' religious teachings in the hope that they would help shape the Nahuas' view of the secular world.

Through instruction on Christian doctrine and sermons, the Nahuas were asked to share the contempt of the friars and the church for the earthly pursuit of social status and power. In a context of unprecedented social mobility that permitted the questioning of traditional sites of authority, these teachings amounted to a plea to reverse time, to return to mythologized old ways. This is apparent in Molina's confession manuals, where he keenly examines the aspirations and weaknesses of Nahua social types. He deemed it necessary for Indian penitents to be asked about what he considered a serious sin: "Did you aspire to obtain a higher rank or honor? Did you wish to become a powerful lord?"[137] This negative view of the quest for earthly goods, which closely reflected monastic values, was not new. Given the many possibilities open to *macehuales* and Indian noblemen not from cacique families, Molina feared that this somewhat minor and often overlooked fault could take on unexpected significance by contributing to the erosion of traditional local authorities and the old social order.

Friars like Molina emphasized the religious dimension of all authority, and initially had considerable input in drafting laws applied to the Indians. A 1546 decree made baptism a precondition for Indians to hold public office.[138] The decree most likely aimed to offer local elites, particularly those members not yet fully committed to the new religion, an incentive to do so; in turn, the Christianization of the native elite was considered key to spreading Catholicism among the lower classes. For Nahua noblemen, baptism marked only the beginning of a religious commitment that could expose them to accusations of having violated Christian precepts and jeopardize their positions in public

---

137. "Desseaste alguna gran dignidad, honra, o cobdiciaste algún gran señorío y governación?" Molina, *Confessionario mayor*, 65r and 78r.
138. Kellogg and Sell, "We Want to Give Them Laws," 353.

office.[139] Simply put, the bar for them was raised higher, and is apparent in the *probanzas de méritos* (proofs of merits) that Nahua noblemen submitted to request recognition for service they or a relative rendered to the crown. As part of this particular legal procedure, for example, in 1536 Don Juan de Guzmán Itzlolinqui, a local lord from Coyoacán, produced witnesses to attest not only that he was a Christian and fulfilled his sacramental obligations, but also that he surpassed all his Indian neighbors in knowledge of Christian doctrine.[140] Along the same lines, penitents from the Nahua nobility were admonished not to take pride in their social rank: "Did you praise yourself by saying very flattering things in front of others because you are of noble lineage and kinship, saying things such as 'I was born from powerful lords and very noble people and I am hair, nails, and part and parcel of them'?"[141] In addressing honor and ancestry in the new Christian society, Molina resorted to the repertoire of metaphors taken from the stylized speeches of senior Nahua noblemen that the missionaries had transcribed and studied. Sahagún showed that he, too, was familiar with the Nahua expression when he included a variation of it in book 6 of his *General History.*[142]

The friars' interest in the Nahua conception of honor is evidenced by Fr. Alonso de Molina's lexicographical research that resulted in the compilation of three bilingual dictionaries: *Aquí comiença un Vocabulario en la lengua castellana y mexicana*, published in 1555, followed by a revised version in 1571, under the title *Vocabulario en lengua castellana y mexicana y mexicana y castellana.* Comparing these to bilingual dictionaries published in Spain makes it immediately apparent that the lexical entries were selected to serve as a linguistic tool for preachers and confessors. The 1571 edition contains, for example, new entries related to "renown" (*fama*) as well as "praise" (*alabanza*). In the case of "praise," the entries do not refer to devotion or ritual action but rather to the dangers of the deadly sin of pride, and include "praising oneself by lying about

---

139. See, for example, the case studied by Judith Francis Zeitlin and Lillian Thomas in "Spanish Justice and the Indian cacique: Disjunctive Political Systems in Sixteenth-Century Tehuantepec," *Ethnohistory* 39, no. 3 (Summer 1992): 285–315.

140. Emma Pérez-Rocha and Rafael Tena, *La nobleza indígena*, 109.

141. "Allabastete mucho y dixiste muchos bienes de ti, delante otros, por ser tu de noble linaje y parentela, diziendo, a mi me engendraron grandes señores, y muy nobles personas, y soy cabellos, uñas, parte y pedaço dellos?" Molina, *Confessionario mayor*, 78r. In Antonine of Florence: "Si alabo a si: o a su linaje.mor[tale], en tres maneras contra la Gloria de dios o despreciando al otro." And: "Alabastes a vos mesmo: o a vuestro linage: allende de lo que erades segun verdad por dar a entender que valaides mas: o que erades mejor que los otros?" Anthonino de Florencia, *La summa de confession llamada defecerunt de fray Anthonino arçobispo de florencia del orden de los predicadores* (Salamanca: Hans Giesser, 1500), 29.

142. "one's hair, one's nails, one's spines, one's thorns, one's beard, one's eyebrows, one's chips, one's fragment." *Florentine Codex*, book 6, chap. 43, 245.

some deed," and closer to the example from the *Confessionario mayor*, "prais-ing oneself with arrogance." Even more exhaustive than Molina's dictionaries in this regard was Juan de Córdoba's 1578 *Vocabulario castellano-zapoteco*.[143] I will come back to the connection between honor and pride in the teachings of the Mexican friars in the conclusion to this chapter.

Despite their critical view of secular and indigenous notions of honor as-sociated with ancestry and social rank, the missionaries relied on these same notions to articulate Christian teachings for a Nahua audience. Molina did just this in a sermon on the sacrament of confirmation, equating the sacrament to the promotion of *macehuales* to the high ranks of the Nahua warriors. He as-sured his audience that those who have been confirmed "will have much honor there in paradise and glory of Heaven, and those who have not received it will not be so renowned and honored," in the same way that knights are more es-teemed than "*macehuales* and humble people."[144] At a time when Nahua war-riors were long gone, and the nobility facing a steady decline, Christianity offered continuity with the past, the accommodation of Nahua secular aspira-tions, and even the replacement of those aspirations with higher, spiritual goals. Molina's sermon, with its promise of spiritual leveling, offered less comfort to the challenged Nahua nobility as the signs of social leveling became more ap-parent in their daily life.

Following well-established tradition, Molina pointed out that penitents who had damaged someone's reputation (*fama*) had to make appropriate resti-tution or could be denied confession. Juan Bautista repeated the same warning years later.[145] Such references do not indicate that confessors actually enforced this restriction. By the end of the sixteenth century, when Juan Bautista was writing, honor no longer seems to be a key concept for friars such as Molina to articulate their teaching of Christianity to appeal to a Nahua audience aware of the new possibilities for social mobility. Juan Bautista conceded that, when an Indian damaged another's reputation, for example, by spreading unfounded ru-mors, the penitent should be asked to make restitution only if the parties were

---

143. Córdoba's treatment of *jactarse* (to boast) in his *Vocabulario* is a case in point. Whereas Molina provided only one entry, Córdoba made room for expressions that covered different aspects of the boasting, such as whether it was done publicly or inwardly. He also included entries that directly addressed the concerns of confessors: boasting of one's lineage, of sins, of things, of deeds, etc. Córdoba, *Vocabulario castellano-zapoteco*, s.v. "jactarse."

144. Molina, *Confessionario mayor*, 92. On Molina's sermon, see Pardo, *The Origins of Mexican Catholicism*, 65–78.

145. "Avias de restituyr la honrra a alguno y no se la restituyste? / Cuix tictemepilizquia in temahuizco auh ahmo ticchiuh?" Juan Bautista, *Confessionario en lengua mexicana*, 41. See also Molina, *Confessionario mayor*, 53r.

nobles steeped in Spanish customs.[146] Juan Bautista's position thus partially co-incided with the approach found in secular legislation. This solution illustrates how important it had become for the friars to acknowledge and preserve the special status of the nobility in the face of its disintegration. Recognizing the higher social rank of Nahua noblemen, however, meant enforcing precepts and sanctions that applied only to the nobility. The approach to the identity of no-blemen in secular legislation and the confessor's manual cannot be extricated from the process of political and cultural assimilation of the Nahua nobility that had been taking place for several decades.

Honor, Authority, and Restitution

In the hands of skillful and somewhat fearless religious men, restitution could be a powerful tool to correct abuses against Indians, as Bartolomé de las Casas demonstrated in the guidelines for confessors that began to circulate in New Spain in manuscript form in 1546 and that he published together with other short treatises in Seville in 1552.[147] His recommendations were not only fol-lowed by members of his order but also incorporated into manuals for confes-sors written in the Peninsula.[148] In these guidelines, the former bishop of Chi-apas instructed the confessors of conquerors, *encomenderos*, and any Spaniard who had reaped economic benefit from the Conquest, to withhold absolution until those penitents made full restitution of goods belonging to the Indians.[149]

---

146. Juan Bautista, *Advertencias para confessores de indios* (Tlatelolco: Melchior Ocharte, 1600), 13r; 14v. Juan Bautista used the word *resabido* to refer to those with an impressive knowl-edge of Christian doctrine who were likely to boast about it. *Resabido* can also describe shrewd individuals aware of their knowledge; this usage is found a few years later in Pedro Sánchez de Aguilar's discussion of idolatry in Yucatán and whether it was the product of ignorance or the work of Indians fully instructed in Christian doctrine. *Informe contra idolorum cultores del obispado de Yucatán*, 3rd ed. (Merida: E. G. Triay, 1937), 11.

147. Helen-Rand Parish and Harold E. Weidman, *Las Casas en México: Historia y obras descon-ocidas* (Mexico City: Fondo de Cultura Económica, 1992), 63–65.

148. For confessors dealing with penitents of high social rank, Bartolomé de Medina wrote: "Lo primero, si el estado, dignidad, mayorazgo y señorio que tienen, le poseen con bueno y justo titulo, y no por tirania, y si los tales señores uvieren venido de Indias, ha se les de preguntar, como adquirieron tantas riquezas, porque si son conquistadores con titulo injusto, hanlo de restituyr todo." Bartolome de Medina, *Instruccion de como se ha de administrar el sacramento de la penitencia* (Alcalá: Juan Gracian, 1591), 205r.

149. Bartolomé de las Casas, *Tratados* (1552), ed. Lewis Hanke and Manuel Giménez Fernán-dez, trans. Agustín Millares Carlo and Rafael Moreno, 2 vols. (Mexico City: Fondo de Cultura Económica, 1965), 2:869. Lohmann Villena, "La restitución por conquistadores y encomenderos: Un aspecto de la incidencia lascasiana en Perú," *Anuario de Estudios Americanos* 23 (1966): 21–89. See also Thomas N. Tentler, *Sin and Confession on the Eve of the Reformation* (Princeton: Princeton University Press, 1977), 367–68.

Las Casas was interested in the goods that made up the main sources of income for the crown and *encomenderos*: lands, tribute, and labor. As for the restitution of intangible goods, Las Casas had no doubt that the Indians were defamed every time that Spaniards equated them to beasts; he did not, however, see the need to advise confessors on dealing with this particular offense.[150] Other ecclesiastical ministers, however, addressed the Spanish attacks on the honor of the new subjects with either words or actions.

One such minister was the Augustinian Gonzalo de Salazar, bishop of Yucatán from 1608 to 1636. Chiefly known for his successful campaigns to rid the province of Cozumel of idols,[151] Gonzalo de Salazar is also remembered in religious chronicles as a staunch defender of ecclesiastical jurisdiction against the encroachment of secular authorities intent on prosecuting idolaters in royal courts. Jurisdictional battles of this kind loomed large in a small but significant episode that would forever be associated with the bishop's name.

According to Pedro Sánchez de Aguilar, a priest, author, and doctor in law who served as deacon of the Cathedral of Mérida in the 1610s, Bishop Gonzalo de Salazar excommunicated the lieutenant governor of Yucatán after the officer refused to hear an appeal by Don Pedro Canche, Indian governor of Tekal.[152] The conflict appears to have started innocently: Don Pedro, on the advice of the town's priest, requested donations from Indian parishioners to buy a silk cape for use in religious functions. The lieutenant governor charged Don Pedro with extracting money from these Indians through the imposition of an additional and unwarranted levy, and sentenced him to be flogged in public.[153] The sentence was carried out despite the intervention of the bishop, who excommunicated the officer and took the case to the Audiencia in Mexico.[154] The high court ordered the restoration of Don Pedro's honor in a public ceremony and fined the lieutenant governor, in effect undoing a previous judicial act.[155]

---

150. Las Casas, *Tratados*, 2:863.

151. Francisco de Cárdenas Valencia, *Relación historial ecclesiástica de la Provincia de Yucatán de la Nueva España, escrita el año de 1639: Con una Nota Bibliográfica por Federico Gómez de Orozco* (Mexico City: Antigua Librería Robredo, de José Porrúa e Hijos, 1937), 43; Gil González Dávila, *Teatro eclesiástico de la primitiva iglesia de la Nueva España en las Indias Occidentales* (1649) (Madrid: J. Porrúa Turanzas, 1959), 2:126; Diego López de Cogolludo, *Los tres siglos de la dominación española en Yucatán (o sea historia de esta provincia)* (1842), 2 vols. (Graz: Akademische Druck- u. Verlagsanst, 1971), 2:455.

152. Sánchez de Aguilar, *Informe contra idolorum*, 130.

153. Sánchez de Aguilar, *Informe contra idolorum*, 130. For the nature of the charges, see López Cogolludo, *Los tres siglos*, 2:453.

154. In 1543, Yucatán was brought under the jurisdiction of the newly created Audiencia y Chancilleria Real de los Confines (also known as Santiago de Guatemala); in 1548, the Real Audiencia de México resumed jurisdiction over Yucatán and Cozumel. Edmundo O'Gorman, *Breve historia de las divisiones territoriales, aportación a la historia de la geografía de México* (Mexico City: Polis, 1937), xxii–xxiii.

155. The sources tend to talk of Don Pedro's *honor*, rather than about his *fame* or *reputation*,

To be sure, this story has remarkably little to do with Don Pedro as an individual, the plight of his people, or questions such as whether the Indians could be said to have honor—questions that had surely crossed the minds of confessors. The likely reason that it was preserved and handed down in religious chronicles and legal treatises such as Sánchez de Aguilar's was because it forcefully illustrated the colonial bishops' successful defense of ecclesiastical jurisdiction against royal intervention or, in language dear to the religious, the power of spiritual over earthly weapons. To Sánchez de Aguilar, a committed defender of the power of the bishop to process Indian idolaters and administer punishments, excommunication was the most efficient weapon available to ecclesiastical authorities, an opinion that secular officers probably shared.[156] Because emerging colonial societies showed deep fractures across religious and secular loyalties, excommunication could tilt the balance of power. For this reason, the crown advised religious authorities to show restraint and resort to excommunication only in very serious cases.[157]

The crown expected similar restraint in the church's handling of the time-honored process for lifting sanctions such as excommunication and censure. For instance, bishops in the colonies had taken to requiring officials under ecclesiastical sanctions to seek absolution in person, turning these affairs into ceremonies of political subordination to religious power. The crown put an end to this practice when it ordered that clergymen especially appointed by the bishop handle absolutions of royal officers, as was traditionally done in Castile.[158]

While González de Salazar's use of the tool of excommunication was important in bringing about justice for Don Pedro, it was the act of restitution that ended the conflict. We do not know the precise form of the ceremony— whether the *cédula* (decree) was read aloud, or if the offending party was present—or the significance that participants and witnesses attached to it. To those who wrote about the episode, González de Salazar was both an alternative purveyor of justice for the Indians and a defender of ecclesiastical prerogatives who fought for the church's right to request donations from Indian parishioners without secular intervention.

---

with no clear indication whether this should be understood as a function of Don Pedro's status as a member of the Indian nobility or the public office he held.

156. On the use of excommunication in the context of colonial groups vying for control of the indigenous population, see Murdo J. Macleod, "La espada de la Iglesia: Excomunión y la evolución de la lucha por el control politico y económico en Chiapas colonial, 1545–1700," *Mesoamérica* 11, no. 20 (December 1990): 199–213.

157. *Recopilación de leyes de los Reynos de las Indias*, prologue Ramón Menéndez y Pidal, preliminary study Juan Manzano Manzano, 4 vols. (Madrid: Ediciones Cultura Hispánica, 1973), book 1, title 7, law 47, 1:68. This advisory was issued by Phillip II in 1560 and again by Phillip III in 1613.

158. The ceremony of absolution included the visit of the official to the church, the uncovering of a cross, and a symbolic wounding with the staff. *Recopilación de leyes de los reynos de las Indias*, book 1, title 7, law 18, 1:59.

From the early years of colonization the crown wanted its new subjects to learn about the established existence of both a temporal and a spiritual power, each with its own representatives, hierarchies, tasks, and jurisdictions. The Indians' understanding of this arrangement was ultimately determined by their varied experiences with these institutions, which handled, among many other important things, the administration of colonial justice. Both royal officers and religious ministers did their part to foster a proper understanding of the justice system among the Indian population, but did not hesitate in some cases to distort information to gain more influence. As we will see in chapter 4, this was especially true of some influential friars who, opposed to any attempt by the crown to bring the Indians under its jurisdiction, did not miss opportunities to discredit or obscure the authority of royal officers of justice.

Don Pedro was an unwitting participant in yet another confrontation between religious and secular officials over ecclesiastical rights. Although all those who witnessed the proceedings may have not been fully aware of this confrontation, the restoration of Don Pedro's honor must have resonated among the Indian population with the force of unambiguous vindication. The royal authorities' willingness, in the name of justice, to undo the harm done to Don Pedro may not have necessarily translated into a vote of Indian confidence. Although the Audiencia ordered the restitution of Don Pedro's honor, one may ask whether the Indians considered honor to be the province of secular Spanish institutions or their parish priests—if they cared about honor at all. On this question, religious sources want to cast the whole episode and its resolution in religious and moral terms, highlighting how important it was for ecclesiastical ministers to count themselves among those who took care of the honor of Indians at one point or another.

It is likely that ecclesiastical involvement helped further undermine the Indians' regard for the secular administration of justice. Restitution, after all, was an obligation of Christians submitting to the sacrament of penance or preparing to die. The missionaries taught that this simple act showed how justice— even at its most elementary—and individual salvation were inextricably linked and within one's reach. Such claims remained largely alien to secular law. It is not entirely surprising that the missionaries, who methodically tried to anticipate how their charges would perceive their teachings, believed that restitution was the most immediately recognizable, concrete, and simple manifestation of justice. To this end, they sought to heighten its significance by scheduling acts of restitution for days of religious celebrations.[159]

---

159. Such was the case of St. Sebastian's Day on January 20, 1552, in Tecamachalco. *Anales de Tecamachalco*, 31.

An anecdote retold by Mercado neatly captures the obstacles that confessors faced when trying to resolve conflicts involving honor. The episode involved Francisco de Vitoria, and as in many of the stories passed on by his disciples, it was meant to highlight his uncompromising moral character and the integrity of his teachings. A hidalgo who had falsely accused a man of a crime for which he was found guilty approached Vitoria and asked how he could unburden his conscience. Vitoria tersely told the troubled man to prepare himself for hell. The dumbfounded hidalgo later relayed this reply to the Franciscan Alfonso de Castro, another theologian from Salamanca, who proceeded to explain the reason behind Vitoria's pronouncement. According to Castro, Vitoria's advice sprang from his certainty that the hidalgo, given the way he was dressed, would not retract before a judge. In short, it was unlikely that an upper-class man so fully invested in preserving the honor that his social status conferred would risk social taint by admitting that he had violated the seventh commandment.

In its critique of the hidalgo class's disproportional preoccupation with honor (and attendant concern with appearances that necessitated the display of expensive clothing), the anecdote echoed an opinion widely shared by reformers, humanists, and religious writers. Confessors were expected, however, to keep their preconceptions to themselves and ensure whenever possible that the reputation of the person making restitution was not irreparably damaged in the process.[160]

Restitution was a procedure intended to compensate individuals or their relatives for losses caused by theft, fraud, slander, insult, physical injuries, or death, not a tool to address systemic social inequalities. And yet it had the potential to become something more than a narrowly circumscribed mechanism of justice. When Las Casas referred to defamation as one of the host of crimes perpetrated by Spaniards that demanded restitution, he raised an interesting practical question: how to undo a verbal offense against an entire population? Taking a cue from the *summae* and manuals for confessors as well as his own reading of Las Casas, the poet Mateo Rosas de Oquendo answered this question when he created the character of a repentant conqueror who before leaving Peru felt compelled to restore the honor of a peaceful tribe from Tucumán whose behavior he had purposely distorted in a *probanza de méritos*.[161] As

---

160. In cases where the offender was of a higher social rank than the victim, monetary compensation without public apology or retraction was deemed an adequate solution. Mercado, *Summa de tratos y contratos*, 165–65v.

161. "Mas pues bien la Quaresma / y tengo de confesarme: / yo rrestituio la honrra / a los pobres naturales, / que ni ellos se defendieron, / ni dieron tales señales; /antes nos dieron la tierra / con muy buenas boluntades, / y partieron con nosotros / de sus asiendas y ajuares." Pedro Lasarte, ed., *Sátira hecha por Mateo Rosas de Oquendo a las cosas que pasan en el Pirú, año de 1598* (Madison, WI: Hispanic Seminary of Medieval Studies, 1990), 43, verses 1717–25.

technicians well versed in blaming and praising, poets took it upon themselves to restore honor in extraordinary cases. In one noteworthy example, Alonso de Ercilla, whose epic poem exalted the values of the Araucanian warrior society, told the "true" story of Dido, queen of Carthage, to restore a reputation that a prestigious literary and historiographic tradition had tarnished.[162]

Some friars in New Spain, falling between the ambitious goals of Las Casas and the symbolic interventions of poets, turned the restitution of indigenous individuals' honor into yet another tool for confronting Spanish officials and secured their place as guardians of indigenous honor, something that many Spaniards believed to be nonexistent among the Mexican Indians. As they observed Spaniards of humble origins adopt the codes, clothing, and sense of entitlement of the upper classes, the friars only became more convinced that the pursuit of honor and reputation could both endanger man's soul and tear apart the social fabric. Although many friars would concede that honor was antithetical to the egalitarian ethos of the Primitive Church on which they sought to model indigenous communities, in the less-than-ideal circumstances that brought together Spaniards and Indians, they did not hesitate to intervene if restoring honor to an Indian also meant settling political scores or challenging their countrymen's assumptions about that odd possession, honor. In doing so the friars, perhaps unwittingly, moved honor closer to the sphere of the spiritual.[163]

Pride and Avarice Go to the Colonies

The friars' interest in the Ten Commandments went far beyond the immediate goals of making Catholic doctrine available to Mexican Indians and preparing the new converts for penance. To this handful of men who never stopped competing with officers and colonists to build authority among the indigenous peoples, the Decalogue offered a useful way to think of the changing configuration of local power in the Indian communities, with a view toward containing

---

162. "Y pues una ficción impertinente / que destruye una honra es bien oída, / y la reina de Tiro injustamente / infama y culpa su inculpable vida, / la verdad, que es la ley de toda la gente, / por quien es en su honor restituida, / ¿por qué no debe ser, siendo cantada, / en cualquiera sazón bien escuchada?" Alonso de Ercilla, *La araucana*, ed. Marcos A. Morínigo and Isaías Lerner, 2 vols. (Madrid: Castalia, 1979), vol. 2, third part, c. 32, stanza 52, 316. On the literary tradition from which Ercilla drew, see María Rosa Lida de Malkiel, *Dido en la literatura española: Su retrato y defensa* (London: Tamesis Books, 1974).

163. Because of its place in society, honor was subjected to both religious and secular forces that shaped its meaning in different historic periods. In this sense, honor did not escape the process of secularization that the Spanish monarchy set in motion and consolidated in the sixteenth century. Maravall, *Poder, honor y élites*, 61–65.

the political ambitions of individuals from the upper and lower social strata. This thinking was then translated into the lessons prepared for Indian penitents on the fourth and seventh commandments. In them, the missionaries laid out the obligations toward civic and ecclesiastical authorities as well as their juridical and religious foundations, advancing the process of political Hispanization already under way at the local government level. They were witnesses to, critics of, and participants in this process. The missionaries' treatment of honor, a matter closely linked to their preoccupation with authority, showed both this same tension between spiritual and earthly values and also that between the exigencies of civil laws and the ideals of a reformed Christianity.

But if the penitential forum was deemed a necessary means to preserve some balance on basic matters of justice, it was certainly not enough, at least not during the years when the missionaries assumed that their close relationship with Viceroy Mendoza would help turn many of their wishes for Christian renewal into realities. The ordinances for Indians that Viceroy Mendoza issued in 1546 spelled out the religious obligations of the new converts such as baptism, attendance at Mass, annual confession, and reverence of sacred images, as well as prohibitions concerning idolatry, unacceptable sexual behavior and marriage practices, thievery, concubinage, and other public sins. Each ordinance also included precise information on the punishment of both first-time offenders and recidivists.[164]

Some of the decrees, especially in their Nahuatl version, are strikingly similar to the questions that Molina would include in his manuals for confessors years later. The twenty-third ordinance, for instance, narrowly focused on a few specific cases of commercial fraud involving the adulteration of cacao beans (still used as currency in the 1540s), honey, and gold through the addition of an alien substance.[165] By necessity the friars took a special interest in the *tian-*

---

164. The *ordenanzas* were brought to light by Edmundo O'Gorman, who referred to them as "una especie de primitivo código penal relativo a los indios." "Una ordenanza para el gobierno de los indios, 1546," 179–94. The ordinances, together with O'Gorman's introduction, was later included as an appendix in Francisco del Paso y Troncoso's *Idolatrías, supersticiones, dioses, ritos, hechicerías y otras costumbres gentílicas de las razas aborígenes de México*, 2nd ed., 2 vols. (Mexico City: Ediciones Fuente Cultural, 1953), 1:410–15. A surviving manuscript containing a translation of the ordinances into Nahuatl, now at the Bancroft Library of the University of California at Berkeley, suggests that Mendoza's request to make them known among Indians did not pass unheeded. The text has been commented on, transcribed, and translated by Barry Sell and Susan Kellogg, "We Want to Give Them Laws," 325–67.

165. "The twenty third [order we give the Indians] no one will embellish cacao, no one will sell cacao under false pretenses. And no one will mix up honey with [other] things, no one will mix it up with lime water or crumbly wood or water. In such a manner people are deceived; absolutely no one will do this. If someone does such once he will be arrested, beaten with a whip and his head will be shaved. . . . Likewise such will be done to him who will sell what is not true gold, what is just embellished or just some [kind] of mixture [of base and precious metals]." Sell and Kellogg, "We

guiz (indigenous markets) and their workings, thus becoming acquainted with the most common practices of fraud among craftsmen, metalworkers, and sellers of a variety of goods from food staples to textiles, much as their medieval counterparts had done in Europe. In this regard, Sahagún's moralized survey of trades and professions was a true guide for confessors, as evinced by the fact that its information on fraudulent practices found its way into Molina's questions on the seventh commandment addressed to Indian penitents.[166] Drafted in close cooperation with the friars, Mendoza's ordinances were meant to serve as a basic legal code for the Nahuas. Rearranged to follow the order of the Decalogue, expanded and enriched in detail, the ordinances enjoyed a parallel life in the manuals for confessors, creating the illusion of a seamless and unified body of law for the Indians that coincided with the teachings of their spiritual fathers.

By way of conclusion, I would like to reflect on some of the historiographic themes to emerge from the topics explored in this chapter. In 1973 Lester K. Little, in his now classic article, explored how and why thirteenth-century theologians turned their focus from pride to avarice.[167] This remarkable shift in Christian thought, traceable in theological works as well as visual and literary representations of the capital sins, closely followed the expansion of the European commercial economy and the transformation of urban life and religious sensibilities. Humility had traditionally been promoted as the virtue through which Christians could defeat pride, thought to be the source of all other sins. In the new moral landscape where the mendicant orders found their calling, the friars taught clergy and laity by word and example that through poverty men could fight their growing appetite for earthly goods and money.

In the sixteenth century, this system, from within which avarice had been made sense of, explained, and dissected in moral treatises, sermons, and works of art, was abandoned in favor of the Ten Commandments. This process, leading to the promotion of the Decalogue as a new moral-pedagogical system across a continent increasingly divided along religious lines, has been explored with characteristic boldness by John Bossy, who qualified this shift as "an event in the moral history of Europe."[168]

Want to Give Them Laws," 359–60.

166. See, for example, Sahagún on bad sellers of cacao beans, *Florentine Codex*, book 10, chap. 18, 65; bad sellers of *aguamiel*, or maguey syrup (compared positively to honey, *necutli*), book 10, chap. 20, 74; and goldworkers, book 10, chap. 7, 25–26.

167. Lester K. Little, "Pride Goes before Avarice: Social Change and the Vices in Latin Christendom," *American Historical Review* 76, no. 1 (February 1971): 16–49.

168. John Bossy, "Moral Arithmetic: Seven Sins into Ten Commandments," in *Conscience and Casuistry in Early Modern Europe*, ed. Edmund Leites (Cambridge: Cambridge University Press; Paris: Editions de la Maison des Sciences de l'Homme, 1988), 214–34. On the treatment of the Ten Commandments in manuals for confessors and cases of conscience of early modern Spain, see

Considered in the context of the transfer of European traditions and institutions to the colonies, the historical sequences of "events" of the kind analyzed by Little and Bossy raise significant methodological and theoretical issues. The ones that I want to examine briefly concern the assumptions that have quietly shaped, if not governed, the ways that intellectual history has conceived of historical change. By focusing too narrowly on historical shifts, intellectual historians have frequently overlooked the fate of their by-products, which are relegated to the status of residual traditions and cease to be phenomena of historical interest.

Regarding the fates of avarice and pride in the colonies, whereas avarice soon became "the sin of the day" among Spanish colonizers, as attested by writers on both sides of the Atlantic, pride was most often on the mind of the missionaries observing the behavior of the Indians under their supervision. In Mexico, as in many other places, missionaries found that building authority required introducing and explaining post-Conquest authorities to the Indians. And so through the teaching of either the Seven Deadly Sins or the Decalogue, some Nahuas learned about immediate and remote authorities and the attendant obligations that bound all Christians to church and state, topics that can be seen in the religious literature produced by the missionaries.

In the 1530s Andrés de Olmos composed a collection of sermons on the Seven Deadly Sins in the Nahuatl language. The work opened with a general exposition on pride (*nepoaliztli, superbia*) followed by a series of sermons, each focused on a different subspecies of that sin, such as disobedience, vanity, self-praise, contempt, slander, and the desire to rule over others. Of all of pride's "children," Olmos dwells most on disobedience. This choice can only be partly explained by reference to the author's chosen literary model and the coexistence of old and new schemes in religious teaching at the moment. In spelling out the many faces of disobedience, Olmos was able to inform an Indian audience of the friars' view on that hotly debated topic: the relation between religious and secular powers.[169]

Olmos's teaching on pride essentially advised subordination to secular and religious authorities such as priests, bishops, royal officers, and heads of households; in short, it comprised the moral injunctions that became associated with the fourth commandment. But Olmos found it necessary to state that the power of secular officers was not boundless. He explained to his potential audience

Antonio González Polvillo, *Decálogo y gestualidad social en la España de la Contrarreforma* (Seville: Universidad de Sevilla, 2011).

169. Andrés de Olmos, *Tratado sobre los siete pecados mortales, 1551–1552*, ed. Georges Baudot (Mexico City: Universidad Nacional Autónoma de México, 1996), 19.

that, as important as it was for Christians to obey secular officials and laws, they nevertheless had the duty to consult with their priest whenever they harbored doubts about the compatibility of secular demands and Christian teachings.[170] Even more significant, Olmos illustrated the moral perils of pursuing public office for fame and recognition by listing those sins likely to be committed by judges with these motivations, which included tampering with evidence and dealing with cases outside their jurisdiction.[171] Commenting on bad judges as a stand-in for public officers was a relatively safe move; it was also in line with similar efforts by some mendicant friars who, alarmed by the growing number of Indian litigants, had resorted to publicly devaluing the efficacy of the secular legal system. The perception that the Mexican Indians thrived on lawsuits took shape gradually, thanks in part to the contributions of friars who, like Andrés de Olmos, believed that the new converts should be solely under ecclesiastical jurisdiction.

The Mexican Indians could learn much about the colonial order and the basic expectations of secular and religious authorities from an explanation of the many facets of pride. The same is not true of avarice. The occasional accounts of Indians who gladly gave up their possessions to embrace poverty were more opportunities for the friars to highlight the appeal of the Franciscan message than they were warnings to the new converts about the moral dangers stemming from the desire for material goods. When Indians became identified with the poor, there was little room for lessons on avarice.

As we have already noted, lexicographic research on the indigenous languages was often guided by the friars' need to teach Christian doctrine. The first folio of the trilingual dictionary *Ayer 1478* at the Newberry Library is a good example of this close relation between evangelization and linguistic inquiry.[172] In it we find the Nahuatl glosses for the Seven Deadly Sins followed by a list of adjectives derived from each. Bilingual dictionaries compiled in Mexico show a limited number of entries related to commercial transactions, notions, and documents. In the world of these dictionaries, Indians engage only in the most basic economic transactions, such as lending, selling, and buying. Similarly, confessors of Indians rarely worried about the complex moral issues that their

---

170. Olmos, *Tratado*, 19.
171. Olmos, *Tratado*, 55.
172. These notes in a different hand are not part of the dictionary. M. Clayton, "A Trilingual Spanish-Latin-Nahuatl Manuscript Dictionary Sometimes Attributed to Fray Bernardino de Sahagún," *International Journal of American Linguistics* 55, no. 4 (October 1989): 391–416. The date and authorship of the dictionary are still being debated. Mary Clayton has offered preliminary evidence suggesting that its author may have been a Nahuatl speaker. "Evidence for a Native-Speaking Nahuatl Author in the Ayer *Vocabulario Trilingüe*," *International Journal of Lexicography* 16, no. 2 (2003): 99–119.

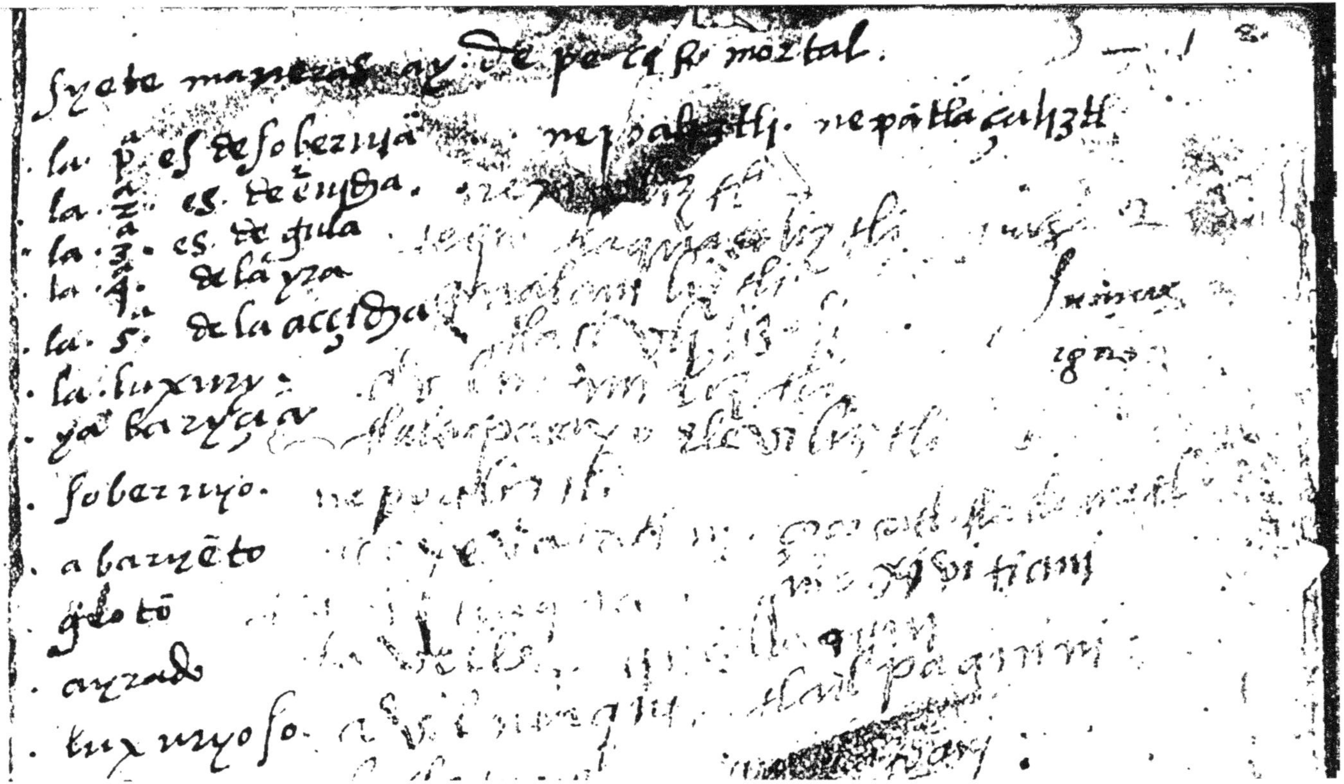

Fig. 2.2. The Seven Deadly Sins. Manuscript Ayer 1478. (Courtesy of the Newberry Library.)

European counterparts had to confront with penitents whose livelihoods depended on increasingly complicated commercial transactions.[173] Comparisons of this sort may seem obvious or inconsequential in isolation, but they become significant when one considers the geographical and temporal scope of historical shifts in intellectual traditions and asks what makes an event belong or not to the moral history of Europe.[174]

173. Mendieta distinguished between the preparation required for confessors of Spaniards and those of Indians. Confessors of Spaniards were expected to be thoroughly familiar with the cases found in any of the well-known *summae*, while for confessors of Indians, he suggested that "basta alguna inteligencia en casos de conciencia, con que sepan razonablemente la lengua." García Icazbalceta, *Códice Mendieta*, 1:76.

174. For a stimulating reflection on closely related historiographical issues, see Reinhart Koselleck, "Perspective and Temporality: A Contribution to the Historiographical Exposure of the Historical World," in *Futures Past: On the Semantics of Historical Time*, trans. Keith Tribe (New York: Columbia University Press, 2004), 128–51.

CHAPTER 3

❦

Missionaries, Oaths, and Indian Testimonies

The Franciscan chronicler Juan de Torquemada reported in his *Monarquía in-diana* (1613) that in earlier times when the honor of a young woman of the Na-hua nobility was put into question, she was given the opportunity to restore her name by taking an oath: swearing her innocence by one of the Nahua gods, she would touch her finger to the ground, take it to her mouth, and kiss it.[1] These simple actions were sufficient to put any doubt about the woman's reputation to rest. The Dominican Bartolomé de las Casas included this bit of ethnographic lore in his *Apologética historia sumaria*, a work that remained unpublished un-til the nineteenth century.[2] And the Franciscan historian Gerónimo de Mend-ieta, on whose work Torquemada drew extensively, had access to Las Casas's work and incorporated the passage in his *Historia eclesiástica indiana*, which was also published in the nineteenth century.[3]

Torquemada highlighted the judicial character of the ritual by presenting it as the familiar *compurgatio* of medieval times, but he also used this information as a preamble to a brief excursus on a type of oath known among the Romans of antiquity. As he reminded his readers, the Romans used to swear by Jupiter while holding a stone in one hand and then throwing it away. By throwing the stone, they dramatized their acceptance of whatever punishment the god might inflict upon one who swore falsely. It was probably not lost on Torquemada that these two rituals were not identical, but whatever their differences, they were insufficient to obscure the apparent similarities that he was interested in

---

1. "Quando alguna era notada de alguna culpa grave, o de infamia (si de ella estaba inocente) para purgarse de aquella acusación, y restituirse en su honra, hacía juramento en esta forma: Por ventura, no me ve Nuestro Señor Dios? Y nombraban el Nombre de su maior Dios, o a otros de esotros, a quienes ellos solían atribuir Deidad, y les eran devotos, y aficionados; y poniendo el dedo en la tierra, lo besaban." Fr. Juan de Torquemada, *Monarquía Indiana*, 3 vols. (Mexico City: Salva-dor Chávez Hayhoe, 1943), book 13, chap. 28, 2:470.

2. Bartolome de las Casas, *Apologética historia sumaria*, ed. Edmundo O'Gorman, 2 vols. (Mex-ico City: Universidad Autónoma Nacional de México, 1967), book 3, chap. 219, 2:419.

3. Mendieta, *Historia eclesiástica indiana*, book 2, chap. 23, 122.

bringing out, namely, the action of incorporating an object into the ritual and attaching a particular meaning to it.

Whereas both Las Casas and Mendieta abstained from generalizing based on this single example, Torquemada ventured that all oaths among the Nahuas followed the same basic pattern and were not unlike their Roman counterpart.[4] Torquemada may have based this conclusion on information found in the writings of his predecessor, the Franciscan Motolinia, who had described how witnesses in Texoco would touch their finger to the ground and take it to their mouth before giving testimony in front of the appointed judges.[5] Or perhaps Torquemada had in mind the Nahuatl gloss for "oath" found in the two dictionaries composed by Fr. Alonso de Molina: *tlalqualiztli*, an expression meaning "the eating of soil."[6] Whatever his ultimate source, Torquemada's words brought home the point that both Nahua and Roman oaths belonged to the past, a safe place where authors could draw parallels between Romans and Mexicans to be enjoyed by readers with a taste for antiquity and alien customs.

The Spanish chronicler Francisco López de Gómara took great interest in the ceremonial swearing with which the supreme lords of the Mexicas took office, a detail that caught the attention of eighteenth-century European writers and readers.[7] For the most part, references to the use of oaths in pre-Conquest Nahua judicial procedures are scarce; they are notably absent from the works of the sixteenth-century observers of indigenous institutions and customs.[8]

---

4. "De los Romanos se dice que, que juraban por el nombre de Jupiter, teniendo una piedra en la mano, y arrojandola, como parece en el Juramento, que en cierta occasion hizo Pompeio; el qual, tomando en sus manos una Piedra grande de pedernal, dijo estas palabras: Si a sabiendas engaño, o miento en esto que juro, arrojeme Jupiter (Padre del Día) sin ofensa, de la Ciudad, de los Exercitos, y de todas las demas cosas pertenecientes a esto como io arrojo esta Piedra de la mano." Torquemada, *Monarquía Indiana*, 2:470.

5. Fr. Toribio de Benavente, *Memoriales o Libro de las cosas de la Nueva España y de los naturales de ella*, ed. Edmundo O'Gorman (Mexico City: Universidad Autónoma Nacional de México, 1971), part 2, chap. 16, 354.

6. The same gloss is found in Molina's *Aqui comiença un vocabulario en la lengua castellana y mexicana* (1555) and *Vocabulario en lengua castellana y mexicana y mexicana y castellana* (1571).

7. Francisco López de Gómara, *Historia de la conquista de México* (Caracas: Biblioteca Ayacucho, 1979), chap. 213, 328. Bernard Picard, for example, found it to be the most interesting feature of Aztec government: "Il juroit aucune, que tant qu'il regneroit, le Soleil donneroit sa lumiere, les pluies tomberoient à propos; que les Rivieres ne feroient point de ravages par leurs débordemens, que les campagnes ne seroient point afligées par la sterilité, ni les homes par les malignes influences du Soleil. Ce pacte, dit l' Auteur de la Conquête du Mexique, a veritablement quelque chose de bizarre ... neanmoins on peut dire, que les sujets prétendoient par ce serment, engager leur Prince à regner avec tant de moderation, qu'il n'attirât point de son chef la colere du Ciel; n'ignorant pas que les chatimens & les calamites publiques, tombent souvent sur les Peuples que soufrent pour les crimes & pour les excés de leurs Rois." *Ceremonies et coutumes religieuses des peoples idolatres represrenseentées par des Figures dessinées de la main de Bernard Picard: Avec une Explication Historique, et quelques Dissertations curieuses* (Amsterdam: Chez J. F. Bernard, 1723), 1:161–62.

8. Mendieta offers a general picture of the way that body of judges holding court in Texcoco, Mexico, and Tacuba heard criminal and civil cases. *Historia eclesiástica indiana*, book 2, chap. 28,

While this was also true of Fr. Bernardino de Sahagún's account of the Nahua judiciary, we do find evidence of the use of oaths in the religious ceremony known as *neyolmelahualiztli* ("the straightening of one's heart") in which the Franciscan identified features similar to those of sacramental penance. I have discussed the significance of Sahagún's account in light of the jurisdictional conflicts between friars and secular officers elsewhere.[9] For the sake of brevity, it suffices to recall that this once-in-a-lifetime purification ceremony, presided over by the goddess Tlazolteotl, allowed perpetrators of serious offenses to receive forgiveness upon completing penitential acts ordered by the officiating priest.[10] Before confessing his or her misdeeds, the penitent took the oath described by Torquemada.[11] Sahagún returned to the subject of oaths when he described how the Nahuas conducted themselves near or within sacred places. According to his informants, all Nahuas regardless of age or gender touched and tasted the ground whenever they were in the presence of idols or temples housing idols, but they also performed these acts as a way of confirming the veracity of their statements.[12]

Thus, according to Sahagún, it was context that turned this seemingly widespread religious act into an oath. Other sources confirm the generalized use of this simple ritual; the *Relación de Epazoyuca* reported that the inhabitants of the town used to worship fire by touching the ground with one hand and then kissing it in a gesture known as *ontlalqua*, the eating of earth.[13] It is worth noting the religious meaning of the eating of earth, especially in the ceremony

---

134. The "Relación de Meztitlan" makes reference to the punishment of perjurers: "Al testigo falso, o delator que levantaba testimonio, daban la misma pena q[ue] al reo se había de dar, siendo convencido." Acuña, *Relaciones geográficas del siglo XVI*, 7:66.

9. Pardo, *The Origins of Mexican Catholicism*, 94–95.

10. Sahagún, *Florentine Codex*, book 1, chap. 12, 8–11.

11. Sahagún, *Florentine Codex*, book 1, chap. 13, 10. "Oído esto el penitente luego hacía juramento de decir la verdad, de la manera que ellos usaban jurar, tocando la tierra con la mano y lamiendo lo que se le había pegado." Bernardino de Sahagún, *Historia general de las cosas de Nueva España*, ed. Alfredo López Austin and Josefina García Quintana, 2 vols. (Madrid: Alianza, 1988), book 1, chap. 13, 1:45.

12. "Usaban una ceremonia generalmente en toda esta tierra, hombres y mujeres, niños y niñas, que cuando entraban en algún lugar donde había imágenes de los ídolos, una o muchas, luego tocaban en la tierra con el dedo, y luego le llegaban a la boca o a la lengua. A esto llamaban 'comer tierra.' Hacíanlo en reverencia de sus dioses. . . . Y en lugar de juramento usaban esto mismo, que para afirmar que decían verdad hacían esta cerimonia, y a los que se querían satisfacer del que hablaba si decía verdad, demandábanle que hiciese esta cerimonia, y luego le creían como juramento." Sahagún, *Historia general de las cosas*, "Apéndiz del Segundo libro," 1:189–90. López de Gómara recorded that the soon-to-be-king and a small entourage kissed the soil upon approaching the image of Huitzilopochtli that presided over the ceremonial swearing of new rulers. *Historia de la conquista de México*, chap. 213, 327.

13. Acuña, *Relaciones geográficas del siglo XVI*, 6:85. Among other rituals observed by the Nahuas, Durán mentioned "el besar la tierra y comerla," although he did not associate this practice with oaths. Diego Durán, *Historia de las Indias de Nueva España*, vol. 1, chap. 1, 13.

of *neyolmelahualiztli*, which functioned as a powerful, if limited, alternative to the everyday justice system. According to Sahagún, Nahuas would later transpose their belief in the efficacy of this ceremony to the sacrament of confession. The paucity of references to vernacular forms of oath-taking becomes more intriguing when considered in light of the well-established tendency of religious writers to draw parallels between native and European features as well as pre-Conquest and contemporary religious practices.

In the reconstruction and interpretation of old Nahua institutions, ceremonies, and beliefs, the missionaries were more often than not guided by immediate needs and goals, such as formulating new policies regarding the conversion of the Mexican Indians, or developing their relationship with other social groups and especially authorities. Some of these concerns had a long history of doubts, questions, and debates that could be traced in theological and canonical literature. In the administration of and teaching about the sacraments, the friars reconstructed Nahua religious and ritual life, an endeavor that required them to revisit old theological debates and accepted solutions. But oaths ranked low among the priorities of the friars, who turned their attention to them only when the Mexican Indians came into contact with Spanish legal institutions. Thus, while teaching about oaths was not a development that the missionaries necessarily welcomed, it quickly became unavoidable. The friars, after all, were well aware of their countrymen's tendency to invoke God, and the new occasions for perjury that lawsuits had created.

As the tradition of the church fathers showed, and scholastic theology confirmed, oaths were not central to the lives of Christians or their salvation. They were, however, a feature of the life of Christians in a society governed by human laws; as such, they were to be approached with caution and reverence. Theologians grappling with the dual nature of oaths determined that the act of swearing could be better conceptualized as an act of religion that should neither be abused nor disavowed or rejected outright.[14] If theologians saw oaths as an act of religion, to Christians they represented a balancing act that could expose them to ecclesiastical, secular, and social sanctions.

In Mexico oaths came onto the missionaries' horizon as a consequence of the transfer of legal and political institutions; the introduction of the Spanish model of municipal government into Indian communities was the most salient feature of this transfer. On both sides of the Atlantic, the *cabildo* was the scene of routine ceremonies that followed the liturgy of the law. In Mexico City, *cabildo* mem-

---

14. For oath-swearing as an external act of religion, see Thomas Aquinas, *Summa theologiae*, 60 vols. (Blackfriars, NY: McGraw-Hill, 1964–81), 2a 2ae, q. 89, a. 4, 39: 212–15.

bers greeted the arrival of royal decrees and approved papal legislation by kissing the documents and placing them over their heads while intoning a formula of obedience.[15] This scene was repeated in indigenous town councils.[16] These brief, cursory, but necessary rituals were duly recorded in the minutes of the governing municipal body, along with the names of witnesses, lending further authority to the proceedings. And, as was the case in the Peninsula, there were plenty of oaths to be administered, taken, and recorded. At the beginning of each year, the elected officers of the *cabildo* were sworn in, a requirement that had been in place in several Spanish municipal councils when Alphonse X codified it for all royal officials.[17] The *regidores* received a staff of office when appointed, which they were obligated to carry and display as a sign of their authority during their tenure; they would swear on the cross that was part of this staff.[18] Indian municipal officers followed the same ceremonial requirements, a practice that extended to other oaths as well. In Tlaxcala, for example, the *corregidor* administering the oaths to Indian officials asked them to swear by kissing a crucifix.[19]

There were oaths for a variety of circumstances. Public oaths by royal officers lent solemnity and a celebratory dimension to official ceremonies. On the occasion of Philip II's accession to the throne, members of the *cabildo* of Mexico swore to serve the new king in an event that took place in the midst of carefully planned street festivities.[20] As part of the ceremony, the Indian governors of Mexico, Texcoco, Tacuba, and Tlatelolco were able to take their oaths of allegiance to the new king through an Indian interpreter.[21] Spanish and Indian interpreters who worked for the *cabildo* and the Audiencia were required to take an oath, as were a number of individuals who worked for the city council either on a regular or ad hoc basis.[22]

15. *Actas de cabildo de la Ciudad de México*, ed. Ignacio Bejarano, paleography Manuel Orozco y Berra, 12 vols. (Mexico City: Municipio Libre, 1889–1900), book 1, 60, 104, 149. On the reception of papal bulls, see book 1, 50.

16. Baltasar Brito Guadarrama, ed., *Códice Chavero de Huexotzingo: Proceso a sus oficiales de república* (Mexico City: Instituto Nacional de Antropología e Historia, 2008), 182.

17. Santos Manuel Corona González, "El Libro de las fórmulas de juramento del Consejo de Castilla," *Anuario de historia del derecho español* 63–64 (1993–94): 985–87.

18. *Actas de cabildo de la Ciudad de México*, March 9, 1566, book 7, 274.

19. *Actas de cabildo de Tlaxcala, 1547–1567*, 238.

20. *Actas de cabildo de la Ciudad de México*, book 6, 291.

21. *Actas de cabildo de la Ciudad de México*, book 6, 292.

22. For example, Martín de Alvear was sworn as interpreter on July 6, 1576. *Actas de cabildo de la Ciudad de México*, book 8, 241. The record notes when the appointed interpreter was an Indian; thus in 1551, "yndio interprete" Hernando Tapia was working for the Audiencia. *Actas de cabildo de la Ciudad de México*, book 6, 23. Also required to take an oath were those interpreters who were on the payroll for the duration of particular public works; see, for example, the record of payment of April 11, 1580, to Juan de Ibarra, interpreter of the Audiencia for eleven days of service related to the planning and measuring of a drainage system. *Actas de cabildo de la Ciudad de México*, book 8, 429. A vast array of individuals who were periodically appointed to oversee the activities

Men of religion were no strangers to oaths, which were required for appointment to ecclesiastical office. The Third Council of Mexico, for example, decreed that ecclesiastical judges should swear to uphold the decrees of both the Council of Trent and the Mexican Council.[23] Canon law stipulated how clergy should approach oaths and also spelled out the strict conditions for priests summoned to serve as witnesses in secular courts, where they could take oaths only with permission from their superior.[24] Religious orders, in turn, imposed their own restrictions on oath-taking on their members. For instance, Dominican friars refused to swear their belief in the Immaculate Conception—a point of contention with the Franciscan order—a policy that led to the relatively long absence of members of that order from the classrooms at the Mexican university. The secular and religious cultures of oaths came together often enough, as they did on January 31, 1561, when two Carthusian brothers seeking to establish a monastery in Mexico appeared before the city council and swore in the manner expected of friars, placing their hands on their chests.[25]

Oaths by royal or ecclesiastical officers belonged to a class that theologians referred to as "promissory oaths."[26] These concerned future behavior and actions, such as the commitments of parties entering into commercial agreements. When an individual affirmed or denied that a particular event had taken place, for example, they took an "assertory oath," whereby swearers make God a witness to their statements, with or without a judge present.[27] The young woman

---

of different trades, such as wine sellers, was also subject to oaths. *Actas de cabildo de la Ciudad de México*, book 6, 69.

23. "Coram Secretario Episcopi jurejurando se obstringant quod Sacrorum Canonum, et Concilij Tridentini Decretis, hujusque Synodi constitutionibus stabunt. Quod Ecclesiasticam Jurisdictionem, immunitatem Ecclesiarum, et earum Ministros tuebuntur, atque defendent." *Concilium Mexicanum Provinciale III*, book 1, title 8, §2, 46.

24. Alonso de la Vega, *Summa llamada nueva recopilación, y práctica del fuero interior, utilissima para Confessores, y penitents . . .* (Madrid: Licenciado Varez de Castro, 1598), chap. 16, 178. For restrictions on priests, see Gratian, *Decretum*, II, 2, c. 5 in *Corpus iuris canonici*, ed. Emil L. Richter and Emil Friedberg (Graz: Akademische Druck-u. Verlagsanstalt, 1955), 1:455.

25. *Actas de cabildo de la Ciudad de México*, book 6, 444. "Quando el Sacerdote es compelido a jurar no a de poner las manos en la vara de justicia ni en la Cruz ni en los Evangelios, mas poniendo la mano en el pecho, y a de jurar por su consagracion como lo manda el Concilio Triburiense." Jerónimo Román y Zamora, *Republicas del mundo. Dividadas en tres partes*, 3 vols. (Salamanca: I. Hernández, 1595), part 1, book 5, chap. 15, 1:292. At the time, only the Augustinians, Dominicans, Franciscans, Jesuits, and Mercedarians were allowed to establish monasteries. Juan de Solórzano Pereira, *Libro primero de la Recopilacion de las cédulas, cartas, provisiones y ordenanzas reales*, ed. Ricardo Levene, 2 vols. (Buenos Aires: Facultad de Derecho y Ciencias Sociales / Instituto de Historia del Derecho Argentino, 1945), title 5, law 6, 1:168. On the *cédulas* concerning the foundation of monasteries, see the information compiled by Solórzano Pereira. 1:169–70.

26. "Quandoque autem inducitur divinum testimonium ad confirmandum aliquid futurum, et hoc dicitur *juramentum promissorium*." Aquinas, *Summa theologiae*, 2a 2ae, q. 89, a. 1, res., 39:204.

27. "Divinum autem testimonium quandoque ad asserendum praesentia vel praeterita, et hoc dicitur *juramentum assertorium*." Aquinas, *Summa theologiae*, 2a 2ae, q. 89, a. 1, res. Sixteenth- and seventeenth-century *summae* and manuals of cases of conscience use different classifications. In some, oaths administered as part of judicial proceedings were considered a separate category. In

that Torquemada mentioned proclaimed her innocence by taking an oath of this kind. By the time that Torquemada put this example into writing, it was yet another token of ancient Nahua wisdom and values that had little relation to the present, and not only because the Nahua gods who could be summoned as witnesses had been proscribed. The world of the Nahua nobility—and the Spanish perception of it—had been forever transformed.

Christianity, like Judaism, had a complicated relationship to oaths, shaped by its long history of encounters with non-Christian peoples and conflicts with secular institutions. In sixteenth-century Mexico, these two elements came into play once again when the friars, especially the Franciscans, turned the administration of oaths into one more source of disagreement over the inclusion and participation of Mexican Indians in the Spanish legal and political system. The history of oaths in early colonial Mexico is inextricably linked to the development of ideas about Indian tutelage that both royal and ecclesiastical authorities eventually came to embrace and turn, however imperfectly, into reality.

Problems New and Old

In 1575 the Augustinian friar and author Jerónimo Román y Zamora published *Repúblicas del mundo*, an encyclopedic work that described the customs and institutions of the nations of the world, from ancient civilizations to societies recently brought into contact with Europeans. The early history of the *Repúblicas*, which was republished in 1595, is inseparable from the obstacles that surrounded its publication and circulation.[28] Like the works of many other Augustinian authors of the time—Fr. Luis de León, for example—royal and Inquisitorial authorities subjected Román y Zamora's work to close scrutiny before allowing it to circulate in revised form.[29]

---

others, authors made several classifications based on different criteria. See, for example, Pedro de Ledesma, *Segunda parte de la summa, en la qual se summa y cifra todo lo moral y casos de conciencia que no pertenecen a los Sacramentos . . .* (Barcelona: Sabastian Matevat, 1620), treatise 11, 859.

28. On the motives behind the censorship of Román y Zamora's work, see Rolena Adorno, "Censorship and Its Evasion: Jerónimo Román and Bartolomé de las Casas," *Hispania* 75, no. 4 (October 1992): 812–27. The document in which the Council of the Indies requested that the first edition of the *Repúblicas del mundo* be taken out of circulation can be found in Fermín de los Reyes Gómez, *El libro en España y América: Legislación y censura (Siglos XV–XVIII)*, 2 vols. (Madrid: Arcos/Libros, 2000), 2:820. The first two parts of Román y Zamora's *Historia de la orden de los frailes ermitaños de San Agustín* was also banned, although many believe this was for exclusively personal reasons. See Virgilio Pinto Crespo, *Inquisición y control ideológico en la España del siglo XVI* (Madrid: Taurus, 1983), 185.

29. The October 29, 1575, letter from Fr. Lorenzo de Villavicencio to Fr. Alonso de la Veracruz mentioning Román y Zamora's troubles with the Inquisition can be found in Burrus, *The Writings of Alonso de la Vera Cruz*, 5:190–93.

Although the topic was not absent from his sources and models, Román y Zamora showed a special interest in oaths, commenting on their variety across human societies and these societies' attitudes toward them. This interest responded in part to concern among clergy and religious authors about an alarming increase in swearing among Spaniards. For religious authorities, priests, and moral reformers, decrying the apparent increase in offensive practices and denouncing the decline of moral standards was part of their job description, and in this sense, the preoccupation with swearing was hardly worthy of notice. The worries that Román y Zamora and contemporary writers voiced point to inveterate pernicious habits and also to the emergence of new ones, both of which needed to be uprooted. In these writers, the timeless indignation at an offense that even pagans found hard to accept,[30] was sharpened by careful observation of the behavior of their flock in all its variety of social types, including noblemen, royal officers, and manual laborers. In this sense, Catholicism's continued engagement with the affairs of the world, as seen in the questions that preoccupied Spanish moral reformers, theologians, and confessors, accompanied the crown's increased efforts to live up to its own image as highest purveyor of earthly justice.

Whatever challenges the present brought could be faced by learning from the past. Román y Zamora explored the ways that European pagans had dealt with oaths, with the goal of shedding some light on the nature of this ritual, the true meaning of which Spaniards continued to ignore.[31] If there was a lesson to learn from the Greeks and Romans, it was that taking an oath was a serious affair; oaths created a sacred obligation and put the swearer at the mercy of the gods, as illustrated by the casting of Jupiter's stone that Torquemada described.[32] Other pagan nations, less attached to oaths, yielded different lessons. The Phrygians, for example, were said to be reluctant to take oaths. The French and some African nations did not think much of them; according to the author, this helped explain these nations' alleged moral indifference toward theft and homicide.[33] A sense of the sacred expressed as a fear of the gods was at

---

30. See, for example, the discussion of the severe penalties for perjury found in the Twelve Tables. Aulus Gellius, *The Attic Nights of Aulus Gellius*, trans. John C. Rolfe, 3 vols. (London: William Heinemann; New York: G.P. Putnam and Sons, 1927), book 20, chap. 1, 427.

31. Román y Zamora, *Repúblicas del mundo*, part 2, book 4, chap. 19, 2:99r and 100v.

32. "Quasi lo mesmo hazian los Romanos en sus sacrificios y juramentos, y tenian una piedra que llamavan la piedra de Iupiter: la cual arrojavan de la mano quando dezian que assi cayesse de su estado, o le sucediesse alguna cosa infelice, como el arrojava aquella piedra, y creo que este fue el mayor juramento, de que usaron los Romanos." Román y Zamora, *Repúblicas del mundo*, part 2, book 4, chap. 19, 2:99v. On oaths among Greek men and women and their gods of choice, see 100r.

33. "Los Phriges fueron en esto moderados, porque se abstenian todo lo possible en jurar. Los Franceses y Affricanos no estimavan en mucho el juramento, y assi no tenian por malo matar hombres y robar." Román y Zamora, *Repúblicas del mundo*, part 2, book 4, chap. 19, 2:100r.

the heart of pagan conceptions of oaths. This particular notion of the sacred explained why some nations were so cautious when it came to oaths. Societies that rejected oaths, according to Román y Zamora, were bound to ignore serious crimes. Thus, besides their immediate practical function, oaths were thought to prevent societies from falling apart.

As the pagan examples showed, oaths were a religious matter. Christianity had to contend with this fact, first as the religion of a persecuted minority and later as an official religion. A strict approach to oaths prevailed in the early Christian church, when Christians learned that they should swear by God alone and that falsehood amounted to a mortal sin.[34] Basing his opinion on the authority of Augustine, who wrote on the topic more than once, Román y Zamora conjectured that the accepted oaths of the Christian past were most likely a single declaration with either God or Christ as witness.[35]

The church prescribed all matters concerning oaths, establishing the formulas to be used, the appropriate days, and the conditions under which women and clergy were permitted to swear.[36] But the history of ecclesiastical legislation reveals that Christianity's relationship with oaths had little to do with the way Christians had come through the ages to relate to this particular religious act. The strict adherence to ecclesiastical precepts that Román y Zamora saw as characteristic of the Primitive Church had given way to the proliferation of superstitious forms of compurgation (duels, ordeals by fire, etc.) born of a demand for visible signs of divine intervention.[37] According to Román y Zamora, the Spanish stood out among all nations as the worst abusers of these judicial ceremonies.

These abuses were condemned and corrected by authorities and the enactment of laws. Many of Roman y Zamora's sources, in fact, are either ecclesiastical or secular legislation. If the old laws of the *Fuero juzgo* attest to a time when ordeals—later banned by papal legislation—were the norm, more recent laws indicated that the crown had heeded the church's call to curb superstitious practices that had become impossible to distinguish from officially sanctioned

---

34. Román y Zamora, *Repúblicas del mundo*, part 1, book 5, chap. 17, 1:292v.
35. On Augustine's response to a Christian who feared pagan oaths, see Claude Lepelley, "Le serment païen malédiction démoniaque: Augustin devant une angoisse des Chrétiens de son temps," in *Le serment*, ed. Raymond Verdier, 2 vols. (Paris: Éditions du centre National de la Recherche Scientifique, 1991), 2:53–61. For Román y Zamora's conjecture, see *Repúblicas del mundo*, part 1, book 5, chap. 17, 1:292v. The bibliography on medieval ordeals and their place in the development of the Western legal system is, of course, inexhaustible. See Henry Charles Lea, *The Duel and the Oath*, ed. Edward Peters (Philadelphia: University of Pennsylvania Press, 1974); Robert Bartlett, *Trial by Fire and Water: The Medieval Judicial Ordeal* (Oxford: Clarendon Press, 1986). For an overview, see Berman, *Law and Revolution*, 1:49–84.
36. Román y Zamora, *Repúblicas del mundo*, part 1, book 5, chap. 17, 1:292v.
37. Román y Zamora, *Repúblicas del mundo*, part 1, book 5, chap. 17, 1:292v.

religious obligations.[38] This was the case with the use of sacred places for taking oaths, a common occurrence at the burial sites of martyred saints in the city of Avila. As Román y Zamora reminded his readers, the Catholic monarchs had banned this practice in Law 67 from the *Leyes de Toro*, issued in 1505 and later incorporated into the *Nueva Recopilación* of 1567.[39] It is worth noting that Law 83 from the *Leyes de Toro* dealt with false testimony in criminal cases; the false witness was subject to the same penalty as that handed down to the person against whom the witness had testified.[40]

Román y Zamora's treatment of oaths across time and space shows that a historical approach to the customs of the European world made an investigation into the development of laws about them all but unavoidable. The laws of a nation, as much as its customs, were part of its makeup. Yet while Román y Zamora saw the church's and crown's legislative attempts to put an end to the abuses surrounding oaths as necessary steps toward the moral development of the Christian republic, the superstitious practices that authorities sought to eliminate remained important to the historian or the student of customs. In the Spanish case, the penchant for swearing and tying one's corporate sense of selfhood and honor to the sacred domain, however mistaken, was a persistent trait that appeared to set Spaniards apart from other Christian nations.[41] For better or worse, it was part of the history of these people who preferred to err on the

---

38. Román y Zamora, *Repúblicas del mundo*, part 1, book 5, chap. 17, 1:293.

39. Román y Zamora, *Repúblicas del mundo*, part 1, book 5, chap. 17, 1:294v. Law 67 reads as follows: "Ningun juramento, aunque el Juez lo mande hacer, o la parte lo pida, no se haga en Sant Vicente de Ávila, ni en el herrojo de Sancta Agueda, ni sobre altar, ni cuerpo sancto, ni en otra Iglesia juradera so pena de diez mil maravedis para la nuestra camara, y fisco, al que lo jurare, y al Juez que lo mandare, y al que lo pidiere, o demandare." *Los códigos españoles concordados y anotados*, vol. 6, law 67, 565. According to the sixteenth-century commentator Antonio Gómez, the rationale for this law was to eradicate surviving superstitions associated with purgations and the expectation of miracles. Pedro Nolasco de Llano, *Compendio de los comentarios extendidos por el Maestro Antonio Gomez, a las ochenta y tres leyes de Toro* (1735) (Valladolid: Editorial Lex Nova, 1981), 324–25. Eighteenth-century commentators on this particular law wondered whether the ban was intended to supersede the law in *Partidas* that not only authorized taking oaths at sacred places but required doing so. The unlikely answer given was that the law, aimed at superstitious uses of sacred places, did not apply to cases where the sacred place was meant to highlight the solemnity of the proceedings. See Sancho de Llamas y Molina, *Comentario crítico-jurídico-literal a las ochenta y tres leyes de Toro* (Madrid: Imprenta de la Compañía de Impresores y Libreros del Reino, 1832), 505; and a similar interpretation in Juan Alvarez Posadilla, *Comentarios a las leyes de Toro, segun su espíritu y el de la legislación de España . . .* , 3rd ed. (Madrid: Don Antonio Martínez, 1826), 373.

40. *Los códigos españoles concordados y anotados*, 6:567. The same penalties were later made applicable to false witnesses in Inquisitorial trials; see petition 54 in *Quaderno de las cortes que en Valladolid tuvo su Magestad del Emperador y rey nuestro señor el año de 1523* (Salamanca: Juan de Junta, 1551), A2r.

41. There seems to be a link between the exacerbated sense of Spanish pride in lineage, as alleged by Tomás de Mercado, and a seeming tendency to abuse oaths; the defense of one's name or honor was often accompanied by the kind of oaths decried by theologians.

side of excessive attachment to the sacred than to keep too much distance from it, as did heretic sects that rejected oaths.[42]

The relationship between customs and laws as seen in Román y Zamora's comparative work is one of unacknowledged tension. In the author's narrative, the mere promulgation of laws barring superstitious oaths appears to make those customs recede progressively into the past and clear the way for future strict religious observance. But until that time comes, abuses would not go away, especially in the courts of law where perjury had taken hold.

From the promulgation of Law 67 to its inclusion in the *Recopilación* and beyond, oaths—in the courtrooms and the streets—remained a matter of unabated concern among royal and ecclesiastical authorities. A 1639 royal decree addressed the abuse of oaths, manifest most perniciously in false testimonies, banning all oaths except those required at courts of law or customary to enter into certain contracts.[43] Offenders faced penalties that included fines and imprisonment; recidivists faced being forced into exile.[44] The decree also required questioning witnesses who gave testimony regarding royal appointments whether the candidate was known to have abused oaths in the past.[45]

If in the abstract, oaths celebrated the idea of a natural union between religion and human affairs, in their social life, oaths were conditioned by human actors who lived under secular and ecclesiastical authorities, with all the attendant tensions and arrangements between the two domains. This is why oaths were often at the center of the jurisdictional disputes that punctuate a significant portion of Spanish legal and political history.[46] Facing rampant unobservance of laws in-

---

42. See André Vauchez, "Le refus du serment chez les hérétiques médiévaux," in *Le serment*, ed. Raymond Verdier, 2 vols. (Paris: Éditions du Centre National de la Recherche Scientifique, 1991), 2:257–63.

43. "Mandamos que ninguna persona de qualquier estado, y calidad que sea, jure el nombre de Dios en vano en ninguna occasion, ni para ningun efeto, y que aquel se diga, y tenga por juramento en vano, que se hiziere sin necessidad, declarando como declaramos, que solo quedan permitidos los juramentos que se hazen en juyzio, o paravalor algun contrato, o otra disposicion, y todos los demas absoluta y generalmente los prohibimos." *Prematica en que su Magestad manda se executen las penas en ellas contenidas, contra los que juraren* (Madrid: Pedro Tazo, 1639), A2v; also in *Recopilación de las leyes destos reynos, hecha por mandado de la Magestad Catolica del rey Don Felipe Segundo nuestro señor*, book 1, title 3, law 10, 1:4–4v.

44. *Prematica en que su Magestad manda se executen*, A2v.

45. *Prematica en que su Magestad manda se executen*, A3r.

46. This phenomenon was not exclusive to Spain and other Catholic countries in post-Tridentine Europe. Due to the scholarly contributions of Paolo Prodi, oaths have come to occupy a significant place in recent historiographical debates about the transformation of the secular and religious dimensions of power resulting from the rise of the confessional states. These debates not only intersect nicely with current scholarship on the shaping of religious beliefs in early modern Europe, but they also provide a provocative framework for challenging inherited notions about the boundaries of social and intellectual history. See Paolo Prodi, *Il sacramento del potere: Il giuramento*

tended to preserve royal jurisdiction, in 1480 the crown called on laymen of all religions to abstain from swearing when formalizing private contracts, an action that put them under ecclesiastical jurisdiction in the event that they violated their sworn obligation.[47] Moreover, the law contained penalties for the notary who certified a transaction under such circumstances. The principle that secular courts had jurisdiction over transactions between private individuals was repeated to notaries across the Atlantic upon being sworn to office; failure to observe this royal provision led to the notary's immediate termination.[48]

Oaths were also a powerful tool that religious officers did not hesitate to use to claim jurisdiction; royal laws were repeatedly issued to warn ecclesiastical authorities against actions considered detrimental to royal jurisdiction.[49] The crown's concern was based on the long-standing arrangement that regulated the basic handling of oaths. Only ecclesiastical authorities had the power to void them. In the case of conflicts arising from unfulfilled obligations in commercial transactions, for example, secular judges had discretion only to persuade the wronged party to annul the oath and reach an agreement. While the king could not void oaths, he could dictate when oaths were required from his subjects and also determine when an oath was not binding because it violated civil or natural law.[50]

In addition to the penalties that royal laws imposed on perjurers, the church could impose its own on laymen. Ecclesiastical law required false witnesses to

---

politico nella storia costituzionale dell'Occidente (Bologna: Il Mulino, 1992); and the collection of essays edited by Nestore Pirillo, *Il vincolo del giuramento e il tribunale della coscienza* (Bologna: Il Mulino, 1993).

47. "Defendemos que ningun lego, christiano, Judio, ni Moro, no haga obligacion, ni se someta a la jurisdiccion Ecclesiastica: ni hagan juramento por la tal obligacion junta ni apartadamente." *Ordenanzas reales de Castilla*, in *Los códigos españoles concordados y anotados*, vol. 6, book 3, title 1, law 6, 345. The law was mainly concerned with usurary loans; see Jerómino Castillo de Bobadilla, *Política para corregidores . . .* , 2 vols. (Madrid: Luis Sanchez, 1597), book 2, chap. 19, 1:1136; and Monterroso y Alvarado, *Pratica civil, y criminal, y instruccion de escrivanos*, 150v. Ecclesiastical authorities opposed the law, complaining about the refusal by notaries to administer oaths even in contracts and situations that required them. See the crown's 1582 response to these complaints in Díaz de Valdepeñas, *Suma de notas copiosas muy sustanciales*, xlix. Spanish lawyers and notaries could rely on specialized treatises to help them navigate the obligations that oaths created in contracts and wills. See, for example, Juan Gutierrez, *Tractatus de iuramento confirmatorio* (1574).

48. *Actas de cabildo de la Ciudad de México*, book 1, 196.

49. "Porque se nos ha hecho relacion, que muchas vezes los obispos, y Arçobispos de las Yglesias de las nuestras indias, y sus provisores, y vicarios, y otros juezes ecclesiasticos se entremeten a usurpar nuestra jurisdicion Real con diferentes colores, que para ello toman, entrando en casas de hombres, y personas legas, ansi Españolas, como indios, y tomandoles juramentos, y haziendo execuciones, y secrestos de bienes, y prendiendo los de su auctoridad, o por engaño en sus cárceles, sin pedir para ello auxilio a las nuestras justicias, y si algunas vezes le piden, es ante los Alcaldes ordinarios, que se le suelen dar, sin ver la justificacion de las causas por que los prenden; a todo lo qual es justo proveer de remedio." Solórzano Pereira, *Libro primero de la Recopilacion*, title 16, law 1, 2:203.

50. Ledesma, *Segunda parte de la summa*, 901–2.

make restitution if their testimonies had damaged the victim; restoration of the individual's reputation was among the contemplated reparatory actions.[51] The 1520 Synod of Córdoba stipulated that perjurers should stand up publicly at the church entrance.[52] The 1565 Council of Granada, although the chapters were never ratified, took a severe stance against such offenders. If the falsely accused individual was damaged by the testimony, the false witness was to be automatically excommunicated; clergy faced penalties that included prison and fines as well as exile and the loss of ecclesiastical benefice.[53] Yet despite the laws and the willingness shown by authorities to bring false witnesses to justice, the petitions of the *cortes* reveal their shared perception that perjurers went largely unpunished.[54] This perception was perpetuated in the text of laws and ordinances themselves.[55]

The Catholic Monarchs Isabel and Fernando made numerous efforts to ensure the proper handling and punishment of a number of offenses that officers of justice had not been interested in prosecuting. This appears to have been the case with judges' passive acceptance of false witnesses in both criminal and civil cases; judges were now required to take any disparity in testimony seriously and initiate an investigation into witnesses' veracity.[56] It was commonly thought that perjurers were more likely to be prosecuted by ecclesiastical than secular courts.[57]

---

51. Valtanás, *Confessionario muy cumplido*, 6v.

52. An ecclesiastical judge was to determine the punishment of a higher social rank. *Constituciones sinodales del obispado de Cordova* (Seville: Jacobo Cromberger, 1521), 23v.

53. Ignacio Perez de Heredia y Valle, *El Concilio Provincial de Granada en 1565: Edición crítica del Malogrado Concilio del Arzobispo Guerrero*, Subsidia num. 26 (Rome: Publicaciones del Instituto Español de Historia Eclesiástica, 1990), 248.

54. *Capitulos generales de las Cortes del año de mil y seyscientos y dos, fenecidas en el de seyscientos y quatro, y publicadas en el de seyscientos y diez* (Madrid: Juan de la Cuesta, 1610), petition 37, folio 6r.

55. See, for example, Ordinance 48 of the provincial and municipal ordinances for "governadores, assistentes, corregidores, juezes de residencia y alcaldes" issued in 1500 and reproduced in Antonio Muro Orejón, "Los capítulos de corregidores de 1500," *Anuario de estudios americanos* 19 (1962): A5r.

56. This law was promulgated in Madrid on December 4, 1502. Muro Orejón, "Los capítulos de corregidores de 1500," folio xli. The search for adequate procedures for deposing witnesses and producing reliable and useful testimonies made it necessary to establish guidelines for the selection of notaries. The quality of testimony presented at a trial depended not only on the moral standing and reliability of the witness, but also the ability of these professionals to extract information. In this regard, it was noticed that young, low-ranking officers lacking the necessary experience were often recording information from witnesses. *Las Cortes de Valladolid del año 1548*, petition 38, B2v; and *Capitulos y leyes discedidos en las cortes que su Magestad del rey don Phelipe nuestro señor tuvo y celebro en la ciudad de Toledo . . .* (Toledo: Juan Ferrer, 1560), petition 69, folio19r.

57. "Caso XIX. Es, quando algun seglar presentado por testigo depusiesse falsamente ante el juez Ecclesiastico: el qual podria entonces previniendo la causa proceder contra el, y castigarle . . . lo qual veo que se castiga mejor en los tribunales Ecclesiasticos que en los seglares, donde se toleran millones de testigos falsos, sin hazer caudal de los males que causan: y mas veo este abuso en los

Unlike French with its well-defined usages for *serment* and *juron*, the Spanish *juramento* refers to oaths such as those taken on a solemn occasion or in
private, as well as profane and unnecessary swearing expressions. The range of
these expressions was (and still is) wide, but theologians from the thirteenth
century onward focused on the far end of the spectrum, where mere profanity
gave way to religious irreverence and sometimes outright derision of sacred
things, scrutinizing periodically to determine what exactly constituted blasphemy.[58] In general, theologians dealt with blasphemy and perjury together;
in many cases Spanish legislation followed suit. Despite the consensus among
theologians that the swearer's intention was an essential component of any
oath, authors of sixteenth- and seventeenth-century manuals for confessors
and related literature paid close attention to expressions used and abused in
everyday life. In the case of oaths, they did so in order to inform confessors
and the public which phrases could be safely employed in a valid oath, and discourage the popular taste for profane, unnecessary, and superstitious forms of
swearing that came dangerously close to blasphemy. The assumption that blasphemy was present in the everyday language of the streets was the basis for the
renewed interest of ecclesiastical and royal authorities, beginning from the time
of the Catholic Monarchs, in controlling speech through the enforcement of
numerous decrees and ordinances that carried a wide array of penalties.[59] The

---

tribunales mayores, como quiera que el testigo que no se pudiesse concordar o salvar, no se devria
perdonar." Castillo de Bobadilla, *Politica para corregidores*, book 2, chap. 17, 1:919. Castillo de Bobadilla's work contains a wealth of information on the use and regulation of oaths in the sixteenth-
century Spanish legal system.
    58. On medieval conceptualizations of the "sins of the tongue," see Casagrande and Vecchio, *I
peccati della lingua*. On the methodological problems posed by the study of blasphemy in the sixteenth century, see Oliver Christin's carefully argued essay, "Sur la condamnation du blaspheme,"
Revue d'histoire de l'Eglise de France 204 (1994): 43–64; Alain Cabantous, *Histoire du blasphème
en Occident, XVIe–XIXe siècle* (Paris: Albin Michel, 1998), especially chaps. 1 and 3. For Spain, see
Flynn, "Blasphemy and the Play of Anger in Sixteenth-Century Spain," 29–56; and Ronald E. Surtz's
case study, "Crimes of the Tongue: The Inquisitorial Trials of Cristóbal Duarte Ballester," *Medieval
Encounters* 12, no. 3 (2006): 519–32. For Mexico, see Javier Villa-Flores, *Dangerous Speech: A Social
History of Blasphemy in Colonial Mexico* (Tucson: University of Arizona Press), 2006.
    59. On July 22, 1492, the Catholic Monarchs made the utterance of certain expressions of reli-
gious disbelief or that challenged God a crime punishable by prison and even exile; third-time offenders risked having their tongue pierced by a nail. *Las pragmaticas del reyno. Recopilacion de algunas
bulas del summo pontifice*, folios 1–1v. Similar concerns were reported at the *cortes* of Toledo in 1525
including the popular belief that only expressions indicating a disavowal of Christ could trigger criminal prosecution. *Las leyes y prematicas reales hechas por sus Magestades en las cortes que mandaron
hazer e hicieron en la ciudad de Toledo 1525* (Salamanca: Juan de Junta, 1550), folios C5v–C6. The determination on the part of authorities to punish verbal offenses such as blasphemy was accompanied
by an equally strong desire to do so without creating a flood of cases of dubious merit. The particular
vulnerability of Spanish men to words related to their sense of honor had prompted authorities to remind officers of justice not to spend time on complaints about *palabras livianas* (light insults) absent
a denunciation from the offended party. See the 1523 *prematica* from Valladolid, which repeated the
content of a 1518 *prematica* issued in the same city. *Reportorio de todas las prematicas y capitulos de
cortes hechos por su magestad, desde el año de mil y quinientos y veynte y tres . . .* (Medina del Campo:

Fig. 3.1. Sins of the tongue. Diego Valadés, *Rhetorica Christiana* (1579). (Courtesy of the John Carter Brown Library at Brown University.)

line between profane swearing and blasphemy was thin and variable. In 1528, for example, authorities suspected that new expressions were being coined in order to circumvent existing ordinances; these included straightforward imprecations as well as a number of irreverent expressions.[60]

In 1526, the Dominican friar Diego de Vitoria took a modest yet unprecedented step toward curbing the violations of the second commandment ("Thou

Pedro de Castro, 1547), folio 73r. Blasphemy was a more serious crime and the evidence easily fabricated. For this reason, judges were instructed to be wary of accusations of blasphemy brought by bailiffs in reliance on the testimony of their aides and servants against individuals they might wish to harm. *Las cortes de Valladolid del año 1548*, petition 51, B6v. Another issue in blasphemy prosecutions was the defense of royal jurisdiction against intrusion by officers of the Inquisition. Those officers were reminded their jurisdiction was limited to crimes of "heregia, apostasia y faturia," and that the intervention of the Inquisition was justified only in cases of "blasphemias hereticales." C7v and C8r. The complaint of overreaching by the officers of the Inquisition was not new. See *Quadernos de las cortes que su magestad de la Emperatriz y reyna nuestra señora tuvo en la ciudad de Segovia el año de MDXXXII* (Salamanca: Juan de Junta, 1549), petition 26, C5.

60. "Por no incurrir en ellas se buscan e inventan otras nuevas maneras de palabras de blasphemias diziendo. Reniego de la fe y de la crisma que rescebi: e jurando como dios es verdad: e como dios es hijo de nuestra señora: e por la virginidad e limpieza de nuestra señora la virgen Maria: y otras palabras semejantes." *Quaderno de las leyes y prematicas reales fechas en las cortes . . .* (Alcalá de Henares: Ioan de Brocar, 1546), petition 69, B4v.

shalt not take the name of the Lord in vain") that had become widely accepted among the populace despite secular and ecclesiastical sanctions. To this end he founded the Cofradía del Santo Nombre de Dios in Burgos, a brotherhood whose members committed themselves to honoring the second commandment and paying a fine each time for every violation of their pledge not to swear. Dominican theologians such as Felipe de Meneses and more notably, Domingo de Soto—both authors of treatises on swearing—championed the brotherhood, and the rest of the order vigorously took up the cause it represented, agreeing at chapters celebrated during the 1550s that preachers should do their part to eradicate the vice.[61] Besides drafting the *cofradía*'s charter, Diego de Vitoria is believed to have written a treatise about oaths.[62] The mission of the brotherhood resonated among religious and laymen in Mexico, where a similar *cofradía* was in existence by the middle of the sixteenth century.[63]

Preaching and the zeal of self-regulating bodies of laymen, however, were not enough; the fast-changing face of sins against the second commandment required confessors to be adequately prepared. Some religious authors such as the Franciscan Francisco de Alcocer set out to fill this gap. In the *Tratado del juego* (Madrid, 1559), Alcocer dealt with every imaginable spiritual and earthly danger that Christians could face in increasingly popular gambling houses. Alcocer saw these dangers as many and serious, since gamblers could break every one of the Ten Commandments when they indulged in their habit.[64] The *Tratado del juego* was something else as well, namely a case study of Christian obligations under both ecclesiastical and royal laws.

According to Alcocer, gambling and all conceivable manifestations of swearing went hand in hand. In the heat of the game, gamblers blasphemed, making their companions unwitting participants in an offense against God. Those with poor luck often found themselves vowing to undertake some pious or religious

---

61. Vicente Beltrán de Heredia, "Ensayo biobibliográfico sobre el P. Diego de Vitoria," in *Miscelánea Beltrán de Heredia: Colección de artículos sobre historia de la teología española,* 4 vols. (Salamanca: Editorial OPE, 1971–73), 2:104. Domingo de Soto published his sermon on swearing in both Latin and Spanish. *Institucion de Fray Domingo de Soto, de la orden de S. Domingo, a loor del nombre de Dios, de como se a de evitar el abuso de los juramentos* (Anvers: Biuda y Herederos de Juan Stelsio, 1569). In addition to Meneses's treatment of the second commandment in his *Luz de alma christiana*—a work translated into the Tarascan language by Fr. Maturino Gilberti—he also wrote a full treatise on the issue of profane swearing, *Tratado de juramentos* (1553).

62. Under the title *Tractatus quibusnam conditionibus juramentum constare debeat.* Beltrán de Heredia, "Ensayo bibliográfico," 106. A work on the Decalogue has also been attributed to him. 109.

63. The *Reglas y constituciones* of the brotherhood, include a transcription of the rules, were published in Mexico in 1567. Joaquín García Icazbalceta, *Bibliografía mexicana del siglo XVI*, 2nd ed. (Mexico City: Fondo de Cultura Económica, 1954), 208–9.

64. Francisco de Alcocer, *Tratado del juego* (Salamanca: Andrea de Portonariis, 1559), 5–14. For Alcocer's thoughts on gambling, see Giovanni Ceccarelli, *Il gioco e il peccato: Economia e rischio nel tardo Medioevo* (Bologna: Il Mulino, 2003).

work as a step toward amending their ways and quitting their vice, but frequently failed to fulfill the promise.[65] Finally, there were the perjurers, who in their desire to win, gave sworn testimony without any consideration for the truth.[66] Despite its gloomy depiction of what transpired in gambling rooms, the treatise was not a single-minded indictment of gambling and call for strict adherence to the highest moral standards, for Alcocer understood that not all games were sinful, and swearing, when done appropriately, was a virtuous act. Furthermore, even blameworthy oaths amounted only to venial sins.[67] Nonetheless, gambling opened up many questions that required the casuist's expert guidance to help confessors make their decisions and teach gamblers to avoid mortal sins.

If gambling houses were a fertile ground for the commission of sins, especially the violation of oaths and proliferation of blasphemy, religious writers and ecclesiastical authorities also cast a vigilant eye toward other social sites. For the Dominican Juan de Ávila, who thought that the governing body of the church was the best model for secular authorities and prominent members of Spanish society interested in the nation's well-being, the most pernicious forms of perjury were found in the administration of justice. He was not referring to false witness, but rather notaries who regularly charged higher fees for their services than those permitted in contravention of their oath of office.[68] As he noted, in the absence of royal efforts to put an end to this abuse, the bishop of Córdoba had instructed priests to withhold the absolution of offenders. Similar violations were also common among lower officers such as the *alguaciles de campo* (sheriffs of the crops). Since no salary was attached to this office, the violation of the oath not to take money for services was all but guaranteed. To Juan de Ávila, the best way to remedy this problem was to forgo the administration of oaths to those individuals who, because of their low station in life, were bound to break them.[69] Implicit in the condemnation of these abuses

---

65. Alcocer, *Tratado del juego*, 7–8.
66. Alcocer, *Tratado del juego*, 8.
67. Alcocer, *Tratado del juego*, 21–22.
68. "Lo primero y que mas pena da, es, ver a Nuestro Señor tan ofendido con juramentos falsos, o diziendo mentira en lo de presente, o no cumpliendo lo que se jura. Y donde mas se usa esta desventura, es donde mas lexos avia de estar, conviene a saber, en el exercicio de la justicia, y cosas tocantes a ella. Los que en este caso mas desenfrenados estan, son los escrivanos, que jurando todos de guardar el aranzel destos Reynos, casi ninguno lo guarda: y aunque es verdad que era cosa muy justa acrecentarles los derechos, pues los tiempos son diferentes, mas no por eso dexan ellos de pecar quebrantando lo jurado: pues Iuramentum debet impleri in specifica forma ni Dios dexa de ser ofendido: y quien dir alas vezes que es esto lo es?" Juan de Ávila, *Obras del padre maestro Juan de Avila, predicador en el Andaluzia. Aora de Nuevo añadida a la vida del Autor . . .* (Madrid: Pedro Madrigal, 1588), 131r.
69. "Yo si pudiera no recibiera juramento de personas de tan baxa suerte y conciencia, por la poca esperança que da de los cumplir." Ávila, *Obras del padre maestro Juan de Avila*, 132v–133r.

was the tension between crown and church and their respective commitments to preserving the integrity of oaths and fulfilling their respective obligations. Ultimately, Ávila wrote, it was up to the crown to eliminate the conditions that enabled the violations of oaths by either adjusting officers' wages or doing away with the obligation to swear. The cases presented by Juan de Ávila were minor ones, but they contained the essence of a jurisdictional conflict that would play out numerous times for decades to come under a fully formulated and unequivocal doctrine of regalism that would only exacerbate these tensions.[70]

Oaths, Witnesses, and Testimonies in
Early Colonial Mexico

Many years before Torquemada compared Nahua and Roman oaths, his brothers within the order had felt compelled to denounce the administration of oaths to the Nahuas, an increasingly common practice with no end in sight. The Franciscan historian was thoroughly familiar with and subscribed to the opinion of other friars such as Fr. Gerónimo de Mendieta. Mendieta believed that the Nahuas should not be required to swear when participating in civil lawsuits. Torquemada recorded that the Franciscans made this their recommendation in 1561 as part of a proposal to rein in the growing number of lawsuits involving Indians. The proposal also contemplated that all civil disputes be heard and resolved at the local level and with minimal, if any, paperwork.[71] From the friars' perspective, the litigiousness of the Indians was compounded by their carefree attitude toward statements made under oath; preventing native litigants from swearing in legal proceedings, the friars argued, could effectively eliminate a common occasion for sin.[72]

In trying to restore or approximate the state of affairs in the past when justice among the Nahuas was allegedly dispensed swiftly and without the trappings of contemporary lawsuits, Mendieta thought that Indian disputes over land should be handled without sworn statements because the parties declared whatever suited them best.[73] Oddly enough, Mendieta justified this measure by stating that the Indians' preoccupation with land and its boundaries was a relatively new phenomenon, born out of the indigenous practice of distributing

---

70. See, for example, Solórzano Pereira's opinion on the accusations of ecclesiastical judges in Peru against *corregidores* who violated their oath of office. *Política Indiana*, book 5, chap. 2, 756.

71. Torquemada, *Monarquía Indiana*, book 5, chap. 16, 1:625.

72. García Icazbalceta, *Nueva colección de documentos*, 1:4–5.

73. García Icazbalceta, *Nueva colección de documentos*, 1:20.

land among their allies.[74] Interestingly, Mendieta was quick to point out that the Nahuas had been motivated exclusively by politics, not justice.[75] Rehashing the familiar arguments about the pernicious effects of the Indian presence in the courts of law, Mendieta did not mince words, declaring that they damned their souls by lying under oath,[76] and that oath-taking was an intrusive Spanish procedure best avoided.

The extant documentation related to a protracted 1565 lawsuit brought by an Indian municipal council against the viceroy and judges of the Real Audiencia during the time of the unwelcome inspection tour of Licenciado Jerónimo de Valderrama offers a glimpse into Indian behaviors during legal proceedings and Spanish misapprehensions about the crown's administration of justice in indigenous communities. The lawsuit charged that the alcaldes still practiced idolatry and accepted bribes, and that they were illiterate and thus ill suited to their offices.[77] In their defense, it was argued that their experience more than compensated for the lack of literacy and, moreover, that no law restricted the access to municipal government of individuals who did not read or write. After all, many alcaldes of Spanish towns fell into the same category.[78]

Due to the unavailability of the interpreters appointed by the Real Audiencia, Diego de León, a new interpreter familiar with Nahuatl, was put in charge of translating the depositions. As was traditional, the interpreter was asked to take an oath, swearing by God and Saint Mary that he would fulfill his duties. The oath also included customary language that its violation constituted a serious offense for which he could expect to be charged with perjury in addition to having to respond before God.[79] The Real Audiencia counted among its officials and administrators a number of appointed interpreters; by a 1563 ordinance, they were required to take an oath promising to perform their job without showing any preference toward the parties to a dispute under penalty of perjury

---

74. Every time the *cabildo* of Mexico City proceeded to grant a Spaniard a parcel of land, it went through the ritual of requesting evidence from Mexican Indians showing (individual or communal) ownership of land and existing boundaries. Failure to provide proof of ownership made any Indian claim invalid. The minutes of the *cabildo* contain numerous examples, such as the cases from November 1563. *Actas de cabildo de la Ciudad de México*, book 7, 148–50.

75. García Icazbalceta, *Nueva colección de documentos*, 1:21.

76. García Icazbalceta, *Nueva colección de documentos*, 1:38.

77. *Códice Osuna: Reproducción facsimilar de la obra del mismo título editada en Madrid, 1878* (Mexico City: Ediciones del Instituto Indigenista Interamericano, 1947), 1, 13–14, and 16.

78. "Y ansimesmo por la leyes de vuestros reynos pueden ser elegidos a los dichos oficios tales personas sabiendo la costumbre y fueros, sin otras letras algunas." *Códice Osuna*, 33.

79. "Y juró por Dios y por Santa María, de usar bien y fielmente del dicho oficio de yntérprete, a su leal saber y entender, y que lo hará bien y fielmente aclarando la verdad, sin quitalla ni mengualla; y si así lo hiciere, dios le ayude, y si no se lo demande como a persona que se perjura y no hace bien su oficio." *Códice Osuna*, 91.

and possible restitution to the wronged individual.[80] An earlier ordinance from 1530 that originated in Spain had called attention to the repeated commission of fraud by interpreters of indigenous languages. To avoid more wrongdoings of this kind, the crown recommended that Indian witnesses testify twice, each time with a different interpreter who was not present for the other testimony.[81] There is evidence that the recommendation was occasionally followed but not without opposition. For instance, in the session of April 25, 1552, the members of the *cabildo* heard two petitions to strip royal inspector Diego Ramírez of his power.[82] According to the petitions, Ramírez had assumed greater powers than those included in his royal appointment. The charges also alleged that Ramírez, accompanied by a notary and bailiffs, had taken to conducting criminal investigations against *encomenderos* whom he then ordered to pay the salaries of his retinue. Interestingly, Ramírez was charged with traveling with two interpreters when only one was required, and opting, in his capacity as judge, for standard and lengthy procedures instead of summary ones in determining whether excessive tributes had been imposed.[83]

A detailed examination of the ways in which interpreters became a permanent fixture of the Audiencia falls outside the scope of this chapter; I will limit myself to suggesting that the two laws I have mentioned, separated by over thirty years, signal a transition from a somewhat tentative approach to ensuring the veracity of Indian testimony to the adoption of standard procedures, notably the appointment of interpreters and other municipal officials. The historical record contains early examples of sworn indigenous witnesses in Inquisitorial

---

80. "Ytem ordenamos y mandamos, que aya numero de interpretes en la dicha nuestra audiencia, y que antes que sean recebidos a usar el oficio juren en forma devida, que usaran sus oficios bien y fielmente declarando e interpretando el negocio y pleyto que les fuere cometido clara y abiertamente, sin encubrir ni añadir cosa alguna, diziendo simplemente el dicho del delito o negocio y testigos que examinaren, sin ser parcial a ninguna de las partes, y sin favorecer mas a uno que a otro, y que por ello no llevaran interesse alguno, mas del salario que les fuere tassado y señalado, so pena de perjuros y del daño e interesse de las partes, y que bolveran lo que ansi llevaren con las setenas, y perdimiento de los officios." Encinas, *Cedulario indiano*, 2:368. When, in 1578, the indigenous community of Huexotzingo filed a lawsuit against its governing body, Christobal Altamirano, the appointed interpreter was informed of the obligations attached to his oath, as well as the penalties for its violation. The instructions, which sketch portraits of the good and bad interpreter, follow and expand upon the 1563 ordinance. Brito Guadarrama, *Códice Chavero de Huexotzingo*, 180–81.

81. Puga, *Provisiones*, folio 41r; also Encinas, *Cedulario indiano*, 2:368.

82. Ramírez was appointed inspector on May 22, 1550 and entrusted with gathering information on reported abuses concerning the collection of Indian tribute. Paso y Troncoso, *Epistolario de la Nueva España, 1505–1818*, 6:12.

83. "por quel puede bisitar lo que su magestad le manda sin alguaziles con un naguatato y no con dos como lleva sin hazer procesos tan costosos solamente saber la berdad sin figuras de juyzio enformandose por testigos de cada parte si se guarda la tasacion o si se esede mandando rrestituyr lo no bien llebado y esto se podra asentar en un libro firmado de su nombre o del escribano para que se supiese lo que haze." *Actas de cabildo de la Ciudad de México*, book 6, 53–54.

and civil courts. For instance, the trials for idolatry overseen by Fr. Juan de Zumárraga in his capacity as apostolic inquisitor between 1536 and 1540 relied on information provided by both sworn and unsworn witnesses.[84] At this early stage, age, gender, and social status were the factors that likely determined whether or not witnesses took an oath. Given Zumárraga's harsh stance against individuals charged with superstition and idolatry, it is difficult to imagine that the administration of oaths to selected indigenous witnesses was carried out without coercion. In the battle against idolaters, what better weapon could there be than oaths to test the allegiance of Christianized Indians and teach about superstition and perjury under the very real threat of punishment?

The incorporation of Indian interpreters into the structure of a municipal government based on the Spanish model was facilitated by the friars' direct involvement in the education of noble Nahua youth. As for the oaths required of witnesses, the documentation related to the 1565 lawsuit recorded that Francisco Ximenez, a principal from the ward of San Sebastian in the city of Mexico, swore by God and Saint Mary and crossed himself before giving testimony.[85] The association between oath-taking and the cross came to be reflected in the Nahuatl language. For "I make an oath," Molina registered both a literal equivalent, *juramento nicchihua*, and also *nicte namiqui yn cruz*, "I encounter/receive the cross."[86]

Officers of justice such as *corregidores* and alcaldes were entrusted with the enforcement of decrees aimed at curbing offenses most often associated with the indigenous population, such as drunkenness and the making and selling of pulque. A set of instructions dating from 1561 also listed perjury among the public misdeeds that these officers were to eliminate, implying that Nahuas were more inclined to perjure themselves than any other group.[87] This view, which reflected

---

84. In the 1536 trial of the Otomi specialists Antonio Tacatecle and Alonso Tanixtecle, two indigenous witnesses, Diego and Andrés, were required to take an oath before giving testimony ("mandó recibir juramento en forma debida de derecho"). *Procesos de indios idólatras y hechiceros* (Mexico City: Publicaciones del Archivo General de la Nación, 1912), 5, 6, and 8. And in February 1537, the Audiencia of Mexico heard testimony from Zapotec witnesses who claimed that Francisco López Tenorio, *corregidor* of Yagavila, had tortured and murdered a Zapotec ruler and high priest and some of his associates. Since they were not yet Christians, the Audiencia had these Zapotec witnesses take an oath "according to their own laws" before they testified. David Tavárez, *The Invisible War: Indigenous Devotions, Discipline, and Dissent in Colonial Mexico* (Stanford: Stanford University Press, 2011), 33.

85. "del qual mediante Joan Grande fue tomado e recibido juramento, y él lo hizo por Dios e por Santa Maria e por la señal de la cruz que hizo con los dedos de su mano." *Códice Osuna*, 20.

86. *Vocabulario en lengua castellana y mexicana*, 73v. Molina's use of "juramento" is consistent with the missionaries' generally favoring this term over the Nahuatl *tlalqualiztli*. The two entries are identical to those found in Molina's earlier dictionary, *Aqui comiença un vocabulario en la lengua castellana y mexicana* (1555).

87. "Y así mismo castigaréis las borracheras y pecados públicos, especialmente los perjurios,

the opinion prevalent among friars and ecclesiastical authorities, went hand in hand with the reluctance in religious quarters to allow Nahuas to redress grievances through the Spanish legal system, as the crown permitted them to do. On this matter, groups as bitterly divided as the friars, bishops, and *encomenderos* found a common voice, albeit for very different reasons.

For example, consider the second archbishop of Mexico, the Dominican Alonso de Montúfar. During his tempestuous tenure as archbishop from 1554 to 1572, Montúfar would repeatedly paint himself before Spanish authorities as the victim of an alliance between the second viceroy, Luis de Velasco, and the friars who sought to curtail his authority and implement the policies designed by the religious orders.[88] The uneasy relationship between Montúfar and the religious men was irreversibly damaged when the friars, with the viceroy's support, rejected the archbishop's demand that tithes be collected from the Indians as they were from all other Christians.

Defending himself from accusations that Indians were being charged legal fees, Montúfar declared to the Council of the Indies that he had tried to ensure that disputes involving Indians be summarily resolved as required by law, and, in those cases where legal process was required, he had made sure that court officials received no fees. Moreover, he had made it a point not to allow Indians to take oaths in legal proceedings because, as he put it, "it is the heaviest burden of conscience in the world."[89] Oaths, as canonists saw them, created a web of obligations, reaching beyond the conscience of the individual oath-taker to implicate the conscience of its administrator. For this reason, known perjurers were barred from serving as witnesses, and even suspicion of false testimony was sufficient cause not to administer an oath to a witness.

Montúfar invoked a similar principle when he refused to ordain a group of Augustinians for their alleged lack of preparation and education. And he construed it as an act of conscience required by his own scruples, but also those of the Dominican prior who, supposedly fearful of ordaining the friars, was inclined to defer to the conscience of the provincial of the order.[90] The crown promptly rebutted Archbishop Montúfar's arguments against the ordination of the friars.[91]

---

porque se entiende con facilidad exceden con esto los indios." "Instrucción a los alcaldes y corregidores de Nueva España." Cuevas, *Documentos inéditos del siglo XVI*, 249.

88. Paso y Troncoso, *Epistolario de la Nueva España*, 9:178.

89. Paso y Troncoso, *Epistolario de la Nueva España*, 8:44. The phrase was common for a long time. See John Spurr, "A Profane History of Early Modern Oaths," *Transactions of the Royal Historical Society* 11 (2001): 38.

90. Paso y Troncoso, *Epistolario de la Nueva España*, 8:191. For the same episode retold by Montúfar, see 9:97.

91. Solórzano Pereira, *Libro primero de la Recopilacion*, title 11, law 8, 1:244.

On another occasion, Montúfar sided with the Indians of Michoacán when, in 1562, they disputed a recent assessment that obliged them to pay an unusually high tribute. The archbishop cast doubt over the assessment procedure, arguing that the information gathered from Indian informers through interpreters had likely been distorted. As support, he pointed out that although there were many local interpreters in the province, only one had been sworn and appointed.[92] Moreover, Montúfar deemed the assessment invalid for the failure to follow the 1531 law regulating the use of interpreters. That law, as we have said earlier, stopped short of requiring the use of two interpreters when taking Indian testimonies, and was intended more as a suggestion that left room for local authorities to devise and implement the administrative steps they thought necessary.

Montúfar was not alone in raising serious doubts about inspections, in particular the collection of information from Indians that served as the basis for assessments. The same year, one critic of the ways inspections were being conducted proposed that judges proceed according to the law by making inquiries of Indian witnesses whose testimonies would be later validated by the inhabitants of the town and checked against the town's painted records.[93]

As some initiatives brewing in the city council show, ecclesiastical authorities and friars were not the only ones to question the administration of oaths to Indians. On October 3, 1561, García de Albornoz, *factor* (tribute administrator) of the *cabildo* of Mexico, who had recently and controversially been chosen to serve as its representative at court in Spain, presented a document to the *cabildo* that contained a number of requests to the king on matters of government. This *Instrucción*, which was read to all members present at the session before it was submitted to Spain for royal approval, touched on a variety of topics, many related to the economic and social consequences of the implementation of the New Laws. And there was, of course, the ever-present issue of tribute. Regarding assessments, the document blamed *nahuatlatos* (Nahua interpreters) and low-ranking members of the native nobility for instigating complaints about excessive tribute and requests for new inspections before the Audiencia; the same culprits were also accused of fostering perjury among Indians by coaching witnesses and showing a total disregard for the truth.[94]

---

92. Paso y Troncoso, *Epistolario de la Nueva España*, 9:190.

93. Paso y Troncoso, *Epistolario de la Nueva España*, 9:243. Morales's recommendation raises the question of the origin of the Nahua practice of authenticating testimonies through the participation of multiple witnesses. Did the Spanish encourage a practice that was already in place? Did they think of it as an acceptable substitute for oaths, as later developments suggest? For a discussion of Nahua forms of authentication, see James Lockhart, "Double Mistaken Identity," 108–9.

94. "Y que los que juran hoy por un pueblo se aprovechan mañana de los mismos por quien

Indian testimony had become a contentious issue among Spaniards chiefly because inspectors routinely depended on it in determining and adjusting tribute. As the *encomenderos* saw it, and their advocates in government reported, tributary contributions were in steady decline due to increasing pressure from Indian communities. The *Instrucción* called on the king to put a swift end to Indian legal demands by preventing the Mexican Indians from taking oaths or acting as witnesses for a period of fifty to sixty years.[95] To justify the request, the document explained that the new converts did not fully grasp oaths' religious underpinnings, and were therefore unaware of the gravity of the sin of perjury. Barring Indians from taking oaths would not only protect them from sinning, but would also protect others from the loss of property and honor as a result of false testimonies.[96]

Neither García de Albornoz nor the document appear to have had much impact because a few months later, on January 9, 1562, the *cabildo* convened again to vote on a set of similar requests that treasurer Don Fernando de Portugal had introduced. And this meeting, too, was fraught with tensions that preceded it. In this case, alleged irregularities in the procedure for examining and approving the document helped further fuel some *cabildo* members' misgivings about a number of provisions that they believed detrimental to Indian well-being. Among them was the request that the king ensure that the Nahuas not serve as witnesses or take oaths for fifty or sixty years. To those that opposed it, this measure went against the very assumptions that underlay current legislation and practice. The most glaring example was the open contradiction between making Indians eligible for municipal government office and denying them the responsibility of being witnesses.[97] Moreover, the objectors argued, Nahuas had become good Christians; many were noblemen by birth and fond of the truth. As such, barring Indians from the courtroom altogether instead of applying the prescribed punishments to those guilty of perjury amounted to an insult, an affront.[98] As these words suggest, this was an issue of the recognition of the honor of the Mexican Indians as well as their personhood before the law, personhood predicated upon the status as Christians that they acquired upon being baptized.[99] Far from exposing a minoritarian view, those who opposed the moratorium on Indian oaths were simply

---

dixeron y en ellos hay gran mal de perjuros y ofensas de Dios." *Actas de cabildo de la Ciudad de México*, book 6, 498.

95. *Actas de cabildo de la Ciudad de México*, book 6, 494.

96. *Actas de cabildo de la Ciudad de México*, book 6, 494.

97. *Actas de cabildo de la Ciudad de México*, book 7, 7.

98. *Actas de cabildo de la Ciudad de México*, book 7, 7.

99. For a wide-ranging reflection on the issue, see Adriano Prosperi, "Batessimo e identità cristiana nella prima età moderna," 65. For the place that the state assigned to baptism, see Hespanha, "Le Droit et la domination coloniale européenne," especially 215–16.

restating principles that reflected the crown's designs for the new subjects. *Encomenderos* and their spokesmen in the city council began to doubt and contest these principles not because they held an alternative view of social order but rather because they sought to protect their own interests, proposing ad hoc solutions to very concrete threats. The crown's assumptions regarding the legal status of Christianized Indians were openly contradicted, as we have seen, when Spaniards refused to acknowledge them as Christians, reserving the term for themselves.[100] When the friars took note of this offense and reported it to royal authorities, they may not have been fully aware of the extent to which their own model of tutelage had contributed to the devaluation of the Indians' legal status in the eyes of other Spaniards. Church authorities, and the friars in particular, occasionally advocated policies that differed very little from those of the party whose ambitions they sought to restrain. After all, it was the missionaries' deep involvement in the most intricate details of their charges' economic life that made it possible to gather information about the existing conditions of labor and tribute collection and communicate it to Spanish authorities in the Peninsula. The crown, for its part, followed well-established legal procedures that aimed to affirm royal jurisdiction and was reluctant to accept the missionaries' sweeping changes that would compromise this jurisdiction.

While Spanish and Indian officials were reminded of the consequences of violating their oaths upon taking office, the rest of the Indian population became familiar with oaths, if at all, through occasional interactions with city government and the justice system. However, the obligations attending this ritual at the intersection of the religious and the secular worlds were included in Christian instruction on the second and eighth commandments. As with many other religious terms and terms related to Spanish legal institutions, both of which were new to Indians, the authors of doctrinal literature for Indians favored the use of the Spanish *juramento* over indigenous expressions.[101] In his 1578 Spanish-Zapotec dictionary, the Dominican Fr. Juan de Córdoba, who, as we have noted, departed from Molina's lexicographical approach, distinguished between Zapotec usages before and after the arrival of the friars.[102] Accord-

---

100. García Icazbalceta, *Códice Mendieta*, 1:298.

101. Sahagún, for example, chose the word *juramento* to translate the admonition against perjury in his Nahua version of the *Book of Wisdom*. See the "Apendiz del primer libro," in *Florentine Codex*, 1:60.

102. See the introduction. Juan de Córdoba was born in 1503 in Spain, where he pursued a military career. He participated in the Coronado expedition before entering the Dominican order in 1543. He was also the author of *Arte en lengua zapoteca*, also published in 1578. Joaquín García Icazbalceta, *Bibliografía mexicana del siglo XVI*, 2nd ed. (Mexico City: Fondo de Cultura Económica, 1954), 290–96. On Córdoba's lexicographic work, see Thiemer-Sachse, "El *Vocabulario castellano-zapoteco* y el *Arte en lengua zapoteca* de Juan de Córdova," 147–74; and Thomas C. Smith

ing to Córdoba, the earlier terms consisted mainly of curses and imprecatory expressions (not unlike those that Spanish laws sought to eradicate), whereas the later ones mirrored acceptable Spanish usage.[103] The same gap between past and present also informed Córdoba's brief section on old Zapotec curses that were reportedly no longer in use.[104] Córdoba's *Vocabulario* also included useful distinctions for the confessor of Indians, with entries for false oaths and those uttered in vain or in a jocular mode. Regarding the word *testigo* (witness), Córdoba, like Molina in his Nahuatl dictionaries, opted not to include its Zapotec gloss.[105]

The courtroom and the obligations of witnesses were very much on the minds of missionaries who were preoccupied by Mexican Indians' growing participation in undesirable secular activities such as legal disputes. This concern had a direct impact on the ways they framed their teachings on the second commandment. For example, the Franciscan Fr. Juan Bautista dealt with it almost exclusively in relation to the administration of justice in his *Confessionario para indios*.[106] Other writers, such as Fr. Domingo de la Anunciación, author of a *Doctrina christiana*

Stark, "La ortografía del zapoteco en el *Vocabulario* de fray Juan de Córdova," in *Escritura zapoteca: 2,500 años de historia*, ed. María de los Ángeles Romero Frizzi (Mexico City: CIESAS, Miguel Ángel Porrúa, CONACULTA-INAH, 2003), 173–240. On Córdoba's *Vocabulario* as a source on Zapotec religion, see Smith Stark, "Dioses, sacerdotes, y sacrificio: Una mirada a la religión zapoteca a través del *Vocabulario en lengua çapoteca* (1578) de Juan de Córdoba," in *La religión de los Binnigula'sa'*, ed. Víctor de la Cruz and Marcus Winter (Oaxaca: Instituto Estatal de Educación Pública de Oaxaca, Instituto Oaxaqueño de las Culturas, 2002), 89–195.

103. Córdoba, *Vocabulario castellano-zapoteco*, 216v. Suárez de Peralta found in the use of oaths among contemporary Nahuas reasons to be equally optimistic about their conversion: "Pues jurar, ni por pienso saben más juramento, de a fe de Dios, y sábelo Dios; que en su lengua dicen así: *Ipaltzinco Dios*; que es, a fe de Dios. *Qui mo, ma chitia, Dios*; que es sábelo Dios. Éste es su ordinario jurar. Antiguamente, antes que recibiesen el bautismo, solían tener por costumbre decir, cuando se les ofrecía, como a nosotros se nos ofrece y decimos muchas veces: ¡Oh! ¡válame Dios, Jesús sea conmigo! Decían: *Matla catecolotl, nech, huica*; que quiere decir: El demonio me lleve." Juan Suárez de Peralta, *Tratado del descubrimiento de las Indias* (Mexico City: Consejo Nacional para la Cultura y las Artes, 1990), chap. 3, 65. A similar conceptualización of pre-Conquest oaths among the Incas is found in Domingo de Santo Tomás, *Grammatica o arte de la lengua general de los indios de los reynos del Peru*, ed. Rodolfo Cerrón-Palomino (Cuzco: Centro Bartolomé de las Casas, 1995), chap. 23, 138–40.

104. "Maldiciones que usavan los Indios vt. mueraste, comante las aves como echan las madres, enojadas a los hijos. Pudranse tus cojones como tierra con la yerva. Ve podrerse. Càtilo, mueraste." Córdoba, *Vocabulario castellano-zapoteco*, 255r. I am grateful to David Tavárez for pointing out to me that some of the expressions that Córdoba describes as Zapotec curses were commonplace expressions that may well have remained in use. For example, *cátilo*, which Córdoba glosses as "muéraste," was the most straightforward way to say "Die!" in Zapotec.

105. One of the entries for "conciencia" reads as follows: "Conciencia pro ut es acto testificativo de lo que hemos o no hemos hecho. To bilào tòbipeayoolani cíeana testigo toconanitono que lahoexihui, laquela nazacanitenino." Córdoba, *Vocabulario castellano-zapoteco*, 84r. Córdoba also has clustered entries related to juridical institutions such as oaths, vows, promises, and oath of allegiance (*omenaje*). 292r.

106. Juan Bautista, *Confessionario en lengua mexicana y castellana*, 44–44v.

breve (1565), were more inclusive, spelling out the conditions required for a valid oath, and highlighting that perjury and blasphemy were offenses to be punished by both secular and ecclesiastical authorities.[107] But the friars' biggest concern was the unsupervised behavior of oath-swearers before secular officials. Taking an oath required preparation in the same way that penitents had to ready themselves for confession. Oath-swearing, after all, took on a quasi-sacramental dimension; it had been referred to in legislation as *sacramentum*. The Augustinian Fr. Juan de la Anunciación emphasized this sacramental dimension in his advice to witnesses included in his *Doctrina* (1574):

> Christian, you are being informed that if at any time it were necessary for you to take an oath, you will first and foremost look inside yourself and reckon, and recall what you know, and those things that you happen to know with much certitude about what Justice may be asking you; you will only testify to what is present in your heart and nothing else, and as to what your heart does not know about what is being asked, you will only testify and give credit to what you have seen with your eyes, and if you have heard it, say so and not that you saw it. And do not take to swearing in the name of our precious Lord in vain, or that of his saint mother, or that of a saint, or sacred thing for each trifle, because even if it is true, swearing in vain is always a sin.[108]

Similar recommendations for those about to swear had been written into the law in the past.[109] The requirement that witnesses specify how they came to know the facts they declared, whether they heard or saw them, is yet another link to medieval legislation.[110] Juan de la Anunciación's focus on the most ritu-

---

107. Domingo de la Anunciación, *Doctrina christiana breve y compendiosa*, 43 and 44–44v.

108. "Por tanto aqui en este libro soys avisados que si alguna vez fuere necessario que hagays juramento, primero y ante todas cosas os examina ynteriormente y entra en quenta con vosotros mesmos, y haze memoria de lo que sabeys, y aquello que con mucha certidumbre supieredes acerca de lo que la justicia os preguntare, eso y no mas testificareys, de la mesma manera que vuestros coraçones lo saben, y si no saben ninguna cosa o parte della acerca de lo que soys preguntados, a solo aquello atestiguad y dad certidumbre que con vuestra vista vistes, y si lo oystes dezid que lo oystes y no que lo vistes. Y no os acostumbreys de siempre con juramento nombrar en vano el nombre precioso de nuestro señor dios o de su madre sancta Maria o de algun sancto, o cosa sagrada por cada cosita: porque aquesto aunque esto sea verdad jamas se haze en vano sin dexar por ello de pecar." Juan de la Anunciación, *Doctrina Christiana muy cumplida, donde se contiene la exposición de todo lo necessario para doctrinar a los Yndios, y administralles los Sanctos Sacramentos* (Mexico City: Pedro Balli, 1575), 76–77.

109. "Debe amar en su corazon si cree sin dubda que sea asi como él responde por su jura." *Las Siete Partidas del Rey Don Alfonso el Sabio*, part. 3, title 11, law 11. Canon law had also required fasting prior to swearing. Aquinas, *Summa theologiae*, 2a 2ae, q. 89, a. 10, res.

110. On what constituted acceptable proof in Spanish medieval legislation, see Marta Madero,

alized and religious aspect of the legal proceeding almost obscures any association with the world of royal institutions and noisy human affairs. Blasphemy
and everyday forms of swearing among the Mexican Indians did not command
the same attention as false testimony's danger of damnation; the concrete and
symbolic space of the court of law, and not the streets, became the arena where
the missionaries sought to alter the balance between human and divine justice.

Indian Testimonies: An Old Opinion in a New Guise

The Society of Jesus was created in 1534 and earned papal recognition in 1540.
News of the religious order and its ambitious goals reached Mexico, where a
handful of religious men, ecclesiastical authorities, and royal officials decided
that the viceroyalty could benefit greatly from the presence of the Jesuit fathers.
It is not a minor detail that both Archbishop Alonso de Montúfar, and the no
less controversial royal inspector Jerónimo Valderrama, two individuals who
maintained relationships of mutual contempt with the mendicant orders, expressed their desire to add members of the Society to the less than harmonious
family of Mexican religious men. In 1572, the first contingent of Jesuit fathers
and brothers arrived in Mexico City; in a few years and backed by a prominent
benefactor, they founded the Colegio de San Pedro y San Pablo there. By the
end of the sixteenth century, they had founded five other educational institutions, in Patzcuaro, Oaxaca, Puebla, Veracruz, and Guadalajara.[111] They had
also become acquainted with the culturally diverse indigenous groups in the
areas surrounding their *colegios*, the result of their periodic excursions for pastoral purposes.

The arrival of the Jesuits marked a significant change in the language of
conversion and pastoral care, not unlike the one that took place in Europe in
the years immediately following the Society's creation. Letters and reports from
New Spain show a disciplined body of priests fully determined to closely follow the apostolic guidelines that in Europe had set the Society apart from other
religious orders. This discipline gave the Jesuits' reports on the spreading of Catholicism in distant corners of the world an inescapable sameness, apparent in
the recurrent use of stock motifs and anecdotes. Although the cumulative effect
of these narratives of conversion and religious reawakening on a contemporary

---

Las verdades de los hechos: Proceso, juez y testimonio en la Castilla del siglo XIII (Salamanca: Ediciones Universidad de Salamanca, 2004), 23–36.

111. Mariano Cuevas, *Historia de la Iglesia en México*, 5 vols. (El Paso: Editorial "Revista
Católica," 1922–28), 2:342.

reader is repetition and predictability, they represented a significant shift at the time. Their novelty is most obvious when the reports of the Jesuits are compared to the dominant version of the evangelization of New Spain conceived, embodied, and told by the mendicant orders.[112] For the purposes of our discussion, it will suffice to take a quick look at the Jesuits' impact on a particular area that had already become a point of pride for the order: confession and the administration of the sacrament of penance.

The Company of Jesus announced its presence in Indian communities with a series of missionary visits, during which the brothers preached, taught the principles of Christian doctrine, and administered the sacraments. Jesuit testimonies from the field about their experience among different indigenous groups expressed that it was still possible to present Christianity in a new fashion to both converted and unconverted Indians. The Jesuits wasted no time in introducing themselves as a new breed of confessors, a select group of technicians skilled in the art of scrutinizing consciences, eradicating shame, and reassuring Christians on their hopes for salvation. And they did so with little concern for the reaction of the mendicant orders that had laid the groundwork for the evangelization of New Spain to the new stories of conversion and religious rejuvenation that were reaching Mexico City and even Europe. Some mendicant friars were as impressed as the Indian communities, judging from the Jesuit account of the story of a group of Augustinians who invited Jesuit missionaries passing through Chietlan to hear the confessions of local Indian penitents.[113]

Jesuit confessors appeared on the scene not to rewrite the history of evangelization in New Spain but rather to perfect that evangelization. In Xalatlaco, a sick Indian woman who had kept a troubling sin to herself for thirty-five years finally declared it to an itinerant Jesuit priest.[114] Similarly, another sick Indian opened up to a Jesuit confessor about a sin (likely of a sexual nature) that he had failed to disclose at his previous confession three years earlier. He had lived with this undeclared sin for years, as if waiting for a qualified or nonjudgmental

---

112. Notwithstanding disagreements and confrontations—some violent—there was a prevailing narrative of the conversion of the Mexican Indians that Franciscans, Dominicans, and Augustinians helped to shape. It is also true that the rosy picture of the history of the evangelization as told and enacted by the friars of the mendicant orders was occasionally contradicted by some of their own members, for example, Durán's hesitation or Sahagún's harsh reservations. The Jesuits had no reservations in proclaiming New Spain "terra nostra" and declaring that their arrival represented a true beginning for Christianity there. See Solange Alberro, *El águila y la cruz: Orígenes religiosos de la conciencia criolla. México, siglos xvi–xvii* (Mexico City: El Colegio de México / Fondo de Cultura Económica, 1999), 85–87.

113. *Monumenta Mexicana*, ed. Félix Zubillaga and Miguel Ángel Rodríguez (Rome: Institutum Historicum Societatis Iesu, 1956–91), 3:9.

114. *Monumenta Mexicana*, 3:13.

priest to appear.[115] When another sick Indian was asked why he had wanted a newcomer to hear his confession, he allegedly answered that the Jesuits were good at examining consciences.[116] These stories share a basic narrative with the less cheerful medieval exempla that illustrate the suffering in hell of those who fail to give a full confession. As mentioned above, medieval exempla found new life in Mexico as sources for friars and their Nahua collaborators in composing sermons and plays in Nahuatl.[117] In his *Confessionario* (1599), Fr. Juan Bautista warned of incomplete confessions by retelling the story of a woman who deliberately omitted confessing to an incestuous relationship, joining the ranks of the damned as a consequence.[118]

The brief and uplifting stories told by the Jesuits as they made their way through indigenous communities quietly hint that the friars' skills may have fallen somewhat short of what was required of confessors tending to the Indians. In this new stage of evangelization, incomplete confessions took on added meaning. It is, then, entirely conceivable that Juan Bautista's exemplum was also a response of sorts to the veiled criticisms contained in the Jesuits' self-congratulatory accounts.[119] The accomplishments of the mendicant orders, however, were implicit in these descriptions: if Indian penitents experienced remorse over the failure to confess, it was due to the teachings of the friars. Jesuit confessors therefore only had to reassure Indian penitents of their chosen path. Meanwhile, to their Spanish constituency, the Jesuits promised a new and lasting alliance with the church.

---

115. Despite the unequivocally technical dimension that the Jesuits brought to the craft of hearing confession, they avoided conflating the images of confessor and judge. They were also dissatisfied with discipline that recalled the secular model that gave authority to judges and prosecutors instead of the model of "fraternal correction" that, in theory at least, was practiced by religious men. A telling example is the unflattering portrait of Father Juan de la Plaza contained in the 1590 "instruction" given to Father Diego de Avellaneda, inspector of the province of Mexico. Strict and unwilling to compromise, Father de la Plaza was known "for a lack of tenderness and simplicity that they notice in him, and his spirit more akin to that of a prosecutor" ("y la falta que le notan de suavidad y sencillez, y demasiado espíritu de fiscal"). *Monumenta Mexicana*, 3:466.

116. "respondióme que porque acá les examinábamos bien sus conciencias, avía pedido le traxesen acá." *Monumenta Mexicana*, 3:27

117. On the transformation and use of European exempla in Jesuit preaching in New Spain, see Danièle Dehouve, *Relatos de pecados en la evangelización de los indios de México (siglos xvi–xviii)* (Mexico City: CIESAS/CEAMCA, 2010), especially 65–78.

118. The exemplum, or *tetzahuitl*, along with one of its possible sources, has been transcribed and translated by Berenice Alcántara Rojas. "El dragón y la mazacoatl: Criaturas del infierno en un *exemplum* en nahuatl de Fray Ioan Baptista," *Estudios de Cultura Náhuatl* 36 (January 2005): 383–420. For an analysis of an exemplum on usury, see Dehouve, *Relatos de pecados en la evangelización de los indios de México*, 101–4.

119. Juan Bautista's exemplum was very much in line with the ways in which the Franciscans opted to respond to the finely calibrated public campaign by the Jesuits to win over Indians and criollos. In the 1590s, for instance, in response to the earlier Jesuit appropriation of Nahua symbols to highlight the affinity between the order and the Nahuas, the Franciscans recast the Nahua symbols of the eagle and the nopal to bolster their order's importance to the Indians and promote St. Francis as an intercessor between God and Indians. See Alberro, *El águila y la cruz*, 98–100.

The Jesuits transformed the language used to describe the conversion and pastoral care of Indians; the word "conscience" became omnipresent and the interest in "cases of conscience" soon resembled a literary fad among the small urban elite. On one level, the Jesuit fathers did little more than rely on the principles and motifs that best expressed the Society's distinctiveness in fashioning their approach to the conversion of Mexican Indians, as the anecdote of the Indian in search of a skillful examiner of conscience illustrates. On another level, however, the overall effect of this somewhat programmatic transposition may not have been fully anticipated. For all their predictability, the stories of success that the Jesuits recorded and circulated featured not only a new type of religious figure as protagonist, but also portrayed Indians with a conscience and psychological depth that deserved the attention of the recently arrived experts.

However conventional their framework, these stories stand out from the ones before them in that they were crafted out of a new stock of conventions. One result is the subtle but tangible shift in the manner of referring to Indian penitents, who appear as morally sophisticated individuals in these accounts. The ideal penitent who has found his or her match in the Jesuit confessor replaced the fleeting ideal of the Mexican Indian engaged in mental prayer and other contemplative and ascetic devotional practices found in the works of Motolinia and Mendieta. This transformation was, of course, less about the Mexican Indians themselves than the ideal types of relationship that the religious orders envisioned establishing with the new converts. When religious groups imagined possible models of authority and subordination, they were bound to touch on issues of their flock's spiritual autonomy in the process. It seems fair to suggest that, at the early stage of contact between the Jesuits and indigenous groups, whatever designs Society members may have had for Indian converts were far from fully articulated.

The Jesuits' annual letter from 1585 mentioned that the Third Mexican Church Council of the same year had asked the Society to contribute to the catechism for Spaniards and Indians and the manual for confessors.[120] When the council finally accepted a catechism, it was not the work of a team as previously envisioned, but that of a sole author, the Jesuit father Juan de la Plaza. After spending several years in Peru, de la Plaza arrived in Mexico in 1580, where he served as provincial of the Society.[121] As it turned out, his catechism

---

120. *Monumenta Mexicana*, 3:80. For catechisms, see *Concilium Mexicanum Provinciale III*, book 1, title 1, §1, 7–8. On the "directorium Confessorum, et poenitentium," see book 5, title 12, §8, 323–24.

121. The complicated history of this catechism and its attribution was first traced by Ernest J. Burrus. "The Author of the Mexican Council Catechisms," *The Americas* 15, no. 2 (October 1958): 171–78. On Juan de la Plaza's contribution to the council, see Llaguno, *La personalidad jurídica del indio*, 46–53. Plaza's *memoriales*, or reports to the council, were first transcribed and published

was not published until after the Fourth Mexican Church Council of 1771, and then in modified form and without the author's name.[122] In the almost two centuries in between, the Jesuit Jerónimo de Ripalda's catechism became hugely popular; it would maintain that status for a very long time.[123] As for the manual of confessors, a *Directorio* was drafted at the time but never published.[124] By 1585, only one comprehensive manual in circulation had been printed in Mexico: the Franciscan Fr. Alonso de Molina's, aimed exclusively at confessors of Indians and the inaugurator of a tradition of sorts.[125] Juan Bautista, who had trained under Molina, developed new works for confessors, preachers, and a small group of literate Nahuas.[126] In 1599 he published the *Confessionario para confessores de indios*; the following year, the same Mexican publisher released his two-part *Advertencias para confessores de indios*.

While the influence of Molina's *Confessionario* loomed large in Juan Bautista's manual (it is difficult to imagine how it could have been otherwise), the work is far from a servile copy. It was, however, the *Advertencias*, a much-needed companion to his own manual, that displayed the full weight of Juan Bautista's authority on the confession of Indians. In the *Advertencias* he set out to address the legitimate concerns and doubts that confessors of Indians might harbor. For those confessors who were tormented by the idea that they had

---

by Félix Zubillaga. "Tercer Concilio Mexicano 1585: Los memoriales del P. Juan de la Plaza S.I.," *Archivum Historicum Societatis Iesu*, extractum and vol. 30 (Rome 1961): 180–244; they also can be found in Carrillo Cázares, *Manuscritos del Concilio Tercero Provincial Mexicano*, vol. 1, part 1, 223–83. For an overview of the council's goals and organization, see Stafford Poole, C.M., *Pedro Moya de Contreras: Catholic Reform and Royal Power in New Spain, 1571–1591* (Berkeley: University of California Press, 1987), 148–203.

122. Burrus, "The Author of the Mexican Council Catechisms," 176. On the Spanish and Latin versions of the catechisms, see Josep-Ignasi Saranyana and Elisa Luque Alcaide, "Fuentes manuscritas inéditas del III Concilio Mexicano," *Annuarium historiae conciliorum* 22 (1990): 273–83. A transcription can be found in Juan Guillermo Durán, "Apéndice documental. A modo de ejemplo: Los Catecismos del III Mexicano," in *Historia de la evangelización de América, Simposio internacional, Ciudad del Vaticano, May 11–14, 1992*, ed. José Escudero Imbert and Victor Manuel Ochoa Cadavid (Vatican City: Librería Editrice Vaticana, 1992), 323–52.

123. Juan Guillermo Durán, "Apéndice documental," 319.

124. On the *Directorio*'s organization, content, and sources, see Carrillo Cázares's introduction to the *Manuscritos del Concilio Tercero Provincial Mexicano*, 5:ix–lxxvi. The Third Council of Lima, which convened in 1583, also agreed to commission a catechism and manual for confessors. The Italian printer Antonio Ricardo published both the *Catecismo para curas de Indios* and the *Confessionario para los curas de indios* in 1585.

125. The Augustinian Alonso de la Veracruz had penned brief guidelines for Spanish confessors that remained unpublished at the time, "Ynstruction para los confesores: cómo se a de aver con los señores de yndios y otras personas." Burrus, *The Writings of Alonso de la Vera Cruz*, 1:135–41.

126. David Tavárez, "Naming the Trinity: From Ideologies of Translation to Dialectics of Reception in Colonial Nahua Texts, 1547–1771," *Colonial Latin American Review* 9, no. 1 (June 2000): 29. As Tavárez has pointed out elsewhere, Juan Bautista Viseo's work was carried out with the active participation of a circle of Nahuas educated at the Colegio de Santa Cruz in Tlatelolco. Tavárez, "Letras clandestinas, textos tolerados, colaboraciones lícitas," 66–68.

granted absolution to Indians who may not have deserved it, Juan Bautista offered a set of guidelines designed to dispel the widespread belief that Mexican Indians lacked both an adequate preparation for confession and true understanding of Christian doctrine.[127] In this sense, the timing of this work by a Franciscan that aimed to unburden the conscience of confessors could not have been more appropriate, given the Jesuits' undeniable success in renewing in a relatively short time the conversation about the role of confession in both religious and lay circles in Mexico. In one indication that Juan Bautista conceived his treatise as a response to this recent development, he discusses the case of penitents who failed to declare some sins to their confessors out of shame or ignorance.[128] The issue was neither minor nor new, having been dealt with in detail in the *summae* for confessors. But what reason might Juan Bautista have had to remind confessors of long-established guidelines other than the Jesuits' insistence that they had encountered numerous Indian penitents who had been absolved after less than perfect confessions? Along the same lines, the author did not share the growing enthusiasm for general confession promoted by the Jesuits, reminding scrupulous confessors that such an authority as the Dominican Martín de Azpilcueta had determined that they were not obliged to inquire about every possible sin, only those more likely to have been committed by an individual of the penitent's rank, trade, or social station.[129]

The literature on confession, closely associated with the Company of Jesus by the end of the sixteenth century, would flourish in hundreds of works on cases of conscience during the following century. Even so, this literature may

127. "Algunas cosas destos naturales desconsuelan notablemente y causan grandes escrupulos a los animos de sus ministros, y aun a algunos los han retraydo deste ministerio apostolico, las quales miradas con pia affeccion y consideracion del poco talento de algunos, causan por una parte lastima, y por otra ponen un Nuevo brio y pecho Christiano, para occuparse en instruyrlos y alumbrarlos en el conocimiento de Dios, provecho y salvacion de sus almas." Juan Bautista, *Advertencias*, 1r.

128. "Lo. 3. Es que haviendo dexado de confessar algunas muy graves culpas mortales por verguença, o veniales, y otras vezes lo que no fue culpa, sino obra meritoria, la tienen por peccado mortal, y por tal lo dexan de confessar por verguença, o por temor, y aun que ay muchos que conoscen esta obligacion, y conforme a ella reyteran las confessiones de su principio, otros ay que si los tienen tres y quarto dias, no dizen sino solo lo que dexaron por verguença diziendo, que ya an dicho lo demas, y que solo aquello es, que como dizen lo uno dixeran lo otro, si ya no lo uvieran dicho a otros padres, y lo propio hazen a la hora y punto de muerte." Juan Bautista, *Advertencias*, 4r–4v.

129. The passage is worth quoting for its unmistakable reference to the trend promoted by the Jesuits: "Los escrupulosos en examinar las consciencias destos naturales adviertan que aunque es verdad que el confessor esta obligado a escudriñar diligentemente la consciencia del peccador, assi como el medico la enfermedad del enfermo, y el Iuez la causa del pleyteante [como dize Sancto Thomas y otros graves autores refferidos por el doctissimo Navarro en su summa cap. 5. Pero que no estan obligados a preguntar e inquirir todo lo que puede haver cometido el penitente, sino solo aquello en que comunmente los de su calidad suelen delinquir, como dize el doctor Navarro en su Manual cap. 5 y el maestro fray Nicolas de Orbelis in. 4. Dist. 17. Q. 2 §.13 por estas palabras." Juan Bautista, *Advertencias*, 13r. On the different meanings of "general confession" in the period, see John W. O'Malley, *The First Jesuits* (Cambridge, MA: Harvard University Press, 1993), 137–39.

have appeared less threatening to the mendicant confessors than the budding presence of the fathers on the Mexican social and geographical landscape. For the particular brand of practical moral theology that would coalesce in the genre of the manuals of cases of conscience that the order made its own was taking shape prior to the arrival of the Jesuit fathers in Mexico and drew on sources familiar to the friars working with the Indians, or teaching at houses of study, or the university. The works of Azpilcueta, which laid the groundwork for the development of casuistry for many scholars, are a case in point.[130]

In the *Advertencias*, Fr. Juan Bautista drew extensively on opinions that the Franciscan Fr. Juan Focher had drafted for a series of unpublished treatises on the theological and legal issues raised by the evangelization of the Mexican Indians, how to determine which unions the church should recognize as legitimate marriages.[131] But while the work acknowledged the contribution and relevance of a pioneer working at a time when writers such as Fr. Gerónimo de Mendieta were taking stock of the Franciscan order's intellectual legacy in Mexico, it also displayed a preference for Spanish theologians who were beginning to be seen as decidedly modern.[132]

Fr. Juan Bautista put the lessons of contemporary treatises on cases of conscience to good use. And he did so in a manner that was entirely his own, while still relying on and paying homage to his order's accumulated experience on matters of evangelization. The Franciscan experience in Mexico had been characterized by the study of indigenous languages and the ethnological investigations that this linguistic knowledge facilitated. These intellectual activities, in turn, made it possible to train brothers and produce new works to assist friars in pastoral activities. Fr. Juan Bautista was both a contributor to and a product of this intellectual tradition, and he examined the literature on confession at his disposal in search of material that would ease the minds and doubts of his fellow confessors. As noted before, these doubts were also a direct result of

---

130. See the chapter "Casuistry, Mental Reservation, and Dr. Navarrus," in Pérez Zagorin, *Ways of Lying: Dissimulation, Persecution, and Conformity in Early Modern Europe* (Cambridge, MA: Harvard University Press, 1990), 153–85. There is even mention that one of Azpilcueta's contemplative treatises was translated into Nahuatl; significantly, it was the *Tratado de alabanza y murmuración*, which addressed issues of the sins of the tongue.

131. Fr. Juan Focher's influential treatise *Itinerarium catholicum proficiscentium ad infideles convertendos* was printed posthumously in Seville in 1574 by his former student, Diego Valadés.

132. Juan Bautista's sources show that he had kept up with recent works on moral theology. A representative sample of these studies includes *Summa theologiae moralis* (Salamanca, 1591) by the Portuguese Jesuit Henrico Henríquez (or Henrico Henriques); *Sylva, y Practica Interior, utilissima para Confesores y Penitentes* (Alcalá, 1594) by Alonso de la Vega; *Instructorium conscientiae* (Salamanca, 1592) by the Dominican Luis López, who spent time in Chiapas, Guatemala, and Oaxaca; *Suma de casos de conciencia* by the Portuguese Franciscan Manuel Rodrigues. All of these works had a successful life in print, with editions in more than one Spanish city and abroad.

those quietly cast by Jesuit priests as they forged their own identity as experts in scrutinizing consciences in a new milieu.

As important as it was for confessors of Indians to be familiar with the *summae* and manuals on cases of conscience, there was no substitute for the knowledge of indigenous languages in determining whether a penitent had sinned, and how seriously. Fr. Juan Bautista made a point of showing several times in the *Advertencias* that what may at first appear to be a grave misdeed might turn out to be a lesser one upon closer inspection of the penitent's words.

Spanish authorities and friars had made much of the Nahuas' excessive consumption of alcohol, but Fr. Juan Bautista placed this fault below fornication in seriousness.[133] There were significant distinctions to be made when talking about drinking, he stated, and a confessor had to keep these distinctions in mind when penitents accusing themselves of indulging in alcohol. According to Juan Bautista, the Nahuatl language had different verbs for drinking to excess and drinking to the point of passing out, a relevant distinction that was lost on confessors unfamiliar with Nahuatl usages.[134] Similarly, Fr. Juan Bautista advised confessors of Indian merchants or individuals of means to inquire whether they had engaged in usurious loans, an economic practice that, although common, was often overlooked among them. Once again, his clarification came in the form of linguistic knowledge, this time regarding a Nahuatl word that closely corresponded to the Spanish term *logro*.[135]

Even more revealing is Juan Bautista's brief and idiosyncratic treatment of sworn statements by Indians. He explained that the Nahuas rarely made straightforward assertive statements, preferring instead to qualify affirmations with the adverb *aço*, an indication of probability that generally translates as "maybe."[136] Sentence-initial qualifiers such as *aço* and the dubitative inter-

---

133. In doing so, Fr. Juan Bautista sought to undermine the argument that the Mexican Indians should not be allowed to receive the Eucharist because of their inclination to drink, a restriction the Franciscan strongly opposed. Bautista, *Advertencias*, 57v.

134. "Advierta el confessor que este verbo tlahuana, propriamente no quiere dezir bever hasta perder el juyzio, o emborracharse, sino lo que en latin, dezimos bibere laute, que es bever en abundancia, aunque sin perder el juyzio. Mas estos verbos Xocomiqui, Ihuinti, Nicpo polohua, nicpopolohua intlanextli. Propriamente quiere dezir emborracharse perdiendo el juyzio. Yo he confessado India que se acuso que preguntandole el confessor, cuix otilahuan, respondio ca quemaca, y no dixo onihuintic. Porque se vea la differencia que ay de lo uno a lo otro. Y assi quando el confessor preguntare, cuix otilaahuan, o el penitente dixere onitlahuan, pregunte luego, cuix huel otihuintic, cuix huel otixocomic: que con esto se quita toda duda." Juan Bautista, *Advertencias*, 77r–77v.

135. "Logro" was a type of loan on which interest was charged. "Ay proprio vocablo de logro, que es, tetechtlaixtlapanaliztli, tetechtlamieccaquixtiliztli, y para dezir diste a logro? Cuix tetech otitlaixtlapan, cuix tech otitlamieccaquisti?" Juan Bautista, *Advertencias*, 15v.

136. "Acerca de los testimonios que estos naturales en sus confessiones dizen haber levantado se advierta que como de su modo de hablar parece claramente, pocas vezes dizen assertivamente. Pedro hurto esto, o Pedro esta amancebado, sino Aço Pedro oquichtec, aço Pedro momecatitinemi

rogative *cuix* appear frequently in the *huehuehtlahtolli*, the traditional Nahuatl speeches that Juan Bautista had studied in detail and even committed to print. It was probably not lost on him that the wide presence of these qualifiers helped reinforce the preference for indirectness, one of the salient rhetorical features of this oral genre.[137]

As puzzling as this linguistic argument may appear on its face, it nonetheless follows the author's overall design, anchoring the discussion in cases of conscience in the tradition his order could legitimately claim to have forged over several decades of work among the Nahuas. But there is something else at work here, too: if Fr. Juan Bautista's authority advice rests on his linguistic knowledge, his argument, however simple or improbable, owes much to the contemporary works of casuistry with which he was conversant. In other words, Fr. Juan Bautista's opinion on sworn statements by Indians constitutes an imaginative transposition of "mental reservation," a much-debated notion among moral theologians of the time. Mental reservation was an operation in which a speaker avoided lying by mentally adding a clause that rendered the false statement that he or she uttered true.[138] To Juan Bautista, the linguistic and ideological feature of the Nahua language that favored indirectness fits nicely with the much-discussed idea of mental reservation. Far from mere intellectual gamesmanship, the discussions of issues that occupied the minds of casuists such as deceit, dissimulation, and the manifold conditions of truth, acquired a dramatic dimension for those forced to make statements of faith during the waves of religious persecution that spread throughout Europe in the sixteenth century.

Although the immediate context of Fr. Juan Bautista's comments was far less urgent, the varying opinions on oaths and mental reservation must have resonated with the Franciscan, who was fully aware of the positions that his brothers and secular officers had taken on Nahua participation in legal disputes. In offering his fanciful solution, Juan Bautista acted as advocate for the Nahuas

---

etc." Juan Bautista, *Advertencias*, 13v. A few decades later, the Jesuit grammarian Horacio Carochi, commented on the uses of this adverb: "*Aço* significa, quiçà; v. g. *àço moztla nihuallaz, ànoço, quin huipila*, quiçà vendrè mañana, ò despues de mañana. Suele ser interrogativo, y servir de lo mesmo, que *cuix*, y entonces se le suele posponer ma, v.g. *àçoma oticmoniachiu inic ye omàxitico in Tlatoani?* Has sabido como ha llegado ya el Governador?" Horacio Carochi, *Arte de la lengua mexicana con la declaracion de los adverbios della* (Mexico City: Juan Ruiz, 1645), 122v. Following existing opinion, Juan Bautista also reminded confessors that even when a witness made an unqualified false statement, if there was no intention to harm, and no harm resulted from the testimony, the witness only committed a venial sin with no expectation of restitution. Juan Bautista, *Advertencias*, 13v.

137. On indirectness in Classical Nahuatl as featured in a collection of speeches closely related to the *huehuehtlahtolli*, see Frances Karttunen and James Lockhart, eds., *The Art of Nahuatl Speech: The Bancroft Dialogues* (Los Angeles: UCLA Latin American Center Publications, University of California Press, 1987), especially 43–51; and Karttunen, "After the Conquest: The Survival of Indigenous Patterns of Life and Belief," *Journal of World History* 3, no. 2 (Fall 1992), especially 250–53.

138. See Jonsen and Toulmin, *The Abuse of Casuistry: A History of Moral Reasoning* (Berkeley: University of California Press, 1988), 195–215; see also Zagorin, *Ways of Lying*, 153–85.

(and his order) and shouldered much of the oath-swearer's burden, projecting a technical subterfuge that comes close to mental reservation into Nahua linguistic usages. The bracketed qualifiers hidden in the speaker's mind reveal the true meaning of his statements, and have appeared in the guise of a Nahuatl adverb. With this explanation, the Franciscans' linguistic research, which had reached a high point in Fr. Juan Bautista's work, converged with the casuists' new interest in examining the use of language. Linguistic ambiguity, for example, was at the center of discussions about moral equivocation and mental reservation at the time. It was also a concern over ambiguity, in this case the desire to dispel it, that guided Fr. Juan Bautista's detailed analysis and critique of the imperfectly translation of the official doctrine of the Trinity into Nahuatl, leaving room for the spread of doctrinal errors.[139]

It can be said that Fr. Juan Bautista's solution, in an odd way, had a modern ring to it, in the sense that it appears informed by the explorations of language and morality that occupied the minds of many sixteenth-century theologians. Yet for all its novelty, his advice on handling the testimonies of the Nahuas came to reinforce his brethren's preexisting opinions and misapprehensions. If not strictly encouraged, the strategy of attaching equivocation to oaths survived in the literature of confession for quite some time. In his *Guía de confessores*, published in Spanish in Mexico in 1653, the Jesuit Gabino Carta offered some practical examples of equivocation that penitents could avail themselves of in everyday life.[140]

A few decades after the *Advertencias* were published, the distinguished legal scholar Juan de Solórzano Pereira wrote extensively on the legal rights and obligations of the American Indians, drawing on what had become a substantial body of legislation and opinions, as well as on the expertise on Indian matters that he had acquired from his years in Peru. By the time Solórzano Pereira was writing his *Política Indiana* it had become widely accepted in royal and religious circles that the legal status of the American Indians best corresponded to what Spanish law labeled *miserables* (orphans, children, and widows). As he

---

139. See Tavárez, "Naming the Trinity."
140. The following quote shows that the author's advice could be applied in the most trivial circumstances: "Aviendo justa causa, puedese jurar con equivocacion; como es, si me piden una cosa que no conviene darla, para que me crean, y quite la importunacion, puedo jurar que no la tengo; es a saber, para darsela a él, o que no la tengo en las manos, y si me amenaçan que les prometa cien escudos, puedo jurar que se los dare, entendiendo si yo querré darselos, y assi de otros casos. Sánchez, lib. 3, c. 6." Gabino Carta, *Guía de confessores*, 47. The same example, along with a discussion of when it is permissible to resort to amphibology and mental reservation, can be found in the widely read *Summa de casos de consciencia*. Manuel Rodriguez, *Summa de casos de consciencia*, vol. 1, chap. 191, 527. See also the detailed account of "equivocal oaths" included by the Quito-born Juan Machado de Chaves in his *Perfeto confessor y cura de almas*, 2 vols. (Madrid: Viuda de Francisco Martínez, 1646), 1:257–58.

pointed out, this status allowed Indian litigants to pursue legal claims in court with very few restrictions. Regarding oaths, however, Solórzano Pereira inherited and embraced many of the doubts about the trustworthiness of the Indian testimonies that had been heard throughout the sixteenth century. Because Indians could not comprehend the obligation to tell the truth, Solórzano Pereira wrote, they should be exempted from oath-taking lest they commit perjury, the seriousness of which they did not or could not fully understand. On this point the author relied on the authority of the Jesuit José de Acosta, who wrote on the topic before the Third Church Council convened in Lima. Solórzano Pereira agreed with Acosta's suggestion that Indians only be sworn in exceptionally serious cases.

Rather than a reasoned opinion, Acosta had formulated something more like practical advice, in line with the Jesuit outlook that left room for flexibility; he thought it desirable that the last word on the issue come from a conciliar and royal legislative body.[141] As it happened, the Third Church Council of Lima, in which Acosta actively participated, touched on the perceived problems of Indian testimonies when discussing how ecclesiastical judges should investigate accusations that Indians made against parish priests.[142] In such instances, the council allowed judges to administer oaths to these Indians proven to be fearful of God, but warned against doing so to neophytes.[143] In Mexico, the Third Council of 1585 followed the legislation of its Peruvian counterpart very closely, including the punishments prescribed for Indian perjurers.[144] Like oaths, and as we shall see in the next chapter, the punishment of Indian offenders was an ever-present topic in the minds of missionaries and ecclesiastical authorities.

Regarding oaths, Solórzano Pereira did not concern himself with the argument about neophytes, which would require accepting that, after decades of evangelization, the American Indians still failed to understand the second and eighth commandments. He did not, therefore, make the progress of Christianity among Amerindians the basis for an opinion either for or against allowing them to take oaths. For Solórzano Pereira, on legal matters—at least in general terms—the Indians should be dealt with as *rudes* or rustics who, following

141. José de Acosta, *De procuranda indorum salute*, ed. Luciano Pereña, 2 vols. (Madrid: Consejo Superior de Investigaciones Científicas, 1984–87), book 3, chap. 23, 1:585.

142. "Demas desto ora se tome la información por vía ordinaria ora por vía extraordinaria contra algún sacerdote, advierta el juez en todo caso que no deve admitir según los sacros Cánones, testimonio alguno de yndios ynfieles, y aun tambien a los yndios fieles o a los hespañoles si fuessen sospechosos (como muchas vezes acaece) no deve admitirlos por testigos, sino a los que son enteros y temerosos de Dios; otrosi advierta grandemente que no tome juramento a estos yndios tan nuevos en la fee, si no fuere en negocio de grande importancia y que no se pueda fenecer de otra suerte." Rubén Vargas Ugarte, *Concilios Limenses (1551–1772)*, 3 vols. (Lima: Tipografía Peruana, 1951–54), vol. 1, chap. 6, 363.

143. Vargas Ugarte, *Concilios Limenses*, vol. 1, chap. 6, 363.

144. *Concilium Mexicanum Provinciale III*, book 2, title 5, §10, 125–26.

Acosta's characterization, had only a tenuous relationship to the truth and a natural tendency to be easily persuaded by parties with bad intentions.

In addition to the conciliar resolution from Peru, Solórzano Pereira had before him a piece of secular legislation that Viceroy Francisco de Toledo enacted in his *Ordenanzas* to instruct judges how to handle Indian testimonies when circumstances required them. As spelled out in the *Ordenanzas*, judges seeking testimonies from Indian witnesses should question them in groups of six; the information obtained through this examination should count as if gathered from a single witness. Numerical equivalences like Toledo's would fascinate commentators for centuries. The eighteenth-century French diplomat François Joseph de Pons interpreted the ordinance as proof of the Indians' inability to become full citizens; almost eighty years later, the Argentinian Domingo F. Sarmiento agreed.[145]

In the early eighteenth century, the Franciscan Francisco de Ávila prefaced his grammar of the Nahuatl language with the recitation of a host of mostly negative features that made up the Indian character. Recognizing that Indian labor was the foundation of colonial society, Ávila nonetheless contended that because of their servile disposition and indolence, the Mexican Indians' aversion to work precluded their moral development.[146] A radical lack of self-worth, noticeable even among the surviving members of the indigenous nobility, prevented the Indians from experiencing shame when engaged in the lowest trades, a moral deficiency that set them apart from Spaniards. While this moral flaw made them immune to offense, it also made them indifferent to generosity.[147] As if to enrich this unflattering characterization, Ávila also complained about the Indians' inclination to fabricate charges against parish priests that they did not like. In collusion with the *principales*, potential witnesses who would testify under oath were frequently coached and bribed.[148] The juxtaposi-

---

145. "L'habitude de mentir leur est si familière; la verité a pour eux si peu de prix, que les lois espagnoles ont, avez raison prévenu les funestes effets que peur causer leurs temoinages à l'innocence; elles ont ordonnés qu'on n'entenda jamais, dans une cause, moins de six Indiens, et que ce que les six auront dit, n'aura pas plus de valeur, dans les tribunaux, que la déclaration, sous serment d'un témoin ordinaire." François Joseph de Pons, *Voyage à la partie orientale de la Terre-Ferme dans l'Amérique Méridionale fait pendant les années 1801, 1802, 1803 et 1804*, 3 vols. (Paris: Colnet, 1806), 1:338. Domingo Faustino Sarmiento translated the passage in *Conflicto y armonías de las razas en América* (Buenos Aires: "La Cultura Argentina," 1915), 85.

146. Francisco de Ávila, *Arte de la lengua mexicana y breves platicas de los mysterios de N. Santa Fee Catholica, y otras para exortacion de su obligacion a los Indios* (Mexico City: Herederos de la Viuda de Miguel de Ribera Calderón, 1717), ii–iii.

147. "Y porque son de animo servil, y no se averguençan de exercitarse en officios viles, aunque sean bien nabcidos. Comen sin asco, y viven sin vergüença. No sienten agravio, ni agradecen beneficio." Ávila, *Arte de la lengua mexicana*, iii.

148. "Para hazer una delacion, o falsa acusacion, hazen junta de los Principales, nombran testigos, y los instruyen en lo que han de jurar, embriaganse todos juntos, hechan derramas, juntan dineros, i gallinas; vistense de la ropa mas rota para parecer ante los Juezes, lloran, se lamentan, y

tion of the allegedly blasé attitude of Mexicans toward an institution central to the Spanish legal system and the implicit charge that they lacked a quality akin to honor was, of course, not coincidental.

Oaths were religious, social, and political tests predicated upon a basic notion of personhood and society that gave meaning to the legal and social sanctions imposed upon perjurers. The perjurer risked the shame of either a public punishment or a declaration of infamy and incapability of serving as witness in the future. According to Ávila, Mexican Indians could break their oaths precisely because they did not share the moral notions at the core of Spanish law, and by extension, Spanish society. It is worth noting that many of the negative moral qualities attributed to the Indians in the eighteenth century are associated with an alleged inability to participate in legal proceedings and follow basic legal rules.[149]

The missionaries opposed the administration of oaths to the Indians in order to save them from the perils of oath-taking that Spaniards regularly faced at their courts of law: shame and punishment. They also sought to prevent the commission of offenses against God. Not only did Spaniards go to court over matters of honor, they also gambled their honor in the process when they took oaths in the courtroom. (Gambling seems an apt if profane metaphor, the implications of which did not pass unnoticed by religious thinkers.) The law made honor a heavy burden, and the missionaries thought that a Christian could do without both honor and the additional complications of the legal system that featured it so significantly. In this risky thought experiment, the friars envisioned a community of Christian Indians governed by a notion of justice that was informed by moral ideas at odds with the moral and social notions underlying the Spanish legal system. It was an odd operation, indeed, full of tensions that negated or failed to acknowledge the long and intimate association between Christianity and European law that had produced the concept of personhood that the friars were questioning. Ávila's warnings to his brothers in religion are an heir to the legacy of sixteenth-century missionaries eager to think outside the framework of the law and its categories. Ironically, however, it was only in referring to the law that the Franciscan was able to construct his portrait of contemporary indigenous peoples.

---

assi hazen creibles sus imposturas, porque se compadesce de ellos el Juez." Ávila, *Arte de la lengua mexicana*, iiii.

149. This is evident from the many examples gathered by William B. Taylor in "'De corazón pequeño y ánimo apocado': Conceptos de curas párrocos sobre los indios en la Nueva España del siglo XVIII," *Relaciones* 39 (1989): 5–67.

CHAPTER 4

❦

How to Punish Indians in Early Colonial Mexico

Not long after the mendicant orders arrived in New Spain, the view emerged among the friars that the subjection of the Mexican Indians to Spanish law might not be as practical and desirable a goal as the crown hoped, at least not for the immediate future. Franciscans, in particular, thought that the transfer and application of long-established legal principles to the Mexican Indians, such as the customary distinction between ecclesiastical and secular jurisdictions, could ultimately hinder rather than facilitate their full conversion to Christianity. For the friars, the administration of justice was a natural extension of the enterprise of evangelization, a point that they made repeatedly in letters and reports.[1] In part, their opposition to subjecting the new converts to secular law stemmed from a general dissatisfaction with the state of legal affairs in the Peninsula, where an alarming increase in lawsuits and legal costs was leading to the further consolidation of a class of *letrados* and appeared to threaten the fabric of social life.

On the surface, it was not so much an issue of the content and underlying principles of existing laws, as one of the institutional framework and sanctioned procedures upon which the administration of justice in secular society had, for better or worse, come to depend. In the case of litigation among Indians, for example, the missionaries strongly opposed both the intervention of lawyers and recourse to traditional litigation, recommending instead that a friar act as a mediator.[2] Litigation, the argument went, was costly and time-consuming, but most importantly, it only enriched Spaniards, leaving Indians poorer and their town coffers. If Christianity was going to take hold in Mexico, Indians had to be protected from the disruptive presence of legal officers. The difficult ques-

---

1. For a useful overview of the structure of the judicial system in colonial Mexico, see Colin M. MacLachlan, *Criminal Justice in Eighteenth-Century Mexico* (Berkeley: University of California Press, 1974), 21–36.
    2. Torre Villar, *Fray Pedro de Gante*, 95; García Icazbalceta, *Nueva colección de documentos*, 1:38.

tion that remained was whether it was possible to shield them from Spaniards without entirely preventing their recourse to Spanish colonial law.

On matters of criminal justice as applied to Indians, the friars' view was basically similar to their thoughts on the settlement of private disputes. To defend such a stand, however, was a riskier and significantly more delicate affair, one that required addressing questions about the nature of authority. It surely did not escape the missionaries' attention that individuals rarely felt the presence and scope of royal power as vividly as when criminal defendants faced their judges and justice was eventually served. But in the years following the conquest of New Spain, the early bishops and Franciscan friars argued that Mexican Indians could dispense with secular judges and the model of authority that they embodied, and be brought instead under the direct supervision of their ministers. Mindful of the possibly troublesome implications of their proposal, the friars carefully modeled their role as arbiters of justice not after judges, but teachers or fathers of Indian pupils or children.[3] This formulation did little to disguise what in essence amounted to an outright rejection of secular jurisdiction. As if to lessen the serious implications of a conclusion of this nature, some friars asserted that the very presence of the religious orders had de facto made the distinction between secular and ecclesiastical spheres moot.[4] Other friars, such as the Franciscan chronicler Gerónimo de Mendieta, argued that inherited notions of civil law were simply not applicable in the new territories.[5]

Whereas distinctions such as the one between a teacher's and a judge's authority were theologically or philosophically meaningful, they proved to be little help in everyday situations. An Indian facing punishment would have surely not found such notions particularly consoling or relevant. How then could the friars ensure that the punishments that they ordered or administered would not be mistaken by the Indians for those they had come to expect from secular officials? And what would prevent Spanish civil and judicial officials from

---

3. This alternative view of authority was embraced by the bishops and religious representatives who participated in the ecclesiastical *junta* that took place in 1539. Joaquín García Icazbalceta, *Don Fray de Zumárraga, primer obispo y arzobispo de México*, ed. Rafael Aguayo Spencer and Antonio Castro Leal, 4 vols. (Mexico City: Editorial Porrúa, 1947), 3:159. The most comprehensive argument was formulated much later by the Franciscan Gerónimo de Mendieta in several letters and *memoriales*. García Icazbalceta, *Nueva colección de documentos*, 1:10–11. On Mendieta's *memoriales*, see Carlos Sempat Assadourian, "Memoriales de Fray Gerónimo de Mendieta," *Historia Mexicana* 37, no. 3 (January–March 1988): 357–422.

4. In 1551, the Franciscan Francisco de Bustamante wrote from Guatemala: "Como en esta tierra esté tan asido lo temporal con lo espiritual, y tan pegado el abono de las almas con la obediencia y sujeción de las personas, que si queremos despegar lo uno de lo otro por fuerza lo hemos de romper todo; a esta causa no podemos dejar de poner mano en entrambas cosas." García Icazbalceta, *Nueva colección de documentos*, 2:184.

5. García Icazbalceta, *Nueva colección de documentos*, 1:17.

perceiving the friars as usurping the role of secular judges? For a number of offenses, the prescription of penitential practices, as we will see, was certainly an option; yet despite official opposition, monasteries in colonial Mexico were equipped with jails and shackles just like their secular counterparts. Missionaries in Mexico were keenly aware of the practical steps needed to bridge the gap between their designs and the untidy reality in which they lived. Understanding how to punish Indians was one of these steps.

Recent studies have helped us to better appreciate the emergence and transformation of colonial legislation by focusing on the ways in which law ceases to be an abstraction and becomes an inextricable part of both Indian and Spanish social experience.[6] As Spaniards conquered and settled new lands, concerns about the treatment of criminals and lesser transgressors were kept alive. If anything, contact with new and widely diverse peoples made the Spanish colonizers more aware of the dangers (and difficulties) of hastily imposed laws or new legal practices that might run against local traditions—provided, of course, that these traditions did not violate Christian norms or European standards.[7] As it happened, the crown and the missionaries working closely with indigenous peoples often had opposing views on how to handle cultural differences when it came to enforcing laws and social norms, and colonial legislation reflected this tension.

As I have noted in previous chapters, the conversion of the indigenous peoples of Mexico, and the colonial enterprise at large, gave the friars many opportunities to grapple with questions that directly or indirectly touched upon the notion of honor. When the friars favored restricting Indians from taking oaths in a court of law, they argued that this restriction would protect them from both perjuring themselves and the severe penalties that perjurers faced. To further justify this recommendation, they also adduced that Indians still did not fully comprehend the connections between truth-telling, reputation, and God that were implicated in swearing, connections that Spanish oath-takers had little difficulty grasping. In order to serve a purpose other than the mechanical application of the law, penalties had to be meaningful. This explains, for example, the recommendation of the Third Mexican Church Council that indigenous

---

6. See Borah, *Justice by Insurance*; and Kellogg, *Law and the Transformation of Aztec Culture*. For a comparative study with a more theoretical bent, see Lauren Benton, *Law and Colonial Cultures: Legal Regimes in World History, 1400–1900* (Cambridge: Cambridge University Press, 2002), especially chap. 2. On the study of punishment and the writing of alternative legal histories in Latin America, see the introductory essay by Carlos Aguirre and Ricardo D. Salvatore in *Crime and Punishment in Latin America: Law and Society since Late Colonial Times*, ed. Ricardo D. Salvatore, Carlos Aguirre, and Gilbert M. Joseph (Durham: Duke University Press, 2001), 1–32.

7. The law was issued in 1555. León Pinelo, *Recopilación de las Indias*, book 2, title 1, law 6, 1:341.

perjurers be punished by shaving their heads, exposing them to public humiliation.[8] Punishments became yet another area that the friars in Mexico sought to infuse with religious meaning, and they did so by relying on what they learned about local notions of honor.

This final chapter addresses the development of a number of related laws concerning the punishment of indigenous subjects from the 1540s to the beginning of the seventeenth century. I have chosen to focus this discussion of corporal punishment on cutting off offenders' hair, a practice that became a point of contention between missionaries and secular officials, and the object of regulation by royal authority.[9] Behind the changes in policy explored here lies an important chapter of the uneasy and shifting relationship between friars and royal officers in New Spain as both groups struggled to build their authority among the native population. As I will show, both groups made claims about the desirability of transforming native cultures that were shaped by their respective views about authority and the function of ecclesiastical and secular laws.

How to Punish Indians

In 1568, the second archbishop of Mexico, Fr. Alonso de Montúfar appointed the *bachiller* Alonso Fernández de Sigura *provisor de indios*, entrusting him with the administration of all ecclesiastical legal matters regarding Indians in the diocese.[10] A year later, Fernández de Sigura's authority was further enhanced when he was elected *visitador general*, responsible for religious affairs and administering justice according to ecclesiastical law to Spaniards and Indians alike.[11] In a report written in 1570, *inspector* Fernández de Sigura in-

---

8. "Si autem falso aliqui jurasse comperti sint, eos, ut ceteri, metu poena terreantur, et cautiores evadant, publique flagellari Judex praecipiat, et ut maiore ignominia afficiantur, detonderi faciant." *Concilium Mexicanum Provinciale III*, book 2, title 5, §10, 126.

9. On the question of why religious men were led to embrace violence as a possible source of transformation in the new territories, see Inga Clendinnen, "Disciplining the Indians: Franciscan Ideology and Missionary Violence in Sixteenth-Century Yucatán," *Past & Present* 94 (February 1982): 27–48. See also Henry Kamen's more general "Clerical Violence in a Catholic Society: The Hispanic World 1450–1720" in *Crisis and Change in Early Modern Spain* (London: Variorum, 1984), 201–16.

10. Luis García Pimentel, ed., *Descripción del Arzobispado de México hecha en 1570* (Mexico City: José Joaquín Terrazas e hijas, 1897), 303–4. The *provisor de indios*, who may or may not be a priest, acted as an assistant to the bishop and was charged with dealing with ecclesiastical legal matters as they applied to Indians. John F. Schwaller, *The Church and Clergy in Sixteenth-Century Mexico* (Albuquerque: University of New Mexico Press, 1987), 24. The first *provisor de indios* appointed by Archbishop Montúfar, Marañón, was already exercising his duties in 1559. Tavárez, *The Invisible War*, 53.

11. García Pimentel, *Descripción del Arzobispado*, 304–6.

formed the Council of the Indies that the inhabitants of San Pablo (one of the four wards that made up Mexico City) practiced a wide variety of trades and had become, for the most part, Christians. The report also mentioned that the Mexican Indians sentenced and punished by Spanish authorities had recently started behaving in unpredictable ways: "[They] no longer consider it an affront to be whipped or have their heads shaven as penitence and punishment; moreover they become more boastful and take pride in this, and consider the Indian who has been punished the most to be the most courageous."[12] Fernández de Sigura's report contradicted the expectations of Spanish colonial officials; the physical punishment of Indian transgressors had somehow failed to produce the desired effect, which was, as the officer's words suggest, to induce a sense of shame that would discourage the commission of further offenses. According to Fernández de Sigura, authorities should replace current punishments with new and more effective ones. The Mexican-born writer Juan Suárez de Peralta, who served as alcalde of Cuauhtitlán around the same time, had a similar view of the transformative effect of flogging and shaving indigenous offenders.[13] He went on to report that in response to this odd development, authorities opted to impose pecuniary fines for drunkenness.[14]

Any attempt at reconstructing and interpreting the events that Fernández de Sigura reports is severely limited by the author's omission of specific information on the nature of the offenses that led to the punishments. We can only guess whether the Indians in question had come to adopt a routine of defiance after what may have been a spontaneous response to punishment, or acted according to some pattern derived from those traces of native cultural traditions that they had managed to preserve. It is equally unclear whether the Indians' behavior, allegedly witnessed by friars and priests, amounted to anything more than the rare and isolated case. Despite these uncertainties, this otherwise unexceptional document raises important questions about the friars' efforts to gain jurisdictional authority over the Indians.

As we have seen, Fernández de Sigura believed that the open display of

---

12. "que no tienen ya por afrenta ser azotados ni tresquilados por penitencia y castigo, antes se precian más y se honran dello." García Pimentel, *Descripción del Arzobispado*, 279.

13. "Que yo vi indios, y aún siendo yo Corregidor por su majestad castigué a muchos, que era la pena ordinaria por borrachos azotarlos públicamente y trasquilarlos las cabezas a panderetes, y después de sueltos de la cárcel tener por mucha honra haberle azotado y trasquilado, y reñir con otros que no lo han sido , y por oprobio y afrenta decirles: *calla, que eres una gallina, que no te han azotado y trasquilado como a mí.*" Suárez de Peralta, *Tratado del descubrimiento de las Indias*, chap. 2, 56.

14. "Y visto tener ellos en poco este castigo, se ha acordado de penarles por las borracheras, en dineros, que esto sienten en extremo, por ser, como son todos en general, laceradísimos, y condenarles a servicio por algunos días." Suárez de Peralta, *Tratado del descubrimiento de las Indias*, chap. 2, 56.

hostility by Indians was a possible response to a form of punishment that had become ineffectual, and needed replacing. Yet he also suggested an alternative diagnosis of the problem, as well as an alternative solution. This report is no exception to the tendency of documents from the period to present information in support of a particular viewpoint on matters of policy somewhat obliquely. If there was something that religious writers learned quickly in their endless exchanges with royal officers, it was to blend information and suggestion in a single statement. In Fernández de Sigura's case, he chose to preface his observations on Nahua rebelliousness with the comment that the administration of justice might be better served if churchmen were allowed to dispense punishments as they saw fit, since they were better acquainted with the Indian population than any other Spanish officials—an opinion that was shared by laymen such as Alonso de Zorita. The inspector thus implied that the difficulty in shaming the Nahuas lay less in the inadequacy of the punishment than in the choice of officer imposing or administering it.[15] To assert, as Fernández de Sigura did in 1570, that secular authorities still lacked the power to command the kind of respect that friars elicited from Indians was probably both a safe description and an exercise in rhetorical persuasion. Although the ultimate cause of the Indians' behavior that Fernández de Sigura described remains elusive, the two explanations that he advanced were practical attempts to deal with a problem that was thought to stem primarily from cultural differences between Indians and Spaniards. Fernandez de Sigura was convinced that only religious ministers were equipped to perceive, if not to account for, minute differences and propose remedies to overcome them. This view was widely shared by the mendicant friars who, since their arrival in Mexico, had sought to assume jurisdiction over Indians in matters of justice for *pecados públicos* (public sins), a desire that secular authorities had repeatedly opposed.[16] At times, the friars based their claim on legal grounds, invoking the papal privileges that allowed them to carry out the activities of any diocesan priest. It is worth recalling that Pope Adrian VI, in the 1522 bull *Exponi novis feciste* (also known as *Omnimoda*), granted the early mendicants authority over the Indians "in utroque

---

15. On the use of violence by regular and secular clergy in colonial Mexico, see Gibson, *The Aztecs under Spanish Rule*, 117–18; see also William B. Taylor, *Magistrates of the Sacred: Priests and Parishioners in Eighteenth-Century Mexico* (Stanford: Stanford University Press, 1996), 215–21.

16. Such opposition started very early on; on July 28, 1525, the *cabildo* of Mexico, upon inspecting the documentation presented by the Franciscans, judged their claim to deal with criminal cases to be suspect. *Actas de cabildo de la Ciudad de México*, 1:49. Some secular officers not only recognized but also welcomed the friars' jurisdiction over certain offenses: "Ellos donde están sirven de curas, bautizan, y confiesan y casan y aun tienen jurisdicción para prender y castigar amancebados, y los indios los quieren mucho, y los respetan." Suárez de Peralta, *Tratado del descubrimiento de las Indias*, chap. 3, 66.

foro."[17] More often, however, as they consolidated their influence over the Indian population, they asked secular authorities to recognize the administration of justice as an integral part of religious supervision. This argument seems to have persuaded the crown to consider granting the friars some limited discretion in the correction of Indians.[18]

There was a fair amount of confusion in the Peninsula over the precise boundaries between royal and ecclesiastical jurisdiction for a variety of crimes. The establishment of the Inquisition had only added to the problem.[19] Things were no different in Mexico, where royal and ecclesiastical officers clashed over the right to intervene in cases concerning public sins despite repeated calls by the crown for bishops to observe the strict jurisdictional separation.[20] Additional conflicts emerged between the ecclesiastical hierarchy and the religious orders over whether friars were allowed to exercise episcopal authority under special circumstances.

A royal decree from 1530, referring to an earlier one from 1525, ordered ecclesiastical judges and officers of the Indies to refrain from arresting laymen without the assistance of secular officials.[21] The 1525 decree noted that this prohibition had been in effect since 1429.[22] If we are to believe the accusations

---

17. Francisco Javier Hernáez, *Colección de bulas, breves y otros documentos relativos a la Iglesia de América y Filipinas*, 2 vols. (Vaduz: Kraus Reprint, 1964), 1:383.

18. Francisco González de Cosío, ed., *Un cedulario mexicano del siglo XVI* (Mexico City: Ediciones del Frente de Afirmación Hispanista, A.C., 1973), 73. This royal *cédula*, issued in February 1538, addressed concerns that Archbishop Zumárraga voiced in the instruction to his representatives to the aborted council of Mantua. Cuevas, *Documentos inéditos del siglo XVI*, 63–71.

19. This already crowded picture is not complete without mentioning the historical significance of seigneurial jurisdiction and its ever-changing relation to royal authority. On the coexistence of several justice systems in Spain, see Michael Weisser, "Crime and Punishment in Early Modern Spain," in *Crime and the Law: The Social History of Crime in Western Europe since 1500*, ed. V. A. C. Gatrell, Bruce Lenman, and Geoffrey Parker (London: Europa Publications, 1980), 76–96, especially 76–82. On jurisdictional conflicts between church and state, see Antonio Domínguez Ortiz, *El Antiguo Régimen: Los Reyes Católicos y los Austrias* (Madrid: Alianza Editorial/Alfaguara, 1973), 220–24.

20. *Pecados públicos* were the province of both religious and secular authorities, and encompassed a wide variety of offenses such as blasphemy, drunkenness, witchcraft, usury, and unions not sanctioned by marriage. See, for example, the order given to the *corregidores* of the colonies in 1530. Encinas, *Cedulario indiano*, 2:23; for Mexico, see the instruction to officers of justice issued in 1561 in which false testimony is added to the list of public sins committed by Indians. Cuevas, *Documentos inéditos del siglo XVI*, 249. The First Mexican Church Council laid out the steps to be followed by bishops and clergy in the treatment of public sins. *Concilios provinciales primero, y segundo*, chap. 6, 47–48. On competing jurisdictions in New Spain, see Richard E. Greenleaf, "The Inquisition and the Indians of New Spain: A Study in Jurisdictional Confusion," *The Americas* 22, no. 2 (October 1965): 138–66. On the types of Indian cases that fell under royal jurisdiction, see Borah, *Justice by Insurance*, 44–52.

21. Encinas, *Cedulario indiano*, 2:32; also in León Pinelo, *Recopilación de las Indias*, book 1, title 16, law 13, 1:237; and a similar order from 1559, book 1, title 16, law 3, 1:223.

22. "Porque assi como nos queremos guardar su jurisdiccion a la Iglesia, y a los Ecclesiasticos Juezes: assaz razon, y derecho es, que la Iglesia, y Juezes Ecclesiasticos, no se entremeten en pertur-

made by the *cabildo* of Mexico City in 1542, ecclesiastical officers intentionally sought to make it difficult for Indians to distinguish between royal and ecclesiastical officers of justice by having the bishop's bailiffs carry the same staff as their secular counterparts.[23] Such deception was surely intended to prevent the Nahuas from fully understanding that the separation of jurisdictions was a fundamental feature of the justice system.[24] Whatever the merits of the charges, the actions reported by the *cabildo* are similar to other methods employed by the friars to further their ascendancy over the Indians.

Religious authorities were not blind to the daily difficulties of colonial administration, and they did not hesitate to point these out to bolster their claims. For instance, when in 1537 Archbishop Zumárraga advocated allowing religious orders to administer justice, he cited the shortage of secular officers as a compelling reason.[25]

Fernández de Sigura's words accurately reflected the friars' belief that their experience and deeper understanding of Indian mores and weaknesses made them the best judges in the land. He quietly used this argument to address an official decree that sought in unmistakable terms to put an end to the friars' interference in secular institutions. It is highly unlikely that when writing to the council, the inspector was unaware that a royal *cédula* from 1560 had banned Franciscan, Dominican, and Augustinian friars from imprisoning and punishing Indians.

The 1560 decree was issued on the heels of serious allegations that the friars had succeeded in gaining authority over the Indians by usurping functions reserved for royal officers and ignoring episcopal jurisdiction. As Archbishop Montúfar wrote to the king in 1558, "The spiritual and temporal government is for the most part in the hands of the religious . . . they judge, pass sentences,

---

bar nuestra jurisdicion real. Y que no sean osados de hacer execucion en los bienes de los legos; ni prender, ni encarcelar sus personas . . . combiene saber, que la Iglesia invoque la ayuda del brazo seglar." *Ordenanzas reales de Castilla*, book 1, title 3, law 7, in *Los códigos españoles concordados y anotados*, 6:263.

23. *Actas de cabildo de la Ciudad de México*, 4:300. Spaniards depended heavily on the Indians' ability to recognize conventional symbols of authority, and the missionaries, as *cabildo* members soon discovered, took full advantage of this. The Nahuatl word *topile* ("holder of the staff") was used in colonial times to designate minor officers, including *alguaciles*. Lockhart, *The Nahuas after the Conquest*, 43. Sahagún states that among the Nahuas the officer charged with the same responsibilities as the Spanish *alguacil* was called *achcauhtli*, and also carried a staff. *Florentine Codex*, appendix to book 3, chap. 5, 55.

24. Jails and staffs were considered "insinias de juredición," Paso y Troncoso, *Epistolario de la Nueva España*, 11:149.

25. Cuevas, *Documentos inéditos del siglo XVI*, 68. The situation was hardly different in 1554, when Viceroy Luis de Velasco wrote to Philip II that "en toda la tierra no conozco diez hombres hábiles para cargos de justicia, y eran menester más de doscientos, que es gran falta." Cuevas, *Documentos inéditos del siglo XVI*, 208.

make arrests and release and decide on ecclesiastical cases with or without consulting prelates . . . they make arrests and undo them in your royal jails outside
of Mexico and some even in Mexico."[26] Montúfar instructed Lorenzo Lebrón de
Quiñones, *alcalde mayor* of New Galicia, to investigate these same charges as
part of his visit to Oaxaca.[27]

The establishment in 1543 of the first indigenous *cabildo* of Cuauhtinchan
also marked the arrival of a new system of justice that inhabitants soon learned
to fear. Justice soon became associated with two especially dreaded forms of
punishment: public whippings and head shavings in the *tianguiz*. The people
of Cuauhtinchan found head shavings particularly insidious because they saw
it as a token of bad luck.[28] Significantly, the 1560 decree explicitly condemned
the widespread use of head shaving, arguing that Mexican Indians found it especially offensive.[29] The law partially acknowledged the friars' justification for
adopting head shaving, but nonetheless rejected this method, finding its very
efficacy excessive. It is unclear whether this particular injunction was intended
to be a broader statement questioning the advisability of punishing the Nahuas
by shaming—assuming that the Spaniards were right to conclude that shame
was the experience that Indians found so threatening. Issued ten years before
the inspector's report, the prohibition may very well explain why Fernández
de Sigura formulated his assessment and recommendations in such a tentative
fashion. As the 1560 *cédula* indicates, royal government had good reason to
suspect that head shaving had become inextricably associated in Indian minds
with the friars' role as administrators of justice. This is why the warning to
the friars alone may not have been considered sufficient, and explicit reference
made to their preferred method of punishment. The charges against the orders
did not go unanswered, nor did the persistent rumors alleging that the friars
continued to administer justice in defiance of the royal order. Early in 1569,
the same year in which Fernández de Sigura wrote his report, the Franciscan
provincial Fray Miguel de Navarro addressed the accusations against his brothers and explained why the friars should be allowed some discretion in the correction of Indians. According to the provincial, the 1560 decree had helped
undermine the authority of the friars among the Indians, who no longer feared

26. Paso y Troncoso, *Epistolario de la Nueva España*, 8:187; on the friars' exercise of episcopal
jurisdiction, see 8:185.

27. Paso y Troncoso, *Epistolario de la Nueva España*, 8:210.

28. *Libro de los guardianes y gobernadores de Cuauhtinchan (1519–1640)*, 45.

29. "A nos se ha hecho relación que los religiosos de las órdenes de Sant Francisco y Sancto
Domingo y Sant Augustin que en essa tierra residen tienen en sus monesterios cepos para poner
en ellos a los indios e indias que quieren y los aprisionan y açotan por lo que les parece y los tres-
quilan que es un género de pena que se suele dar a los yndios, lo que ellos sienten mucho." Puga,
Provisiones, 201v.

any reprisal if they skipped Mass.[30] As if echoing the words of the *encomendero* Jerónimo López that I mentioned in chapter 2, Navarro expressed the widespread view among Spaniards that the Indians' knowledge of the laws protecting them was sooner or later bound to have negative consequences. Navarro responded to the charges contained in the 1560 law by exploiting its ambiguities. He carefully limited his discussion of punishments to cases of Indians who failed to fulfill their religious obligations such as attending Mass and catechism; the friars' actions were thus presented as tools that enabled conversions and lacked any legal weight or meaning. Provincial Navarro's reluctance to discuss issues of legal competence directly betrays the seriousness of the charges launched against the brothers under his supervision. Just a few years earlier, two issues, excessive use of violence and the usurpation of jurisdiction, had been at the center of charges faced by Diego de Landa, bishop of Yucatán.[31] The Landa affair, which became an almost mandatory point of reference in future discussions of the jurisdictional authority of religious orders, cast a wide shadow over both the accusations against the Franciscans and the friars' responses. As to the suggestion that the friars had been directly involved in the flogging or shaving of individuals, the Franciscan replied that Indians appointed by the viceroy to assist the missionaries actually carried out the punishments.[32] This seemingly minor distinction was significant from both the secular and the ecclesiastical perspective, since, as the First Mexican Church Council had declared in 1555, the clergy was prohibited from administering physical punishments to slaves or servants.[33] As explained by the Third Mexican Council, by abstaining from violence themselves, priests were safely protected from the possibility of crossing the fine line that separated brotherly correction from vengeance.[34]

The legislation of the Third Mexican Church Council consolidated once and

---

30. García Icazbalceta, *Códice Mendieta*, 1:110.

31. An account of the investigation can be found in Clendinnen, *Ambivalent Conquests: Maya and Spaniard in Yucatan, 1517–1570* (Cambridge: Cambridge University Press, 1987), 93–111. In 1536 the crown banned missionaries in Chiapas from shaming Indians in public, a form of punishment that Landa later used in Yucatán. Luis Weckmann, *La herencia medieval de México*, 2nd ed. (Mexico City: Fondo de Cultura Económica, 1994), 438. It should be added that when asked to comment on the charges against Landa, the Augustinian Alonso de la Veracruz and other theologians found that the bishop had not overstepped his jurisdiction. France V. Scholes and Eleanor B. Adams, eds., *Don Diego Quijada, Alcalde Mayor de Yucatán, 1561–1565*, 2 vols. (Mexico City: Antigua Librería Robredo, 1938), 2:425–29.

32. The order by Viceroy Luis de Velasco is included in García Icazbalceta, *Códice Mendieta*, 1:112–14.

33. "Otrosi estatuimos, y mandamos, que ningun Clérigo castigue por su propria Persona a ningun esclavo, o esclava, ni criado suyo, si no fuere castigo moderado y humano, porque lo contrario está prohibido por los Sacros Cánones." *Concilios provinciales primero, y segundo*, chap. 60, 133.

34. *Concilium Mexicanum Provinciale III*, book 3, title 5, §5, 181.

for all the status of the Mexican Indians as neophytes in need of supervision. Under the tutelage of the church, the Indians were exempt from certain obligations and restricted from pursuing avenues open to other Christians, such as the priesthood. Concerning penalties, conciliar authorities agreed that those who violated ecclesiastical laws should be shown some leniency rather than given harsh punishments, except for unrepentant idolaters and dogmatizers.[35]

The church had traditionally reserved for itself the exclusive use of "spiritual weapons" for censuring or disciplining sinners, including members of the clergy.[36] These weapons, which included different kinds of excommunication, imposed restrictions on the ability to fully partake in Catholic worship. As mentioned above, friars expressed doubts about the effectiveness of such weapons on individuals new to the faith; the Mexican council, following the Third Council of Lima (1582–83), embraced this view and exempted Indians from these spiritual sanctions.[37] But when the church determined that punishments were to be considered in light of the Indians' ongoing education in the new religion, not everyone was ready to dismiss tougher secular as well as spiritual sanctions as inherently at odds with doctrinal teaching. Pedro de Feria, then bishop of Chiapas, certainly was not. In a report that he submitted to the council, he resented the limits that the crown imposed on ecclesiastical judges to prevent them from handing down the sentences they saw fit. Taking exception to the blanket characterization of converted Indians as "neophytes," the bishop recommended that members of the indigenous nobility not be exempted from physical punishments or ecclesiastical sanctions in cases of idolatry or incest, especially considering how well acquainted they had become with Spanish mores.[38]

Either because the rumors acquired a life of their own or because the friars continued to ignore the 1560 royal order, or both, in 1574 new accusations emerged that Franciscan friars had usurped ecclesiastical and royal jurisdiction by executing sentences against Indians. According to several witnesses a group

---

35. *Concilium Mexicanum Provinciale III*, book 5, title 4, §1, 292.

36. According to canon law, excommunication, together with suspension and interdiction, fell under the category of "censures," which differed from "penalties" proper; a systematic exposition of these distinctions can be found in the guidelines for confessors written by the Jesuit Juan de la Plaza in accordance to the Third Mexican Council. Carrillo Cázares, *Manuscritos del Concilio Tercero Provincial Mexicano*, 5:112–49. For a concise overview of the historical development of excommunication, see Helmholz, *The Spirit of Classical Canon Law*, 370–93.

37. Vargas Ugarte, *Concilios Limenses*, action 4, chap. 7, 1:364.

38. "No tendría por errado, sino por muy açertado, que de delitos graves, de los arriba referidos, y por otros semejantes, ubiese de quando en quando algunos castigos ejemplares y rigurosos, mayormente en los indios principales, y en los vezinos de los pueblos que están en comarca de españoles, los cuales están ya muy ladinos y demasiado bachilleres, y esta gente no sabe juzgar de la gravedad de los peccados sino por la gravedad y rigor de la pena con que son castigados." Carrillo Cázares, *Manuscritos del Concilio Tercero Provincial Mexicano*, vol. 1, part 1, 299.

of friars acting as a parallel court of justice had ordered the flogging, cutting of hair, and imprisonment of several individuals.[39] The accusations suggest that the friars were able to get away with this behavior because the Indian population had been taught from the pulpit to seek justice exclusively through their religious guides.[40] The accusations centered on the guardian of the monastery of Tlatelolco, Alonso de Molina, whose antipathy for Archbishop of Mexico Pedro Moya de Contreras was no secret. It should be noted that the charges paralleled almost point by point the infractions referred to in the decree from 1560, a document well known to the accusers. Augustinians and Dominicans were not spared similar accusations.[41]

The enemies of the orders made the 1560 law into a template for elaborating further accusations against the friars. But the law also happened to touch on a number of significant themes and issues that would occupy religious and secular writers for quite some time.[42] One such theme was the changing relation between practices and meanings in the colonial context and the forces at work in shaping of colonial traditions.

Punishments Old and New

Sixteenth-century religious and secular writers commented approvingly on the ancient laws of the land, to which they attributed Nahua success in building and preserving an ordered society. Spanish authors praised the severity of these

---

39. "E asimismo perteneciendo el conocimiento de todos los negocios e causas eclesiásticas in foro contencioso al ordinario y sus provisores y vicarious, el guardian y frailes del dicho monasterio questan en el dicho barrio de Tlatelolco se han entremetido de hecho a conocer e conocen de las causas y negocios de los indios de dicho barrio, ansí civiles como criminales y los prenden y los ponen en la cárcel con cepo e prisiones y los azotan y trasquilan." Paso y Troncoso, *Epistolario de la Nueva España*, 9:148. See 9:154 and 158 for references on the court-like system.

40. Paso y Troncoso, *Epistolario de la Nueva España*, 11:154. Testimony given in the case reported that the friars formed what amounted to a parallel court of justice with its own officers. 11:154 and 158.

41. On Augustinians, Paso y Troncoso, *Epistolario de la Nueva España*, 11:158. The controversial inspector Jerónimo de Valderrama, who found himself at odds with the Dominican bishop of Oaxaca Bernardo de Albuquerque, wrote to the king in 1564 that the Dominicans "have become spiritual and temporal lords and they resent more than others relinquishing their status and authority" ("estado y señorío"). *Colección de documentos inéditos, relativos al descubrimiento, conquista y organización de las antiguas posesiones españolas de América y Oceanía, sacados de los archivos del reino, y muy especialmente del de Indias*, 42 vols. (Madrid, 1864–84), 13:372. In 1560 Albuquerque had given other Dominicans, such as Pedro Guerrero, full authority to punish Indian idolaters. David Tavárez, *The Invisible War*, 59 and 64–65. On the activities of these Dominicans in Oaxaca, see Cuevas, *Historia de la Iglesia en México*, 1:263.

42. In 1613 Pedro Sánchez de Aguilar, dean of the Cathedral of Yucatán, commented on this same law in a treatise written as a defense of the right of bishops to punish Indian idolaters without secular interference. Sánchez de Aguilar, *Informe contra idolorum*, 29–32.

laws, and, not unlike other Europeans, were particularly fascinated by the variety of Mexican methods for the execution of criminals. Fr. Diego Durán, for example, always ready to correct fellow writers in matters of native traditions and customs, felt the need to dispel the myth that the Nahuas executed criminals by hanging.[43] But more importantly, Spanish writers concluded that in prescribing penalties according to the seriousness of each crime, the Nahuas had shown the keen sense of justice that was an essential feature in any civilized society.[44]

In Spain, the public administration of lashes was considered an effective way of shaming minor offenders from the lower social strata; shaming became a standard form of punishment of women delinquents.[45] Soon after the fall of Tenochtitlán, head shaving, sometimes combined with public whipping, became a common method of punishing Indian transgressors.[46] In 1536, for instance, Antonio Tacatecle and Alonso Tanixtecle were found guilty of idolatry and sentenced to be publicly whipped and have their heads shaven.[47] Indians convicted of speaking openly against Christianity met similar punishments.[48] In 1545, a small group of Indian merchants and noblemen from Nueva Galicia had their hair cut in public and were sentenced to labor for having engaged in the selling of free fellow tribesmen.[49] Around the same time in Yanhuitlán,

---

43. Fr. Diego Durán, *Historia de las Indias de Nueva España*, 1:184. For the opposite view, see Las Casas, *Apologética historia sumaria*, 2:399–400. Writing in 1581, the author of the *relación de Tasco* conceded that he was not able to gather information on traditional punishments. Acuña, *Relaciones geográficas del siglo XVI*, 7:126–27. As several codices attest, Spanish methods of execution may have exerted a similar fascination over the Nahuas. Juan José Batalla Rosado, "La pena de muerte durante la colonia—siglo XVI—a partir del análisis de las imágenes de los códices mesoamericanos," *Revista española de antropología americana* 25 (1995): 71–110.

44. On similarities between the Ten Commandments and Aztec law, see Fr. Diego Durán, *Historia de las Indias de Nueva España*, 1:35–36.

45. Ruth Pike, "Crime and Punishment in XVIth-Century Spain," *Journal of European Economic History* 5, no. 3 (1976): 690–91. In the eighteenth century, the legal reformer Manuel de Lardizábal y Uribe still believed that, properly applied, this kind of punishment "can produce very healthy effects." Manuel de Lardizábal y Uribe, *Discurso sobre las penas contrahido a las leyes criminales de España para facilitar su reforma* (Madrid: Joaquín Ibarra, 1782), 195. Scourging or whipping was also the penalty most commonly imposed by the Spanish Inquisition. Henry Charles Lea, *A History of the Spanish Inquisition*, 4 vols. (New York: Macmillan, 1922), 3:136–37. On the use of torture and physical punishments in sixteenth-century Valencia, see Emilia Salvador Esteban, "Tortura y penas corporales en la Valencia foral moderna: El reinado de Fernando el Católico," *Estudis* 22 (1996): 263–87.

46. Public whippings seem to have been the method of choice for punishing Spaniards, at least in cases not involving religious offenses or serious crimes. A set of legal regulations related to the administration of mines issued by Viceroy Antonio de Mendoza in 1539 prescribed one hundred lashes for the failure to appear in person to report on the amount of silver extracted every week. Paso y Troncoso, *Epistolario de la Nueva España*, 3:251. An overview of legal punishments in colonial Mexico can be found in Weckmann, *La herencia medieval de México*, 434–43.

47. *Procesos de indios idólatras y hechiceros*, 15.

48. *Procesos de indios idólatras y hechiceros*, 77.

49. Paso y Troncoso, *Epistolario de la Nueva España*, 4:186–87. The author of the report makes clear that Indians feared shame more than death: "puso tanto temor el castigo y fué de tanta eficacia

a town in the Mixteca region, a Dominican friar ordered that a group of Indian women accused of practicing divination be flogged and have their hair cut.[50] While these crimes were considered serious offenses against the Catholic faith, a mid-sixteenth-century Nahuatl translation of *ordenanzas* that closely reflected the friars' concerns in 1546 shows that shaming was also prescribed for lesser faults.[51] Head shaving became the method of choice for shaming Indians who had violated Christian precepts and moral norms.[52] For baptized Indians convicted of their first act of idolatry, the ordinances prescribed both one hundred lashes and head shaving.[53] The same penalty applied to those arrested a second time for drunkenness.[54] A method of shaming reserved for diviners and local healers involved the public display of the offender tied to a post in the marketplace and wearing a crown of paper thorns.[55] In what appears to be a plan to take possession of his property in 1608 the alcalde of San Bartolomé was the fatal victim of an attack in Tehuacán; the physical assault involved some kind of shaving.[56]

Deciding on the most appropriate ways to punish Indians proved to be a delicate task for colonial administrators and missionaries. How, for example, were religious orders to deal with the overwhelming number of baptized In-

---

por ser los condenados principales y verlos servir con hierros, que del todo este delicto se ha remediado . . . no se les dió más riguroso castigo por ser cosa muy acostumbrada entre estos bárbaros y aún porque tienen por mayor castigo verlos servir con hierros que no en la horca."

50. Wigberto Jiménez Moreno and Salvador Mateos Higuera, eds., *Códice de Yanhuitlan* (Mexico City: Museo Nacional, 1940), 42. This information was provided by an Indian witness in the Inquisitorial process against the cacique and the two governors of Yanhuitlán; the women in question were reportedly found in the house of Don Francisco, one of the governors.

51. It is thought that the original document was translated between 1546 and 1555. Sell and Kellogg, "We Want to Give Them Laws," 326–27. On the ecclesiastical meeting or *junta* of 1546, see Fernando Gil, *Primeras "Doctrinas" del Nuevo Mundo: Estudio histórico-teológico de las obras de fray Juan de Zumárraga (†1548)* (Buenos Aires: Publicaciones de Teología de la Pontificia Universidad Católica Argentina "Santa María de los Buenos Aires," 1992), 248–70.

52. Sell and Kellogg rightly highlight the connection between punishment and race that emerges from this document. "We Want to Give Them Laws," 339. A revealing example can be found in the 1590 city ordinances of Guayaquil that reserve head shaving for Indians and blacks. Interestingly, these two groups are not always treated similarly with respect to punishment for the same offenses. While blacks caught playing cards were to be whipped and sent to jail for four days, Indians would receive the same jail time and be "trasquilados." Francisco de Solano, *Normas y leyes de la ciudad hispanoamericana (1492–1600)*, 2 vols. (Madrid: Consejo Superior de Investigaciones Científicas, Centro de Estudios Históricos, 1996), 1:261–62.

53. Sell and Kellogg, "We Want to Give Them Laws," 353.

54. Sell and Kellogg, "We Want to Give Them Laws," 356. Scourging and head shaving were the most common punishments administered by the *verdugo* appointed by the Indian *cabildo* in Tlaxcala; in 1548 the town agreed to pay the officer four *maravedíes* per offender. *Actas del cabildo de Tlaxcala, 1547–1567*, 280. See also note 14 to this chapter.

55. Sell and Kellogg, "We Want to Give Them Laws," 356. Public infamy remained the prescribed penalty for diviners and those accused of resorting to potions and spells. *Concilium Mexicanum Provinciale III*, book 5, title 6, §1, 299–300.

56. *Anales de Tepeteopan*, 63.

Fig. 4.1. Punishment of a petty thief in sixteenth-century Spain. Christoph Weiditz, *Das Trachtenbuch*. (Courtesy of the Germanisches Nationalmuseum, Nuremberg.)

dians who kept concubines? When religious authorities posed this question to the crown in 1537, they hoped to receive guidance as well as broader power over the Indians.[57] The source of the problem was a royal decree from the previous year instructing that Indians living in unions not recognized by the church not be fined as a penalty, as was customary for Spaniards.[58] Constrained by this prohibition and the crown's mandate to show moderation toward new converts, the friars looked for acceptable solutions that would not compromise their authority over cases concerning Christian morals. Signs of the search for a middle ground are apparent in the course of action against Indian offenders that was laid out in the Nahuatl version of the *ordenanzas* of 1546. These included verbal warnings and public whippings, plus the possibility of unspecified penitential acts.[59] Alarmed by reports of false accusations of women living in unlawful unions, the crown laid out the circumstances under which those charges could be brought, and banned the physical punishment of pregnant women.[60] Colonial authorities also asked for guidance on in response to the New Laws of 1542, which banned enslavement and branding, two standard punishments for Indians who had either participated in rebellions or been captured in battle.[61]

Soon after their arrival, the friars learned from native informants that head shaving had been one of several current methods of punishment among the Nahuas. Motolinia, for instance, reported that drunkards had their hair shaved in the *tianguiz*, a penalty similar to the one prescribed in the 1546 decrees.[62] The *Codex Mendoza*, a pictorial manuscript designed to convey the customs, rituals, and life cycle of the Nahuas to a European audience, depicts a young man being subjected to such punishment. A summary of the old laws of the Mexican Indians states that young people who misbehaved risked having their

---

57. González de Cosío, *Un cedulario mexicano del siglo XVI*, 51

58. Puga, *Provisiones*, 110v. In 1560 Philip II issued a decree banning ecclesiastical judges from imposing pecuniary penalties on Indians. Encinas, *Cedulario indiano*, 4:336; also in León Pinelo, *Recopilación de las Indias*, book 1, title 16, law 7, 1:235. The exemption seems to have been adopted much earlier, as attested by a petition signed by Zumárraga on December 4, 1537. Cuevas, *Documentos inéditos del siglo XVI*, 153. The Third Mexican Council upheld this decision. *Concilium Mexicanum Provinciale III*, book 5, title 9, §1, 305–6. The Franciscans working in Guadalajara did not miss the opportunity to use this restriction to their advantage when, in 1569, they made their case against secular judges, whom they accused of just fining Indians without any concern for their moral well-being. García Icazbalceta, *Nueva colección de documentos*, 2:159.

59. Sell and Kellogg, "We Want to Give Them Laws," 354. The Spanish version omits any consideration of mitigating circumstances. O'Gorman, "Una ordenanza para el gobierno de los indios," 185.

60. Paso y Troncoso, *Epistolario de la Nueva España*, 8:215.

61. Paso y Troncoso, *Epistolario de la Nueva España*, 4:196–97; 5:87.

62. Motolinia, *Memoriales*, 362. This information was later repeated by Gerónimo de Mendieta. *Historia eclesiástica indiana*, book 2, chap. 30, 139. Mendieta also mentions the same punishment for venal judges. *Historia eclesiástica indiana*, book 2, chap. 28, 135.

Fig. 4.2. Punishment of a young offender. *Codex Mendoza*. (Courtesy of the Bodleian Library, Oxford University.)

Fig. 4.3. Head-shaving of Indian delinquents in Tlaxcala. Diego Muñoz Camargo, *Relación geográfica de Tlaxcala*. (Courtesy of the library of the University of Glasgow, Scotland.)

hair shorn, although the punishment seems to have been left to parents or relatives rather than government officials.[63] More dramatically, Nahua priests who

---

63. "El modo que tenían de castigar a sus hijos y hijas siendo mozos, cuando salían viciosos y desobedientes y traviesos, era tresquilarlos y traerlos mal tratados, y punzarle las orejas y los muslos y brazos." García Icazbalceta, *Nueva colección de documentos*, 3:284. This document from 1543 was authored by Fr. Andrés de Alcobiz in Spain. It coincides word for word with the text found in Las Casas, *Apologética historia sumaria*, book 3, chap. 213, 2:387–92. The same text was later used by Jerónimo Román y Zamora in his *Repúblicas del mundo*, part 3, book 2, chap. 5, 3:157–58. On the legal system in pre-Conquest Mexico, see Jerome A. Offner, *Law and Politics in Aztec Texcoco* (Cambridge: Cambridge University Press, 1983), especially 242–55.

committed crimes had their distinctive long hair cut before being executed.[64] The Nahuas may have continued to use head shaving as punishment after the arrival of the Spaniards.

The friars were quick to put this information to use, turning head shaving into their signature method for punishing and correcting Indian behavior. This choice went hand in hand with their resolution to administer justice among the Nahuas despite the clear opposition of colonial authorities, who repeatedly denounced the ministers' disregard for secular officers and their jurisdiction. To the friars, who should punish and how to punish became one question in which ideology and practical concerns converged. By continuing a tradition familiar to Indians (albeit one that they may not have been keen to see maintained), the religious orders sought to set themselves apart from the crown's officers of justice. Interestingly enough, those parties that denounced the friars' actions also commented on their lack of judgment when imposing penalties. In the words of a close associate of the controversial Archbishop Montúfar, religious ministers "have punished light offenses harshly and serious ones lightly, exaggerating and underestimating crimes without any discretion."[65] To their opponents, not only did the friars' claims lack legitimacy, but they also did not know how to punish.

As time went on and their familiarity with Nahua culture and traditions deepened, the missionaries came to learn why the Nahuas had chosen to shave the heads of transgressors. Their inquiries into those traditions revealed that the painstakingly choreographed ceremonies that accompanied the capture and sacrifice of enemy warriors often involved cutting hair from the crown of the captive's head, as was the case during the annual ceremony of *Tlacaxipehualiztli*.[66] In this ritual, the captor was instructed to keep the victim's hair after it had been removed.[67] According to Sahagún, by taking the enemy's hair, the warrior was taking his reputation and making it his own.[68] The Nahuas believed that hair helped to preserve and transfer a vital force known as *tonalli* (*tetonal*), a hot element thought to be related to an individual's destiny and located pri-

---

64. Acuña, *Relaciones geográficas del siglo XVI*, 6:203.

65. Cuevas, *Documentos inéditos del siglo XVI*, 260. The document also makes reference to the cruelty of the punishments inflicted by the friars, such as "encorozar" Indians (that is, to place on the head a "coroza," or conical paper hat with drawings depicting the crime committed by the wearer), a practice more often associated with the Inquisition. See 252.

66. Sahagún, *Florentine Codex*, book 2, chap. 21, 47.

67. Sahagún, *Florentine Codex*, book 2, chap. 21, 49.

68. Sahagún, *Florentine Codex*, book 2, chap. 21, 49. The significance of this action is further highlighted by the ceremonial events that followed the victim's sacrifice. The ritual required the captor wear the victim's skin for several days, after which it would be buried. On the day of the burial, according to the *relación de Acolman*, the warrior "recorría todo el campo y, a las personas que hallaba labrando sementeras, les tresquilaba la coronilla de la cabeza, y el tal tresquilado quedaba por exclavo. Y cuando no hallaba pers[on]a algu[n]a, en lugar de los cabellos que había de traer, c[or]taba pencas de maguey." Acuña, *Relaciones geográficas del siglo XVI*, 7:227.

marily in the individual's head.[69] As the friars learned, the notion of *tonalli* was central to the indigenous understanding of the life cycle in which the orders of biology, society, and morality mirrored each other. *Tonalli* was, according to the lexicographer Alonso de Molina, apportioned to each individual; it was akin but not identical to personhood.[70] The Spanish idea of personhood or individual worth was often associated with honor; they found further evidence of this connection through their study of Nahua lore as codified in speeches transmitted from generation to generation of members of the nobility. Among the commonly used metaphors and figures of speech that Fr. Bernardino de Sahagún selected from the Nahuatl language was the expression "I protect thy hair, thy head," which he glossed as "That is, [I do this] in order thus to admonish thee, to take care of thy honor so that nothing may defame it, so that no affliction may befall thee."[71] Thus, hair, a body part that carried *tonalli*, was conceptualized as a site of honor and renown.[72]

The transfer of the enemy's *tonalli* was only one step in a process that gave Nahua warriors a new social identity, or, as the ceremonial speeches put it, a new face. It is significant that the Nahuas bestowed honor upon their warriors by changing their hair according to carefully prescribed patterns.[73] A warrior who distinguished himself on the battlefield by taking numerous captives had his hair shaven except for one long tuft; he was also given the military title of *quachic*, "the shorn one."[74] If, as the treatment of captives suggests, *tonalli* could be transferred, the haircuts that represented or sealed the warrior's newly acquired rank can be seen as a necessary ritual step that completed the delicate harnessing of this force that was essential to life on earth.

---

69. The literature on *tonalli* is vast and often controversial. Among the interpretive works focusing on sixteenth-century sources, see Alfredo López Austin, *The Human Body and Ideology: Concepts of the Ancient Nahuas*, trans. Thelma Ortíz de Montellano and Bernard Ortíz de Montellano, 2 vols. (Salt Lake City: University of Utah Press, 1988), 1:204–29; and Jill L. Mackeever Furst, *The Natural History of the Soul in Ancient Mexico* (New Haven: Yale University Press, 1995), 63–130.

70. A full exploration of this topic falls outside the scope of this study. As their use of names shows, the Nahuas' concept of the individual was inseparable from their understanding of ancestry. MacKeever Furst, *The Natural History*, 76–85.

71. Sahagún, *Florentine Codex*, book 6, chap. 43, 241.

72. For a comment on this passage, see MacKeever Furst, *The Natural History*, 126–27.

73. Sahagún, *Florentine Codex*, book 2, chap. 21, 75–77. This feature was noticed and recorded by early observers, such as the Conquistador Anónimo. García Icazbalceta, *Colección de documentos para la historia de México*, 2:371. Sahagún's chapter offers an excellent example of how the Nahua elite's conceptualization of the life cycle and related notions such as childhood, maturity, and masculinity were inseparable from their ideology and institutions of warfare. For an account of the making of a Nahua warrior, see Ross Hassig, *Aztec Warfare: Imperial Expansion and Political Control* (Norman: University of Oklahoma Press, 1988), 27–47; and Clendinnen, *Aztecs*, 112–28.

74. Fr. Diego Durán, *Historia de la Indias de Nueva España*, 1:114. On the virtues of the *quachic*, see Sahagún, *Florentine Codex*, book 10, chap. 6, 23. The author of the *relación de Huaxtepeque* mistakenly rendered *quachic* as "cresta de cabellos." Acuña, *Relaciones geográficas del siglo XVI*, 6:204.

Fig. 4.4. *Quachic* with captive. *Codex Mendoza*. (Courtesy of the Bodleian Library, Oxford University.)

From their knowledge of the tradition of head shaving as punishment and the rituals of the bygone world of Nahua warriors, the missionaries concluded that the Mexican Indians were as driven by the pursuit of honor and the avoidance of shame as their Spanish counterparts. Shaming, more than any punishment that inflicted physical pain, had the power to directly affect what the friars saw as the only possible source of moral and religious transformation: the Nahuas' sense of self. It was a spiritualized version of the physical punishments so closely associated with the world of secular officers, *encomenderos*, and even the Inquisition.[75] As a distinctive form of punishment, shaming still spoke the language of the law. In its intended effect, however, it took on meanings and values more often associated with penitential practices, a dimension that was not lost on the friars and that they hoped the Indians would duly note.[76] Spiritualizing the eminently social notion of shame amounted to transforming it into individual "guilt."

As for the punishment of friars who committed offenses, there appeared to be no agreed-upon approach. Some forms of shaming that friars devised to punish offending brothers were found unacceptable. Especially insidious, in the eyes of the clergy, was requiring brothers disciplined for serious misdeeds to wear the habit of secular priests in public.[77] In Mexico's polarized religious milieu, this punishment carried a larger message that reflected the friars' less than kind view of their immediate competitors.

Regarding head shaving, the missionaries' arguments in favor of adopting and promoting this old Nahua practice may have been merely the visible justification for restoring another practice, one that reached back to a bygone Christian institution that fed the imagination of Spanish missionaries who longed for religious reform: public penance. According to conciliar legislation from Visigothic Spain, the ceremony that accompanied canonical penance included shaving the male penitent's head in front of the community.[78] This connection

75. Instead of favoring spiritual penance, the Spanish Inquisition adopted pecuniary and physical punishments. Lea, *A History of the Spanish Inquisition*, 3:131. Mexico was not an exception. Solange Alberro, *Inquisición y sociedad en México, 1571–1700* (Mexico City: Fondo de Cultura Económica, 1988), 193. For a chart showing the distribution of penalties, see 208.

76. Processions of penitents became an integral part of the Nahuas' religious life under the Spaniards. On October 8, 1581, the Indians from Tecamachalco flogged themselves in public as part of a religious celebration. *Anales de Tecamachalco*, 86.

77. The written complaint was brought to the attention of the Third Church Council by a priest called Bartolomé Díaz de Pisa. Carrillo Cázares, *Manuscritos del Concilio Tercero Provincial Mexicano*, vol. 1, part 1, 194.

78. The Third Council of Toledo, held in 1589, prescribed that male penitents be shaven before they were given penance. Francisco-Javier Lozano Sebastián, *La penitencia canónica en la España romano-visigoda* (Burgos: Ediciones Aldecoa, 1980), 43–46. It should be noted that the twelfth-century *fuero de Cuenca* included head shaving and scourging among the penalties for certain crimes. Serra Ruiz, *Honor, honra e injuria en el derecho medieval español*, 74.

seems even more likely when one considers both the Franciscans' interest in promoting penitential practices among the Indians and their interpretation of Nahua purification rituals in terms that resembled the acts of public satisfaction required for the reconciliation of serious sinners.[79]

The missionaries' confidence in the enduring power of native beliefs made them alternatively distrustful and optimistic as their efforts to keep selected traditions alive ran up against the inevitable and uncontrollable forces of social change. For head shaving to be effective, the missionaries counted on Mexican Indian males to continue to wear their hair long.[80] By the time that Fernández de Sigura was puzzling over the apparent failure of this traditional method of punishment, however, Indian males had already started to favor shorter haircuts and even shaven heads.[81]

Fernández de Sigura's report of a seemingly minor episode involving head shaving is an example of the strategies that the Mexican missionaries deployed to articulate their claims to criminal jurisdiction over the Nahuas. This claim was based on the idea that the Indians were more likely to respond and obey if

---

79. Sahagún's interpretation of Nahua rituals in light of the sacrament of penance was shaped in part by the dispute over jurisdictions. Pardo, *The Origins of Mexican Catholicism*, 94–95.

80. Commenting on Indian grooming and clothing, Fr. Diego Durán wrote: "En las cabezas jamás usaron de sombreros, ni de otra cobertura, sino sólo el cabello largo, cercenado por abajo de las orejas." *Historia de las Indias de Nueva España*, vol. 1, chap. 11, 116.

81. The author of the *relación de Chiconauhtlan* appears to have been well aware of this change when he stressed the contrast between past and present in the following description: "Y el traje que traían antiguamente es el propio de ahora: una manta y un paño ceñido para tapar sus vergüenzas, y los cabellos largos, y tenían por afrenta que los trasquilasen. Ahora traen camisa y zaragüeles de algodón, y manta de lo mismo, y la mayor parte dellos andan trasquilados y con sombreros de fieltro en las cabezas." Acuña, *Relaciones geográficas del siglo XVI*, 6:235–36, a very similar description appears in Suárez de Peralta, *Tratado del descubrimiento de las Indias*, chap. 3, 61. We can only speculate about the possible connection between short hair and the Indians' use of hats. The adoption of shorter hair is implied in the *relación de Citlaltepec*. Acuña, *Relaciones geográficas del siglo XVI*, 7:199; see also 68 and 206. It has been suggested that the male custom of wearing long tufts of hair on the side of shaven heads, or *balcarrotas*, which is well attested to in eighteenth-century *casta* paintings, may have developed as the result of the shavings administered as punishment; see Jaime Cuadriello, *The Glories of the Republic of Tlaxcala: Art and Life in Viceregal Mexico*, trans. Christopher J. Follett (Austin: University of Texas Press / Teresa Lozano Long Institute of Latin American Studies, 2011), 277 n. 2. By the eighteenth century *balcarrotas* had become an integral part of what Spaniards and criollos took to be the traditional attire of Christianized Indians. For example, in 1767, and following episodes of social unrest in San Luis Potosí, the visitor general Don José de Gálvez sought to enforce stricter demarcations among ethnic groups: "I have ordered, among other things, that the justices not permit the Indians to carry any arms, penalty of death, nor wear the clothes of Spaniards which they injustly used, but that they go about with *balcarrota* and *tilma*, according to the usage of such Indians." Quoted in David Frye, "The Native Peoples of Northeast Mexico," in *The Cambridge History of the Native Peoples of the Americas*, vol. 2, *Mesoamerica*, ed. Richard E. W. Adams and Murdo J. MacLeod (Cambridge: Cambridge University Press, 2000), 2:25. In other circumstances the proud display of *balcarrotas* amounted to an affirmation of ethnic identity. William B. Taylor, *Magistrates of the Sacred*, 234–35. In Peru, the jurist Juan de Matienzo recommended that Indians working closely with Spaniards be persuaded, but not compelled, to wear short hair. Juan Matienzo, *Gobierno del Perú* (Buenos Aires: Compañía Sud-Americana de Billetes de Banco, 1910), chap. 23, 47.

they operated within a familiar framework and under the direct supervision of the Spaniards who understood them best. For the friars, cultural competence was both the key to successful control of Indians and a potentially useful political weapon. The crown, for its part, was unwilling to recognize the role that the friars had assigned themselves as the sole authorities on matters of Indian culture. As we will see in the next section, the crown turned to the defense of native customs as a way to exert further control over the missionaries in the colonies.

The Luxury of Custom: Indian Hair and Moral Reform

Beneath the disagreements over the appropriate punishment of Indians lurked incompatible views of the meaning of punishment. Even so, both sides recognized that the cultural traditions of the increasingly diverse peoples that came under Spanish rule had to be taken into account.

After the 1560 decree that prohibited friars from administering punishments, especially head shaving, several similar decrees aimed at parish priests as well as friars followed.[82] At the same time, the crown learned that missionaries across the territories had taken to cutting the hair of new converts soon to be baptized. This news was cause for concern and in 1581 the king issued a *cédula* addressed to the archbishop of Nueva Granada (present-day Colombia), ordering that the ministers promptly address this matter, lest the Indians abandon Christianity out of fear. The reasons behind the decree read as follows: "We have been informed that the Indians indigenous to that province wear long hair down to the waist or back, an ancient custom among them, and because they think of it as their most significant and venerable ornament, they cannot conceive of any greater punishment than seeing their hair cut; those whom the caciques or judges have sentenced to have their hair cut for the commission of excesses or offenses are considered defamed and affronted."[83]

The passage blends new and familiar issues. On the familiar side, the document acknowledges that hair cutting had become an accepted form of punish-

---

82. They date from 1594, 1614, and 1624. *Recopilación de leyes de los Reynos de las Indias,* book 1, title XIII, law 6.

83. "Nos somos informados que los indios naturales de essas provincias traen el cabello largo hasta la cinta, o las espaldas que ha sido antigua costumbre entre ellos, y por tenello por principal y venerable ornato es el mayor castigo que se les puede hazer y que mas sienten el cortarselos, y ansi entre ellos es tenido por infame y afrentado el a quien los caciques o juezes de comission lo quitan por algún excesso o delicto." Encinas, *Cedulario indiano,* 4:360.

ment used by caciques and colonial judges alike, without elaborating on the
origin of the practice. As in the Mexican case, the natives of Nueva Granada are
said to associate long hair with honor and to experience its taking by another as
infamy. The emphasis on the power of custom and the conceptualization of the
Indians' hair as ornamentation—a subject to which I will return—are depar-
tures from previous legislation. How were the Indians to distinguish between
preparing to receive the sacrament—in this case a positive step meant to highlight the significance and dignity of the ritual—and the sacrament itself?[84] And,
more importantly, how were the Indians to discern both religious and secular
meanings in a single ritualized action? Without spelling out these questions,
the decree suggested that the activities of religious ministers had led the Indians
to begin to associate the sacrament of baptism with punishments administered
by local authorities.

The particular circumstances of the Indians of Nueva Granada gave the
crown an opportunity to appear to be looking after the interest of the church at
the same time that it asserted its power to intervene in ecclesiastical matters. Instead of leaving it up to the missionaries to find an adequate solution, the *cédula*
recommended that all Indians, Christian and non-Christian alike, be asked to
wear their hair short, allowing them to keep one longer tuft in deference to
their traditions.[85] This proposal illustrates once again the calculated accommo-
dations that went into preserving the crown's delicate balance between ecclesiastical and secular powers, and traditional Nahua and new Christian customs.

A few years later, the crown found it necessary to issue another, very similar
law. On this occasion, however, the law addressed the predicament of a group of
Chinese merchants (or *sangleyes*) living in Manila whose ministers asked them
to cut their hair before being baptized.[86] By this time, the Spaniards were acquainted with some basic information about Chinese customs through reports
and letters written and circulated by missionaries based in the Philippines.[87]
These early sources made up the best-selling *Historia de las cosas más notables,
ritos y costumbres del gran Reyno de la China* (1585), written in Mexico by Juan
González de Mendoza. Among the many aspects of Chinese culture that Europeans found worth recording and commenting on was their fondness for wear-

---

84. This issue was raised during the baptismal controversy that divided the religious orders in
sixteenth-century Mexico. Pardo, *The Origins of Mexican Catholicism*, 26–32.

85. Encinas, *Cedulario indiano*, 4:360–61.

86. *Recopilación de leyes de los Reynos de las Indias*, book 1, title 1, law 18, 1:4.

87. On the origins of missionary activities in the Philippines, see John Leddy Phelan, *The Hispanization of the Philippines: Spanish Aims and Filipino Responses, 1565–1700* (Madison: University
of Wisconsin Press, 1959), 41–71.

ing their hair long and their devotion to its care, which González de Mendoza interpreted as superstition.[88]

As the law of 1587 pointed out, the Chinese, not unlike some indigenous groups in the American colonies, viewed hair cutting as an especially brutal punishment that brought infamy on the punished. This concern may have had few consequences if the Chinese merchants had remained in the Philippines, where they made up an important and influential sector of the population. But their profession required them to make frequent trips to Chinese lands where they would certainly face derision and, depending on the provinces they visited, possibly even death.

In issuing both of these laws, the crown found compelling reasons to intervene, given that baptism also conferred legal personhood. However, what distinguishes the law regarding the Chinese merchants from the previous one pertaining to the Indians of Nueva Granada is the absence of any attempt to meet the missionaries halfway in this matter of baptismal preparation. Instead, the crown ordered the friars in unmistakable terms to abandon the practice and allow Chinese and Indians alike to wear their hair as they pleased.[89]

The question that remains is whether the missionaries, who were certainly familiar with Chinese customs, ever considered the possible ramifications of their actions. The law did not address these possibilities directly, but in providing the missionaries with information about Chinese customs and beliefs, information that the missionaries had themselves helped to gather, the crown was more forcefully assuming the role of ultimate arbiter in matters of policy and cultural diversity.

Seventeenth-century legal scholars commented on the important issues raised by the crown's position on these two related laws. The jurist Juan Solórzano Pereira, like many before him, asserted the principle that laws should always respond to the cultural characteristics of the peoples for whom they were

88. "Crian todos uñas muy largas en las manos izquierdas, trayendo cortadas las de las derechas. Traen el cabello largo, y curan del mucho. Y assi esto, como lo de las uñas, no carece de superstición: porque dizen, han de ser llevados por el al cielo." Juan González de Mendoza, *Historia de las cosas mas notables, ritos y costumbres del gran Reyno de la China* (Madrid: Pedro Madrigal, 1586), 16v. The passage blends two sources: the *Relación* by the Augustinian missionary Martín de Rada in the Philippines, and the *Tractado* by the Portuguese Dominican friar Gaspar da Cruz. See C. R. Boxer, ed., *South China in the Sixteenth Century* (London: Hakluyt Society, 1953), 282 and 138, respectively. On Rada's hopes to set up a mission in China, see his letters to the provincial of the Augustinians in México in Burrus, *The Writings of Alonso de la Vera Cruz*, 5:194–224.

89. "Encargamos a los Prelados, que a los Chinos, e Indios que se Baptizaren no se les corte el cabello, y dexen a su voluntad el traerlo, o dexarlo de traer, y los consuelen, animen y aficionen con prudencia a ser Christianos." *Recopilación de leyes de los Reynos de las Indias*, book 1, title 1, law 18, 1:4.

issued, a basic tenet of government that, as he conceded, was known even to Indian lords before the Spanish arrival.[90] Since transforming Indians into full Christians was a long and difficult process, it was in the crown's best interest to tolerate those customs that did not violate natural law or Christian precepts.[91] Solórzano Pereira asserted that the crown had acted wisely in allowing Indians to preserve a custom like long hair that contradicted neither natural nor religious principles. There were, however, reasons to be particularly cautious about accepting seemingly harmless customs: "Because truly, if the converted Indians who wear long hair take to treasure in excess this or some other custom, these customs may rekindle memories of their heathen past, becoming a sign that they never left it behind completely; if this were the case, one should proceed with more severity to eliminate such attachment."[92]

At issue here was the dilemma that generations of Catholic missionaries had faced as they struggled to distinguish acceptable from unacceptable customs and traditions among those they set out to convert. In the sixteenth century, the Dominican Diego Durán described several customs that the converted Nahuas had not yet abandoned, and that his brothers had learned to tolerate, as neutral.[93] Solórzano Pereira referred to them as "indifferent," neither good nor pernicious.[94] But, as the jurist León Pinelo saw it, these latter customs could be prohibited under certain conditions, because what was indifferent one day might be harmful in the future.[95] This very possibility informs Solórzano Pereira's not-so-hypothetical case, in which he aptly described the resignification of indigenous practices in a colonial context. According to this troublesome scenario, paying excessive attention to their customs could transform

---

90. Solórzano Pereira, *Política Indiana*, book 2, chap. 25, 210. Solórzano Pereira's *Indiarum Iure* was published in Madrid in 1629, and its second part ten years later. The Spanish version prepared by the author himself was originally printed in 1648 under the title *Política Indiana*.

91. Solórzano Pereira, *Política Indiana*, book 2, chap. 25, 210–11.

92. "I verdaderamente, si esta costumbre de traer largo el cabello los Indios ya convertidos, i preciarse de ella, o otras semejantes les pudiessen avivar la memoria i deseo de su infidelidad, o dar indicio de que no estaban bien apartados de ella, entonces se avria de proceder con mas severidad a quitarsela." Solórzano Pereira, *Política Indiana*, book 2, chap. 25, 213.

93. Fr. Diego Durán, *Historia de las Indias de Nueva España*, 1:55. The problems raised by these conceptualizations of customs and practices remain crucial to any discussion on the historical reconstruction of cultural change. On vestigial practices and meaning, see Perry Anderson, "Nocturnal Enquiry: Carlo Ginzburg," in *A Zone of Engagement* (London: Verso, 1992), 207–29; especially 223–27.

94. Solórzano Pereira, *Política Indiana*, 213.

95. "Lo que es indiferente, que llamamos malo por prohibido y prohibido porque aunque no es por sí malo, se usa ordinariamente mal de ello, y así produce efectos malos." Antonio de León Pinelo, *Velos en los rostros de las mujeres: sus consecuencias y daños* (1641), 2 vols. (Santiago de Chile: Centro de Investigaciones de Historia Americana, 1966), chap. 25, 2:287.

these customs into something else. Custom, accordingly, ceases to be "second nature" and becomes a consciously sought form of behavior with unforeseen consequences that would haunt the Spaniards in the long run.

When Solórzano Pereira was writing on the legal questions posed by the customs of colonial subjects, Spain was being swept by legislation that aimed to reform the mores of a society that Philip believed to be losing its moral compass. A good example was the royal court itself, where in matters of fashion Spaniards appeared to have been seized by an unstoppable desire for all things French. As Palafox y Mendoza put it when restraining himself from mocking the elaborate headpieces worn by the Tartars: "for in matters of clothing, we Spaniards are not allowed to laugh at anyone, because everybody laughs at us for plenty of reasons, and the Tartar should not be so confident that we are not going to steal what he wears, even those ridiculous things on their heads, because before stealing from them we have stolen from other nations at which we laugh very much."[96]

To put an end to this state of affairs, starting in 1623 the crown issued a set of sumptuary laws meant to regulate, among other things, the ways in which Spanish men and women dressed and presented themselves in public.[97] As with similar efforts, Spanish citizens spent more time talking about these royal *pragmáticas* than observing them.[98] Writers such as Francisco de Quevedo did not miss the opportunity to poke fun at both the follies of his countrymen and the laws enacted to correct them. A satirical poem inspired by the 1539 *pragmática* banning men from sporting *guedejas* (long tufts of curly hair) is a good example.[99] Along with the stipulation that *guedejas* should not be worn past the ears, the edict prescribed penalties for those who violated its restrictions or contributed to its violation—in this case, barbers.[100]

96. Juan Palafox y Mendoza, *Historia de la conquista de la China por el Tártaro* (Paris: Antonio Bertier, 1670), 376–77.

97. On Philip IV's first set of *pragmáticas*, see Ruth Lee Kennedy, "Certain Phases of the Sumptuary Decrees of 1623 and Their Relation to Tirso's Theater," *Hispanic Review* 10, no. 2 (April 1942): 91–115. An overview of sumptuary laws from the period that remains useful can be found in Juan Sempere y Guarinos, *Historia del luxo y de las leyes suntuarias de España*, 2 vols. (Madrid: Imprenta Real, 1788), 2:117–32.

98. Some contemporary thinkers who fully supported the crown's efforts, however, had reservations about the power of the *pragmáticas* to bring about reform. Pedro Fernández Navarrete, *Conservación de monarquías y discursos políticos* (1626), ed. Michael D. Gordon (Madrid: Instituto de Estudios Fiscales, 1982), discurso 38, 311–20.

99. Francisco de Quevedo, *Poesía original completa*, ed. José Manuel Blecua (Madrid: Planeta, 1999), no. 689, 744.

100. "Ningun hombre pueda traer copete o jaulilla, ni guedejas con crespo u otro rizo en el cabello, el qual no pueda pasar de la oreja; y los barberos que hicieren qualquiera de las cosas suso dichas, por la primera vez caigan e incurran en pena de veinte mil maravedís y diez dias de cárcel . . . y a las personas que traxeren copete, o guedejas y rizos en la forma dicha, no se les dé entrada en la Real presencia, ni en los Consejos." *Novísima recopilación de las leyes de España dividida en XII libros, 1805–1829*, 6 vols. (Madrid, 1805–29), book 6, title 12, law 7, 3:188–89.

Religious writers, jurists, and the cast of assorted characters who became known as *arbitristas* found little amusement in the turn that Spanish mores had taken. Although they welcomed the *pragmáticas*, they may have sensed that the royal edicts, though clear in spelling out restrictions, somehow failed to convey the seriousness of both the moral and the national economic reasons behind their enactment. A variety of moral treatises printed in this period intended to bring this point home, and Solórzano Pereira was thoroughly familiar with this literature.

It was not by chance that, when discussing alien customs in general, and the Indian fondness for long hair in particular, Solórzano Pereira had in mind the comments of fellow writers on the odd directions the customs of their countrymen had taken. In their opinions he found a way to bring the missionaries' perspective on indigenous customs back into his legal commentary, a perspective that the crown, for practical reasons, had chosen to set aside in its laws. Were the missionaries justified in requiring the Indian catechumens to give up their long hair in order to receive baptism? From a strictly legal point of view, they were not, since the custom did not run counter to any Christian precept or interfere with the normal administration of baptism.[101] The same could be said about *guedejas*, which did not contravene natural law either. It is worth noting that despite the penalties for failing to observe the *pragmáticas'* guidelines regarding clothing and luxury items, their violation did not, strictly speaking, constitute a *delito* (crime).[102]

In their search for authoritative sources to justify their attacks on fashion, Spanish writers privileged religious over legal texts. Alonso Carranza, for instance, an author quoted by Solórzano Pereira, relied on St. Paul and his commentators to remind his readers that wearing long hair was the strict prerogative of women, and that the men who imitated them would know no honor.[103] According to Carranza, nature had provided men and women with *ornatos* exclusive to their sex: men had been given beards and women abundant hair and any transgression of these boundaries was against the natural order.[104]

Of particular interest to our analysis, the laws of 1581 and 1587 that Solór-

---

101. Solórzano Pereira, *Política Indiana*, 212.

102. The legal literature of the period opted for the terms *casos* or *contravenciones*. Francisco Tomás y Valiente, *El derecho penal de la Monarquía absoluta (Siglo XVI—XVII—XVIII)* (Madrid: Tecnos, 1969), 212. On the status of sumptuary laws in early modern Spanish penal law, see especially 210–14.

103. Alonso Carranza, *Rogación en detestación de los grandes abusos en los traxes y adornos nuevamente introducidos en España* (Madrid: María de Quiñones, 1636), 24. For his reliance on Tertullian, see 31–33.

104. Carranza, *Rogación en detestación*, 25v. The same principle was invoked to argue against the use of veils to cover women's faces. León Pinelo, *Velos en los rostros de las mujeres*, chap. 14, 2:186.

zano Pereira commented on referred to the Indians' long hair as their most esteemed *ornato*.[105] For Solórzano Pereira and other writers, the term had become inextricably associated with luxury and excess, sources of the social evils that had taken over Spain. Far from an innocent pastime, the excessive attention that Spaniards paid to their physical appearance had resulted in the promotion of indecency, envy, and immoderate expenditure. As imagined (and feared) by Solórzano y Pereira, the undue interest of American Indians in their long hair would most likely indicate an undue interest in their own customs and traditions, which would oblige the crown to intervene. To borrow the language of the moral reformers whose arguments inform Solórzano Pereira's observations, custom could be construed as a luxury item in certain circumstances. In America, interest in custom could mean a return to idolatry or the prospect of Indian revolts. In the Peninsula, on the other hand, moralists could only hope that Spanish men and women would return to the simpler customs they had abandoned.

Solórzano Pereira's exegesis, informed by the legal scholar's perspective and the moral reformer's concerns, brings together questions both new and old. While the laws he commented on may have put an end to particular practices of the missionaries in Nueva Granada or Manila, the crown could not afford to ignore the problems that religious ministers continued to wrestle with in the colonies. Despite the distance between their worlds, Solórzano Pereira understood that the missionaries working among indigenous peoples, like his contemporaries in Spain, were driven by ideals of reform. As we have seen, he found that the writings of the reformers shed light on the missionaries' determination to uproot some native customs though they did not represent an immediate or serious challenge to Christian teachings. Yet at the same time, he remained faithful to the general principle that laws should be enacted according to the particular characteristics of each people. As applied to these laws, this principle had less to do with a design by the crown to respect the cultural autonomy of colonized populations than with the central authorities' resolve to have the last word on decisions concerning native customs. When the crown addressed issues of local customs and practices, it did so in response to the missionaries' unflagging determination to change native mores by adopting ad hoc policies that infringed on royal jurisdiction. By questioning the relevance of officially sanctioned distinctions between secular and ecclesiastical jurisdictions, the friars in Mexico made indigenous customs their exclusive domain.

---

105. There is a curious logic at work here. As mentioned earlier, the law considered all of the hair on the Indians' heads to be ornament, and the solution proposed to the friars called for Indians to wear only a single tuft of long hair.

This domain, as many of them saw it, was better dealt with by relying on direct experience instead of law. This shift allowed them to conceptualize actions against Indian offenders as corrective rather than punitive. Once removed from the juridical context, traditional notions of punishment could be reconfigured in light of what the friars had learned about the traditions and practices of the Mexican Indians. Ultimately, the real meaning of the missionaries' attempts to change the Indians' ways remained tied to the changing course of their mutual perceptions, not conceptual niceties over the precise meaning of correction and judicial punishment. From the beginning of the evangelization in Mexico, discussions about indigenous customs and authority over the Indians went hand in hand. Thus, questions about cultural autonomy and change became inextricably linked to the ongoing struggle between missionaries and royal officials over jurisdictional authority. The policies regarding the punishment of Indians and other ethnic groups that I have discussed here reflect this struggle, and recount the story of the fading power of the missionaries to transform their unique knowledge of alien cultures into a source of authority.

Conclusion

In 1649, months after he was recalled by the crown from the bishopric seat of Tlaxcala, Juan de Palafox y Mendoza returned to Spain, where he would spend his remaining years as bishop of the far less wealthy diocese of Osma. Years of bitter confrontations with viceregal administrators, the mendicant orders, and above all, the Jesuits, had badly tarnished his reputation; yet he still hoped, somewhat naively, that it could be restored if he regained the king's confidence. His death in 1659 did little to mollify those who saw him as a ruthless enemy of the Society of Jesus.[1] The bishop may have had the last word, however. After a long and divisive process that began in 1694, his beatification became a reality in April 2011.

Back in Spain, when a prompt return to America still seemed likely, Palafox y Mendoza wrote *De la naturaleza del indio*, the brief tract on the moral disposition of the indigenous people for which he is known today. According to his original plan, reflecting the long-held notion that laws should respond to the character of those they govern, *De la naturaleza del indio* was to have two companion treatises that were never written: one on the most urgent problems facing the indigenous population, and another on policies to solve them.[2]

Having served as general inspector, viceroy, and bishop, Palafox y Mendoza considered himself uniquely qualified to dispense advice to viceroys and royal administrators who, by the very nature of their office, rarely attained more than partial knowledge of the needs of the Indians under their supervision.[3]

---

1. For a comprehensive study of the invectives and satires that Palafox y Mendoza inspired during and after his lifetime, see Gregorio Bartolomé Martínez, *Jaque mate al obispo virrey* (Mexico City: Fondo de Cultura Económica, 1991).

2. Juan de Palafox y Mendoza, *Manual de estados y profesiones* and *De la naturaleza del indio* (Mexico City: Coordinación de Humanidades/Miguel Angel Porrúa, 1986), 52. This treatise has also been published under the title *Virtudes del indio*.

3. Palafox y Mendoza, *De la naturaleza del indio*, 49–50. Viceroys saw the scope of their duties and obligations in very different terms. See, for example, the account that Martín Enríquez left for his successor Lorenzo Suárez de Mendoza (1580–83), in Ernesto de la Torre Villar, ed., *Instrucciones y memorias de los virreyes novohispanos*, 2 vols. (Mexico City: Editorial Porrúa, 1991), 1:177–78.

Although there is little in *De la naturaleza del indio*'s portrait of the Indians as paragons of moral virtue that their defenders (and in some cases, even their detractors) had not said before, the treatise represents the most elaborate expression of the indigenous peoples of New Spain as *personas miserables*. It also harbors no doubts as to the success of the conversion of the Indians, doubts that even members of the mendicant orders had voiced since the last quarter of the sixteenth century. As evidence of this success, Palafox y Mendoza pointed to the regular sight of numerous men and women participating in processions, the widespread presence of religious images in their households, and the care with which they prepared their bodies for communion through fasting and cleansing.[4] The Franciscan Gerónimo de Mendieta praised the first generation of converts for adopting inner forms of devotion such as mental prayer; decades later, the post-Tridentine reformer Palafox y Mendoza found proof of the success of the Mexican church in the strict adherence to Catholic rituals.[5] If Indian spirituality existed, it was expressed through and in liturgical celebrations where order took precedence over individual devotion.[6]

While the pious observance of Christian ceremonies could be evidence of Catholicism's successful transplantation to New Spain, the many iterations of rituals that indigenous officers of local governments performed as part of their duties barely seemed to register, even when they had an unmistakable religious imprint. To acknowledge them would have meant acknowledging as well the degree of autonomy that Indian communities enjoyed; although well known to both criollos and Spaniards, many chose to gloss over this fact. Concerning this apparent blind spot, it is worth noting one particular portrait of a purportedly exceptional indigenous nobleman. I am referring to Cristóbal de la Cueva, a cacique from Miltepec in Oaxaca. The Dominican historian Francisco de Burgoa elaborately praised Don Cristóbal, even referring to him as Baldus,

---

4. Palafox y Mendoza, *De la naturaleza del indio*, chap. 2, 57–58.

5. As bishop of Puebla, Palafox y Mendoza tried to make rituals more uniform in the diocese. To this end, in 1642 he ordered the publication of the *Manual de los santos sacramentos* sanctioned by Paul V. He also took steps to ensure the preservation of the solemnity of religious services in all churches, regardless of their wealth. Particularly valuable for its transcription of a set of guidelines by Palafox y Mendoza for the furnishing of churches is Ricardo Fernández Gracia's essay, "Juan de Palafox: Directrices para templos y su exorno artístico," in *Varia Palafoxiana: Doce estudios en torno a don Juan de Palafox y Mendoza*, ed. Ricardo Fernández Gracia (Pamplona: Gobierno de Navarra, 2010), 71–112.

6. "La devocion, y puntualidad en el rezar, y decir la doctrina en voz alta, es notable, y al irse a cantar a la Misa, y la division con que están en las Iglesias, apartados los hombres de las mujeres, assistiendo con admirable reverencia en los Templos, los ojos bajos, el silencio profundissimo, las humillaciones, genuflexiones concertadas, las postraciones tan uniformes, y la orden tan grande, que dudo mucho haya Religion tan perfecta, y observante, que este culto exterior con mayor humildad le egercite, y ofrezca." Palafox y Mendoza, *De la naturaleza del indio*, chap. 2, 59.

after the medieval jurist. The first time Burgoa caught a glimpse of Cristóbal de la Cueva at his home, the cacique was sitting at a table, wearing glasses and surrounded by well-known contemporary legal works, fully absorbed by legal questions that people had brought to him.[7] As presented by Burgoa, this image of an indigenous *letrado* immersed in his work has an almost visionary dimension, as if the chronicler had been granted a peek at an idealized version of the future in which indigenous autonomy was the direct result of the colonizer's gift of the law.[8] This figure of the cacique *letrado* calls to mind that of the "holy man" whose source of knowledge of Scriptures or nature remains shrouded in mystery and confounds the learned; in this case Don Cristóbal's judgments on civil and criminal matters suggested years of university studies or secret instruction from a supernatural entity.[9] Cristóbal de la Cueva seemed to simultaneously embody the *buen varón* (virtuous nobleman) of days gone by and the modern *letrado*; the cacique thus stood in stark contrast to a new generation of impoverished caciques who, according to Burgoa, chose to earn their livings (and reputations) by promoting lawsuits among towns.

In any event, contemporary Spanish laymen on either side of the Atlantic would have seen few similarities between themselves and the Indians who populate *De la naturaleza del indio*, with their indifference to material possessions, the promise of riches, or the opportunity to rise above their station in life by pursuing public office; this was precisely one of the points that Palafox y Mendoza wanted to bring home. In showing criollos and Spaniards an inverted im-

---

7. "Y cogímosle sin avisarle por cogerlo descuidado, y excusarle el regalo que suelen hacer a personas de respeto. Y llegados al patio le vimos en medio de la sala, sentado a una mesa, con anteojos puestos, y algunos libros: la Curia Filípica, Escrituras de Palomares, y otros de pleitos de litigantes, y una campanilla cerca de sí, con que hacía señal a la gente de su servicio, y a los negociantes." Burgoa, *Geográfica descripción*, vol. 2, chap. 31, 13.

8. As Terraciano has shown, a significant number of Mixtec noblemen were literate and wrote in both Spanish and their particular Ñudzahui language. Based on indirect testimony he also suggests that it was common for members of the nobility to exchange correspondence; of particular interest here is his reference to a document from a Mixteca nobleman who delivered letters between the cacique Felipe de Velasco and his nephew, the very same Cristóbal de la Cueva. Terraciano, *The Mixtecs of Colonial Oaxaca*, 54. Cristóbal de la Cueva's name also appears in the legal record from 1622, when an ecclesiastical dispensation was requested to allow the marriage of Diego de Velasco y Arellano, son of Felipe de Velasco, and Doña Micaela, daughter of Cristóbal de la Cueva in 1622. See *Mesoamerican Voices: Native Language Writings from Colonial Mexico, Oaxaca, Yucatan, and Guatemala*, ed. Matthew Restall, Lisa Sousa, and Kevin Terraciano (Cambridge: Cambridge University Press, 2005), 192–94.

9. "Y con tanta resolución despachaba peticiones, demandas con términos tan propias del derecho civil, y criminal, que parecía haber cursado mucho tiempo en alguna universidad o tener algún espíritu que le instruía." Burgoa, *Geográfica descripción*, vol. 2, chap. 31, 13. On the holy man's sources of knowledge in the context of colonial Mexico, see Osvaldo F. Pardo, "Contesting the Power to Heal: Angels, Demons and Plants in Colonial Mexico," in *Spiritual Encounters: Interactions between Christianity and Native Religions in Colonial America*, ed. Nicholas Griffiths and Fernando Cervantes (Birmingham: University of Birmingham Press, 1999), 163–65.

age of themselves, the bishop reminded them that the economic benefits they had reaped in New Spain depended on preserving its labor force but also on the entirely distinct moral world of indigenous laborers.[10] This is how Palafox y Mendoza, reformulating an idea already present among the first friars, conceptualized the relation between the republic of Spaniards and the republic of Indians, the volatile legal and administrative composite that constituted New Spain.[11] By construing the republic of Indians as a spiritual reservoir in need of protection, the church hoped to secure its participation in policy decisions.

Four decades later, the criollo scholar and former Jesuit Carlos de Sigüenza y Góngora turned Palafox y Mendoza's portrait of the indigenous masses on its head when he chronicled the riots that shook Mexico City in 1692.[12] Almost point by point, he refuted Palafox y Mendoza's catalog of Indian behaviors. Rather than devoted Christians, the Nahuas remained attached to their old religion, which enabled them to better challenge criollos and Spaniards. More significantly, the urban indigenous peoples were driven by greed, oblivious to the negative consequences of their actions in pursuit of profit. In Sigüenza y Góngora's account, the Indian poor, as encountered or imagined by the first friars and later recast by Palafox y Mendoza, turned into a mob of Nahua street vendors and vagrants, who roamed around the *traza* of Mexico City in the company of idle mestizos and *castas* and spread the revolt until it culminated in the burning of the viceregal palace and other public buildings.[13] Although

---

10. On the other hand, Palafox y Mendoza did not hesitate to side with *criollo* landowners to the detriment of the welfare of indigenous laborers when he deemed it necessary. As Álvarez de Toledo has pointed out, the bishop paved the way for the establishment of the system of peonage when in 1641 he signed an edict that made Indian workers indebted to a landowner a part of the landowner's estate. Isabel Álvarez de Toledo, *Politics and Reform in Spain and Viceregal Mexico: The Life and Thought of Palafox, 1600–1659* (Oxford: Oxford University Press, 2004), 90–91.

11. Throughout the sixteenth century the viceroys of New Spain expressed their doubts about the two-republic model in no uncertain terms. As Viceroy Luis de Velasco II warned his successor in 1595, the coexistence of two republics under different legal regimes and with opposite interests posed enormous challenges for the administration of justice. Torre Villar, *Instrucciones y memorias*, 1:317. In 1566, *cabildo* officials complained about the difficulty of creating unity out of what they described as three republics living side by side ("la una despañoles y las dos de yndio y dentro de un circuito de cibdad y las casas despañoles e yndios todas entretexidas mas entre otras"). *Actas de cabildo de la Ciudad de México*, book 6, 492. On the Spanish notion of *república* in America, and its historical antecedents, see Mario Góngora, *Studies in the Colonial History of Spanish America*, trans. Richard Southern (Cambridge: Cambridge University Press, 1975), 98–119; and Alejandro Cañeque, *The King's Living Image: The Culture and Politics of Viceregal Power in Colonial Mexico* (New York: Routledge, 2004), 214–22.

12. For a thorough discussion of the riots and the events leading up to them, see R. Douglas Cope, *The Limits of Racial Domination: Plebeian Society in Colonial Mexico City, 1660–1720* (Madison: University of Wisconsin Press, 1994), chap. 7.

13. Contrary to what Sigüenza y Góngora suggested, a majority of those charged and sentenced in connection with the riots turned out to be indigenous artisans. Cope, *The Limits of Racial Domination*, 158. For Sigüenza y Góngora's perspective on the composition of the crowd that participated in the riots, see Cañeque, *The King's Living Image*, 225–28.

opinions unfavorable to Viceroy Galves abounded at the time, Sigüenza y Góngora had only praise for the viceroy's efforts to avert a grain shortage and any resulting social unrest in the city. While the viceroy fulfilled his role as protector, the indigenous masses proved undeserving of the many legal privileges that the crown had unwisely granted them.[14]

Palafox y Mendoza took the wisdom of the legal privileges accorded to the Indians as self-evident; to Sigüenza y Góngora, those privileges were largely unwarranted. Their opposite perspectives hint at two different ways of conceiving the relationship between the two republics, the principle of protection, and the obligations of church and crown. They also disagree in their assessments of what the church and the law had accomplished in New Spain. Palafox y Mendoza had little doubt that the church had something to show for its decades of evangelization and pastoral care. In contrast, Sigüenza y Góngora saw the riots as a demonstration that the laws enacted for the benefit of Indians had failed.[15]

The views of seventeenth-century legal scholars differed from those of both the bishop and the criollo polymath. According to Solórzano Pereira, the crown had taken the right approach to governance in predicating the Indians' many legal privileges on their status as "miserables y pobres."[16] These privileges included summary trials and the rights to dispute petitions drafted by their lawyers, introduce new evidence, and call witnesses.[17] In spiritual matters, the church acted along the same lines, under the assumption that indigenous

---

14. "gente la más ingrata, desconocida, quejumbrosa e inquieta que Dios crió, la más favorecida con privilegios y a cuyo abrigo se arroja a iniquidades y sinrazones, y las consigue." Carlos de Sigüenza y Góngora, *Seis obras*, ed. William G. Bryant (Caracas: Biblioteca Ayacucho, 1984), 115.

15. Sigüenza y Góngora did not concern himself with the larger questions, such as the power of law to effect change, implicit in his harsh criticism of royal legislation. As could be expected, learned eighteenth-century travelers through America found the issue unavoidable, and wondered why Amerindians had failed to join the ranks of their civilized *criollo* neighbors despite the existence of beneficial laws. One such traveler was François Raymond Joseph de Pons: "Tous les efforts du législateur, pour leur inspirer un certain amour propre, qui créât en eux des facultés, ou qui développat le peu qu'ils peuvent avoir reçues de la nature, on été inutiles. Ni l'accueil qu'ils ont reçu, en entrant dans la société, ni les distinctions avec lesquelles ils sont traités, n'ont pu dégoûter de la vie sauvage, bien qu'ils ne la connoissent que par tradition . . ." de Pons, *Voyage à la partie orientale*, 1:337. De Pons was thoroughly familiar with the work of Solórzano Pereira, as can be gathered from his summary of Indian legal privileges. See pages 1:324–30.

16. The phrase is found in Ordinance 51 issued by Philip II in 1571 and calling on the *fiscal* of the Council of the Indies to ensure that all policies aimed at protecting the Indians were implemented ("especialmente lo que es en favor de los Indios, de cuya protection y amparo, como de personas miserables y pobres, se tenga por muy encargado"). Encinas, *Cedulario Indiano*, 1:16. Duve has traced the development of the notion of *persona miserabile* from its medieval roots to its transformation in colonial law. See Thomas Duve, *Sonderrecht in der Frühen Neuzeit. Studien zum ius singulare und den privilegia miserabilium personarum, senum und indorum in Alter und Neuer Welt* (Frankfurt am Main: Vittorio Klostermann, 2008); in relation to the views of seventeenth-century legal scholars, see especially 181–93.

17. Solórzano Pereira, *Politica Indiana*, book 2, chap. 28, 233–34.

converts should be considered neophytes regardless of their actual proficiency in Christian doctrine or even whether they had been raised in the faith. For example, the number of fasting days was reduced; the number of religious holidays was also reduced; no special authorization was required to marry within the third or fourth degree of consanguinity; and work on religious holidays was strictly voluntary.[18]

Honor had no apparent place in the extreme portraits of Indian character sketched by Palafox y Mendoza and Sigüenza y Góngora. However, when scholars such as Solórzano Pereira or the Jesuit Diego de Avendaño (*Thesaurus Indicus*, 1668) examined colonial legislation and the privileges granted to indigenous subjects, they knew that the question of Indian honor was not easily ignored. Solórzano Pereira collected opinions as authority for the classification of the Indians as "miserable"; most of these came from friars or other religious men who had worked in New Spain and depicted its inhabitants as living in a state of utter abjection. Solórzano Pereira was well aware that the royal laws he commented on did not respond to the pious exaggerations of the early religious observers that he relied on, but rather to a more accurate view of the everyday reality of indigenous communities in the American territories. That reality included conflicts and disputes between Indians and Spaniards that required resolution according to enduring principles of distributive justice, which included, for example, considering social condition. In the case of an injurious act perpetrated by a Spaniard against an Indian, the first step in adjudication was to establish whether the Indian had honor. Relying on the opinion of Fernando Zurita, Solórzano Pereira concluded that they did; as a consequence, a Spaniard found guilty of such an act would be subjected to penalties, although less harsh than those that applied if the victim were also Spanish, because indigenous people were of a lower condition.[19] Although some commentators had interpreted the monarch's obligation to protect the new subjects to mean that

---

18. Solórzano Pereira, *Politica Indiana*, book 2, chap. 29, 239–40.

19. "I resuelve, que por barbaros que sean i infieles que ayan sido, pudieron, i pueden tener a su modo verdadera nobleza, i verdadero i proprio derecho de su fama, i hazienda, como lo enseña santo Tomas." Solórzano Pereira, *Politica Indiana*, book 2, chap. 28, 233. In the same passage Solórzano Pereira commented on the condition of the Indians: "por ser los Indios de mas baxa i humilde condicion, i que se embriagan facilmente, i no se curan mucho de estas injurias, ni se alteran, ni enojan gravemente si las reciben." Concerning how Indians should be compensated for insults, Zurita wrote: "Quo circa, si qui Indorum parum sobrii sint, vel que magis dolere soleat, quod pecuniolam amiserint, quam quod acceperint alapam: ijs quidem gravis ex obiecto & genere contumelia, leviori satisfactione poterit recompensari." Zurita, *Theologicarum de Indis quaestionum*, propositio 5, 14v. Avendaño agreed with Solózano Pereira's characterization of the Indians and his approach to handling offenses against honor when neither noblemen nor physical violence were involved. Diego de Avendaño, *Thesaurus Indicus*, vol. 1, *Tit. X–XI y complementos* (Pamplona: EUNSA, 2009), complement to title 11, chap. 1, corollary, §2, 275–76.

Indians should be considered above Spaniards in determining punishments, this scheme seemed to violate well-established practice.[20] As for the fact that Indians were permitted to seek redress for offenses against honor, Solórzano Pereira reminded his readers that in Athens even slaves enjoyed this right.[21]

Solórzano Pereira returned to the question of honor when discussing legislation that prevented Indians from being ordained, as well as the opinions of other jurists in support of it. Although he considered this restriction to have been amply justified in the early days of the colony, given the new converts' undisputable condition as neophytes, it had become difficult to defend after several generations of Indians had been raised in the Christian faith.[22] "Neophyte" was clearly a slippery category when it came to the Indians. As a general rule (which also applied to the classification "miserable"), Solórzano Pereira argued that Indians should be considered neophytes only in those cases that clearly favored them—as in the restrictions on the administration of oaths to Indians.[23] For the case at hand, he agreed with those who believed that Indians should no longer be considered neophytes ten years after their baptism, and thus should not be denied access to ecclesiastical benefices and public offices.[24] In short, Indians did not fall under the pure-blood statutes that applied to Jews and Moors.[25] There remained the question of benefits that required statutes of

---

20. Avendaño, on the other hand, thought that the measure could be justified based on the idea that the Indians were considerably more vulnerable than Spaniards, and hence in need of stronger protection. Avendaño, *Thesaurus Indicus*, complement to title 11, chap. 1, corollary, §2, 273–74.

21. Solórzano Pereira, *Política Indiana*, book. 2, chap. 28, 233. Concerning honor, slavery posed its own particular set of problems on account of slaves' dual status as both property and person. In the Deep South of the United States, for instance, the honor and moral character of slaves became a matter of discussion in courtrooms, despite the fact that slaves were considered to be outside the system of honor. Ariela J. Gross, *Double Character: Slavery and Mastery in the Antebellum Southern Courtroom* (Princeton: Princeton University Press, 2000), 72–83. Moreover, although slaves were barred from testifying in court, witnesses quoted their words; those words made it into the legal record and in some instances had considerable impact on the outcome of the trial. See pages 68–70.

22. Solórzano Pereira, *Política Indiana*, book. 2, chap. 29, 242. See Thomas Duve, "Derecho canónico y la alteridad indígena: Los indios como neófitos," in *Esplendores y miserias de la evangelización de América: Antecedentes europeos y alteridad indígena*, ed. Wulf Oesterreicher and Roland Schmidt-Riese (Berlin: De Gruyter, 2010), 73–94.

23. "Pero oy, aunque para lo que les es favorable, se juzgan tambien por Neophitos, I gozan, como tales, los privilegios, i gracias que he referido; verdaderamente no lo son los mas de ellos, i mucho menos sus descendientes." Solórzano Pereira, *Política Indiana*, book 2, chap. 29, 242.

24. Solórzano Pereira, *Política Indiana*, book 2, chap. 29, 242.

25. "Que los Indios ya de antiguo convertidos, aunque desciendan de padres, i abuelos, que fueron infieles, deben ser admitidos al Sacerdocio, i a todos los beneficios, i dignidades Eclesiasticas, cargos, i oficios publicos, en que no quiere Dios, ni el derecho regularmente, que aya excepcion, o acepcion de personas, i que no halla ley, que los excluya de ellos, y mucho menos que los comprehenda en los Estatutos de Iglesias, ordenes, o Colegios, que excluyen de su ingresso Judios, i Moros, i los que de ellos descendieren por qualquier via." Solórzano Pereira, *Política Indiana*, 242. To bolster his argument, Solórzano Pereira asked, in the case that the restriction of Indians was found to be legally sound, whether the descendants of Spanish noblemen who married indigenous women should also be excluded. Solórzano Pereira, *Política Indiana*, 243.

nobility, such as joining military orders. Solórzano Pereira posed that, in the absence of the positive proofs of nobility that were standard in Spain, indigenous noblemen could prove noble ancestry according to the procedures customarily followed in their respective communities. According to him, the conditions that traditionally warranted the exclusion of particular groups from organizations such as military orders were largely absent in the case of indigenous men seeking to join the priesthood. As with the conversion of currencies, nobility could be measured across cultural boundaries, as the long-standing practice of inducting foreigners of noble families into the knight orders of Spain showed, and indigenous noblemen should be no exception.[26]

In sixteenth-century New Spain, the friars made Indian honor—understood as both an attribute of members of the indigenous elites (vertical honor) and an individual trait (horizontal honor)—an important part of the conversation about justice.[27] The issue was unavoidable, as *encomenderos* and their descendants pretended to be noblemen while waiting in vain for the crown to give in to their demands. At the same time, the friars could not do without the notion of nobility, however contrary it was to their religious ideals, since they pinned the evangelization's success on the conversion of the Nahua elite whose members would then be elected local authorities and officials. While these conditions shaped the conversion of the indigenous peoples of New Spain and their transformation into royal subjects, so did the particular legal regime that governed them.

As I hoped to have shown, another chapter of the history of honor was played out in the Spanish territories overseas. The regime of protection of indigenous subjects that the friars promoted and the crown partially came to embrace, however, transformed the same notion of honor that it meant to preserve. As Solórzano Pereira worried, it also potentially affected some basic principles of justice. Considering the well-known hypothetical case of a nobleman facing imminent danger from an attacker, Tomás de Mercado pointed out that the victim was under no obligation to avoid confrontation if avoidance might damage his honor.[28] This case serves as an example of the type of autonomy that social status could confer, one that became unnecessary in a way as authorities, especially religious ones, took on the role of protectors of Indians and their honor.

Solórzano Pereira had no doubt that the crown had lived up to its promise to protect its indigenous subjects in order to facilitate their full political and religious development. Echoing the Jesuit José de Acosta, Solórzano Pereira

---

26. Solórzano Pereira, *Politica Indiana*, book 2, chap. 29, 243.
27. On the concepts of horizontal and vertical honor, see Frank H. Stewart, *Honor* (Chicago: University of Chicago Press, 1994): 54–63.
28. Mercado, *Summa de tratos y contratos*, 161.

agreed that the laws to which Spaniards had become accustomed were far too harsh ("rigurosas") for the Indians.[29] The many laws introduced from the early days of the Spanish settlement to protect the welfare of the Indians confirmed that the crown had put this guiding principle into practice.

In many of the sources I have drawn from, the word "rigor" is closely associated with the law. The Nahuas lived under rigorous laws before the Spanish arrival, and, according to Fr. Diego Durán, their enforcement was also rigorous.[30] Franciscan friars referred to the Nahuas' civic and religious obligations as "burdensome," a term rich with scriptural associations. With those associations in mind, Motolinia stated that through the Spaniards, God had freed the Nahuas from both harsh laws and religious observances and brought their bodies and souls under his gentle yoke.[31]

Solórzano Pereira's characterization of Spanish laws tells us something about the way Spaniards had come to think of themselves and also those to whom the laws would apply. In New Spain, many friars, especially Franciscans, would have concurred with him, although for very different reasons; as we have seen, they viewed any legal approach to the administration of indigenous affairs as inherently misguided. Although the friars failed to gain jurisdiction over the Indians, they were instrumental in pushing the church to redefine its relationship with Indians in nonjudicial terms. On many occasions the crown, drawing on the friars' recommendations and language, advised its administrators to exert their authority over Indians without relying exclusively on the coercive power of their office.

Laws were not meant to elicit warm feelings, which were more appropriately directed toward their source, the king. According to Solórzano Pereira, Spaniards were able to reconcile the harshness of the law with their love for the king (or somehow turn the law's harshness into love for the king). Implicitly, he took this particular way of experiencing citizenship as a point of national or ethnic pride.

---

29. Solórzano Pereira, *Política Indiana*, book 2, chap. 25, 210.

30. "Había muchas maneras de hacer esclavos por la ley de la repúblicas de estos indios. Las cuales quiero poner por su orden, porque había en las repúblicas, leyes y ordenanzas, puestas por los reyes y por sus consejos y ministros; así había gran rigor en las ejecutar." Fr. Diego Durán, *Historia de las Indias de Nueva España*, vol. 1: chap. 20, 182. On mandatory days of fasting, see vol. 1, chap. 17, 160. On the enforcement of sumptuary laws in America compared to Spain, see vol. 1, chap. 11, 116. "Extraño rigor" was applied in cases of drunkenness and adultery. Vol. 1, chap. 21, 188.

31. "El trabajo de éstos demás de trabajar como hombres, también tenían el de las bestias, de llevar cargas, muriendo por los caminos, e ya por una parte ha multiplicado Dios e multiplica todo género de ganados y animales, y por otra son favorecidos de la justicia, que no sean cargados como solían, y ansí les quita Dios la carga pesada corporal y la muy grave servidumbre que al demonio hacían, y les pone su yugo suave y muy ligero, con el cual hallarán holganza para sus ánimas." Motolinia, *Memoriales*, part. 1, chap. 50, 158. On the question of Christianity's relation to Jewish law as addressed by the church fathers, see Rémi Brague, *The Law of God: The Philosophical History of an Idea* (Chicago: University of Chicago Press, 2007), 209–16.

In the American territories, the crown, following the opinion of churchmen, hoped that indigenous populations would learn to love the king first through his acts of justice, sparing them the laws that both tested and strengthened the Spanish love for the monarch.[32] With its religious echoes, the loved-based relation between teacher and disciple eventually emerged as an acceptable solution to the complexities inherent in the ways Spaniards related to king, God, and human and divine laws, as well as their Christian and political selves.

Oaths illustrate why jurists such as Solórzano Pereira thought of Spanish laws as burdensome, even if he did not say it in so many words. He agreed that in preventing indigenous witnesses from testifying under oath, ecclesiastical authorities protected them from the penalties that could result from perjury charges. In order for privileges of this sort—which amounted to restrictions—to be perceived as such, Indians needed to witness the punishment of perjurers. As this particular example shows, teaching Indians about the law was not a straightforward process. While it was assumed that Indians were not fully prepared to grasp the binding force of oaths—and the particular notion of moral agency attached to them—they were expected to understand that the laws and procedures from which they had been partially exempted were harsh. In light of this approach to both content and transmission, the entries in Juan de Córdoba's Zapotec dictionary for a concept as important to moral theology and law as conscience look oddly out of place, like remnants of a lesson in basic moral and political principles that was never delivered. Notwithstanding the pronouncements of royal and religious authorities, the colonial enterprise turned into truncated lessons on civic life, Christianity, commerce, and history. From the perspective of colonial power, however, the impasse was a consequence of the inability of the new subjects to learn. Thus, the model of teacher and pupil that was once thought to be a viable alternative to a purely secular understanding of power, authority, and social change, ultimately failed.

---

32. In a 1532 report to the king, Sebastián Ramírez de Fuenleal, bishop of Santo Domingo and president of the Real Audiencia of New Spain, observed: "Y pues los naturales van amando el apellido real, tanto que [como tengo dicho] muchos me han venido a rogar que los tome para V.M. trayendo razones para ello, razon es que estos conozcan a V.M. por universal señor, y se tengan por sus vasallos, [y tomallos ha de ser su conservacion y acrecentamiento]." García Icazbalceta, *Colección de documentos para la historia de México*, 185. Written at a time when the crown was still figuring out the legal and economic implications of the conquerors' actions and demands vis-à-vis the control of the indigenous population, Ramírez de Fuenleal's report recommended in the strongest possible terms that the conquerors not be granted jurisdiction over the Indians, "porque las personas y vidas de los indios son de los españoles en tan poco tenidas, que diciendo verdad no se podrá creer por los que no lo han visto; y porque los indios muestran mucho contentamiento cuando se les da a entender que son de V. M., y algunos dicen, y delante de mí, que los que los tienen en encomienda son calpixques y macehuales de V.M., y que ellos son de V.M. y no suyos. " García Icazbalceta, *Colección de documentos para la historia de México*, 167–68.

Bibliography

Primary Sources

Actas de cabildo de la Ciudad de México. Edited by Ignacio Bejarano. Paleography by Manuel Orozco y Berra. 12 vols. Mexico City: Municipio Libre, 1889–1900.

Actas de cabildo de Tlaxcala, 1547–1567. Edited by Eustaquio Celestino Solís, Armando Valencia R., and Constantino Medina Lima. Mexico City: Archivo General de la Nación; Tlaxcala: Instituto Tlaxcalteca de la Cultura, 1984.

Acosta, José de. *De procuranda indorum salute.* Edited by Luciano Pereña. 2 vols. Madrid: Consejo Superior de Investigaciones Científicas, 1984–87.

Acuña, René, ed. *Relaciones geográficas del siglo XVI: México.* 10 vols. Mexico City: Universidad Nacional Autónoma de México, 1982–88.

Ajofrín, Francisco. *Diario del viaje que por orden de la Sagrada Congregación de Propaganda Fide hizo a la América septentrional, en el siglo xviii el P. Fray Francisco Ajofrín.* 2 vols. Madrid: Real Academia de la Historia, 1958.

Alcocer, Francisco de. *Confessionario breve y muy provechoso para los penitentes.* Salamanca: Juan de Cánova, 1568.

Alcocer, Francisco de. *Tratado del juego.* Salamanca: Andrea de Portonariis, 1559.

Alfonso X el Sabio. *Las Siete Partidas del Rey Don Alfonso el Sabio cotejadas con varios codices antiguos por la Real Academia de la Historia.* 3 vols. Madrid: Imprenta Real, 1807.

Alva, Bartolomé de. *Confessionario mayor y menor en lengua mexicana.* Mexico City: Francisco Salbago, 1634.

Alvarez Posadilla, Juan. *Comentarios a las leyes de Toro, segun su espíritu y el de la legislación de España, en que se tratan las cuestiones prácticas, arreglando sus decisiones a las leyes y resoluciones mas modernas que en el día rigen.* 3rd ed. Madrid: Don Antonio Martínez, 1826.

Anales de Tecamachalco, 1398–1590. Edited by Eustaquio Celestino Solís and Luis Reyes García. Mexico City: Fondo de Cultura Económica, 1992.

Anales de Tepeteopan: De Xochitecuhtli a don Juan de San Juan Olhuatecatl, 1370(?)–1675. Edited by Blanca Lara Tenorio, Eustaquio Celestino Solís, and Elisa Pérez Alemán. Mexico City: CIESAS/CONACYT/CONACULTA/ INAH, 2009.

Annals of the Cakchiquels. In *Annals of the Cakchiquels* and *Title of the Lords of Totonicapan*, edited by Adrián Recinos and translated by Adrián Recinos, Delia Goetz, and Dionisio José Chonay, 43–159. Norman: University of Oklahoma Press, 1953.

Anonymous conqueror. "Relación de algunas cosas de la Nueva España, y de la gran ciudad de Temestitán México." In *Colección de documentos para la historia de México*, edited by Joaquín García Icazbalceta, 1:368–98. 1858–86. Reprint, Nendeln, Liechtenstein: Kraus Reprint, 1971.

Anthonino de Florencia. *La summa de confession llamada defecerunt de fray Anthonino arçobispo de florencia del orden de los predicadores.* Salamanca: Hans Giesser, ca. 1500.

Antúnez y Acevedo, Rafael. *Memorias históricas sobre la legislación, y gobierno del comercio de los españoles con sus colonias en las Indias Occidentales.* Madrid: Imprenta de Sancha, 1797.

Anunciación, Domingo de la. *Doctrina christiana breve y compendiosa por via de dialogo entre un maestro y un discipulo, sacada en lengua castellana y mexicana.* Mexico City: Pedro Ocharte, 1565

Anunciación, Juan de la. *Doctrina Christiana muy cumplida, donde se contiene la exposición de todo lo necessario para doctrinar a los Yndios, y administralles los Sanctos Sacramentos.* Mexico City: Pedro Balli, 1575.

Aquinas, Thomas. *Summa theologiae.* 60 vols. Blackfriars, NY: McGraw Hill, 1964–81.

Arte para bien confessar fecha por un devoto hieronymo: Agora de nuevo corregida. Seville: Juan Cronberger, 1537.

Aulus Gellius. *The Attic Nights of Aulus Gellius.* Translated by John C. Rolfe. 3 vols. London: William Heinemann; New York: G. P. Putnam and Sons, 1927.

Avendaño, Diego de. *Thesaurus Indicus*, vol. 1. *Tít. X–XI y complementos.* Pamplona: EUNSA, 2009.

Ávila, Francisco de. *Arte de la lengua mexicana y breves platicas de los mysterios de N. Santa Fee Catholica, y otras para exortacion de su obligacion a los Indios.* Mexico City: Herederos de la Viuda de Miguel de Ribera Calderón, 1717.

Ávila, Juan de. *Obras del padre maestro Juan de Avila, predicador en el Andaluzia: Aora de Nuevo añadida a la vida del Autor, y las partes que ha de tener un predicador del Evangelio, por el padre fray Luys de Granada, de la orden de Santo Domingo, y unas reglas de bien bibir del Autor.* Madrid: Pedro Madrigal, 1588.

Azpilcueta, Martín de. *Manual de confessores, y penitentes, que clara y brevemente contiene la universal, y particular decission de quasi todas la dubdas, que en las confessiones suelen ocurrir de los peccados, absoluciones, restituciones, censuras, irregularidades.* Toledo: Juan Ferrer, 1554.

Azpilcueta, Martín de. *Tractado de alabança y murmuracion en el qual se declara quando son merito, quando peccado venial, y quando mortal.* Valladolid: Adrian Ghemart, 1572.

Benavente, Toribio de (Motolinia). *Historia de los indios de la Nueva España.* Edited by Georges Baudot. Madrid: Castalia, 1985.

Benavente, Toribio de (Motolinia). *Memoriales o Libro de las cosas de la Nueva España y los naturales de ella.* Edited by Edmundo O'Gorman. Mexico City: Universidad Nacional Autónoma de México, 1971.

Bernardus Papiensis. *Summa Decretalium.* Edited by Theodor Laspeyres. Ratisbon: Joseph Manz, 1860.

Boxer, C. R., ed. *South China in the Sixteenth Century.* London: Hakluyt Society, 1953.

Brito Guadarrama, Baltazar, ed. *Códice Chavero de Huexotzingo: proceso a sus oficiales de república.* Mexico City: Instituto Nacional de Antropología e Historia, 2008.

Bujanda, J. M. de. *Index de L'Inquisition Espagnole 1551, 1554, 1559.* Sherbrooke, Quebec: Centre d'Études de la Renaissance; Geneva: Librarie Droz, 1984.

Burgoa, Francisco de. *Geográfica descripción de la parte septentrional del polo ártico de la América y, nueva iglesia de las Indias occidentales, y sitio astronómico de esta Provincia de Predicadores de Antequera Valle de Oaxaca.* 2 vols. 1674. Reprint, Mexico City: Editorial Porrúa, 1989.

Burrus, Ernest J., ed. *The Writings of Alonso de la Vera Cruz.* 5 vols. Rome: Jesuit Historical Institute; St. Louis: St. Louis University, 1967–72.

Cajetan (Tommasso de Vio). *Summa Caietana, trasladada en lingoajem Portugues com annotaoes de muytas duvidas, & casos de consciencia. Por ho Doctor Paulo de Palacio.* Coimbra: Ioão de Barreyra, 1566.

Capitulos generales de las Cortes del año de mil y seyscientos y dos, fenecidas en el de seyscientos y quarto, y publicadas en el de seyscientos y diez. Madrid: Juan de la Cuesta, 1610.

Capitulos y leyes discedidos en las cortes que su Magestad del rey don Phelipe nuestro señor tuvo y celebro en la ciudad de Toledo: que se començaron el año passado de MDLIX y se fenescieron y acabaron este presente año de mil y quinientos sesenta. Toledo: Juan Ferrer, 1560.

Cárdenas Valencia, Francisco de. *Relación historial ecclesiástica de la Provincia de Yucatán de la Nueva España, escrita el año de 1639: Con una Nota Bibliográfica por Federico Gómez de Orozco.* Mexico City: Antigua Librería Robredo, de José Porrúa e Hijos, 1937.

Carochi, Horacio. *Arte de la lengua mexicana con la declaracion de los adverbios della.* Mexico City: Juan Ruiz, 1645.

Carranza, Alonso. *Rogación en detestación de los grandes abusos en los traxes y adornos nuevamente introducidos en España.* Madrid: María de Quiñones, 1636.

Carrillo, Martín. *Memorial de Confessores.* Zaragoza: Miguel Ximeno Sánchez, 1596.

Carrillo Cázares, Alberto, ed. *Manuscritos del Concilio Tercero Provincial Mexicano (1585).* 5 vols. Zamora, Michoacán: El Colegio de Michoácan/Universidad Pontifica de México, 2006.

Carta, Gabino. *Guía de confessores.* Mexico City: Biuda de Bernardo Calderón, 1653.

Cartagena, Alonso de. *Defensorium unitatis christianae.* Edited by Manuel Alonso. Madrid: Publicaciones de la Escuela de Estudios Hebraicos, 1943.

Cartas de religiosos de Nueva España, 1589–1594. Mexico City: Salvador Chavez Hayhoe, 1941.

Castillo de Bobadilla, Jerónimo. *Politica para corregidores, y señores de vassallos en tiempos de paz, y de guerra, y para Prelados en lo espiritual, y temporal entre legos, Juezes de Comission, regidores, Abogados, y otros Oficiales publicos, y de las jurisdiciones, preeminencias, residencias, y salarios de ellos; y de lo tocante a las de Ordenes, y Cavalleros de ellas.* 2 vols. Madrid: Luis Sanchez, 1597.

Catecismo mexicano que contiene toda la Doctrina Christiana con todas sus Declaraciones, en que el Ministro de Almas hallará, lo que a estas debe enseñar; y estas hallaran lo que, para salvarse, deben saber, creer y observar. Mexico City: Imprenta de la Bibliotheca Mexicana, 1758.

Catecismos políticos españoles arreglados a las constituciones del siglo XIX. Introduction by Miguel A. Ruíz de Azúa. Madrid: Comunidad de Madrid / Consejería de Cultura, 1989.

Cedulario americano del siglo XVIII. Edited by Antonio Muro Orejón. 3 vols. Seville: Escuela de Estudios Hispano-Americanos, 1956–77.

Celano, Thomas of. *Vita prima.* In *Le due Vite e il Trattato dei Miracoli di San Francesco d' Assisi,* edited by Luigi Macali. Rome: Angelo Signorelli, 1954.

Chimalpahin, Don Domingo de San Antón Muñón. *Annals of His Time.* Edited and translated by James Lockhart, Susan Schroeder, and Doris Namala. Stanford: Stanford University Press, 2006.

Chobbam, Thomas de. *Thomae de Chobham Summa confessorum.* Louvain: Éditions Nauwelaerts; Paris: Bêatrice-Nauwelaerts, 1968.

Cline, S. L. *The Book of Tributes: Early Sixteenth-Century Censuses from Morelos.* Los Angeles: UCLA Latin American Center Publications, 1993.

Cline, S. L., and Miguel León-Portilla, eds. *The Testaments of Culhuacan.* Los Angeles: UCLA Latin American Center Publications / University of California, Los Angeles, 1984.

The Code of Cuenca: Municipal Law on the Twelfth-Century Castilian Frontier. Edited by James F. Powers. Philadelphia: University of Pennsylvania Press, 2000.

Códice Osuna: Reproducción facsimilar de la obra del mismo título editada en Madrid, 1878. Mexico City: Ediciones del Instituto Indigenista Interamericano, 1947.

Colección de documentos coloniales de Tepeaca. Edited by Hildeberto Martínez. Mexico City: Instituto Nacional de Antropología e Historia, 1984.

Colección de documentos inéditos, relativos al descubrimiento, conquista y organización de las antiguas posesiones españolas de América y Oceanía, sacados de los archivos del reino, y muy especialmente del de Indias. 42 vols. Madrid, 1864–84.

Concilios provinciales primero, y segundo, celebrados en la muy noble, y muy leal ciudad de México, presidiendo el illmo. Y rmo. Señor d. fr. Alonso de Montúfar, en los años de 1555, y 1565. Mexico City: Joseph Antonio de Hogal, 1769.

Concilium Mexicanum Provinciale III. Mexico City: Joseph Antonio de Hogal, 1770.

Constituciones sinodales del obispado de Cordova. Seville: Jacobo Cromberger, 1521.

Córdoba, Antonio de. *Quaestionarium theologicum sive Sylva amplissima decisionum, et variarum resolutionum casuum conscientiae.* Venice: Beretii, 1604.

Córdoba, Juan de. *Relación de la fundación, capítulos y elecciones que se han tenido en esta Provincia de Santiago de ésta Nueva España, de la Orden de Predicadores de Santo Domingo, 1569.* Mexico City: Vargas Rea, 1944.

Córdoba, Juan de. *Vocabulario castellano-zapoteco.* 1578. Reprint edited by Wigberto Jiménez Moreno, Mexico City: Instituto Nacional de Antropología e Historia, 1942.

Córdova, Antonio de. *Tratado de casos de conciencia.* Barcelona: Sanson Arbus, 1581.

Corpus iuris canonici. Edited by Emil L. Richter and Emil Friedberg. 2 vols. 1878–81. Reprint, Graz: Akademische Druck-u. Verlagsanstalt, 1955.

Cuevas, Mariano, ed. *Documentos inéditos del siglo XVI para la historia de México.* 2nd ed. Mexico City: Editorial Porrúa, 1975.

D'Assisi, San Francesco. "Prima regola dei fratri minori." In *Gli scritti,* edited by Giacomo V. Sabatelli. Assisi: Edizioni Porziuncola, 1971.

Dávila Padilla, Agustín. *Historia de la fundación y discurso de la Provincia de Santiago de México, de la Orden de Predicadores.* Edited by Agustín Millares Carlo. Mexico City: Editorial Academia Literaria, 1955.

Daza, Bernardino, trans. *Las Instituciones Imperiales (o Principios del Derecho Civil) dirigidas al Principe Don Philippe nuestro señor traduzidas por Bernardino Daza, Legista, natural de Valladolid,* by Justinian. Tolosa: Guion Bodauila, 1551.

Díaz de Montalvo, Alfonso. *Los códigos españoles concordados y anotados.* 12 vols. Madrid: Imprenta de la Publicidad a cargo de M. Rivadeneyra, 1847–51.

Díaz de Valdepeñas, Hernando. *Suma de notas copiosas muy sustanciales y compendiosas.* Toledo: Hernando Díaz y Juan de Medina, 1543.

Dificultad imaginada, Facilidad verdadera: En la practica de testamentos, reducida a ocho Documentos, en que se manifiesta la facilidad, con que se pueden tener en sana salud otorgados los Testamentos: se ponen patentes las tentaciones diabolicas, que los retardan; se dan los remedios de las dificultades; y se expressan las reglas, que facilitan su disposicion, y otorgamiento. Mexico City: Viuda de Miguel de Ribera Calderon, 1714.

Doctrina cristiana en lengua española y mexicana por los religiosos de la orden de Santo Domingo. 1548. Reprint, Madrid: Ediciones Cultura Hispánica, 1944.

Durán, Fr. Diego. *Historia de las Indias de Nueva España e islas de la Tierra Firme.* Edited by Angel Ma. Garibay K. 2 vols. Mexico City: Editorial Porrúa, 1967.

Durán, Juan Guillermo. "Apéndice documental. A modo de ejemplo: Los Catecismos del III Mexicano." In *Historia de la evangelización de América: Trayectoria, identidad y esperanza de un continente. Simposio internacional, Ciudad del Vaticano, May 11–14, 1992,* edited by José Escudero Imbert and Victor Manuel Ochoa Cadavid, 317–52. Vatican City: Libreria Editrice Vaticana, 1992.

Durán, Juan Guillermo. *Monumenta Catechetica Hispanoamericana.* 2 vols. Buenos Aires: Facultad de Teología de la Pontificia Universidad Católica Argentina Santa María de los Buenos Aires, 1984.

Encinas, Diego de. *Cedulario indiano.* 4 vols. 1596. Reprint edited by Alfonso García Gallo, Madrid: Ediciones Cultura Hispánica, 1945.

Ercilla, Alonso de. *La araucana.* Edited by Marcos A. Morínigo and Isaías Lerner. 2 vols. Madrid: Castalia, 1979.

Escobar, Andrés de. *Modus confitendi.* Paris: Antoine Caillaut, ca. 1483.

Feria, Pedro de. *Doctrina Christiana en lengua Castellana y çapoteca compuesta por el muy Reverendo padre Pedro de Feria.* Mexico City: Pedro Ocharte, 1567.

Feria, Pedro de. "Memorial del Obispo Fray Pedro de Feria." In *Manuscritos del Concilio Tercero Provincial Mexicano (1585),* edited by Alberto Carrillo Cázares, vol. 1, part 1, 284-436. 5 vols. Zamora, Michoacan: El Colegio de Michoacán / Universidad Pontificia de México, 2006.

Feria, Pedro de. "Revelación sobre la reincidencia en sus idolatrías de los indios de Chiapa después de treinta años de cristianos." In *Tratado de las idolatrías, supersticiones, dioses, ritos hechicerías y otras costumbres gentílicas de las razas aborígenes de México,* edited by Francisco del Paso y Troncoso, 1:381–92. Mexico City: Ediciones Fuente Cultural, 1953.

Fernández del Castillo, Francisco. *Libros y libreros en el siglo XVI.* Mexico City: Fondo de Cultura Económica, 1982.

Fernández Navarrete, Pedro. *Conservación de monarquías y discursos políticos.* Edited by Michael D. Gordon. Madrid: Instituto de Estudios Fiscales, 1982.

Gaius. *The Institutes of Gaius.* Translated and introduction by W. M. Gordon and O. F. Robinson. Ithaca, NY: Cornell University Press, 1987.

García, Francisco. *Tratado utilísimo y muy general de todos los contratos (1583).* Pamplona: Ediciones Universidad de Navarra, 2003.

García Icazbalceta, Joaquín. *Códice Mendieta.* 2 vols. 1892. Reprint, Guadalajara: Edmundo Aviña Levy, 1971.

García Icazbalceta, Joaquín, ed. *Colección de documentos para la historia de México*. 2 vols. 1858–86. Reprint, Nendeln, Liechtenstein: Kraus Reprint, 1971.

García Icazbalceta, Joaquín. *Don Fray de Zumárraga, primer obispo y arzobispo de México*. Edited by Rafael Aguayo Spencer and Antonio Castro Leal. 4 vols. Mexico City: Editorial Porrúa, 1947.

García Icazbalceta, Joaquín, ed. *Nueva colección de documentos para la historia de México*. 3 vols. Mexico City: Salvador Chávez Hayhoe, 1941.

García Pimentel, Luis, ed. *Descripción del Arzobispado de México hecha en 1570*. Mexico City: José Joaquín Terrazas e hijas, 1897.

Gerson, Jean. *Tripartito del Christianissimo y Consolatorio Doctor Juan Gerson de Doctrina Christiana a cualquiera muy provechosa*. 1544. Reprinted with prologue by Alberto Ma. Carreño, Mexico City: Ediciones "Libros de México," 1949.

Gilberti, Maturino. *Vocabulario en Lengua de Michoacan*. Transcription by Agustín Jacinto Zavala. Zamora, Michoacan: El Colegio de Michoacán / Fideicomiso Teixidor, 1997.

Gómez de Cervantes, Gonzalo. *La vida económica y social de Nueva España al finalizar el siglo XVI*. Edited by Alberto María Carreño. Mexico City: Antigua Librería Robredo de José Porrúa e Hijos, 1944.

González, Angel Martín, ed. *Gobernación espiritual de Indias: Código Ovandino, Libro 1º*. Guatemala City: Instituto Teológico Salesiano, 1978.

González Dávila, Gil. *Teatro eclesiástico de la primitiva iglesia de la Nueva España en las Indias Occidentales*. 1649. Reprint, Madrid: J. Porrúa Turanzas, 1959.

González de Cossío, Francisco, ed. *Un cedulario mexicano del siglo XVI*. Mexico City: Ediciones del Frente de Afirmación Hispanista, A.C., 1973.

González de Mendoza. *Historia de las cosas mas notables, ritos y costumbres del gran Reyno de la China*. Madrid: Pedro Madrigal, 1586.

Gutierrez, Juan. *Tractatus de iuramento comfirmatorio, et aliis in iure variis resolutionibus*. Salamanca: Herederos de Juan de Cánova, 1574.

Gutierrez de los Ríos, Gaspar. *Noticia general para la estimacion de las artes y de la manera que se conocen las liberales de las que son mecanicas y serviles*. Madrid: Pedro Madrigal, 1600.

Henríquez, Ioan. *Compendio de casos morales ordinarios*. Seville: Francisco de Lyra, 1634.

Hernáez, Francisco Javier. *Colección de bulas, breves y otros documentos relativos a la Iglesia de América y Filipinas*. 2 vols. Brussels: Imprenta de Alfredo Vromant, 1879. Reprint, Vaduz: Kraus Reprint, 1964.

Historia de la nación mexicana (Códice Aubin). 1634. Reprint edited by Charles E. Dibble, Madrid: J. Porrúa Turanzas, 1963.

Horozco Covarrubias, Sebastián de. *Tesoro de la Lengua Castellana o Española*. Edited by Martín de Riquer. Barcelona: S. A. Horta, I. E., 1943.

Huarte de San Juan. *Examen de ingenios*. Edited by Guillermo Serés. Madrid: Cátedra, 1989.

Instrucciones y memorias de los virreyes novohispanos. Edited by Ernesto de la Torre Villar. 2 vols. Mexico City: Editorial Porrúa, 1991.

Jiménez Arias, Diego. *Lexico ecclesiasticum latino-hispanicum ex sacris bibliis, conciliis, pontificum decretis, ac theologorum placitis, divorum vitiis, variis dictionariis, aliisque probatissimis scriptoribus concinnatum, servata ubique vera etymologiae, orthographiae, et accentus ratione*. Barcelona: Ioannes Piferrer, 1739.

Jiménez Moreno, Wigberto, and Salvador Mateos Higuera, eds. *Códice de Yanhuitlan.* Mexico City: Museo Nacional, 1940.

Juan Bautista. *Advertencias para confessores de indios.* Tlatelolco: Melchior Ocharte, 1600.

Juan Bautista. *Confessionario en lengua mexicana y castellana.* Tlatelolco: Melchior Ocharte, 1599.

Justinian. *Justinian's Institutes.* Translated and introduction by Peter Birks and Grant McLeod. Ithaca, NY: Cornell University Press, 1987.

Körntgen, Ludger, and Francis Bezler. *Paenitentialia hispaniae.* Turnholt: Brepols, 1998.

Lagunas, Juan Baptista de. *Arte y dictionario con otras obras en lengua michoacana.* Edited by J. Benedict Warren. Morelia, Michoacan: Fimax Publicistas Editores, 1983.

Lardizábal y Uribe, Manuel de. *Discurso sobre las penas contrahido a las leyes criminales de España para facilitar su reforma.* Madrid: Joaquín Ibarra, 1782.

Las Casas, Bartolomé de. *Apologética historia sumaria.* Edited by Edmundo O'Gorman. 2 vols. Mexico City: Universidad Nacional Autónoma de México, 1967.

Las Casas, Bartolomé de. *Tratados.* 2 vols. 1552. Reprint translated by Agustín Millares Carlo and Rafael Moreno and with prologues by Lewis Hanke and Manuel Giménez Fernández, Mexico City: Fondo de Cultura Económica, 1965.

Las cortes de Valladolid del año 1548. Valladolid: Fernández de Cordova, 1549.

Las pragmaticas del Reyno. Recopilacion de algunas bulas del summo pontifice: concedidas en favor de la jurisdiccion real: con todas las pragmaticas: y en algunas leyes del reyno: hechas para la buena governacion y guarda de la justicia: y muchas pragmaticas y leyes añadidas que hasta aqui no fueron impressas. Valladolid: Juan de Villaguiran, 1540.

Ledesma, Pedro de. *Segunda parte de la summa, en la qual se summa y cifra todo lo moral y casos de conciencia que no pertenecen a los Sacramentos, con todas las dudas con sus razones brevemente puestas.* Barcelona: Sebastian Matevat, 1620.

León, Martín de. *Camino del Cielo en Lengua Mexicana, en todos los requisitos necessarios para conseguir este fin, con todo lo que un Christiano deve creer, saber, y obrar, desde el punto que tiene uso de razon, hasta que muere.* Mexico City: Diego López Dávalos, 1611.

León Pinelo, Antonio de. *Recopilación de las Indias.* Edited by Ismael Sánchez Bella. 3 vols. Mexico City: Miguel Ángel Porrúa, 1992.

León Pinelo, Antonio de. *Velos en los rostros de las mujeres: sus consecuencias y daños.* 2 vols. Santiago de Chile: Centro de Investigaciones de Historia Americana, 1966.

Leyes y ordenanças nuevame[n]te hechas por su Magestad /para] la governacion de las Indias y buen tratamiento y conservacion de los Indios: que se han de guardar en el Consejo y audiencias reales q[ue] en ellas residen. Alcala de Henares: Juan de Brocar, 1543.

Las leyes y prematicas reales hechas por sus Magestades en las cortes que mandaron hazer e hicieron en la ciudad de Toledo 1525. Salamanca: Juan de Junta, 1550.

Libro de los guardianes y gobernadores de Cuauhtinchan (1519–1640). Edited by Constantino Medina Lima. Mexico City: CIESAS, 1995.

Llamas y Molina, Sancho de. *Comentario crítico-jurídico-literal a las ochenta y tres leyes de Toro.* Madrid: Imprenta de la Compañía de Impresores y Libreros del Reino, 1832.

Lockhart, James, Frances Berdan, and Arthur J. O. Anderson, eds. *The Tlaxcalan Actas: A Compendium of the Records of the Cabildo of Tlaxcala (1545–1627).* Salt Lake City: University of Utah Press, 1986.

López de Cogolludo, Diego. *Los tres siglos de la dominación española en Yucatán (o sea historia de esta provincia)*. 2 vols. 1842–45. Reprint, Graz: Akademische Druck- u. Verlagsanst, 1971.

López de Gómara, Francisco. *Historia de la conquista de México*. Caracas: Biblioteca Ayacucho, 1979.

Lorenzana y Buitron, Francisco Antonio. *Cartas pastorales y edictos del Illmo. Señor Don Francisco Antonio Lorenzana y Buitron, Arzobispo de México*. Mexico City: Joseph Antonio de Hogal, 1770.

Los códigos españoles concordados y anotados. 12 vols. Madrid: Imprenta de la Publicidad a cargo de M. Rivadeneyra, 1847–51.

Los títulos primordiales del centro de México. Edited by Paula López Caballero. Mexico City: CONACULTA, 2003.

Loyola, St. Ignatius of. *The Spiritual Exercises of St. Ignatius*. Translated by Anthony Mottola. New York: Image Books / Doubleday, 1989.

Lucian. *Discurso de Luciano que no deve sarse credito facilmente a la murmuracion*. Lisbon: Pedro Craesbeeck, 1626.

Machado de Chaves, Juan. *Perfeto confessor y cura de almas*. 2 vols. Madrid: Viuda de Francisco Martínez, 1646.

Manipulus curatorum officia sacerdotum. Cologne: Heinrich Quentell, 1498.

Matienzo, Juan. *Gobierno del Perú*. Buenos Aires: Compañía Sud-Americana de Billetes de Banco, 1910.

Matthew of Krakow. *De modo confitendi et de puritate conscientiae cuilibet confessori et confiteri volenti per utilis et necessarius*. Paris: Denis Roce, [1501?].

Medina, Bartolomé de. *Breve instruccion de como se a de administrar el sacramento de la penitencia, dividida en dos libros*. Zaragoza: Juan Alterache, 1580.

Medina, Bartolomé de. *Instruccion de como se ha de administrar el sacramento de la penitencia*. Alcala: Juan Gracian, 1591.

Medina, Juan de. *De Poenitentiae, Restitutione, & Contractibus*. 2 vols. Ingolstadt: David Sartori, 1581. Reprint, Farnborough, UK: Gregg Press, 1967.

Mendieta, Gerónimo de. *Historia eclesiástica indiana*. Mexico City: Antigua Librería, 1870. Reprint, Mexico City: Editorial Porrúa, 1993.

Mercado, Tomás de. *Summa de tratos y contratos*. Seville: Hernando Díaz, 1571.

Mesoamerican Voices: Native Language Writings from Colonial Mexico, Oaxaca, Yucatan, and Guatemala. Edited by Matthew Restall, Lisa Sousa, and Kevin Terraciano. Cambridge: Cambridge University Press, 2005.

Molina, Alonso de. *Aquí comiença un vocabulario en la lengua castellana y mexicana*. 1555. Reprint edited by Manuel Galeote, Malaga: Universidad de Málaga, 2001.

Molina, Alonso de. *Confessionario breve, en lengua Mexicana y Castellana*. Mexico City: Antonio de Espinosa, 1565.

Molina, Alonso de. *Confessionario mayor en la Lengua Mexicana y Castellana*. Mexico City: Universidad Nacional Autónoma de México, 1984.

Molina, Alonso de. *Nahua Confraternities in Early Colonial Mexico: The 1552 Nahuatl Ordinances of Fray Alonso de Molina, OFM*. Translated and edited by Barry D. Sell. Berkeley: Academy of Franciscan History, 2002.

Molina, Alonso de. *Vocabulario en lengua castellana y mexicana y mexicana y castellana*. 1571. Reprint with introduction by Miguel León-Portilla, Mexico City: Editorial Porrúa, 1977.

Monterroso y Alvarado, Gabriel de. *Pratica civil, y criminal, y instruccion de escrivanos. Dividida en nueve Tratados. Agora d enuevo emendada, y añadida en esta postrera impression la carta de trueque y cambio, y especialmente en el quinto Tratado: y con sus anotaciones en la margen conforme a la nueva Recopilacion.* Madrid: Pedro Madrigal, 1603.

Monumenta Mexicana. Edited by Félix Zubillaga and Miguel Ángel Rodríguez. Rome: Institutum Historicum Societatis Iesu, 1956–91.

Murillo Velarde, Pedro. *Practica de testamentos en que se resuelven los casos mas frequentes, que se ofrecen en la disposicion de las ultimas voluntades.* Manila: Imprenta de la compañía de Jesús por Nicolás de la Crua Bagay, 1745.

Muro Orejón, Antonio. "Los capítulos de corregidores de 1500." *Anuario de estudios americanos* 19 (1962): 699–724.

Muro Orejón, Antonio. "Las Ordenanzas de 1571 del Real y Supremo Consejo de las Indias. Texto facsimilar de la edicion de 1585." *Anuario de estudios americanos* 14 (1957): 363–423.

Nolasco de Llano, Pedro. *Compendio de los comentarios extendidos por el Maestro Antonio Gomez, a las ochenta y tres leyes de Toro.* 1735. Reprint, Valladolid: Editorial Lex Nova, 1981.

Novísima recopilación de las leyes de España dividida en XII libros, 1805–1829. 6 vols. Madrid, 1805–29.

O'Gorman, Edmundo. *Breve historia de las divisiones territoriales: Aportación a la historia de la geografía de México.* Mexico City: Polis, 1937.

O'Gorman, Edmundo. "Una ordenanza para el gobierno de los indios, 1546." *Boletín del Archivo General de la Nación* 11, no. 2 (1940): 179–94.

Olmos, Andrés de. *Arte para aprender la lengua mexicana.* Edited by Rémi Siméon. Paris, 1875. Reprint, Guadalajara: Edmundo Aviña Levy, 1972.

Olmos, Andrés de. *Tratado sobre los siete pecados mortales.* Edited by Georges Baudot. Mexico City: Universidad Autónoma de México, 1996.

Ortíz Lucio, Francisco. *Compendio de todas las summas que comunmente andan, y recopilacion de todos los casos de conciencia mas importantes y comunes, assi para el penitente examinar su conciencia, como para el confessor exercitar bien su oficio.* Mallorca: Gabriel Guasp, 1599.

Palafox y Mendoza, Juan. *Historia de la conquista de la China por el Tártaro.* Paris: Antonio Bertier, 1670.

Palafox y Mendoza, Juan. *Manual de estados y profesiones* and *De la naturaleza del indio.* Mexico City: Coordinación de Humanidades / Miguel Angel Porrúa, 1986.

Paso y Troncoso, Francisco del. *Epistolario de la Nueva España.* 14 vols. Mexico City: Antigua Librería Robredo de José Porrúa e Hijos, 1939.

Paso y Troncoso, Francisco del. *Idolatrías, supersticiones, dioses, ritos, hechicerías y otras costumbres gentílicas de las razas aborígenes de México.* 2nd ed. 2 vols. Mexico City: Ediciones Fuente Cultural, 1953.

Perez de Heredia y Valle, Ignacio. *El Concilio Provincial de Granada en 1565. Edición crítica del malogrado concilio del Arzobispo Guerrero.* Subsidia num. 26. Rome: Publicaciones del Instituto Español de Historia Eclesiástica, 1990.

Pérez de Vargas, Bernardo. *De re metalica: En el qual se tratan muchos y diversos secretos del conocimiento de toda suerte de minerales.* Madrid: Pierre Cosin, 1569.

Picard, Bernard. *Ceremonies et coutumes religieuses des peuples idolatres représentées par des Figures dessinées de la main de Bernard Picard: Avec une Explication Historique, et quelques Dissertations curieuses.* Amsterdam: Chez J. F. Bernard, 1723.

Pizzigoni, Caterina, ed. and trans. *Testaments of Toluca.* Stanford: Stanford University Press; Los Angeles: UCLA Latin American Center Publications, 2007.

Pomar, Juan. "Relación de Tezcoco." In *Relaciones geográficas del siglo XVI: México,* edited by René Acuña. 3 vols. Mexico City: Universidad Nacional Autónoma de México, 1986.

Pons, François Joseph de. *Voyage à la partie orientale de la Terre-Ferme dans l'Amérique Méridionale, fait pendant les années 1801, 1802, 1803, et 1804.* 3 vols. Paris: Colnet, 1806.

Pragmática en que se da la orden y forma que se ha de tener y guardar, en los tratamientos y cortesias de palabra y por escripto, y en traer coroneles, y ponellos en qualesquier partes y lugares. Alcala: Juan Iñiguez de Lequerica, 1586.

Prematica en que su Magestad manda que se guarden las que ultimamente se promulgaron en cinco de Enero, y doze de Abril de seiscientos y onze, y los Capitulos de reformacion de onze de Hebrero de seiscientos y veinte y tres, en razon de las cortesias con las declaraciones y penas que en ella se declara. Madrid: Maria de Quiñones, 1636.

Prematica en que su Magestad manda se executen las penas en ellas contenidas, contra los que juraren. Madrid: Pedro Tazo, 1639.

Procesos de indios idólatras y hechiceros. Mexico City: Publicaciones del Archivo General de la Nación, 1912.

Puga, Vasco de. *Provisiones, Cédulas, Instrucciones para el Gobierno de la Nueva España.* 1563. Reprint, Madrid: Ediciones Cultura Hispánica, 1945.

Quaderno de las cortes que en Valladolid tuvo su magestad del Emperador y rey nuestro señor el año de 1523. Salamanca: Juan de Junta, 1551.

Quaderno de las leyes añadidas a la Nueva Recopilacion que se imprimio el año de 1598 en que van las leyes y prematicas que desde el dicho año, hasta principio deste de 1610 se han publicado. Madrid: Juan de la Cuesta, 1610.

Quaderno de las leyes y prematicas reales fechas en las cortes que su Magestad del Emperador y rey nuestro señor mando celebrar en la noble villa de Madrid en el año 1528 años. Alcala de Henares: Ioan de Brocar, 1546.

Quadernos de las cortes que su magestad de la Emperatriz y reyna nuestra señora tuvo en la ciudad de Segovia el año de MDXXXII. Salamanca: Juan de Junta, 1549.

Quevedo, Francisco de. *Poesía original completa.* Edited by José Manuel Blecua. Madrid: Planeta, 1999.

Raymond of Penyafort. *Summa de poenitentia, et matrimonio cum glossis Ioannis de Friburgo.* Rome: Johannes Tallini, 1603. Reprint, Farnborough, UK: Gregg Press, 1967.

Recopilación de las leyes destos reynos, hecha por mandado de la Magestad Catolica del Rey Don Felipe Segundo nuestro señor, que se ha mandado imprimir, con las leyes que despues de la ultima impression se han publicado, por la Magestad Catolica Felipe Quarto el Grande nuestro señor. Madrid: Catalina de Barrio y Angulo y Diego Diaz de la Carrera, 1640.

Recopilación de leyes de los Reynos de las Indias. 4 vols. 1681. Reprint with prologue by Ramón Menéndez Pidal and preliminary study by Juan Manzano Manzano, Madrid: Ediciones Cultura Hispánica, 1973.

Remesal, Antonio de. *Historia general de las Indias Occidentales y particular de la gobernación de Chiapa y Guatemala.* 2 vols. Mexico City: Editorial Porrúa, 1988.

Reportorio de todas las prematicas y capitulos de cortes hechos por su magestad, desde el año de mil y quinientos y veyinte y tres, hasta el año de mil y quinientos y quarenta y quarto: hecho por el licenciado Andres Martinez de Burgos vezino de Astorga. Medina del Campo: Pedro de Castro, 1547.

Resines, Luis, ed. *Catecismo del Sacromonte y Doctrina Christiana de Fr. Pedro de Feria: Conversión y evangelización de moriscos e indios*. Madrid: Consejo Superior de Investigaciones Científicas, 2002.

Resines, Luis, ed. *Catecismos de Astete y Ripalda*. Madrid: Biblioteca de Autores Cristianos, 1987.

Rodriguez, Manuel. *Summa de casos de consciencia con advertencias muy provechosas para Confessores con un Orden judicial a postre en la qual se resuelve lo mas ordinario de todas las materias morales*. 2 vols. Salamanca: Juan Fernandez, 1595.

Rojas Rabiela, Teresa, Elsa Leticia Rea López, and Constantino Medina Lima, eds. *Vidas y bienes olvidados: Testamentos indígenas novohispanos*. 5 vols. Mexico City: CIESAS, 1999–2004.

Román y Zamora, Jerónimo. *Repúblicas del mundo. Dividas en tres partes*. 3 vols. Salamanca: I. Hernández, 1595.

Rosas de Oquendo, Mateo. *Sátira hecha por Mateo Rosas de Oquendo a las cosas que pasan en el Pirú, año de 1598*. Edited by Pedro Lasarte. Madison, WI: Hispanic Seminary of Medieval Studies, 1990.

Ruiz de Alarcón, Hernando. *Treatise on the Heathen Superstitions That Today Live among the Indians Native to This New Spain, 1629*. Edited and translated by J. Richard Andrews and Ross Hassig. Norman: University of Oklahoma Press, 1984.

Sahagún, Bernardino de. *Coloquios y doctrina cristiana con que los frailes de San Francisco, enviados por el papa Adriano IV y por el emperador Carlos V, convirtieron a los indios de la Nueva España, en lengua mexicana y española de Bernardino de Sahagún, 1524*. Edited by Miguel León-Portilla. Mexico City: Universidad Nacional Autónoma de México, 1986.

Sahagún, Bernardino de. *Florentine Codex: General History of the Things of New Spain*. Edited and translated by J. O. Anderson and Charles E. Dibble. 12 vols. Santa Fe, NM: School of American Research; Salt Lake City: University of Utah, 1953–82.

Sahagún, Bernardino de. *Historia general de las cosas de Nueva España*. Edited by Alfredo López Austin and Josefina García Quintana. 2 vols. Madrid: Alianza, 1988.

Sahagún, Bernardino de. *Psalmodia Christiana*. Translated by Arthur J. O. Anderson. Salt Lake City: University of Utah Press, 1993.

Sánchez de Aguilar, Pedro. *Informe contra idolorum cultores del obispado de Yucatán*. 3rd ed. Merida: E. G. Triay, 1937.

Sánchez de Arévalo, Rodrigo. *Spejo de la vida humana*. Zaragoza: Paulo Brus, 1491. Reprint, Valencia: Librerías "Paris-Valencia, S.L.," 1996.

Santo Tomás, Domingo de. *Grammatica o arte de la lengua general de los indios de los reynos del Peru*. 1560. Reprint edited by Rodolfo Cerrón-Palomino, Cuzco: Centro Bartolomé de las Casas, 1995.

Saravia de la Calle, Doctor. *Instrucion de mercaderes muy provechosa*. Medina del Campo: Pedro de Castro, 1547.

Sarmiento, Domingo Faustino. *Conflicto y armonías de las razas en América*. Buenos Aires: "La Cultura Argentina," 1915.

Scholes, France V., and Eleanor B. Adams, eds. *Cartas del Licenciado Valderrama y otros documentos sobre su visita al gobierno de Nueva España.* Mexico City: José Porrúa e Hijos, 1961.

Scholes, France V., and Eleanor B. Adams, eds. *Don Diego Quijada, Alcalde Mayor de Yucatán, 1561–1565.* 2 vols. Mexico City: Antigua Librería Robredo, 1938.

Scholes, France V., and Eleanor B. Adams. *Sobre el modo de tributar los indios de Nueva España a Su Majestad, 1561–1564.* Mexico City: José Porrúa e Hijos, 1958.

Sell, Barry D., and Louise M. Burkhart. *Nahuatl Theater: Death and Life in Colonial Nahua Mexico.* Norman: Oklahoma University Press, 2004.

Sempere y Guarinos, Juan. *Historia del luxo y de las leyes suntuarias de España.* 2 vols. Madrid: Imprenta Real, 1788.

Sigüenza y Góngora, Carlos de. *Seis obras.* Edited by William G. Bryant. Caracas: Biblioteca Ayacucho, 1984.

Solano, Francisco de. *Normas y leyes de la ciudad hispanoamericana (1492–1600).* 2 vols. Madrid: Consejo Superior de Investigaciones Científicas, Centro de Estudios Históricos, 1996.

Solórzano Pereira, Juan de. *Libro primero de la Recopilacion de las cédulas, cartas, provisiones y ordenanzas reales.* Edited by Ricardo Levene. 2 vols. Buenos Aires: Facultad de Derecho y Ciencias Sociales / Instituto de Historia del Derecho Argentino, 1945.

Solórzano Pereira, Juan de. *Política Indiana.* Madrid: Diego Díaz de la Carrera, 1648.

Soto, Domingo de. *Deliberacion en la causa de los pobres.* Salamanca: Juan de Junta, 1545.

Soto, Domingo de. *Institucion de Fray Domingo de Soto, de la orden de S. Domingo, a loor del nombre de Dios, de como se a de evitar el abuso de los juramentos.* Anvers: Biuda y Herederos de Juan Stelsio, 1569.

Suárez de Figueroa, Christoval. *Plaza universal de todas ciencias y artes.* Madrid: Luis Sanchez, 1615.

Suárez de Peralta, Juan. *Tratado del descubrimiento de las Indias.* Mexico City: Consejo Nacional para la Cultura y las Artes, 1990.

Sullivan, Thelma D., ed. *Documentos tlaxcaltecas del siglo XVI.* Mexico City: Universidad Nacional Autónoma de México, 1987.

Talavera, Hernando de. *Confessional.* In *Breve y muy provechosa doctrina de lo que deve saber todo christiano con otros tractados muy provechosos conpuestos por el Arçobispo de Granada.* Granada: Meinardo Ungut and Juan Pegnitzer, [1496?].

Tapia, Carlos de, Marqués de Belmonte. *Espejo de murmuradores. Traduzido de la lengua italiana por Francisco de Tapia y Leyva.* Madrid: Viuda de Alonso Martín, 1623.

Tira de Tepechpan. Edited by Xavier Noguez. 2 vols. Mexico City: Biblioteca Enciclopédica de Estado de México, 1978.

Torquemada, Fr. Juan de. *Monarquía Indiana.* 3 vols. Mexico City: Salvador Chávez Hayhoe, 1943.

Torre Villar, Ernesto de la, ed. *Fray Pedro de Gante, maestro y civilizador de América.* Mexico City: Seminario de Cultura Mexicana, 1973.

Torre Villar, Ernesto de la, ed. *Instrucciones y memorias de los virreyes novohispanos.* 2 vols. Mexico City: Editorial Porrúa, 1991.

Tylor, Edward B. *Anahuac: Or Mexico and the Mexicans, Ancient and Modern.* London: Longman, Green, Longman, and Roberts, 1861. Reprint, New York: Bergman Publishers, 1970.

Valtanás, Domingo de. *Confessionario muy cumplido con un tractado de materia de excomuniones y de usura, de matrimonio, y de votos . . . Agora nuevamente corregido y añadido en esta tercera impression.* Seville: Sebastián Trugillo, 1555.

Vargas Ugarte, Rubén. *Concilios Limenses (1551–1772).* 3 vols. Lima: Tipografía Peruana, 1951–54.

Vega, Alonso de la. *Summa llamada nueva recopilación, y práctica del fuero interior, utilissima para confessores, y penitentes, con varias resoluciones de casi innumerables casos de consciencia, tocantes a todas las materias theologicas, canonicas y iuridicas, conforme a la doctrina de los Santos, y mas graves autores antiguos y modernos.* Madrid: Licenciado Varez de Castro, 1598.

Verdín-Díaz, Guillermo, ed. *Alonso de Cartagena y el Defensorium Unitatis Christianae.* Oviedo: Universidad de Oviedo, 1992.

Villavicencio, Lorenzo de. *De oeconomia sacra circa pauperum curam a Christo instituta, Apostolis tradita, & in universa ecclesia inde ad nostra usque tēmpora perpetua religione observata, cum quarundam propositionum, quæ huic sacræ œconomiæ adversantur, confutatione libri tres.* Paris: Michael Sonnium, 1564.

Vitoria, Francisco de. *Confessionario muy util y provechoso. Agora nuevamente corregido y enmendado.* Valladolid: Francisco Fernández de Córdoba, 1568.

Vitoria, Francisco de. *On Homicide, and Commentary on Summa theologiae II-IIae Q. 64.* Introduction and translation by John P. Doyle. Milwaukee: Marquette University Press, 1997.

Yrolo Calar, Nicolás de. *La política de escrituras.* Edited by María del Pilar Martínez López-Cano, Ivonne Mijares Ramírez, and Javier Sanchiz Ruíz. Mexico City: Universidad Nacional Autónoma de México, 1996.

Zapata y Sandoval, Juan. *De iustitia distributiva et acceptione personarum ei opposita disceptatio.* Edited by C. Baciero, A. M. Barrero, J. M. García Añoveros, and J. M. Soto. Madrid: Consejo Superior de Investigaciones Científicas, 2004.

Zavala, Lorenzo de. *Ensayo crítico de las revoluciones de México.* In *Obras: El Historiador y el Representante Popular,* edited by Manuel González Ramírez. Mexico City: Editorial Porrúa, 1969.

Zavala, Silvio. *Fuentes para la historia del trabajo en Nueva España.* 5 vols. Mexico City: Fondo de Cultura Económica, 1939.

Zuazo, Alonso de. *Cartas y memorias (1511–1539).* Edited by Rodrigo Martínez Baracs. Mexico City: CONACULTA, 2000.

Zorita, Alonso de. *Breve y sumaria relación de los señores de la Nueva España.* Mexico City: Universidad Nacional Autónoma de México, 1942.

Zorita, Alonso de. *Cedulario de 1574.* Introduction by Beatríz Bernal. Mexico City: Miguel Ángel Porrúa, 1985.

Zorita, Alonso de. *Colección de libros y documentos referentes a la historia de América.* Vol. 9, *Historia de la Nueva España por el Doctor Alonso de Zorita (siglo XVI).* Madrid: Victoriano Suárez, 1909.

Zorita, Alonso de. "Parecer de Alonso de Zorita sobre lo que debian tributar y los indios de Mexico y Santiago. 1562." In *Colección de libros y documentos referentes a la historia de América.* Vol. 9, *Historia de la Nueva España por el Doctor Alonso de Zorita (siglo XVI).* Introduction by Manuel Serrano y Sanz. Madrid: Victoriano Suárez, 1909.

Zurita, Fernando. *Theologicarum de Indis quaestionum: Enchiridion primum.* Madrid: Querino Gerardo, 1586.

Secondary Sources

Adorno, Rolena. "Censorship and Its Evasion: Jerónimo Román and Bartolomé de las Casas." *Hispania* 75, no. 4 (October 1992): 812–27.

Aguilar Piedra, Carlos H. *La orfebrería en el México precortesiano.* Mexico City: Acta Anthropologica II:2, 1946.

Aiton, Arthur Scott. "Real Hacienda in New Spain under the First Viceroy." *Hispanic American Historical Review* 6, no. 4 (November 1926): 232–45.

Alberro, Solange. *El águila y la cruz: Orígenes religiosos de la conciencia criolla. México, siglos xvi–xvii.* Mexico City: El Colegio de México / Fondo de Cultura Económica, 1999.

Alberro, Solange. *Inquisición y sociedad en México, 1571–1700.* Mexico City: Fondo de Cultura Económica, 1988.

Alcántara Rojas, Berenice. "El dragón y la mazacoatl: Criaturas del infierno en un *exemplum* en náhuatl de Fray Ioan Baptista." *Estudios de Cultura Náhuatl* 36 (January 2005): 383–420.

Alcina Franch, José. *Calendario y religión entre los zapotecos.* Mexico City: Universidad Nacional Autónoma de México, 1993.

Álvarez de Toledo, Isabel. *Politics and Reform in Spain and Viceregal Mexico: The Life and Thought of Palafox, 1600–1659.* Oxford: Oxford University Press, 2004.

Anderson, Perry. "Nocturnal Enquiry: Carlo Ginzburg." In *A Zone of Engagement.* London: Verso, 1992, 207–29.

Baldwin, John W. *The Medieval Theories of the Just Price: Romanists, Canonists, and Theologians in the Twelfth and Thirteenth Centuries. Transactions of the American Philosophical Society.* Philadelphia: American Philosophical Society, 1959.

Barahona, Renato. *Sex Crimes, Honour and the Law in Early Modern Spain: Vizcaya, 1528–1735.* Buffalo: University of Toronto Press, 2003.

Barrio Lorenzot, Francisco del. *Ordenanzas de gremios de la Nueva España.* Mexico City: Dirección de Talleres Gráficos, 1921.

Bartlett, Robert. *Trial by Fire and Water: The Medieval Judicial Ordeal.* Oxford: Clarendon Press, 1986.

Bast, Robert James. *Honor Your Fathers: Catechisms and the Emergence of a Patriarchal Ideology in Germany, 1400–1600.* Leiden: Brill, 1997.

Batalla Rosado, Juan José. "La pena de muerte durante la colonia—siglo XVI—a partir del análisis de las imágenes de los códices mesoamericanos." *Revista española de antropología americana* 25 (1995): 71–110.

Baudot, Georges. *Utopía e Historia en México: Los primeros cronistas de la civilización mexicana (1520–1569).* Madrid: Espasa-Calpe, 1983.

Bauer. Arnold J. *Goods, Power, History: Latin America's Material Culture.* Cambridge: Cambridge University Press, 2001.

Beltrán de Heredia, Vicente. "Ensayo biobibliográfico sobre el P. Diego de Vitoria." In *Miscelánea Beltrán de Heredia: Colección de artículos sobre historia de la teología española.* 4 vols., 2: 93–111. Salamanca: Editorial OPE, 1971–73.

Benton, Lauren. *Law and Colonial Cultures: Legal Regimes in World History,1400–1900.* Cambridge: Cambridge University Press, 2002.

Berdan, Frances B. *The Aztecs of Central Mexico: An Imperial Society.* New York: Holt, Rinehart and Winston, 1982.

Berman, Harold J. *Law and Revolution.* 2 vols. Cambridge, MA: Belknap Press of Harvard University Press, 1983–2003.

Borah, Woodrow. *Justice by Insurance: The General Indian Court of Colonial Mexico and the Legal Aides of the Half-Real.* Berkeley: University of California Press, 1983.

Boureau, Alain. "Droit et théologie au XIIIe siècle." *Annales* 47, no. 6 (November–December 1992): 1113–25.

Bossy, John. "Moral Arithmetic: Seven Sins into Ten Commandments." In *Conscience and Casuistry in Early Modern Europe*, edited by Edmund Leites, 214–34. Cambridge: Cambridge University Press; Paris: Editions de la Maison des Sciences de l'Homme, 1988.

Brague, Rémi. *The Law of God: The Philosophical History of an Idea.* Chicago: University of Chicago Press, 2007.

Bravo Lozano, Jesús, and Patricio Hidalgo Nuchera. *De indianos y notarios.* Madrid: Colegios Notariales de España, 1995.

Broda, Johanna. "El tributo en trajes guerreros y la estructura del sistema tributario mexica." In *Economía política e ideología en el México prehispánico*, edited by Pedro Carrasco and Johanna Broda, 115–74. Mexico City, CIS-INAH (Centro de Investigaciones Superiores del Instituto Nacional de Antropología e Historia) / Editorial Nueva Imagen, 1978.

Brown, David. "Anselm on Atonement." In *The Cambridge Companion to Anselm*, edited by Brian Davies and Brian Leftow, 279–302. Cambridge: Cambridge University Press, 2004.

Brumfiel, Elizabeth M. "Elite and Utilitarian Crafts in the Aztec State." In *Specialization, Exchange, and Complex Societies*, edited by Elizabeth M. Brumfiel and Timothy K. Earle, 102–18. Cambridge: Cambridge University Press, 1987.

Bryson, Frederick Robertson. *The Point of Honor in Sixteenth-Century Italy: An Aspect of the Life of the Gentleman.* New York: Columbia University / Publications of the Institute of French Studies, 1935.

Burrus, Ernest J. "The Author of the Mexican Council Catechisms." *The Americas* 15, no. 2 (October 1958): 171–78.

Bustamante García, Jesús. "El conocimiento como necesidad de estado: Las encuestas oficiales sobre Nueva España durante el reinado de Carlos V." *Revista de Indias* 60, no. 218 (2000): 33–55.

Calnek, Edward E. "El sistema de Mercado de Tenochtitlan." In *Economía política e ideología en el México prehispánico*, edited by Pedro Carrasco and Johanna Broda, 95–114. Mexico City: CIS-INAH (Centro de Investigaciones Superiores del Instituto Nacional de Antropología e Historia) / Editorial Nueva Imagen, 1982.

Cañeque, Alejandro. *The King's Living Image: The Culture and Politics of Viceregal Power in Colonial Mexico.* New York: Routledge, 2004.

Caro-Baroja, Julio. "Honour and Shame: A Historical Account of Several Conflicts." In *Honour and Shame: The Values of Mediterranean Society*, edited by J. G. Peristiany, 81–137. Chicago: University of Chicago Press, 1966.

Carrasco, Pedro. "La economía del México prehispánico." In *Economía política e ide-*

ología en el México prehispánico, edited by Pedro Carrasco and Johanna Broda, 58–64. Mexico City: CIS-INAH (Centro de Investigaciones Superiores del Instituto Nacional de Antropología e Historia) / Editorial Nueva Imagen, 1978.

Carrera Stampa, Manuel. "The Evolution of Weights and Measures in New Spain." *Hispanic American Historical Review* 29, no. 1 (February 1949): 2–24.

Carrera Stampa, Manuel. *Los gremios mexicanos: la organización gremial en Nueva España 1521–1861*. Mexico City: EDIAPSA, 1954.

Casagrande, Carla, and Silvana Vecchio. *I peccati della lingua: Disciplina ed etica della parola nella cultura medievale*. Rome: Istituto della Enciclopedia Italiana, 1987.

Ceccarelli, Giovanni. *Il gioco e il peccato: Economia e rischio nel tardo medioevo*. Bologna: Il Mulino, 2003.

Chamoux, Marie Noëlle. "Dire le savoir-faire en nahuatl classique." In *Dire le savoir-faire: Gestes, techniques et objects*, edited by Salvatore D'Onofrio and Frédéric Joulian, 37–54. Paris: L'Herne, 2006.

Chase, Arlen F., and Diane Z. Chase. "Mesoamerican Elites: Assumptions, Definitions, and Models." In *Mesoamerican Elites: An Archaeological Assessment*, edited by Diane Z. Chase and Arlen F. Chase, 3–17. Norman: University of Oklahoma Press, 1992.

Charlton, Thomas H., and Patricia Fournier. "Pots and Plots: The Multiple Roles of Colonial Red Wares in the Basin of Mexico." In *Enduring Conquests: Rethinking the Archaeology of Resistance to Spanish Colonialism in the Americas*, edited by Matthew Liebmann and Melissa M. Murphy, 127–48. Santa Fe, NM: School for Advanced Research, 2010.

Charlton, Thomas H., Cynthia L. Otis Charlton, and Patricia Fournier García. "The Basin of Mexico A.D. 1450–1620: Archaeological Dimensions." In *The Postclassic to Spanish-Era Transition in Mesoamerica: Archaeological Perspectives*, edited by Susan Kepecs and Rani T. Alexander, 49–63. Albuquerque: University of New Mexico Press, 1995.

Chauchadis, Claude. *La loi du duel: Le code du point d'honneur dans l'Espagne des XVIe–XVIIe siècles*. Toulouse: Presses Universitaires du Mirail, 1997.

Christin, Oliver. "Sur la condamnation du blasphème." *Revue d'histoire de l'Eglise de France* 204 (1994): 43–64.

Clanchy, Michael. "Law and Love in the Middle Ages." In *Disputes and Settlements: Law and Human Relations in the West*, edited by John Bossy, 47–67. Cambridge: Cambridge University Press, 1983.

Clavero, Bartolomé. *Antidora: Antropología católica de la economía moderna*. Milan: Giuffrè Editore, 1991.

Clayton, Mary. "Evidence for a Native-Speaking Nahuatl Author in the Ayer *Vocabulario Trilingüe*." *International Journal of Lexicography* 16, no. 2 (2003): 99–119.

Clayton, Mary. "A Trilingual Spanish-Latin-Nahuatl Manuscript Dictionary Sometimes Attributed to Fray Bernardino de Sahagún." *International Journal of American linguistics* 55, no. 4 (1989): 391–416.

Clendinnen, Inga. *Ambivalent Conquests: Maya and Spaniard in Yucatan, 1517–1570*. Cambridge: Cambridge University Press, 1987.

Clendinnen, Inga. *Aztecs: An Interpretation*. Cambridge: Cambridge University Press, 1991.

Clendinnen, Inga. "Disciplining the Indians: Franciscan Ideology and Missionary Violence in Sixteenth-Century Yucatan." *Past & Present* 94 (February 1982): 27–48.

Cline, Howard F. "The Relaciones Geográficas of the Spanish Indies, 1577–1648." In *Handbook of Middle American Indians*, edited by Robert Wauchope. Vol. 1, *Guide to Ethnohistorical Sources*, edited by Howard F. Cline, 183–93. Austin: University of Texas Press, 1972.

Cline, S. L. *Colonial Culhuacan, 1580–1600*. Albuquerque: University of Mexico Press, 1986.

Cline, S. L. "Fray Alonso de Molina's Model Testament and Antecedents to Indigenous Wills in Spanish America." In *Dead Giveaways: Indigenous Testaments of Colonial Mesoamerica and the Andes*, edited by Susan Kellogg and Matthew Restall, 13–33. Salt Lake City: University of Utah Press, 1998.

Coleman, Janet. "Medieval Discussions of Property: *Ratio* and *Dominium* According to John of Paris and Marsilius of Padua." *History of Political Thought* 4, no. 2 (1983): 209–28.

Constable, Olivia Remi. *Trade and Traders in Muslim Spain: The Commercial Realignment of the Iberian Peninsula, 900–1500*. Cambridge: Cambridge University Press, 1994.

Cope, R. Douglas. *The Limits of Racial Domination: Plebeian Society in Colonial Mexico City, 1660–1720*. Madison: University of Wisconsin Press, 1994.

Corona González, Santos Manuel. "El Libro de las fórmulas de juramento del Consejo de Castilla." *Anuario de historia del derecho español* 63–64 (1993–94): 985–87.

Cuadriello, Jaime. *The Glories of the Republic of Tlaxcala: Art and Life in Viceregal Mexico*. Translated by Christopher J. Follett. Austin: University of Texas Press/Teresa Lozano Long Institute of Latin American Studies, 2011.

Cuevas, Mariano. *Historia de la Iglesia en México*. 5 vols. El Paso: Editorial "Revista Católica," 1922–28.

Cutter, Charles R. *The Legal Culture of Northern Spain, 1700–1810*. Albuquerque: University of New Mexico Press, 1995.

Dehouve, Danièle. *Relatos de pecados en la evangelización de los indios de México (siglos xvi–xviii)*. Mexico City: CIESAS/CEAMCA, 2010.

Diel, Lori Boornazian. *The Tira de Tepechpan: Negotiating Place under Aztec and Spanish Rule*. Austin: University of Texas Press, 2008.

Dionisotti, Carlo. "La letteratura italiana nell'età del concilio di Trento." In *Geografia e storia della letteratura italiana*. Turin: Einaudi, 1999.

Domínguez Ortíz, Antonio. *El Antiguo Régimen: Los Reyes Católicos y los Austrias*. Madrid: Alianza Editorial/Alfaguara, 1973.

Donkin, A. *Spanish Red: An Ethnogeographical Study of Cochineal and the Opuntia Cactus*. Transactions of the American Philosophical Society. New Series, vol. 67, no. 5 (1977).

Duve, Thomas. "Derecho canónico y la alteridad indígena: Los indios como neófitos." In *Esplendores y miserias de la evangelización de América: Antecedentes europeos y alteridad indígena*, edited by Wulf Oesterreicher and Roland Schmidt-Riese, 73–94. Berlin: De Gruyter, 2010.

Duve, Thomas. *Sonderrecht in der Frühen Neuzeit. Studien zum* ius singulare *und den* privilegia miserabilium personarum, senum *und* indorum *in Alter und Neuer Welt.* Frankfurt am Main: Vittorio Klostermann, 2008.

Erspamer, F. *La biblioteca di don Ferrante: Duello ed onore nella cultura del Cinquecento.* Rome: Bulzoni, 1982.

Escalante Gonzalbo, Pablo. "El patrocinio del arte indocristiano en el siglo XVI: La iniciativa de las autoridades indígenas en Tlaxcala y Cuautinchan." In *Patrocinio, colección y circulación de las artes,* edited by Gustavo Curiel, 215–35. Mexico City: Universidad Nacional Autónoma de México, 1997.

Estrada de Gerlero, Elena Isabel. "El Códice Cuetlaxcoapan." In *Estudios acerca del arte novohispano: Homenaje a Elisa Vargas Lugo,* 29–41. Mexico City: Universidad Nacional Autónoma de México, 1983.

Fernández Gracia, Ricardo. "Juan de Palafox: Directrices para templos y su exorno artístico." In *Varia Palafoxiana: Doce estudios en torno a don Juan de Palafox y Mendoza,* edited by Ricardo Fernández Gracia, 71–112. Pamplona: Gobierno de Navarra, 2010.

Flynn, Maureen. "Blasphemy and the Play of Anger in Sixteenth-Century Spain." *Past & Present* 149 (1995): 29–56.

Flynn, Maureen. *Sacred Charity: Confraternities and Social Welfare in Spain, 1400–1700.* Ithaca, NY: Cornell University Press, 1987.

Foriers, Paul. "Les Utopies et le Droit." In *Les Utopies à la Renaissance.* Brussels: Presses Universitaires de Bruxelles; Paris: Presses Universitaires de France, 1963.

Frye, David. "The Native Peoples of Northeast Mexico." In *The Cambridge History of the Native Peoples of the Americas.* Vol. 2, *Mesoamerica,* edited by Richard E. W. Adams and Murdo J. MacLeod, 89–135. Cambridge: Cambridge University Press, 2000.

García-Gallo, Alfonso. "Del testamento romano al medieval: Las líneas de su evolución en España." *Anuario de historia del derecho español* 47 (1977): 425–97.

García Icazbalceta, Joaquín. *Bibliografía mexicana del siglo XVI.* 2nd ed. Mexico City: Fondo de Cultura Económica, 1954.

Garibay K., Angel Ma. "Frases y modos de hablar, elegantes y metafóricos, de los indios mexicanos." *Estudios de Cultura Náhuatl* 6 (1966): 11–27.

Garnsey, Peter. *Thinking about Property from Antiquity to the Age of Revolution.* Cambridge: Cambridge University Press, 2007.

Gaudemet, Jean. "Persona." In *La doctrine canonique médiévale.* London: Variorum, 1994, 465–91.

Geremek, Bronislaw. *La potence ou la pitié: L'Europe et les pauvres du Moyen Âge à nos jours.* Translated by Joanna Arnold-Moricet. Paris: Gallimard, 1987.

Gibson, Charles. "The Aztec Aristocracy in Colonial Mexico." *Comparative Studies in Society and History* 2, no. 2 (January 1960): 169–96.

Gibson, Charles. *The Aztecs under Spanish Rule: A History of the Indians of the Valley of Mexico, 1519–1810.* Stanford: Stanford University Press, 1964.

Gil, Fernando. *Primeras "Doctrinas" del Nuevo Mundo: Estudio histórico-teológico de las obras de fray Juan de Zumárraga (†1548).* Buenos Aires: Publicaciones de Teología de la Pontificia Universidad Católica Argentina "Santa María de los Buenos Aires," 1992.

Góngora, Mario. *Studies in the Colonial History of Spanish America.* Translated by Richard Southern. Cambridge: Cambridge University Press, 1975.

González Polvillo, Antonio. *Decálogo y gestualidad social en la España de la Contrarreforma*. Seville: Universidad de Sevilla, 2011.

Greenleaf, Richard E. "The Inquisition and the Indians of New Spain: A Study in Jurisdictional Confusion." *The Americas* 22, no. 2 (October 1965): 138–66.

Gross, Ariela J. *Double Character: Slavery and Mastery in the Antebellum Southern Courtroom*. Princeton: Princeton University Press, 2000.

Gruzinski, Serge. *The Conquest of Mexico: The Incorporation of Indian Societies into the Western World, 16th–18th centuries*. Translated by Eileen Corrigan. Cambridge: Polity Press, 1993.

Guardiola, Conrado. "Los primeros datos documentales sobre Guido de Monte Roquerio, autor del 'Manipulus Curatorum.'" *Hispania: Revista española de historia* 48, no. 170 (1988): 797–826.

Gutierrez, Ramón A. "From Honor to Love: Transformations of the Meaning of Sexuality in Colonial New Mexico." In *Kinship Ideology and Practice in Latin America*, edited by Raymond T. Smith, 237–63. Chapel Hill: University of North Carolina Press, 1984.

Hanawalt, Patricia. "Costume and Control: Aztec Sumptuary Laws." *Archaeology* 33, no. 1 (January–February 1980): 33–43.

Hanks, William F. *Converting Words: Maya in the Age of the Cross*. Berkeley: University of California Press, 2010.

Harnack, Adolph. *History of Dogma*. Translated by Neil Buchanan. 7 vols. New York: Dover Publications, 1961.

Haskett, Robert. *Indigenous Rulers: An Ethnohistory of Town Government in Colonial Cuernavaca*. Albuquerque: University of New Mexico Press, 1991.

Haskett, Robert. "Paper Shields: The Ideology of Coats of Arms in Colonial Mexican Primordial Titles." *Ethnohistory* 43, no. 1 (Winter 1996): 99–126.

Hassig, Ross. *Aztec Warfare: Imperial Expansion and Political Control*. Norman: University of Oklahoma Press, 1988.

Hassig, Ross. *Trade, Tribute, and Transportation: The Sixteenth-Century Political Economy of the Valley of Mexico*. Norman: University of Oklahoma Press, 1985.

Haviland, John Beard. *Gossip, Reputation, and Knowledge in Zinacantan*. Chicago: University of Chicago Press, 1977.

Helmholz, R. H. *The Spirit of Classical Canon Law*. Athens: University of Georgia Press, 1996.

Herzog, Tamar. *Defining Nations: Immigrants and Citizens in Early Modern Spain and Spanish America*. New Haven: Yale University Press, 2003.

Hespanha, Antonio Manuel. "Le Droit et la domination coloniale européenne: Le cas de l'Empire oriental portugais." In *Lois, justice, coutume: Amérique et Europe latines (16e–19e siècles)*, edited by J. C. Garavaglia and J-F. Schaub, 203–26. Paris: Éditions de l' EHESS, 2005.

Horn, Rebecca. *Postconquest Coyoacan: Nahua-Spanish Relations*. Stanford: Stanford University Press, 1997.

Hosler, Dorothy. 2003. "Metal production." In *The Postclassic Mesoamerican World*, edited by Michael E. Smith and Frances E. Berdan, 159–71. Salt Lake City: University of Utah Press.

Hosler, Dorothy. *The Sounds and Colors of Power: The Sacred Metallurgical Technology of Ancient West Mexico*. Cambridge, MA: MIT Press, 1994.

Johnson, Lyman L., and Sonya Lipsett-Rivera, eds. *The Faces of Honor: Sex, Shame and Violence in Colonial Latin America*. Albuquerque: University of New Mexico Press, 1998.

Jonsen, Albert R., and Stephen Toulmin. *The Abuse of Casuistry: A History of Moral Reasoning*. Berkeley: University of California Press, 1988.

Kagan, Richard L. *Lawsuits and Litigants in Castile, 1500–1700*. Chapel Hill: University of North Carolina Press, 1981.

Kamen, Henry. "Clerical Violence in a Catholic Society: The Hispanic World 1450–1720." In *Crisis and Change in Early Modern Spain*. London: Variorum, 1984.

Karttunen, Frances, and James Lockhart, eds. *The Art of Nahuatl Speech: The Bancroft Dialogues*. Los Angeles: UCLA Latin American Center Publications, University of California Press, 1987.

Karttunen, Frances. "After the Conquest: The Survival of Indigenous Patterns of Life and Belief." *Journal of World History* 3, no. 2 (Fall 1992): 239–56.

Kaye, Joel. *Economy and Nature in the Fourteenth Century*. Cambridge: Cambridge University Press, 1998.

Kellogg, Susan. *Law and the Transformation of Aztec Culture, 1500–1700*. Norman: University of Oklahoma Press, 1995.

Kennedy, Ruth Lee. "Certain Phases of the Sumptuary Decrees of 1623 and Their Relation to Tirso's Theater." *Hispanic Review* 10, no. 2 (April 1942): 91–115.

Klein, Elka. *Jews, Christian Society, and Royal Power in Medieval Barcelona*. Ann Arbor: University of Michigan Press, 2006.

Koselleck, Reinhart. "Perspective and Temporality: A Contribution to the Historiographical Exposure of the Historical World." In *Futures Past: On the Semantics of Historical Time*, translated by Keith Tribe. New York: Columbia University Press, 2004, 128–51.

Lambertini, Roberto. "La proprietá di Adamo: Stato d'innocenza ed origine del *dominium* nel *Commento alle Sentenze* e nell *Improbacio* di Francesco d'Ascoli." *Bulletino dell' Istituto Storico Italiano per il Medio Evo e Archivio Muratoriano* 99, no. 2 (1994): 201–51.

Langholm, Odd. *Economics in the Medieval Schools: Wealth, Exchange, Value, Money and Usury according to the Paris Theological Tradition, 1200–1350*. Leiden: E.J. Brill, 1992.

Lavrin, Asunción, ed. *Sexuality and Marriage in Colonial Latin America*. Lincoln: Nebraska University Press, 1989.

Lauwers, Michel. "Le cimetière dans le Moyen Âge latin: Lieu sacré, saint et religieux." *Annales: Histoire, sciences sociales* 5 (September–October 1999): 1047–72.

Lea, Henry Charles. *The Duel and the Oath*. Edited by Edward Peters. Philadelphia: University of Pennsylvania Press, 1974.

Lea, Henry Charles. *A History of the Spanish Inquisition*. 4 vols. New York: Macmillan, 1922.

Lee, Raymond L. "Cochineal Production and Trade in New Spain to 1600." *The Americas* 4, no. 4 (April 1948): 449–73.

Le Goff, Jacques. *La bourse et la vie*. In *Un Autre Moyen Âge*. Paris: Gallimard, 1999.

Le Goff, Jacques. *Pour un autre Moyen Âge: Temps, travail, et culture en Occident: 18 essais*. Paris: Gallimard, 1977.

León-Portilla, Ascensión H. de. "El Códice de Cuetlaxcohuapan y los primeros escribanos nahuas." In *Códices y Documentos sobre México: Segundo Simposio*, edited by Salvador Rueda Smithers, Constanza Vega Sosa, and Rodrigo Martínez Baracs, 2:311–31. Mexico City: Instituto Nacional de Antropología e Historia. Dirección de Estudios Históricos / Consejo Nacional para la Cultura y las Artes, 1997.

León-Portilla, Ascensión H. de. *Tepuztlahcuilolli: Impresos en Náhuatl*. 2 vols. Mexico City: Universidad Nacional Autónoma de México, 1988.

León-Portilla, Miguel. *Los franciscanos vistos por el hombre náhuatl*. Mexico City: Centro de Estudios Bernardino de Sahagún, S. A., 1985.

Lepelley, Claude. "Le serment païen malédiction démoniaque: Augustin devant une angoisse des Chrétiens de son temps." In *Le serment*, edited by Raymond Verdier, 2:53–61. Paris: Éditions du centre National de la Recherche Scientifique, 1991.

Lewis, Oscar. "The Possessions of the Poor." In *Anthropological Essays*. New York: Random House, 1970, 441–60.

Lida de Malkiel, María Rosa. *Dido en la literatura española: Su retrato y defensa*. London: Tamesis Books, 1974.

Little, Lester K. "Pride Goes before Avarice: Social Change and the Vices in Latin Christendom." *American Historical Review* 76, no. 1 (February 1971): 16–49.

Little, Lester K. *Religious Poverty and the Profit Economy in Medieval Europe*. Ithaca, NY: Cornell University Press, 1978.

Llaguno, José A. *La personalidad jurídica del indio y el III Concilio Provincial Mexicano (1585)*. Mexico City: Editorial Porrúa, 1963.

Lockhart, James. "Double Mistaken Identity: Some Nahua Concepts in Postconquest Guise." In *Of Things of the Indies: Essays Old and New in Early Latin American History*. Stanford: Stanford University Press, 1999.

Lockhart, James. *The Nahuas after the Conquest: A Social and Cultural History of the Indians of Central Mexico, Sixteenth through Eighteenth Centuries*. Stanford: Stanford University Press, 1992.

Lockhart, James. "Views of Corporate and Self and History in Some Valley of Mexico Towns, Late Seventeenth and Eighteenth Centuries." In *Nahuas and Spaniards: Postconquest Central Mexican History and Philology*. Stanford: Stanford University Press; Los Angeles: UCLA Latin American Center Publications / University of California, Los Angeles, 1991.

Lohmann Villena, Guillermo. "La restitución por conquistadores y encomenderos: Un aspecto de la incidencia lascasiana en Perú." *Anuario de Estudios Americanos* 23 (1966): 21–89.

Long, Pamela O. *Openness, Secrecy, Authorship: Technical Arts and the Culture of Knowledge from Antiquity to the Renaissance*. Baltimore: Johns Hopkins University Press, 2001.

López Austin, Alfredo. *The Human Body and Ideology: Concepts of the Ancient Nahuas*. Translated by Thelma Ortíz de Montellano and Bernard Ortíz de Montellano. 2 vols. Salt Lake City: University of Utah Press, 1988.

López Sarrelangue, Delfina Esmeralda. *La nobleza indígena de Pátzcuaro en la época virreinal*. Mexico City: Universidad Nacional Autónoma de México / Instituto de Investigaciones Históricas, 1965.

Lozano Sebastián, Francisco-Javier. *La penitencia canónica en la España romano-visigoda*. Burgos: Ediciones Aldecoa, 1980.

Luján Muñoz, Jorge. *Los escribanos en las Indias occidentales*. 3rd ed. Mexico City:

Universidad Nacional Autónoma de México / Instituto de Estudios y Documentos Históricos, A.C., 1982.

Luque Colombres, Carlos. "El Formulario de Testamentos del P. Gerónimo de Zeballos S.J." *Revista de historia del derecho* 7 (1980): 347–433.

MacCormack, Sabine. *On the Wings of Time: Rome, the Incas, Spain, and Peru.* Princeton: Princeton University Press, 2007.

MacCormack, Sabine. "Social Conscience and Social Practice: Poverty and Vagrancy in Spain and Early Colonial Peru." In *Home and Homelessness in the Medieval and Renaissance World*, edited by Nicholas Howe, 91–123. Notre Dame: University of Notre Dame Press, 2004.

Macías Rosendo, Baldomero. *La correspondencia de Benito Arias Montano con el Presidente de Indias.* Huelva: Universidad de Huelva, 2008.

MacKay, Ruth. *"Lazy, Improvident People": Myth and Reality in the Writing of Spanish History.* Ithaca, NY: Cornell University Press, 2006.

Mackeever Furst, Jill L. *The Natural History of the Soul in Ancient Mexico.* New Haven: Yale University Press, 1995.

MacLachlan, Colin M. *Criminal Justice in Eighteenth-Century Mexico.* Berkeley: University of California Press, 1974.

MacLeod, Murdo, J. "La espada de la Iglesia: Excomunión y la evolución de la lucha por el control político y económico en Chiapas colonial, 1545–1700." *Mesoamérica* 11, no. 20 (1990): 199–213.

Madero, Marta. *Manos violentas, palabras vedadas: La injuria en Castilla y León (siglos XIII–XV).* Madrid: Taurus, 1992.

Madero, Marta. *Las verdades de los hechos: Proceso, juez y testimonio en la Castilla del siglo XIII.* Salamanca: Ediciones Universidad de Salamanca, 2004.

Malagón-Barceló, Javier. *La literatura jurídica española del siglo de oro en la Nueva España. Notas para su estudio.* Mexico City: Universidad Nacional Autónoma de México, 1959.

Manzano Manzano, Juan. *Historia de las recopilaciones de Indias.* 2 vols. Madrid: Ediciones Cultura Hispánica, 1950.

Maravall, José Antonio. "La imagen de la sociedad expansiva en la conciencia castellana del siglo XVI." In *Estudios de historia del pensamiento español.* 3 vols. Madrid: Cultura Hispánica, 1984, 2: 271–315.

Maravall, José Antonio. *Poder, honor y élites en el siglo XVII.* Madrid: Siglo Veintiuno de España, 1979.

Martínez, Gregorio Bartolomé. *Jaque mate al obispo virrey.* Mexico City: Fondo de Cultura Económica, 1991.

Martínez Baracs, Rodrigo. *Caminos cruzados: Fray Maturino Gilberti en Perivan.* Zamora, Michoacan: El Colegio de Michoacán, 2005.

Martz, Linda. *Poverty and Welfare in Habsburg Spain: The Example of Toledo.* Cambridge: Cambridge University Press, 1983.

Maurtúa, Victor M. *Antecedentes de la Recopilacion de Yndias.* Madrid: Imprenta de Bernardo Rodríguez, 1906.

Maza, Francisco de la. "La mitra Mexicana de El Escorial," *Artes de México* 17, no. 137 (1971): 71–72.

Michaud-Quantin, Pierre. *Sommes de casuistique et manuels de confession au moyen âge (xii–xvi siècles).* Louvain: Edit. Nauwelaerts; Lille: Librairie Giard, 1962.

Mollat, Michel. *The Poor in the Middle Ages: An Essay in Social History*. New Haven: Yale University Press, 1986.

Moorman, John. *A History of the Franciscan Order from Its Origins to the Year 1517*. Oxford: Clarendon Press, 1968.

Oakley, Thomas Pollock. *English Penitential Discipline and Anglo-Saxon Law in Their Joint Influence*. Studies in History, Economics and Public Law 107, no. 2. New York: Columbia University, 1923.

O'Callaghan, Joseph F. *The Learned King: The Reign of Alfonso X of Castile*. Philadelphia: University of Pennsylvania Press, 1993.

Offner, Jerome A. *Law and Politics in Aztec Texcoco*. Cambridge: Cambridge University Press, 1983.

O'Hara, Matthew. *A Flock Divided: Race, Religion, and Politics in Mexico, 1749-1857*. Durham: Duke University Press, 2010.

O'Malley, John W. *The First Jesuits*. Cambridge, MA: Harvard University Press, 1993.

Ortíz Salazar, Teresa. "The Feather Adarga of Philip II and the Escorial Miter." *Coloquios: Nuevo Mundo Mundos Nuevos*, 2006. http://nuevomundo.revues.org/1468.

Pardo, Osvaldo F. "Contesting the Power to Heal: Angels, Demons and Plants in Colonial Mexico." In *Spiritual Encounters: Interactions between Christianity and Native Religions in Colonial America*, edited by Nicholas Griffiths and Fernando Cervantes, 163–84. Birmingham: University of Birmingham Press, 1999.

Pardo, Osvaldo F. "How to Punish Indians: Law and Cultural Change in Early Colonial Mexico." *Comparative Studies in Society and History* 48, no. 1 (2006): 79–109.

Pardo, Osvaldo F. *The Origins of Mexican Catholicism: Nahua Rituals and Christian Sacraments in Sixteenth-Century Mexico*. Ann Arbor: University of Michigan Press, 2004.

Parish, Helen-Rand, and Harold E. Weidman. *Las Casas en México: Historia y obras desconocidas*. Mexico City: Fondo de Cultura Económica, 1992.

Pedraza Gracia, Manuel José. "La introducción de la imprenta en Zaragoza: La producción y distribución del *Manipulus Curatorum* de Guido de Monterroterio, Zaragoza, Matheus Flanders, 15 de octubre de 1475." *Gutenberg-Jahrbuch* 71 (1996): 65–71.

Peña y Cámara, José María de la. "Nuevos datos sobre la visita de Juan de Ovando al Consejo de Indias." *Anuario de historia del derecho español* 12 (1935): 425–38.

Pérez-Rocha, Emma, and Rafael Tena. *La nobleza indígena del centro de México después de la conquista*. Mexico City: Instituto Nacional de Antropología e Historia, 2000.

Perlstein Pollard, Helen. "The Political Economy of Prehispanic Tarascan Metallurgy." *American Antiquity* 52, no. 4 (October 1987): 741–52.

Phelan, John Leddy. *The Hispanization of the Philippines: Spanish Aims and Filipino Responses, 1565-1700*. Madison: University of Wisconsin Press, 1959.

Pike, Ruth. "Crime and Punishment in XVIth-Century Spain." *Journal of European Economic History* 5, no. 3 (1976): 689–704.

Pineda, Victoria. "La retórica epideíctica de Menandro y los cuestionarios para las *Relaciones geográficas de Indias*." *Rhetorica* 18, no. 2 (May 2000): 147–73.

Pinto Crespo, Virgilio. *Inquisición y control ideológico en la España del siglo XVI*. Madrid: Taurus, 1983.

Pirillo, Nestore, ed. *Il vincolo del giuramento e il tribunale della coscienza*. Bologna: Il Mulino, 1993.

Pitt-Rivers, Julian. "Honour and Social Status." In *Honour and Shame: The Values of*

Mediterranean Society, edited by J. G. Peristiany, 19–77. Chicago: University of Chicago Press, 1966.

Pitt-Rivers, Julian. Review of *Honor* by Frank Henderson Stewart. *L'Homme* 143 (July–September 1997): 215–17.

Poole, Stafford. *Juan de Ovando: Governing the Spanish Empire in the Reign of Philip II*. Norman: University of Oklahoma Press, 2004.

Poole, Stafford. *Pedro Moya de Contreras: Catholic Reform and Royal Power in New Spain, 1571–1591*. Berkeley: University of California Press, 1987.

Prodi, Paolo. *Il sacramento del potere: Il giuramento politico nella storia costituzionale dell'Occidente*. Bologna: Il Mulino, 1992.

Prosperi, Adriano. 2006. "Batessimo e identità cristiana nella prima età moderna." In *Salvezza delle anime, disciplina dei corpi: Un seminario sulla storia del battesimo*, edited by A. Prosperi, 1–65. Pisa: Edizioni della Normale, 2006.

Rendón, M. Juan José. "Nuevos datos sobre el origen del Vocabulario en lengua zapoteca del padre Córdova." *Anales de Antropología* 6 (1969): 115–29.

Resines, Luis. *Catecismos americanos del siglo XVI*. 2 vols. Castile and Leon: Consejería de Cultura y Turismo, 1992.

Resines, Luis. *La catequesis en España: Historia y textos*. Madrid: Biblioteca de Autores Cristianos, 1997.

Reyes Gómez, Fermín de los. *El libro en España y América: Legislación y censura. (Siglos XV–XVIII)*. 2 vols. Madrid: Arcos/Libros, 2000.

Ricard, Robert. *The Spiritual Conquest of Mexico*. Translated by Lesley Byrd Simpson. Berkeley: University of California Press, 1966.

Rodríguez-Alegría, Enrique. "Consumption and the Varied Ideologies of Domination in Colonial Mexico." In *The Postclassic to Spanish-Era Transition in Mesoamerica*, edited by Susan Kepecs and Rani T. Alexander, 35–48. Albuquerque: University of New Mexico, 2005.

Romero de Terreros y Vinent, Manuel. *Las artes industriales en la Nueva España*. Mexico City: Librería de Pedro Robredo, 1928.

Roover, Raymond de. *San Bernardino of Siena and Sant' Antonino of Florence*. Boston: Baker Library / Harvard Graduate School of Business Administration, 1967.

Rubial García, Antonio. *La hermana pobreza: El franciscanismo de la Edad media a la evangelización novohispana*. Mexico City: Facultad de Filosofía y Letras, Universidad Nacional Autónoma de México, 1996.

Salvador Esteban, Emilia. "Tortura y penas corporales en la Valencia foral moderna: El reinado de Fernando el Católico." *Estudis* 22 (1996): 263–87.

Salvador y Conde, José. "Fray Pedro de Feria y su *Doctrina Zapoteca* (estudio Bio-Bibliográfico." *Missionalia Hispánica* 4, no. 12 (1947): 417.

Salvatore, Ricardo D., Carlos Aguirre, and Gilbert M. Joseph. *Crime and Punishment in Latin America: Law and Society since Late Colonial Times*. Durham: Duke University Press, 2001.

Sánchez Bella, Ismael. "El 'Título de las Descripciones' del código de Ovando." In *Dos estudios sobre el Código de Ovando*. Pamplona: Ediciones Universidad de Navarra, 1987.

Sánchez Silva, Carlos, and Miguel Suárez Bosa. "Evolución de la producción y comercio mundial de la grana cochinilla, siglos xvi–xix." *Revista de Indias* 66, no. 237 (2006): 473–90.

Saranyana, Josep-Ignasi, and Elisa Luque Alcaide. "Fuentes manuscritas inéditas del III Concilio Mexicano." *Annuarium historiae conciliorum* 22 (1990): 273–83.

Schwaller, John F. *The Church and Clergy in Sixteenth-Century Mexico.* Albuquerque: University of New Mexico Press, 1987.

Seed, Patricia. *To Love, Honor, and Obey in Colonial Mexico: Conflicts over Marriage Choice, 1574-1821.* Stanford: Stanford University Press, 1988.

Sell, Barry D., and Susan Kellogg. "We Want to Give Them Laws: Royal Ordinances in a Mid-Sixteenth Century Nahuatl Text." *Estudios de Cultura Náhuatl* 27 (1997): 325–367.

Sempat Assadourian, Carlos. "Memoriales de Fray Gerónimo de Mendieta." *Historia Mexicana* 37, no. 3 (January–March 1988): 357–422.

Serra Ruiz, Rafael. *Honor, honra e injuria en el derecho medieval español.* Murcia: Sucesores de Nogués, 1969.

Shaw, Judith. "Corporal and Spiritual Homicide, the Sin of Wrath, and the 'Parson's Tale.'" *Traditio* 38 (1982): 281–300.

Sherman, William H. *Used Books: Marking Readers in Renaissance England.* Philadelphia: University of Pennsylvania Press, 2008.

Shuger, Debora K. *The Renaissance Bible: Scholarship, Sacrifice, and Subjectivity.* Berkeley: University of California Press, 1994.

Sicroff, Albert A. *Les controverses des statuts de "pureté de sang" en Espagne du XVe au XVIIe siècle.* Paris: Didier, 1960.

Sigal, Pete. "The *Cuiloni*, the *Patlache*, and the Abominable Sin: Homosexualities in Early Colonial Nahua Society." *Hispanic American Historical Review* 85, no. 4 (2005): 555–93.

Skinner, Quentin. *The Foundations of Modern Political Thought.* 2 vols. Cambridge: Cambridge University Press, 1978.

Smith, Michael E. "Household Possessions and Wealth in Agrarian States: Implications for Archaeology." *Journal of Anthropological Archaeology* 6 (1987): 297–335.

Smith Stark, Thomas C. "Dioses, sacerdotes, y sacrificio: Una mirada a la religión zapoteca a través del *Vocabulario en lengua çapoteca* (1578) de Juan de Córdova." In *La religión de los Binnigula'sa'*, edited by Víctor de la Cruz and Marcus Winter, 89–195. Oaxaca: Instituto Estatal de Educación Pública de Oaxaca, Instituto Oaxaqueño de las Culturas, 2002.

Smith Stark, Thomas C. "La ortografía del zapoteco en el *Vocabulario* de fray Juan de Córdova." In *Escritura zapoteca: 2,500 años de historia*, edited by María de los Ángeles Romero Frizzi, 173–240. Mexico City: CIESAS, Miguel Ángel Porrúa, CONACULTA-INAH, 2003.

Spurr, John. "A Profane History of Early Modern Oaths." *Transactions of the Royal Historical Society* 11 (2001): 37–63.

Stewart, Frank H. "De l' honneur." *L'Homme* 147 (1998): 237–46.

Stewart, Frank H. *Honor.* Chicago: University of Chicago Press, 1994.

Strauss, Gerald. *Law, Resistance, and the State: The Opposition to Roman Law in Reformation Germany.* Princeton: Princeton University Press, 1986.

Suárez, Jorge A. "La clasificación de las lenguas zapotecas." In *Homenaje a Jorge A. Suárez: Lingüística indoamericana e hispánica*, edited by Beatríz Garza Cuarón, 41–68. Mexico City: El Colegio de México, 1990.

Surtz, Ronald E. "Crimes of the Tongue: The Inquisitorial Trials of Cristóbal Duarte Ballester." *Medieval Encounters* 12, no. 3 (2006): 519–32.

Tavárez, David E. *The Invisible War: Indigenous Devotions, Discipline, and Dissent in Colonial Mexico.* Stanford: Stanford University Press, 2011.

Tavárez, David E. "Letras clandestinas, textos tolerados, colaboraciones lícitas: La producción textual de los intelectuales nahuas y zapotecos en el siglo xvii." In *Élites intelectuales y modelos colectivos: mundo ibérico (siglos xvi-xix)*, edited by Mónica Quijada and Jesús Bustamante, 60–82. Madrid: Consejo Superior de Investigaciones Científicas, 2000.

Tavárez, David E. "Naming the Trinity: From Ideologies of Translation to Dialectics of Reception in Colonial Nahua Texts, 1547–1771." *Colonial Latin American Review* 9, no. 1 (June 2000): 21–47.

Taylor, Scott K. *Honor and Violence in Golden Age Spain.* New Haven: Yale University Press, 2008.

Taylor, William B. "'De corazón pequeño y ánimo apocado': Conceptos de curas párrocos sobre los indios en la Nueva España del siglo XVIII." *Relaciones* 39 (1989): 5–67.

Taylor, William B. *Magistrates of the Sacred: Priests and Parishioners in Eighteenth-Century Mexico.* Stanford: Stanford University Press, 1996.

Tentler, Thomas N. *Sin and Confession on the Eve of the Reformation.* Princeton: Princeton University Press, 1977.

Terraciano, Kevin. *The Mixtecs of Colonial Oaxaca: Ñudzahui History, Sixteenth through Eighteenth Centuries.* Stanford: Stanford University Press, 2001.

Thiemer-Sachse, Ursula. "El problema de la definición de regalos, impuestos y tributos en el estado zapoteco en el tiempo precolonial." *Anales de antropología* 33 (1996–99): 285–318.

Thiemer-Sachse, Ursula. "El *Vocabulario castellano-zapoteco* y el *Arte en lengua zapoteca* de Juan de Córdova—intenciones y resultados (Perspectiva antropológica)." In *La descripción de las lenguas amerindias en la época colonial*, edited by Klaus Zimmermann, 147–74. Frankfurt am Main: Vervuert; Madrid: Iberoamericana, 1997.

Thomas, Yan. "*Res Religiosae*: On the Categories of Religion and Commerce in Roman Law." In *Law, Anthropology, and the Constitution of the Social*, edited by Alain Pottage and Martha Mundy, 40–72. Cambridge: Cambridge University Press, 2004.

Tierney, Brian. *The Idea of Natural Rights.* Grand Rapids, MI: William B. Eerdmans, 1997.

Todeschini, Giacomo. *I mercanti e il tempio: La società cristiana e il circolo virtuoso della ricchezza fra Medioevo ed Età Moderna.* Bologna: Società Editrice Il Mulino, 2002.

Tomás y Valiente, Francisco. *El derecho penal de la Monarquía absoluta (Siglo XVI-XVII-XVIII).* Madrid: Tecnos, 1969.

Trexler, Richard C. *Church and Community, 1200–1600: Studies in the History of Florence and New Spain.* Rome: Edizioni di Storia e Letteratura, 1987.

Turrini, Miriam. "Il giudice della coscienza e la coscienza del giudice." In *Disciplina dell'anima, disciplina del corpo e disciplina della società tra medioevo ed età moderna*, edited by Paolo Prodi, 279–94. Bologna: Il Mulino, 1994.

Twinam, Ann. *Public Lives, Private Secrets: Gender, Honor, Sexuality, and Illegitimacy in Colonial Latin America.* Stanford: Stanford University Press, 1999.

Ulloa H., Daniel. *Los predicadores divididos. (Los dominicos en Nueva España, siglo XVI).* Mexico City: El Colegio de México, 1977.

Van Den Hoven, Birgit. *Work in Ancient and Medieval Thought: Ancient Philosophers,*

Medieval Monks and Theologians and Their Concept of Work, Occupations and Technology. Amsterdam: J. C. Gieben, 1996.

Van Houdt, Toon, and Jan Papy. "*Modestia, Constantia, Fama*: Towards a Literary and Philosophical Interpretation of Lipsius's *De Calumia Oratio*." In *Iustus Lipsius Europae Lumen et Columen: Proceedings of the International Colloquium, Leuven 17–19 September 1997*, edited by G. Tournoy, J. de Landtsheer, and J. Papy, 186–220. Leuven: Leuven University Press, 1999.

Van Zantwijk, Rudolph. *The Aztec Arrangement: The Social History of Pre-Spanish Mexico.* Norman: University of Oklahoma Press, 1985.

Vauchez, André. "Le refus du serment chez les hérétiques médiévaux." In *Le serment*, edited by Raymond Verdier, 257–63. Paris: Éditions du Centre National de la Recherche Scientifique, 1991.

Vigil, Ralph. *Alonso de Zorita: Royal Judge and Christian Humanist, 1512–1585.* Norman: University of Oklahoma Press, 1987.

Villa-Flores, Javier. *Dangerous Speech: A Social History of Blasphemy in Colonial Mexico.* Tucson: University of Arizona Press, 2006.

Viñas y Mey, Carmelo. *Doctrinas de los tratadistas españoles de los siglos XVI y XVII sobre el comunismo.* Madrid: Escuela Social de Madrid, 1945.

Vodola, E. F. "Fides et culpa: The Use of Roman Law in Ecclesiastical Ideology." In *Authority and Power: Studies in Medieval Law and Government Presented to Walter Ullmann on His Seventieth Birthday*, edited by Brian Tierney and Peter Linehan, 83–97. Cambridge: Cambridge University Press, 1980.

Weckmann, Luis. *La herencia medieval de México.* 2nd ed. Mexico City: Fondo de Cultura Económica, 1994.

Weisser, Michael. "Crime and Punishment in Early Modern Spain." In *Crime and the Law: The Social History of Crime in Western Europe since 1500*, edited by V. A. C. Gatrell, Bruce Lenman, and Geoffrey Parker, 76–96. London: Europa Publications, 1980.

Whitecotton, Joseph W. *The Zapotecs: Princes, Priests, and Peasants.* Norman: University of Oklahoma Press, 1984.

Witte, John Jr. *Law and Protestantism: The Legal Teachings of the Lutheran Reformation.* Cambridge: Cambridge University Press, 2002.

Wood, Stephanie. "The Social vs. Legal Context of Nahuatl Titles." In *Native Traditions in the Postconquest World*, edited by Elizabeth Hill Boone and Tom Cummins, 201–31. Washington, DC: Dumbarton Oaks Research Library and Collection, 1998.

Zagorin, Perez. *Ways of Lying: Dissimulation, Persecution, and Conformity in Early Modern Europe.* Cambridge, MA: Harvard University Press, 1990.

Zavala, Silvio. "El humanismo de Vasco de Quiroga." In *Ideario de Vasco de Quiroga*. Mexico City: El Colegio de México, 1941.

Zeitlin, Judith F., and Lillian Thomas. "Spanish Justice and the Indian Cacique: Disjunctive Political Systems in Sixteenth-Century Tehuantepec." *Ethnohistory* 39, no. 3 (1992): 285–315.

Zubillaga, Félix. "Tercer Concilio Mexicano 1585: Los memoriales del P. Juan de la Plaza S.I." *Archivum Historicum Societatis Iesu*, extractum and vol. 30 (1961).

Zucchini, Giampaolo. "Critica del diritto, difetti della giurisprudenza e problemi di legislazione in utopie del Cinque e Seicento." *Rivista internazionale di filosofia del diritto* (1986): 409–23.

Index

Acosta, José de, 160, 201
Alcocer, Francisco de, 107, 138–39
Alphonse X, King of Castile, 15, 89, 127
Antoninus of Florence, 36, 109n141
Antonio Valeriano, 7
Anunciación, Domingo de la, 106, 149, 170
Augustinians, 7, 128n25, 129, 144, 151, 174
authority: ecclesiastical, 63; friars and, 8; of indigenous local lords, 86; royal, 63; sources, 3, 6; traditional indigenous forms, 108. *See also* friars; jurisdictions; justice
Avendaño, Diego de, 199, 200n20
Ávila, Francisco de, 161–62
Ávila, Juan de, 139–40
Azpilcueta, Martín de, 20n47, 96n99, 100–1, 156

baptism, 14, 108; of Chinese merchants, 187–88; and head shaving, 186–87; legal implications, 15; Nahua interpretation, 15; and naming, 51–52; and personhood, 188
bells, 47n97, 48, 50
Benavente, Fr. Toribio de (Motolinia), 22, 41, 52, 65; on laws, 202; on Nahua witnesses, 124; on punishments, 178; on usury, 38n58
blasphemy, 100n113, 136–37, 139, 149–50, 169n20. *See also* public sins
Bossy, John, 118–19
Buen varón, 97, 196
Burgoa, Francisco de, 195–96

Carranza, Alonso de, 191
Casas, Bartolomé de las, 111–12, 115–16, 123–24
catechisms, 2, 25–27, 32n38, 34, 92; pictorial, 9–10; 153–54. *See also names of individual authors*
censers, 44–45
Chimalpahin, Domingo Francisco de San Antón Muñon, 39, 47
cochineal, 45, 47
confession, 19, 117; and commerce, 36; of indigenous officers, 92; and offenses against honor, 94; in Tarascan language, 12; and trades, 35, 42. *See also* Ten Commandments
conscience, 13, 148n105, 152–153, 203. *See also* confession; Jesuits
conversos, 15
Córdoba, Juan de, 13–14, 30n26, 110, 147–48, 203. *See also* goods
Córdoba, Pedro de, 26–28
Cortés, Hernán, 41, 79, 88
Covarrubias, Sebastián de Horozco, 33

Daza, Bernardino, 33
Decalogue, 35, 116, 118–19, 138n62. *See also* Ten Commandments
Díaz de Toledo, Fernán, 15n34
doctrinal texts: on confession, 154–56; on goods, 20; and indigenous cultures, 34, 40; and legal norms, 7–8; and Mexican reading public, 2–3. *See also* catechisms; *and names of individual authors*